THE THEOLOGY OF JOHN MACQUARRIE (1919-2007)

A Comprehensive and Contextual Exploration

Owen F. Cummings

With a Foreword by
Thomas E. Hosinski

The Edwin Mellen Press
Lewiston•Queenston•Lampeter

Library of Congress Cataloging-in-Publication Data

Cummings, Owen F.
    The theology of John Macquarrie (1919-2007) : a comprehensive and contextual
exploration / Owen F. Cummings ; with a foreword by Thomas E. Hosinski.
        p. cm.
    Includes bibliographical references and index.
    ISBN-13: 978-0-7734-3611-4
    ISBN-10: 0-7734-3611-1
    1. Macquarrie, John. I. Title.
    BX4827.M25C87 2010
    230'.3092--dc22
                                                    2010026740

hors série.

A CIP catalog record for this book is available from the British Library.

Front cover photo: John Macquarrie, courtesy of the author

The Edwin Mellen Press   The Edwin Mellen Press
Box 450   Box 67
Lewiston, New York   Queenston, Ontario
USA 14092-0450   CANADA L0S 1L0

The Edwin Mellen Press, Ltd.
Lampeter, Ceredigion, Wales
UNITED KINGDOM SA48 8LT

Printed in the United States of America

In memory of

John Macquarrie

(June 27, 1919-May 28, 2007)

i

TABLE OF CONTENTS.

FOREWORD

This is a fine, comprehensive study of the most important Anglican theologian of the twentieth century. John Macquarrie has been influential, but paradoxically is perhaps the most neglected of important twentieth century theologians. Professor Cummings' study shows why Macquarrie's greatest influence may yet lie in the future.

This book is well-written, comprehensive, balanced, insightful, and interesting. It is fundamentally appreciative while also recognizing controversial aspects of Macquarrie's thought. Beginning with an informative biographical sketch, this study presents a careful, nuanced analysis of every major aspect of Macquarrie's theology, including his interest in mysticism. Cummings broad knowledge of various currents in philosophy and theology enables him to situate Macquarrie's theology very well in the context of both past and present discussions and controversies. While Cummings deals with various critics of Macquarrie's theology, he writes in the same irenic tone and spirit that characterized Macquarrie's own approach to theological discussion. Reading this book, you are in the hands of a guide you can trust.

This book, while it would be difficult for all but the most advanced undergraduates, will be very useful to seminary students and graduate students seeking a comprehensive introduction to Macquarrie's theology. It ought to be in any library holding a collection in theology. Professional theologians will also find the book informative and enlightening, most especially because of Cummings' personal acquaintance with John Macquarrie and his extensive interest in the full range of theological topics, much like Macquarrie's own. Cummings' book does this service for Macquarrie's theology, showing him to be an important voice for tolerance, ecumenism, and balance in our current pluralistic situation in theology.

Thomas E. Hosinski, C.S.C.
Professor of Theology
University of Portland, OR

INTRODUCTION

Every reader, and perhaps especially every theologian, has a community of the heart, authors who speak in a profound way, to whom recourse is made again and again for wisdom, insight and enrichment. This is what David Ford is talking about when he says: "No one on earth has an 'objective' standpoint that would require being able to stand outside it all in some way. For all the importance of being as intelligent as possible about our beliefs... it is hard to imagine any ultimately convincing argument one way or the other. There are huge issues here, but let me go straight to what I see as the crucial one: whose testimony do we trust?"[1] Necessarily, then, autobiography and critical reflection go hand in hand, and in my life and work as a theologian, as I attempt to be as intelligent as possible about my beliefs, I have been trusting the testimony of John Macquarrie for over forty years.

It began in spring 1968. As an undergraduate reading Semitic Languages at University College Dublin, I found a paperback copy of Macquarrie's *An Existentialist Theology*. I devoured it. His expository contrast of Heidegger and Bultmann was just what I needed at the time for two reasons. First, my father was dying, and Macquarrie's mediation of Heidegger's understanding of man as a "being-unto-death" was enormously helpful to me in my struggle with bereavement. Second, the particular course I had chosen in Semitic Languages involved a study of Hellenistic Greek, including texts by Philo and Polybius and several of St. Paul's letters. Macquarrie's mediation of Bultmann's understanding of St. Paul was illuminating, to say the least. My copy of *An Existentialist Theology* was underlined heavily and annotated frequently, and it remains on my shelves. Since then I have read virtually everything John Macquarrie has written. Moving on to read for the B.D. at the University of Dublin, Trinity College, Professor Macquarrie of Oxford University was the external examiner. When Macquarrie was slated as one of the preachers at the Sunday evening ecumenical service in Trinity College Chapel, the Anglican Dean of Residence, the Rev. Peter Hiscock, invited me to join him and Macquarrie after the service for a pint in a Dublin pub. That was autumn 1972. Much later, as senior lecturer in theology at Newman University College Birmingham I invited Professor Macquarrie to lecture and preach.

Finally, in 1998 I had the great joy of spending some days with him in Oxford in preparation for the book, *John Macquarrie, A Master of Theology.*[2] Lawrence Cunningham of the University of Notre Dame has described this book as a work of *pietas.* It is a fair description of the book. Although the present work contains material from that 2002 essay, it differs substantially in the following ways.

First, the scope of the present work is more comprehensive, taking account both of Macquarrie's more recent and final publications and also of published critical evaluations of different aspects of Macquarrie's corpus. A treatment of Macquarrie's anthropology and eschatology is provided.[3] The critical reflections of such scholars as Niall Coll, Charles Hefling, David Jenkins, Georgina Morley, Vernon Purdy and Douglas Pratt are woven into the conversation. Second, some issues are dealt with more analytically and systematically than in the earlier volume, notably his teaching on God, taking account of ongoing critiques of "classical theism" and panentheism. Third, Macquarrie will be considered as a mystical theologian through not only his teaching on prayer but also his increasing concern with mystics and mystical awareness. "Mysticism" and "mystic" are often problematic words in theology. It is necessary at this point to provide some minimal understanding of how these terms are understood in this study, and the theologian of Christian mysticism and Teilhardian scholar, Ursula King, provides a good entry point: "A mystic is a person who is deeply aware of the powerful presence of the divine Spirit: someone who seeks, above all, the knowledge and love of God, and who experiences to an extraordinary degree the profoundly personal encounter with the energy of divine life. Mystics often perceive the presence of God throughout the world of nature and in all that is alive, leading to a transfiguration of the ordinary all around them. However, the touch of God is most strongly felt deep within their own hearts."[4] If this fairly typical description by King is judged adequate, then it becomes also a description of mystical Macquarrie. He is deeply aware of the powerful presence of God, throughout the world of nature as well as in people, but "the touch of God is most strongly felt deep within (his) own heart." It is impossible to come away from Macquarrie's writings without this touch of God. Mystical Macquarrie will be fully engaged in the chapter on prayer and mysticism.

Finally, here and there throughout the book I have used other authors with whom to contrast the theology of John Macquarrie, and I have also drawn to a limited extent on personal correspondence with him. The last communication I had from John Macquarrie was in December 2006. On that occasion he sent me a copy of the book *In Search of Humanity and Deity: A Celebration of John Macquarrie's Theology*,[5] along with comments concerning the present manuscript, much of which he had seen. *In Search of Humanity and Deity* was published by Macquarrie's first publisher, SCM Press of London, and edited by his Oxford theology colleague and friend Robert Morgan to celebrate the fiftieth anniversary of the publication of his first book, *An Existentialist Theology*. The twenty-seven essays with a foreword by Rowan D. Williams, Archbishop of Canterbury, are a timely testimony to the man and his message. It is the author's hope that through this book others will continue to be drawn to the work of John Macquarrie, not only for theological insight but for personal enrichment in Christian living.

---

[1] See David F. Ford, *The Shape of Living* (London: HarperCollins, 1997), 19.

[2] Owen F. Cummings, *John Macquarrie, A Master of Theology* (New York-Mahwah, NJ: Paulist Press, 2002).

[3] In a review of my earlier *John Macquarrie, A Master of Theology* Professor Kerry Walters of Gettysburg College made the important point that I had neglected Macquarrie's anthropology and especially his book on peace. The neglect has been remedied in the present book, and I am beholden to Dr. Walters for drawing attention to this deficit.

4

[4] Ursula King, *Christian Mystics: The Spiritual Heart of the Christian Tradition* (New York: Simon and Schuster, 1998), 6.

[5] Robert Morgan, ed., *In Search of Humanity and Deity: A Celebration of John Macquarrie's Theology* (London: SCM Press, 2006).

1. INTRODUCING JOHN MACQUARRIE (1919-2007)

*Looking back, it seems that my life has been shaped as much or even more by
events that just seemed to happen than by deliberate choices.*
John Macquarrie.[1]

*Ian has always been a theologian of the Church — not in a narrow or sectarian
way, but out of the conviction that the language of theology is answerable to more
than just the academy at the end of the day. His own example of patient
intellectual work inseparably combined with personal devotion and humility has
been a beacon for many.*
Rowan Douglas Williams,
Archbishop of Canterbury.[2]

The theology of John Macquarrie (1919-2007), always known as "Ian"
by his friends, ranks among the most influential in the English-speaking
theological world of the twentieth century. It has an appeal to open-minded
Christians of almost every confession. This opening chapter situates Macquarrie's
theology within the context of his life and career.

John Macquarrie's lifelong commitment to the theological enterprise
begins with participation in a religious faith. He has never been a thinker who
reflects on Christianity from a distance, but always from the within of the
Christian community and tradition. Through a theological contribution that has
been critically constructive, always courteous, even with positions and insights
with which he finds himself in serious disagreement, John Macquarrie put his life
at the service of the Christian faith throughout much of the twentieth century, and
into the twenty-first.

Early Life and Education

John Macquarrie was born on June 27, 1919, in Renfrew, Scotland, the
only child of John and Robina (née McInnes) Macquarrie. His father was born in
1873, also in Renfrew. His parents had married in 1914 and they had a son who

died in infancy. His mother told him that he himself barely survived. Macquarrie's grandfather, a Gaelic-speaker also named John Macquarrie, had come from the Island of Islay, off the west coast of Scotland, to work on Clydeside. His family was not poor but they were certainly not affluent. His father worked in the shipbuilding industry as a pattern maker. Though it was a skilled occupation, he would not have earned more than three pounds per week.

Both of John Macquarrie's parents were very devout, his father being an elder in the Presbyterian Church, but Macquarrie says of himself that he never had *what might be called a conversion experience.*[3] Commenting on his religious background, Eugene T. Long writes: "Macquarrie's upbringing fostered in him a sense of deep religious commitment that has always been balanced by tolerance and an openness toward others. He recognized early both the importance of religious conviction and the legitimacy of religious diversity. Indeed, both a spirit of charity and a depth of conviction equally characterize his work."[4] Long has been a student of Macquarrie's, both directly and indirectly, since the 1960s, and his characterization of Macquarrie is both entirely accurate and points to one of the most attractive features of his thought.

Reflecting on his initial interest in the ministry and theology, Macquarrie notes that motives are always mixed. He describes positively the influence of a minister in his home town of Renfrew: *I think to some extent a bit of hero-worship comes into it. Our pastor at the time was a man of considerable learning who had a first-class degree in philosophy, who practiced what he preached.* At the same time, *being a minister of the Kirk was quite a nice position in society.* The minimum stipend which most ministers of the Church of Scotland received was about three hundred pounds a year along with a house. Although there was no dramatic moment when he received a call to the ministry, the first time he recalls being conscious of the ministry as a personal vocation was when he completed an application form for Glasgow University. He had been studying the normal range of high school subjects at Paisley Grammar School, and in the fifth year of the course he entered and won a Glasgow University bursary competition that would take him for seven years through both an arts and a divinity degree. It was worth forty-seven pounds a year, adding almost another pound to the weekly household budget, and without it he probably would not have gone to university. Part of the university application form inquired about the candidate's vocational aspirations, and Macquarrie found himself writing "the Christian ministry." Even at this early stage of his professional life and career, and while still an active member of the Church of Scotland (Presbyterian) he found himself strongly attracted to the Episcopal Church.[5] He began his university education at the University of Glasgow in 1936, receiving his first degree, the M.A., with first class honors in Mental Philosophy in 1940.[6] He was a student of Charles Arthur Campbell, Professor of Logic and Rhetoric, to whom in 1972 he dedicated his book, *Existentialism.*

The University of Glasgow and Theology

The University of Glasgow was founded in a bull of 1450 by Pope Nicholas V and is the second of the Scottish universities, the first being the University of St. Andrews established some thirty-two years earlier. The founding bull of 1450 provides the mission of the University: "to promote the Catholic faith," and the royal confirmation of the University's institution adds "to defend the orthodox faith more vigorously."[7] The University had a strong philosophical tradition from its inception, but, of course, allied to theology. In this earliest phase, notes the church historian Ian Hazlett, "The general theological tint in Glasgow was decidedly Thomist."[8] In 1518, at the very beginning of the Reformation, the university star in philosophy and theology was the great Scotsman John Mair, author of forty-six published works in philosophy, Scripture and theology, and who came to Glasgow from the Sorbonne. Although John Mair remained firmly attached to the Catholic Church, his Nominalism distanced him from his Thomist predecessors.

With the onset of the Reformation the distinguished scholar Andrew Melville (1545-1613) was the principal architect in the revision of the theological curriculum. Theology students would undergo a six-year formation, three years in arts (especially Latin, Greek, Hebrew, logic, metaphysics and ethics), and three years in theology. Hazlett describes Melville's achievement in these words: "In regard to theological education, with its strong humanist and philosophical props, his program survived conceptually unchanged for almost four hundred years."[9] In other words, Hazlett is claiming that there was no substantive change in the theological curriculum until the twentieth century. In Macquarrie's time this meant that a student for the Presbyterian ministry proceeded first to the MA, Master of Arts, before going on to the BD, Bachelor of Divinity.

The years 1729 to 1746 at the university were informed by the contribution of the Ulster Presbyterian Francis Hutcheson (1694-1746). Hutcheson stood for a new way of doing theology --- what Ian Hazlett calls an "open minded way of doing theology" --- a way of doing theology that had as much of Athens in it as Jerusalem. It is also noteworthy that Hutcheson opened up his presentations in religion and theology to the public at large in Glasgow "so as to increase access to philosophical and theological discourse and encourage people to think for themselves."[10] Hutcheson's outlook and theology in these aspects anticipate the outlook and theology of John Macquarrie. Macquarrie stood with both feet firmly in both Athens and Jerusalem, but, as an obituary notes, "he was always ready to accept an invitation to preach in an Oxfordshire village church or to give a paper to a group of parish clergymen."[11] Theology was most certainly not to be confined to the academy.

A student of the university and a minister of Ayr, William McGill, published in 1786 his *Practical Essay on the Death of Jesus Christ*. The essay caused quite a stir for various reasons, not least McGill's severe critique of Anselmian atonement theology as received in Scottish Calvinism. The Church of Scotland took him to task and the affair died down, but Ian Hazlett points out that it lived on in Scottish culture through the pen of McGill's friend, the Ayrshire poet Robert Burns, in his poem *The Kirk's Alarm*:

Doctor Mac, Doctor Mac, ye should stretch on the rack,

To strike evildoers wi' terror;
To join Faith and Sense, upon any pretence,
Was heretic, damnable error.
Doctor Mac! 'Twas heretic, damnable error.

While he did not draw upon "The Kirk's Alarm," Macquarrie published in 1974 an appreciative essay on Robert Burns, whom he considered to be in his own way "poet, prophet, philosopher."[12]

Although not on the faculty of theology, John MacLeod Campbell (1800-1872) was a student at the university for nine years, including three in theology, and he too got into difficulties for his beliefs on the atonement, election and assurance. He was formally condemned as a heretic by the Church of Scotland in 1831, but continued to work as a minister. In an essay given over to Campbell's understanding of the atonement, Macquarrie writes: "He was a man ahead of his times, and his ideas are relevant to current theological discussions. As we look back to the nineteenth century, it would be difficult to dissent from the judgment of an historian of British religious thought in that period, B. M. G. Reardon, that 'Campbell's is the outstanding name in Scottish theology during the last century.'"[13]

Concluding his essay on theology in Scotland up to the middle of the nineteenth century, Ian Hazlett writes: "If it is true that 'Scotland has produced marvelously little constructive theology', and if by 'constructive' is meant at least 'legitimately innovative' or 'critically reflective', then on the basis of this essay it can be argued that Glasgow has had relatively more than her fair share of the tranches of bolder thinking that were in circulation."[14] It is a very fair comment indeed. Perhaps it is true of all academic faculties of philosophy and theology to some degree, but it is certainly true of Glasgow that there has been a fairly regular desire to reach beyond the lineaments of received orthodoxy, not so much to subvert them as hospitably to enlarge and to extend them, a desire we might say to move from a rigid orthodoxy to a generous orthodoxy. In Glasgow we may see a movement from Thomism to Nominalism, from various forms of Calvinist dogmatics to Hutchesonian Enlightenment humanism, to the liberalizing protests of McGill and Campbell. When we come to comment later on theologians Ian Henderson and Ronald Gregor Smith as well as John Macquarrie himself we shall see this fine tradition continuing to be represented in the twentieth century. Now, however, it is important to turn to the immediate philosophical tradition in which Macquarrie was nurtured in Glasgow.

F. H. Bradley and C. A. Campbell

Among all the philosophers he studied "the one who really bowled (him) over" was F. H. Bradley (1846-1924), who had been a Fellow of Merton College, Oxford.[15] Bradley's *Appearance and Reality* had a considerable influence on him, a work described by the anonymous author in *The Oxford Dictionary of the Christian Church* as "the most original work in British metaphysics in the nineteenth century."[16] Subsequently, Macquarrie was to describe Bradley in equally positive terms: "Undoubtedly the most brilliant of the neo-idealists and probably the greatest British philosopher of any school in recent times."[17] Although standing loosely in the Hegelian tradition, Bradley differed from Hegel. This is how Macquarrie puts it: *Hegel was, to use the technical term, panlogist, so that the real was the rational and the rational was the real. Bradley was more of a mystic. The Absolute for him --- he did not speak so much of God as of the Absolute --- is the ultimate reality and is supra-rational. It is beyond our grasp. This became a kind of mystical element in his philosophy. But he also thought that the study of metaphysics is the way in which a lot of people experience religion. The Absolute is the Whole and for Bradley "God" is not the form of the Absolute. "God" is, as it were, this side of the Absolute. God, shall we say, is a kind of rationalized version of the Absolute.* The description of Bradley here as "more of a mystic" is most interesting for two reasons. First, it seems accurately to represent Bradley's understanding of reality and the Absolute, an understanding that Macquarrie will describe later as reaching towards a "higher pantheism," a pantheism that is not reductionist, but rather reaching to the "God beyond God."[18] Secondly, this could be a description of John Macquarrie himself, something that will be commented on from time to time throughout this book.

Macquarrie finds a passage in Bradley's *Principles of Logic*, particularly revealing. While we were discussing how Bradley's philosophy influenced him, he left his study and disappeared up a ladder into the attic of his home where his library was stored, found the particular passage immediately, and read it to me:

> Suppose (let us say) a man convinced of the truth of Christianity and rightly or wrongly to understand Christianity as the unity of God with finite souls, a reality at once consummated and eternal and yet temporal and progressive. Christianity is to such a man a main aspect of the Universe, conscious of itself above time, and yet revealing itself in the historical growth of spiritual experience. And imagine the same man asked to compare with this principle the truth about some happening in time. I will not instance such events as the virgin birth and bodily ascension of Jesus of Nazareth, but I will take the historical assertion that Jesus actually at a certain time lived and taught in Galilee and actually died at Jerusalem on the cross. And by 'actually' I mean so that, if *we* had been there, we should have seen these things happen. 'All such events,' our supposed man might reply, are, if you view them as occurrences, of little importance. Enquire by all means whether and how far there is good evidence for their happening. But do not imagine that Christianity is vitally concerned with the result of your enquiry. Christianity, as I conceive it, covers so much ground, fills such a space in the Universe, and makes such a difference to the world, that, without it, the world would be not so much changed as destroyed. And it counts for much that this eternal truth should have happened on our planet (as presumably elsewhere), and should here (we hope) be developing itself more and more fully. But the rest, if you will take it as mere event and occurrence, is an affair so small --- a matter grounded by the very nature of its world on so little --- that between the two things there can be hardly a comparison.[19]

Here is a large panoramic vision of reality that stands in clear contrast with a narrow religious vision, even though it fails to appreciate the importance of history. Macquarrie says of this passage that: *It made a big impression on me. I don't hold it nowadays because I do think that historical truth is important. I changed my mind about that.* It is rather tempting to see in Macquarrie's summation of Bradley's metaphysics his own self-reflection when he writes, "The aim of metaphysics is to satisfy the intellect. The intellect is satisfied only by that which is one and free from contradiction; this is *reality*."[20]

He sees the idealist tradition of Bradley continued in his own teacher, C. A. Campbell. In his discussion of Campbell again it is not difficult to see Macquarrie's own image. Outlining Campbell's appropriation of Rudolf Otto's doctrine of the numinous, Macquarrie concludes: "This means that our language about God is not literally applicable, but is symbolic of a reality which is in itself unknown. But if our talk of God is not to be utterly empty, we would need to suppose that there is some affinity between our symbols and what they symbolize... Campbell argues further that the symbolical knowledge of God of which he speaks is no more agnostic, it would seem, than the knowledge permitted by scholastic philosophy's doctrine of analogy."[21] The connection of Campbell with scholasticism is important. As shall be noted in the chapter on God, what the scholastics intended by the doctrine of analogy is not only instanced in Campbell but also becomes Macquarrie's own position, even if it is not always named as such. We see here in his observations of Bradley and Campbell some of the characteristics of his own mature theology, the need and importance of metaphysics in theology and the care with which language must be used of God. Macquarrie makes reference to Campbell in the introduction to his translation with Edward Robinson of Heidegger's *Being and Time*. It seems reasonable to assume that he had been in contact with Campbell about some aspects of Heidegger's philosophy.

Theology and Ministry

Macquarrie then proceeded to the study of theology also at the University of Glasgow, then housed at Trinity College, a magnificent structure looking down upon Charing Cross and Sauchiehall Street. During his years at Trinity College, Macquarrie worked at the parish church of Dumbarton, and for two years helped to start a new congregation in Paisley. The town had experienced an increase in the worker population in a wartime factory, but Macquarrie "being somewhat introverted and shy," apparently did not find this work particularly satisfying.[22] In theology while he found biblical criticism and church history interesting, he disliked systematic theology, especially Calvin and Barth, whom he described as "specially insufferable."[23] A course offered on Buddhism by Dr. A. J. Gossip also interested him, as well as a course on Islam by Dr. James Robson. He was awarded the degree of B.D. in 1943, and was offered a scholarship to do further theological studies at Westminster College, Cambridge. He declined the offer, and served in the British Army as a chaplain from 1945-1948. As an army chaplain, Macquarrie's principal responsibility was the oversight of German prisoner-of-war camps in the Middle East.

After army service, Macquarrie became the minister of St. Ninian's Church, Brechin, in 1948. He was to remain in Brechin until 1953. In 1949 he married Jenny Welsh --- who had been a student of mathematics and physics at the University of Glasgow which is where they met --- and they had three children, two boys and a girl: John Michael, Catherine Elizabeth and Alan Denis. During his time at Brechin, as the result of a suggestion made by a former theology professor from Glasgow, Dr. J. G. Riddell, he embarked on theological research and completed his Ph.D. in theology under the supervision of Ian Henderson (1910-1969), who was among the first to introduce the work of Rudolf Bultmann to the English-speaking world, with his book, *Myth in the New Testament*.[24] Macquarrie's doctoral dissertation, a comparison of Rudolf Bultmann and Martin Heidegger, was to be published as *An Existentialist Theology* in 1955, and was dedicated to his parents. It is interesting to note that Macquarrie like Rudolf Bultmann had served for a time as an army chaplain. Undoubtedly this experience led both of them to recognize the urgency of seeking out more contemporary expressions of Christian faith. From the preface to *An Existentialist Theology*, we are given a sense of the scope of the work: "... the right of the apologist to make use of current philosophical concepts; the claim that there is a special relation between the philosophy of existence and the work of theology; and an affinity between the concepts of existentialism and those of biblical thought."[25] Macquarrie speaks warmly of Henderson in the preface, and in a later essay, published after his death, considers Henderson "in the first rank of Scottish theologians of this century."[26] In 1953, one year before completing the dissertation, Macquarrie began his academic career as a colleague of Henderson's, as lecturer in Systematic Theology at the University of Glasgow. The next ten years or so, his years in Glasgow and his early years in New York City, represent Macquarrie's "existentialist phase." Every thinker thinks in a particular context, and so Georgina Morley points out about Macquarrie that:

> The influence of colleagues and institutions during his career provide the temporal narrative which account for the particular directions his work takes... It is in the very alchemy of subjecting the best characteristics of existentialist theology to the sociopolitical concerns and process interests of colleagues at Union Theological Seminary, New York, and then to the ecclesiastical and philosophical traditions of Oxford, that Macquarrie's mature theology offers a mediating position between gift and being.[27]

Macquarrie's theology then proceeds to develop alongside and in interaction with the places and friends and colleagues among whom he lived. A close friend and an influence during his time as a professor in the faculty of Divinity at Glasgow was Ronald Gregor Smith.

Lecturer at the University of Glasgow

In 1956, Ronald Gregor Smith (1913-1968) joined the Glasgow divinity faculty as Primarius Professor of Divinity. Gregor Smith, as editor of the London-based Student Christian Movement Press, had been responsible for a new series of publications, the Library of Theology and Philosophy, and Macquarrie's *An Existentialist Theology* was the first volume to be published. He was six years Macquarrie's senior, and the two men make an interesting contrast.

Gregor Smith was born in Edinburgh, son of a marine biologist, Macquarrie in Glasgow, son of a Clydeside shipyard craftsman. Gregor Smith graduated from the University of Edinburgh, first with an M.A. in English Language and Literature (1934) and then with a B.D. (1937), Macquarrie from the

University of Glasgow with an M.A. in Mental Philosophy, and then the B.D. As Macquarrie (in conjunction with E. Robinson) was to translate into English Martin Heidegger's *Being and Time*, so Gregor Smith translated Martin Buber's *I and Thou*.[28] As Macquarrie says of Smith, "his academic background was literary rather than philosophical."[29] Gregor Smith, having spent further time in theological studies at the Universities of Munich and Marburg and having married a German, was keenly interested in building bridges between the German theological world and the English speaking world.[30]

Both of them, however, were keenly interested in Rudolf Bultmann. One commentator on Gregor Smith writes: "If there was one theologian to whom he was most indebted both intellectually and personally it was Rudolf Bultmann."[31] Both Gregor Smith and Macquarrie could be said to have been in their existentialist phase in Glasgow together, though unfortunately there grew an estrangement between Gregor Smith and Ian Henderson.

Probably the most outstanding expression of the joint work of Macquarrie and Gregor Smith during their Glasgow years was their joint supervision of the doctoral dissertation of Eugene Thomas Long, a comparison of Rudolf Bultmann and Karl Jaspers.[32] Initially Macquarrie was his dissertation supervisor, and when he left for Union Theological Seminary in New York, Gregor Smith took over.[33] Long remained faithful to both his Glasgow teachers. After Gregor Smith's premature death in a car accident in 1968, Long put together a *Festschrift* in his memory.[34] He also wrote an excellent introduction to the thought of John Macquarrie, *Being and God: An Introduction to the Philosophical Theology of John Macquarrie*.[35] He was also co-editor with another of Macquarrie's students, Alistair Kee, of the 1986 *Festschrift* for Macquarrie.[36]

Both Gregor Smith and Macquarrie were to develop in quite distinct theological directions, the former decisively influenced by "secular Christianity," informed in various ways by Dietrich Bonhoeffer and Friedrich Gogarten, the latter moving in a decisively Anglo-Catholic direction both ecclesiologically and doctrinally so much so that the Scottish Presbyterian theologian, Alasdair Heron, was to describe him in 1980 as "perhaps the leading Anglican theologian of the present day."[37] Of Macquarrie Gregor Smith says "(he) has done much to restore philosophical theology to a position of reasoned assurance in recent times."[38] Discussing Gregor Smith's "secular theology" Macquarrie remarks that

> At the end of his life, the late Ronald Gregor Smith was struggling with the question of God. He was in violent reaction against classical theism, and especially against the notion of an unchanging God, throned above the chances and changes of time. Though a secular theologian --- and he understood that to mean an historicizing theologian --- he did not run away from the God question, as many of the secularizers did.[39]

Gregor Smith's brand of "secular theology" was undoubtedly philosophically searching, but it was never his intention to suggest "that God is something less than our forefathers believed him to be."[40] Both men remained critically aware and appreciative of each other's theology, and each in his own way tried to "lift (the name of God) out of the dust," to make it speak to contemporary people.[41]

Another well-known member of the divinity faculty at this time was the popular New Testament scholar, William Barclay (1907-1978), who was a minister in Renfrew when Macquarrie was a boy. He is described by Macquarrie as *an old-fashioned liberal, an evangelical minus the fundamentalism.* Although Macquarrie is mentioned a number of times in Barclay's authorized biography, we are not given any sense of relationship between them, though Macquarrie speaks of him fondly.[42] Theologically there would have been serious differences between them, Macquarrie with an increasingly Catholic ecclesiology, Barclay an evangelical free churchman by conviction. The late Robert P. Carroll, an Irish student of the great Hebraist Jacob Weingreen of Trinity College Dublin and Old Testament scholar at the University of Glasgow for many years, penned an essay in which, though laudatory in some regards with respect to William Barclay, also described him in very negative terms:

> He was about the ugliest, unfittest man I have ever met, but he was also astonishingly generous, good-natured and friendly. Yet he intrigues me. Ugly, gruff, deaf, stinking of tobacco and a great toper, he was a legendary

figure in his own lifetime as a communicator of the Christian gospel... Because he was a legend, millions believed him to be a confirmed ascetic and teetotaler, yet he was a gourmand, a heavy smoker and as close to being an alcoholic, without actually being one, as it is possible to be.[43]

In private conversation Macquarrie told me how much he disagreed with this description and that he had written to Professor Carroll to lodge his disagreement. This is absolutely typical of Macquarrie --- ever ready to see the good side, invariably kind and fair, always courteous.

We are given a different insight into John Macquarrie in the reminiscence of a Scottish Jesuit spiritual theologian, Gerard W Hughes. Hughes, who had been brought up in Glasgow, completed his theological formation at the Jesuit Faculty of Theology in Frankfurt. Expressing an interest in Scottish theology after his ordination to the priesthood, Hughes inquired among his Glasgow Jesuit colleagues about their contact with Church of Scotland ministers. The reminiscence is best given in his own words:

> They had none, so I went to the Church of Scotland office and asked to see their directory of clergy in Glasgow. I found the divinity faculty at Glasgow University, took a phone number at random and arranged to meet a lecturer, John Macquarrie, with whom I had two three-hour sessions, which ended with supper in the kitchen with his wife and himself. John Macquarrie was far better read in Catholic theology than I, yet he had never in his life spoken with a Catholic priest... I was delighted to meet him again after fifteen years when Glasgow University gave him an honorary doctorate.[44]

Although Hughes is not explicit, it is clear from the Catholic representatives in his *Twentieth Century Religious Thought* that Macquarrie was reading people like Karl Rahner, Romano Guardini and Hans Urs Von Balthasar.

Union Theological Seminary, New York

Macquarrie took up a post at Union Theological Seminary in New York City in 1962, having first delivered the Hastie Lectures at the University of Glasgow on "The Problem of Theological Language." He had been recommended to Union by Professor John Baillie of the Faculty of Divinity at Edinburgh University.[45] Along with other essays, papers and lectures given in the United States there came *God-Talk: An Examination of the Language and Logic of Theology* (1962). His 1962 inaugural lecture at Union was entitled, "How Is Theology Possible?" and that year also saw his translation, along with Edward Robinson of the University of Kansas, of Martin Heidegger's *Sein und Zeit*.[46] In 1963, at the invitation of the editorial staff of Harper and Brothers he published his *Twentieth Century Religious Thought*, dedicated to his three children. The ferment in theology at the time made such a book invaluable to the student of theology trying to understand how to take the pulse of theological pluralism in the early 1960s. Macquarrie realized the magnitude of the task that he had been invited to assume, but in his typically humble way, he wrote in the preface: "At first I shied away from so wide and laborious an undertaking. But on reflection, it occurred to me that if I were to make the attempt --- and surely someone ought to make it --- then even if no one else were to profit from my book, I should at least educate myself a little better in writing it."[47] In this book, acclaimed almost universally for its even-handedness and fairness so much so that it has been issued in an updated form three times (in 1971, 1981 and 2001), he outlines and critically responds to over one hundred and fifty philosophers and theologians. Eugene T. Long says of this book that it "testifies to Macquarrie's responsibility to sum up the essential aspects of a theory or system of thought in a few words. Macquarrie's critical commentary also provides a guide to the maturation and development of his own thought."[48] Hard on its heels in 1966 came his *Principles of Christian Theology*, in which he drew heavily on Heidegger's philosophy as a vehicle through which to express the tradition of Christian doctrine. Macquarrie refers to the genesis of the book in these terms: "The most daunting obligation that I took upon myself before leaving Glasgow arose out of a letter in 1961 from the New York publishing house Charles Scribner's Sons... The letter enquired whether I would undertake to write a one-volume systematic theology."[49] It was daunting not least because Macquarrie was only forty-two at the time, whereas the great Paul Tillich, one of his theological heroes, was sixty-seven when he published the first volume of his systematic theology. It seems that the title, *Principles of Christian Theology* was patterned after F. H. Bradley's *Principles of Logic*.[50] Macquarrie writes of systematic theology: "It is an attempt to think Christianity as a whole. When you begin to do so, you are at once astonished by the coherence and consistency of this vision. One doctrine flows into another, each supports the other and strengthens the other, and the whole is a vision of incredible strength and beauty. One never, of course, entirely comprehends this, and so there can never be a final systematic theology."[51]

In this much-used and applauded book, in reality an ecumenical systematic theology, he moves decisively out of an existentialist mold into what he calls the "existential-ontological" method. A later successor to John Macquarrie in the Lady Margaret Chair of Divinity at Oxford, John Webster, has high praise for *Principles*:

> *Principles of Christian Theology* is one of a handful of enduring texts of Anglican divinity from the 1960s, and the only comprehensive account of Christian doctrine of any substance written by an Anglican in at least the last sixty years... *Principles* has not been superseded. Classroom texts such as Owen Thomas's *Introduction to Theology* or McGrath's *Christian Theology* are pedestrian by contrast and have nothing of Macquarrie's constructive grandeur or philosophical acumen. Anglicanism still awaits another attempt of similar stature.[52]

While Webster succeeded Macquarrie to the Lady Margaret Chair after Rowan Williams his immediate successor had been elevated to the episcopate, he was no disciple. He has been much appreciative of the Barthian tradition, both in respect of Barth himself and of Eberhard Jüngel, one of the most prominent and influential of the Barthians.[53] Given Macquarrie's at least partial distaste for Barthian theology, Webster's positive evaluation is significant. At the same time, Webster finds fault with Macquarrie's lack of engagement with Scripture and historical theology: "Biblical exegesis is only lightly scattered throughout the book, as are references to classical authors; and only rarely does Macquarrie place himself with respect to the other leading systematicians of his day, such as Tillich or Barth."[54] It is certainly true that he does not position himself often with regard to Karl Barth, nor indeed with the Calvinist tradition generally, but he is very aware of Paul Tillich. True enough, his awareness does not stretch to frequent citation, reference and engagement, but that is probably because Macquarrie judges that Tillich is drawing on Heidegger, and he turns directly to the primary Heideggerian texts themselves.[55] When it comes to biblical exegesis, Webster is correct. Macquarrie does not spend much time on detailed exegesis, something that has been noticed by others, for example, the Anglican Bishop John Austin Baker.[56] This emerges clearly in an article written for the *Church Times* in the nineties on the infancy narratives of the Gospels of Sts. Matthew and Luke. Macquarrie acknowledges that the core historical truth of the narratives is the actual birth of Jesus, and that many of the other details in the narratives --- the three *magoi*, the guiding star, etc. --- play a symbolic and not a historical role.[57] In this respect Macquarrie would probably find himself in the company of many if not most New Testament scholars. Probably his dominant approach to the Scriptures was the historical-critical. In a review of his Oxford colleague Andrew Louth's book, *Discerning the Mystery*, while Macquarrie appreciates his use of philosophers such as Hans-Georg Gadamer in a renewed theological methodology, he shows little sympathy for Louth's re-appropriation of other approaches to Scripture from the patristic and medieval traditions.

> Some readers (and one suspects Macquarrie himself in the first rank) may find a long chapter commending allegory less convincing, and it is not very well integrated into the argument of the book as a whole. It may remind us of the enthusiasm shown for the allied subject of typology by biblical theologians a quarter of a century ago. Their work has not stood out very well.[58]

The 1960s witnessed some radical movements in theology, especially the "Death of God" theology associated with Thomas J. J. Altizer, William Hamilton and Paul M. van Buren. Forms of secular or religionless Christianity advocated by Harvey G. Cox and connected with varying degrees of accuracy to Dietrich Bonhoeffer were widespread. In response to such movements, Macquarrie wrote

God and Secularity (1967). This book according to his own analysis in "Pilgrimage in Theology" marks a turning point in his theological development. From now on he would turn his attention more and more to articulating the themes of Christian doctrine enunciated in his *Principles of Christian Theology*.

Macquarrie's appointment to Union also brought him into contact with process theology, especially in the person and work of a colleague for whom he had enormous respect, Daniel Day Williams. In an essay written in appreciation of Williams after his premature death, Macquarrie writes that "I was (Williams') close colleague for eight years, and we often discussed theological questions."[59] Later in his Gifford Lectures, *In Search of Deity*, Macquarrie describes something of their theological relationship: "(Williams) looked to Whitehead for his categories of theological explanation, while I looked to Heidegger, and we used to compare the merits and demerits of these two philosophers. I had to concede that Whitehead provided a much more adequate theology of nature, but Williams in turn admitted that Heidegger had the more profound understanding of the human person..."[60] It must be acknowledged that process theologians have found in Macquarrie a sympathetic fellow, and to this we shall return in the chapter "Speaking of Deity." This reflects their joint appreciation of the necessity of metaphysics for theology, but also their dynamic views of reality. Norman Pittenger, for example, teaching at the Anglican school, General Theological Seminary, during Macquarrie's stay in New York, says that if he did not find the thought of Whitehead and Hartshorne so compelling, he would opt for and endorse the thought of John Macquarrie.[61]

The years at Union Theological Seminary not only chart Macquarrie's theological development, but also his ecclesial affiliation. Macquarrie became a good friend of the Union New Testament scholar, John Knox. Shortly after Macquarrie arrived in New York, Knox gave him a copy of his latest book, *The Church and the Reality of Christ*, in which "Christ and the Church comprise together the unity of the Christ-event."[62] Although a Methodist, Knox's developing ecclesiology was taking him in another direction and in fact, in

December 1962, he was ordained a priest in the Anglican Communion. Macquarrie's theological pilgrimage was taking him in the same direction too, and so in January 1965 he was ordained deacon and in June priest in the Anglican Communion by Bishop Horace Donegan of New York. Macquarrie dedicated his *Principles of Christian Theology* to John Knox, mentioning in the preface his indebtedness to Knox's "profound insights into the nature of the Church." Macquarrie did not feel that he was renouncing his Reformation upbringing, but rather was taking it into a larger room, the Anglican Communion, that "had preserved some things of great value that had been lost by the majority of Protestant churches; namely, a liturgy that is continuous with the worship of the early church, and a ministry of bishops, priests, and deacons which stood in historic succession to the ministry of the apostles who had been appointed by Christ himself."[63] Although he has never written formally on the issue of race relations, Macquarrie with his family used to worship at St. Mary's Church of Manhattanville, a mainly Black Episcopalian church.

University of Oxford

In the autumn of 1970, Macquarrie returned to the United Kingdom to become the Lady Margaret Professor of Divinity in the University of Oxford. As well as the official letter from Oxford came a personal letter from Henry Chadwick, Regius Professor of Divinity at the university, strongly encouraging the move. It was a difficult decision for the Macquarrie family. John's wife, Jenny, had become a very successful and popular teacher of mathematics at an Episcopal school in New York, St. Hilda's and St. Hugh's. Their eldest child, John Michael Macquarrie, suffered from autism and had just been offered a place at Manhattan College. However, at a family meeting over the question all the children expressed a desire to return to Britain, and so the difficult decision was made, as also were arrangements for John Michael to continue his studies. The chair of divinity at Oxford went with a canonry of Christ Church Cathedral. Macquarrie describes his duties: "As one of the canons, I had regular duties in the cathedral as well as my teaching duties. There are services in the cathedral every day of the year -- -- matins at 7:15 a.m., followed by a Eucharist, then at 6 p.m. evensong is sung by the choir. On Sundays matins and the Eucharist are also sung. In describing my life at Union... I spoke of 'an ideal situation for writing theology', but my new situation at Christ Church, though very different, was equally ideal!"[64] With the position the Macquarries had a large mansion of over thirty rooms in the heart of the college, and it is said that they made rooms in the house available to students whose financial means made it difficult to find appropriate accommodation in Oxford.[65]

Macquarrie succeeded in the Lady Margaret Chair Frank Leslie Cross (1900-1968), the patristic scholar, best known as convener of the First International Conference on Patristic Studies in 1951 and editor of *The Oxford Dictionary of the Christian Church*. Macquarrie held this chair until 1986 when he in turn was succeeded by Rowan D. Williams, another scholar whose competence reached into the patristic tradition as well as into contemporary Orthodox theology, and who is now the 104th Archbishop of Canterbury. When Macquarrie arrived in Oxford, a new syllabus in undergraduate theology was under construction. It was an attempt to expand the theology offerings beyond the traditional philological and doctrinal horizon "From the Garden of Eden to the Council of Chalcedon." The new syllabus was to include courses on particular theologians, and Robert Morgan reports that "Macquarrie's specialty was always Schleiermacher."[66] Macquarrie has had an abiding interest in Schleiermacher. The first published note occurs in *The Scope of Demythologizing* (p. 55), followed by the substantial essay "Schleiermacher Reconsidered" in the 1975 volume *Thinking About God* (pp. 157-166), and then the careful Christological consideration in the 1990 *Jesus Christ in Modern Thought* (pp. 192-211), with many occasional Schleiermacherian sprinklings in between. This is an indication of what may be called a growing mystical awareness in Macquarrie. In the 1990 book Macquarrie cites Schleiermacher:

The Redeemer assumes believers into the power of his God-consciousness, and this is his redemptive activity... Such a presentation of the redeeming activity of Christ as has been given here, which exhibits as the establishment of a new life common to him and us (original in him, in us new and derived), is usually called by those who have *not* had the experience, 'mystical.' This expression is so extremely vague that it seems better to avoid it.[67]

Then Macquarrie proceeds to comment on this passage as follows: "That paradigmatic humanity realized in Jesus Christ is imparted to the believers in the corporate experience of redemption in the community. If we ask more closely about the nature of this redeeming relation to Christ, Schleiermacher is prepared to describe it as 'mystical', though... he is not very happy about the term."[68] Mystical means here something like an abiding consciousness of Christ-in-God, and so may not be reduced to a mere subjectivism. It is in some respects conceptually close to Bradley's "higher pantheism." The mystical Macquarrie is emerging in and through these theological engagements.

Equally involved in the expansion of the theology syllabus was Macquarrie's long term Oxford colleague and friend, Maurice F. Wiles, the Regius Professor of Divinity, who had arrived shortly before Macquarrie. Wiles was a distinguished patristic scholar whose interests had moved into the arena of modern doctrinal interpretation. Wiles had been a contributor to the 1977 iconoclastic *Myth of God Incarnate*, edited by the Presbyterian theologian at the University of Birmingham, John H. Hick. While Macquarrie was genuinely appreciative of Wiles' contribution, he found much in this christological collection distasteful and both theologically and pastorally unhelpful. Both he and Wiles make an interesting contrast similar to the contrast between Macquarrie and Ronald Gregor Smith at the University of Glasgow. It is well captured by Robert Morgan: "Their collegial relationship was always cordial and became warm, but their very different backgrounds, expertise, and churchmanship meant they pursued similar theological goals while ploughing rather different furrows."[69] Their differences were not only to do with their respective training and interests, with Wiles being a classicist and patristic scholar and Macquarrie a philosopher and systematic theologian. Wiles belonged to the English establishment and to the Evangelical wing of the church, while Macquarrie came from the Scottish working-class and was a very articulate Anglo-Catholic. From his collegial interaction with Wiles Macquarrie learned the importance of patristic theology. He had long been interested in St. Athanasius --- see, for example, the many references to him in the 1965 book *Studies in Christian Existentialism* --- but through Wiles he came to a deeper appreciation of the patristic period: "I have often wished that I myself had received the thorough grounding in the Fathers that Headlam had imparted to his students, but our tradition in Scotland was very different and (at the time when I was a student in Glasgow) definitely deficient in patristics. The subject was included in church history rather than theology."[70] He never developed a strong competence in patristic theology. Macquarrie wrote a sensitive obituary when Maurice Wiles died in 2005, and an essay entitled "The Theological Legacy of Maurice Wiles."[71] The essay is a sensitive hermeneutic of Wiles' theological project and does justice to Wiles' intentions, the method characteristic of John Macquarrie, but he also indicates clearly where he departs from Wiles. During the Second World War, Wiles had been assigned to the secret British establishment at Bletchley Park, where intellectuals were engaged in deciphering the coded messages of Germany and Japan. Macquarrie draws a parallel between the code cracking work of Wiles and his later doctrinal work. "A friend of mine has pointed out that, although no one was aware of it at the time, Maurice's work at Bletchley Park was also a preparation for his life's work of cracking the codes of traditional biblical and theological teachings so that they might be available to the people of today's world."[72] Wiles was an advocate of what he called doctrinal criticism, the application to the creeds and texts of the tradition of the apparatus of criticism that had been applied to the Holy Scriptures. Macquarrie contrasts Wiles in theology with Derrida in philosophy, both involved in the project of deconstruction, opening the way to new interpretations of the Christian faith. He points out that Wiles was cautious, attempting to demonstrate in his own way that "the idea of radical discontinuity in doctrine is not strictly conceivable."[73] If he contrasts Wiles with Derrida, he also contrasts him with Karl Rahner who believed that the creeds and conciliar statements of the tradition "derive their life from the fact that they are not the end but the beginning, not the goal but the means – truths which open the way to the ever greater Truth."[74] However, when it comes to Wiles' treatment of the incarnation, a treatment in which he judges that the divinity of Christ is not necessarily "an unquestionable axiom," Macquarrie demurs, and holds fast to the traditional position of the Church.[75]

Since his return to the United Kingdom, a stream of books on different aspects of Christian doctrine has poured from Macquarrie's pen. *Paths in Spirituality* (1972) was devoted to prayer, worship and spirituality. In the new edition of this book published in 1992, there are three additional chapters: "Eucharistic Sacrifice," "The Reconciliation of a Penitent," and "Rest and Restlessness in Christian Spirituality." *Three Issues in Ethics* (1970) is taken up with moral theology. *Christian Unity and Christian Diversity* (1975) demonstrates his interest in and commitment to ecumenism, and William Green remarks of this book that "Macquarrie takes up John Knox's argument that the Roman Catholic Church must be the center of visible unity."[76] He suggests that Church unity might be structured after the pattern of the Uniate Churches, a pattern that allows communion with Rome as well as a measure of self-determination and autonomy. Contemporary dissatisfaction with uniatism as an ecumenical method might put his approach in a different light, but it would not seem to deflect from his central conviction that the only realistic approach to healing past divisions is some form of unity with Rome, but without absorption. Particular issues in the *Quaestiones disputatae* chapters of the book have been further refined by Macquarrie, especially his understanding of the Blessed Virgin Mary and the Petrine Ministry. *Christian Hope* (1978) develops Macquarrie's approach to eschatology. Beginning with a phenomenology of human hope in general terms, he goes on to outline the history of eschatology before making his own proposals for a contemporary understanding. In terms of individual eschatology, his central conviction is that if God is indeed as he is manifest in the person of Jesus Christ, he could not permit death to wipe out his care for his personal creatures. *The Faith of the People of God* (1972), a fine example of a systematic theologian writing for a non-specialist audience, *Thinking About God* (1975), a collection of essays and papers which finds its focus in a more organic relationship between God and the world and eschews any spectatorial or monarchic image of God and *The Humility of God* (1978), a series of provocative meditations on the articles of the Creed --- all wide-ranging explorations of Christian doctrine and Christian theologians. In 1977 he published a revised edition of his *Principles of Christian Theology*, about which he writes: "The fundamental teachings remain unaltered, but there is a good deal of new material, also clarifications and explanations to meet the criticisms of (Alistair) Kee and (Huw Parri) Owen particularly, though I have not actually named them... The new edition has some fresh material on most topics..."[77] William Green provides a most useful summary of the principal areas of doctrine which have been supplemented in this revised edition:

> 1) The philosophical criticisms of natural theology have been expanded and separated from the theological ones, and a more affirmative stance taken toward traditional natural theology; 2) there is less emphasis on human finitude and more on the inborn drive toward human transcendence; 3) greater balance has been given to the treatment of the person and work of Christ; 4) consideration of the Blessed Virgin is now supplemented by positive statements regarding her immaculate conception and assumption; 5) the concept of 'ministerial collegiality' makes its appearance for the first time.[78]

Beginning in the 1980s, Macquarrie took up various themes from the *Principles* for yet further development and exploration. *In Search of Humanity* (1982) offers an account of his anthropology that goes well beyond the anthropology of the *Principles*. For example, there are chapters on "Embodiedness," "Love," "Art" and "Hope" as well as aspects of an existentialist anthropology so well represented in *Principles*. As he works through the many and various elements of what it means to be human, an important ingredient in his understanding is dialectic, a willingness to enter as far as one can into mutually opposing systems of thought or action in order to find and if possible reconcile the insights on both sides. This is vintage Macquarrie, a scholar in whom "conflicting points of view were embraced in a generous orthodoxy – *odium theologicum* was unknown to (him)…"[79]

This perspective is taken further in respect of God in the next book. *In Search of Deity* (1984), his Gifford Lectures in the University of St. Andrews, takes further his interest in natural theology, in which Macquarrie demonstrates his progression from the "panentheism" of his earlier work to "dialectical theism." As he articulates his dialectical theism, he considers a series of contrasts about God: knowability and incomprehensibility, transcendence and immanence, impassibility and passibility, eternity and temporality. In his careful treatment of these opposites, Macquarrie comes close to paradox as the least inadequate way to speak of God. *Theology, Church and Ministry* (1984) gathers up a wide range of contemporary and, at times, controverted topics that reflect the title, for example: "Pride in the Church," "The Meeting of Religions in the Modern World: Opportunities and Dangers," "The Bishop and the Theologian" and "The Ordination of Women to the Priesthood." In the essay, "The Bishop and the Theologian," Macquarrie reflects on the importance of theology to the ministry of the bishop, something to which he returns even more emphatically in his recent *A Guide to the Sacraments*. It is probably true to say, however, with Bishop John Austin Baker that, while Macquarrie has been concerned with issues in Christology, ecclesiology, Eucharistic theology, and Mariology, these issues and areas of thought "have not engaged him as constantly as the divine mystery." There has been a greater concern with the doctrine of God above all else.[80]

It is intriguing, to say the least, that while Macquarrie throughout his entire professional career as a theologian attempted to remain in contact with philosophy, there is no obvious evidence of philosophers in the United Kingdom being conversant with the work of Macquarrie. For example, during the length of his tenure in Oxford, Sir Anthony Kenny was teaching philosophy. Kenny has always shown an interest in the philosophy of religion even though he professes to be an agnostic. Yet there is no reference to Macquarrie in any of Kenny's writings of which I am aware. Even given the somewhat necessary if too extended turf protection in the various disciplines of the academy, Kenny could not have been totally unaware of Macquarrie.[81]

Retirement in Oxford

In retirement, John Macquarrie has continued to be prolific. In point of fact, he states the obvious: "If someone has been studying, teaching and writing for three or four decades, these activities have become so much a part of his/her life that the person concerned cannot give them up. I have noticed that when such a person has, for one reason or another, been compelled to give up these activities, on retirement, very often there has been a steady decline."[82] He never gave up his theological activities. *Jesus Christ in Modern Thought* (1990), which won the Harper Collins Religious Book Prize, represents his mature christology. For years, apart from the synthetic treatment of *Principles*, Macquarrie has been putting out papers reflecting different issues in christology. Thus, he has written on such diverse christological topics as "The Humility of God"; responses to the British *The Myth of God Incarnate* debate in the late 1970s; "Kenoticism Reconsidered," "Tradition, Truth and Christology," "The Humanity of Christ," to name but a few. The 1990 book brings all this material together in an ordered fashion. The first part of the book deals with the New Testament sources of christology, the emergence of classical christology, and its development through the Reformation. In the second part, he plots a trajectory through modern christology, all of which prepares for the third part, his own contemporary expression of belief in Jesus Christ. In 1998 he published *Christology Revisited*, the Albert Cardinal Meyer Memorial Lectures delivered at the University of St. Mary of the Lake/Mundelein Seminary in the Archdiocese of Chicago. In his own words, after publishing *Jesus Christ in Modern Thought* "as soon as the book was finished and fixed in print, I began to realize that some things that might have been said had not been said, that many things could have been said better, while still other things should perhaps not have been said at all."[83] In *Mary for All Christians* (1990), on the encouragement of Dom Alberic Stacpoole, O.S.B., a colleague from Benet Hall, Oxford, Macquarrie published an accessible mariology, accessible both ecumenically and to the lay reader.

In his Hensley-Henson Lectures at Oxford in 1993-94, published as *Heidegger and Christianity* (1994), Macquarrie returns to the work of the philosopher Martin Heidegger. When asked if starting all over again in theology whether Heidegger would still be a central philosophical dialogue partner Macquarrie answered in the affirmative. *I think for various reasons he has never been taken very seriously in England, partly because English philosophy in the last fifty years or so has been very much tied to the analytic tradition. Heidegger combines both analysis and synthesis, and there are theological elements in Heidegger. His view of Being is not unlike Bradley's Absolute, because Heidegger does not equate Being with God. Being is somehow beyond God. You could think of it in various ways as somehow like those early theologians such as Dionysius. Dionysius speaks of the thearchy beyond divinity. The idea comes up in Tillich too, the 'God beyond God.' There are depths in God which we simply cannot grasp.* He notes that even the supposed atheist theologian, Don Cupitt, in his most recent work speaks of the *Fountain,* a term found also in Heidegger. *Being is the Fountain, that which gives itself, that which is the foundation of other things. In his latest books Cupitt talks about the religion of Being, which is very Heideggerian. I don't think Cupitt has sufficiently studied Heidegger, but it seems a more promising line than some of his earlier work. Heidegger says of himself that he is neither a theist nor an atheist, but it depends so much on how these terms are defined. His last essay was an interview which he gave to a journalist from Der Spiegel, and he called it "Only a God Can Save Us."In that essay Heidegger says that we cannot bring God back. There is a mystical element of waiting for God.* Notice particularly that judgment on Heidegger's interview, "There is a mystical element of waiting for God." Macquarrie's acknowledgment of this "mystical element" in Heidegger is a feature also of his growing awareness of mysticism.

Invitation to Faith (1995) was originally published as *Starting From Scratch: The Nature of Christian Faith*, a series of lectures given in Lent 1994 in St. Andrew's Church, Old Headington, Oxford. It is a fine example of Christian apologetics, not least because after every chapter, we are provided with some of the ensuing discussion between Macquarrie and the participants. *Mediators Between Human and Divine* (1996) brings him back to something in which he has been interested since his B.D. days in Glasgow, the great religious traditions of the world. *A Guide to the Sacraments* (1997) which grew out of lectures at Nashotah House in July of 1996, is thoroughly ecumenical in character, offering an understanding of sacramental theology that speaks broadly to all Christian traditions.

Stubborn Theological Questions (2003) gathers together Macquarrie's contribution to the topic that provides the title! He ranges over difficult theological terrain, usually through scholarly contributions, for example of Moltmann, Mascall, Berdyaev, DuBose, Ian Ramsey, Kant, and the collection is dedicated to his Oxford colleague, Maurice Wiles, "friend, colleague and fellow struggler with the stubborn questions." *Two Worlds Are Ours: An Introduction to Christian Mysticism* came out in 2004. In it Macquarrie considers an ecumenical array of mystics and their writings in between a carefully crafted introduction and conclusion that provides his own mind on the matter. While his theme is very definitely mysticism, one has the strong impression that he was working on the history of Western theology more generally, and also revealing something of his own mystical side. The dedication reads "Remembering Hazel." His daughter-in-law, Hazel, married to his son, the Scottish church historian and librarian, Alan Macquarrie, died in Glasgow on Christmas Day, 2003.

It would be most unfortunate if the impression were given that John Macquarrie's retirement was spent in publishing theological articles and books. He was a regular assistant in his local parish church of St. Andrew's, Headington.

In a letter to the author dated July 4, 2004, he wrote: "I still do a certain amount of voluntary work for the local parish, e.g., occasionally preaching, taking communion to the aged, etc..." His pastoral involvement also took him further afield. For example, John Macquarrie was the only priest of the Church of England who was able to preach in Scottish Gaelic at the Presbyterian services at the Crown Court Church of Scotland in London. His last engagement there was on May 22, 2005.[84]

Evaluations and Responses

In anyone's theological journey some theologians will figure more centrally than others. For me, as has been noted in the preface, John Macquarrie has been the paradigm of mature Christian theology, and a constant reading companion since 1968. Not everyone, however, will find his theology equally attractive and appealing. Balanced, critical accounts may be had in James J. Bacik, *Contemporary Theologians*,[85] and Daniel W. Hardy, "Theology Through Philosophy."[86] Bacik, a Catholic theologian who did his doctoral work on Karl Rahner under Macquarrie at Oxford, offers a most positive assessment of his supervisor: "Macquarrie has been a most valuable guide precisely because of his balance, clarity and respect for tradition. His creative work is solid because it is deeply rooted in a long and diverse tradition."[87] In the preface to his doctoral dissertation, Bacik again acknowledges Macquarrie's theological scholarship: "His great breadth of scholarship and fine human sensitivity are impressive to me..."[88]

Hardy, an Anglican theologian, is more critical. He points out that "Reason and philosophical insight enjoy a special position in Macquarrie's work, as the means of investigating human nature and discerning the patterns and universal structures of human existence, and developing a theological anthropology to which revelation contributes, and for which Scripture and tradition serve as the norms." He shows "the steady development" in Macquarrie's theology from the influence of Bradley, through his existentialism to his comprehensive systematic theology. Hardy points to a certain tension between a general religious faith and the very particular claims of Christian faith. Hardy's judgment seems right here. Macquarrie certainly refuses to isolate Christian faith from an innate and universal human religiosity, but equally he takes with great seriousness the objective fabric of Christian doctrine. There is an unavoidable tension here, and Macquarrie's chosen theological methodology refuses to dissolve it in favor of the one or the other, general religious faith or the specificity of Christian faith.

In the first edition of his justly celebrated synthesis of Catholic doctrine, *Catholicism*, Richard P. McBrien compares his project to Macquarrie's *Principles of Christian Theology:*

> The final product... is slightly more akin to Anglican theologian John Macquarrie's *Principles of Christian Theology*...than to Catholic theologian Hans Küng's *On Being a Christian...* Macquarrie's work deliberately seeks a balance between what Macquarrie calls the existentialist and the ontological approaches to Christian theology: the one emphasizing the personal and the subjective, the other emphasizing the essential and the objective.[89]

One has the impression that the way in which McBrien has shaped *Catholicism* owes not a little to Macquarrie's inspiration --- in fact he says so himself --- and in the new edition published in 1994, one will find over thirteen references to various aspects of Macquarrie's theology. At the same time, McBrien is not uncritical of Macquarrie. Writing as a Catholic, McBrien considers *Principles of Christian Theology* "insufficient (in) historical and doctrinal content" and judges "its existentialist approach to the major theological issues... not completely suited to a predominantly Catholic student-body."[90] There is some truth to this criticism. There is in Macquarrie, at times, an insufficiently historical perspective as he reaches for theological insight into important doctrinal issues, and this will be acknowledged in subsequent chapters. However, while McBrien is right to note the existentialist approach, he fails to acknowledge an equal emphasis on ontology. Macquarrie's approach to theology at the time of his *Principles* is best described as existential-ontological. He cannot be judged simply as an existentialist theologian. McBrien also acknowledges the support that Macquarrie gave him when he visited him at Union Theological Seminary. "I had recently begun a weekly column for various Catholic papers and wondered if it was a mistake to invest so much time and effort in popularizing academic theology. (Macquarrie) unhesitatingly insisted that theologians have a responsibility to share the fruits of theological scholarship with a wider and increasingly educated public."[91] That is exactly what John Macquarrie has done. Bishop John Austin Baker has written of Macquarrie's attempt to reach the wider Christian public as follows: "Macquarrie's aim is always to write for the thoughtful and interested Christian or enquirer on the central issues raised by religious belief. He has been acutely aware of the theological and devotional clichés that make conventional Christianity so largely unintelligible in contemporary culture."[92] Mediating Christianity in an intelligible way to contemporary culture recalls Schleiermacher's defense of Christian faith to the cultured despisers of religion, and Macquarrie fits so well as a latter day Schleiermacher.[93]

The noted Jesuit theologian, Avery Dulles, later a cardinal, delivered in 1970 a most appreciative lecture on Macquarrie's recently published *Principles of Christian Theology*.[94] He considers *Principles* "of extraordinary interest" and "highly ecumenical." Dulles noted that it was being used in many Catholic colleges and institutions as a textbook, although Dulles took issue with Macquarrie's approach to the doctrine of God: "I would respect John Macquarrie as a theologian very much, I think he is a brilliant man, but nevertheless he is far from Catholic doctrine in his doctrine of God, it seems to me..."[95] Dulles is proposing essentially a Thomist approach to God --- in point of fact, one of his earliest publications was a contribution to Thomist philosophy. On that presupposition Macquarrie's doctrine of God would necessarily be found wanting, but the question remains whether this approach is the only approach, an issue that will be taken up in some detail in the chapter on God. When Dulles was in Oxford delivering the Martin D'Arcy Lectures at Campion Hall in 1983, he had the occasion for theological encounter with Macquarrie, reporting that he found his theological work even more engaging, not least his explicitly ecumenical publications.[96] One could go on adding to the list of theologians who have been influenced or helped by Macquarrie, and such references abound in his *Festschrift*. Singling out these references and testimonies has but one purpose, that is, to establish something of the warm ecumenical appreciation of Macquarrie's work. Whatever individual differences one might have with specific aspects of his theology, the words that constantly come to mind in describing his contribution are: scholarship, sensitivity, balance, respect.

However, one especially stinging reaction to Macquarrie's work came from the pen of the late Donald M. Mackinnon, a Scottish theologian teaching at Cambridge. Stories, often embellished, abound about Mackinnon, and his theology has been helpful to many. Daniel Hardy counts among those who have been deeply influenced by Mackinnon the following theologians working in the United Kingdom today: Sarah Coakley, David Ford, Fergus Kerr, Nicholas Lash, Richard Roberts, (now Archbishop) Rowan Williams[97], and Frances Young.[98] Their contribution has been and continues to be very substantive. Let us take some examples more closely to focus on Mackinnon's influence. The Methodist theologian, the Rev. Professor Frances M. Young of the University of Birmingham, in her moving account of personal pain and suffering as she struggled with a severely handicapped son, is a witness to Mackinnon's penetrating lectures on the problem of evil. By way of contrast to superficial treatments of theodicy he demanded clear and conscious engagement with the sheer horror of evil.[99] In a similar way, Dr. Robert Runcie, former Archbishop of Canterbury, attended lectures by Mackinnon when he was a student at Oxford. The benefit was real albeit not immediate. Runcie says, "If you took down what Donald said, you couldn't understand it at the time, but you gradually worked your way into something which was really significant."[100] Again, the Catholic theologian, Professor Nicholas L. A. Lash, Mackinnon's successor in the Norris-Hulse Chair of Divinity at Cambridge, testifies to Mackinnon's influence as a teacher: "That Christian theology discovers and maintains its peculiar *akribeia* only in the measure that philosophy is 'complicated' by agony is, I think, amongst the more important lessons that Donald Mackinnon has helped me to learn."[101] There can be no doubt concerning Mackinnon's importance not only for those who came individually under his tuition as exemplified above, but also for the development of British theology more generally. Some would go further and point to his "chief influence" as coming through "his long-running interaction with the intellectual life of Britain."[102] None of this is in dispute.

Nonetheless, there was an unnecessarily acerbic side to Mackinnon. In a lengthy review of Macquarrie's *Studies in Christian Existentialism* Mackinnon begins: "Students of contemporary theology must welcome the appearance of this collection of essays by Professor John Macquarrie, as they provide an excellent introduction to the tendencies of which he is a very influential spokesman. He is a lively, if often superficial writer, self-confident, repetitive, likely to prove very persuasive to those who, through lack of the proper philosophical equipment, may be tempted to find in his favoured nostrums an intellectual panacea."[103] He goes on to contrast Macquarrie most unfavorably with Hans Urs Von Balthasar, a theologian whose work was congenial to Mackinnon and whose then untranslated *Herrlichkeit* he was introducing to the English theology-reading public. Describing his own philosophical bias as "impenitently realist" Mackinnon goes on to suggest that Macquarrie "needs (and I must add that a careful study of his over-praised *Twentieth Century Religious Thought* abundantly confirms this) to deepen and enlarge his philosophical perceptions." Even allowing for the strong contrast that Mackinnon wishes to draw between Macquarrie's theology and his own, this is unduly harsh and destructive. The Scottish Dominican theologian, Fr. Fergus Kerr, who was a student of Mackinnon's at the University of Aberdeen, makes some interesting remarks *a propos* of the idealist-realist debate which help to throw light on Mackinnon's views. Kerr notes that in the mid fifties Mackinnon's insistence on what he took to be "realism" was well established, but "A decade later his attitude to tendencies that he detected in modern theology had greatly hardened."[104] Kerr contextualizes Mackinnon's hardened position, but that cannot justify the rudeness and crudity of expression. About Mackinnon's own style of theology Macquarrie says, *I must confess that it doesn't appeal particularly to me. It's difficult to know. It's kind of nebulous, and I'm not quite sure what he's on about. Mackinnon was subject to some very strong likes and dislikes. I am not the only victim of his displeasure. John Knox, the New Testament scholar, also fell victim. Mackinnon was quite vicious in that review in the Journal of Theological Studies, and I remember (Dennis) Nineham saying to me, 'That review is actionable.' I don't know if he even bothered to read the book because the review did not touch on the substance of the book at all. The review brought me letters from various people, for example, John N. D. Kelly and Eric L. Mascall, assuring me that Mackinnon's view was not widely shared nor supported. Mascall was quite critical of existentialism --- in fact, he thought that Rahner was too much under the spell of Heidegger --- but he considered that Mackinnon was wide of the mark in this review.* I pointed out to Macquarrie the contrast between Mackinnon's mean-spirited review and the review of *Principles of Christian Theology* that came from the pen of John N. D. Kelly, the patristic theologian and Principal of St. Edmund Hall, Oxford. Kelly describes *Principles* as a "one-volume *Summa*," which demonstrates "a masterly grasp of theological issues and unrivalled clarity of exposition" as its author presents a "highly successful restatement of traditional Christian beliefs within the framework of a new-style natural theology inspired mainly by the writings of Martin Heidegger."[105] Macquarrie then showed me a letter that he received in New York from Kelly before he left for Oxford and the Lady Margaret Chair. In Kelly's letter the following passage may be found:

> Although we both have a Glasgow connection, I do not think that we have ever met, but in spite of this I should like, if I may, to congratulate you on your recent book *Principles of Christian Theology*. I have read this recently with absorbed interest and admiration, and would like to say how impressed I am by your skill at presenting our faith so persuasively in the context of an ontological existentialism... May I also say how distressed I was to read our friend Donald Mackinnon's savage attack on your *Studies*

in Christian Existentialism in the recent issue of the J.T.S. Some of his comments are grossly unfair, but I suppose we must accept them as examples of the neurotic obsessions which Donald all his life has had from time to time with particular issues. In any case the review is so unbalanced that I cannot think it will do your work much harm.[106]

Kelly has been proved right by the enormous receptivity to Macquarrie's work, especially but not only in the English-speaking theological world.

The early Mackinnon was greatly influenced by Karl Barth, especially his christocentrism and the sheer, gratuitous givenness of revelation. Macquarrie, on the other hand, has been rather critical of Barth's theology. He gives a more positive role to the innate human quest for God and to the pre-reflective or un-reflective experience of God as Holy Being. Macquarrie and Mackinnon represent quite contrasting theological viewpoints. Their differing philosophies or metaphysics also come into play. Mackinnon has been consistently critical of Bradley's metaphysics, and it may be, as Fergus Kerr avers, that Mackinnon in his passionate support of realism sought to expose "sometimes with a great ferocity" what he considered to be an idealist tendency in much modern theology, but that will not do. A fierce defense of one's theology or philosophy does not warrant discourtesy either to a text or to a living person. A courteous hearing and a vigorous response seem to be moral requirements in any publicly credible intellectual exchange.

While I was speaking to Macquarrie one morning, he received a phone call from Hong Kong to do with some legal difficulties of copyright in a Chinese translation of one of his books. Pursuing the matter further, he took down from his shelves the Chinese translations of a number of his books. Guanghu He, a professor of religious studies at Renmin University of China in Beijing gives us an indication of the influence of Macquarrie's theology in China: "(Macquarrie) is one of the few Western theologians with a high reputation among, and increasing influence upon, today's Chinese teachers and students who are interested in theology or religious thought."[107] The fact that an English language theologian is translated into Chinese and Japanese as well as European languages (see the details in the bibliography published in his *Festschrift*) gives some indication of his accessibility to the believing community and his contribution to the upbuilding of Christian faith. "Reception" by Christian theologians and people is an important hermeneutical principle in "faith seeking understanding." The global reception, both geographical and ecumenical, that John Macquarrie enjoyed is more than adequate testimony to his status as an important Christian theologian.

The Eirenic Theologian

A suggested title for the 2006 celebratory volume, *In Search of Humanity and Deity*, edited by Macquarrie's friend, the Oxford New Testament scholar Robert Morgan, had been *The Eirenic Theologian*. Whatever its merits as a book title, "the eirenic theologian" is an apt description for John Macquarrie in his treatment of others' work. As Ronald Stone points out, "He has no taste for polemics. The scholarly consensus has been that in his exposition of others' work he has been fair."[108] The contributors to this congratulatory volume would all stand behind that statement, even when they differ with Macquarrie. The book celebrated the fiftieth anniversary of the publication of his first book with SCM Press of London, *An Existentialist Theology*. Typical of this gentle, generous and good man, he sent me a copy of this volume in December 2006.

Eugene Long, Macquarrie's former doctoral student at the University of Glasgow, describes his final meeting with his former teacher in Oxford in June 2006. "The occasion was the publication by SCM Press of a collection of articles by students, friends, and colleagues celebrating the golden jubilee of one of its most distinguished authors. In addition to the presentation at the Deanery in Christ Church, we had a Sunday lunch in a nearby pub and a quiet dinner at the Macquarries' home. On our last day, which happened to be Ian's 87th (and last) birthday, we brought a cake, lit a candle, and sang happy birthday."[109] The stomach cancer which had plagued him for the last few years finally won out and John Macquarrie died on May 29, 2007, one month short of his eighty-eighth birthday. His books and papers had been given to the Graduate Theological

Federation of South Bend, Indiana, in the spring of 2007, and it is certain that the theological wisdom and balance and *eirene* of John Macquarrie will enrich many for a long time to come. Jenny Macquarrie followed John in death on July 19, 2008, at St. Luke's Nursing Home, Oxford.

Conclusion

David Tracy has suggested that there are two basic forms of the Christian imagination, the analogical and the dialectical, the former reflecting in the main the Catholic and Orthodox traditions, the latter the Reformation tradition.[110] The analogical imagination tends to emphasize the immanence of God in his creation, the dialectical God's transcendence, but seldom if ever are these shapes of the Christian imagination encountered in a pure form. Although he does not use Tracy's terminology, Macquarrie seems to share his perspective when he writes "Post-Reformation Christianity has, on the whole, stressed God's transcendence at the expense of his immanence."[111] The good theologian, recognizing the infinite complexity of his or her subject-matter will acknowledge each form as the corrective of the other. It is a matter of balance as one reverences the Mystery of God and his dealings with us, both-and and not either-or. John Macquarrie, it seems to me, is an excellent example of such balance at work, demonstrating throughout his work a sense of God's immanence and transcendence. He exemplifies both modes of the Christian imagination in fruitful tension. Here is a systematic theologian from whom much may be learned, a theologian described by Louis Bouyer as having "a positive sense of Protestantism, but who is also *très catholicisant.*"[112] Very high praise indeed from Louis Bouyer, but I wish to draw this chapter to a close with words from the obituary written about Macquarrie by Robert Morgan: "The more important memory is of a holy and humble man of heart and endlessly patient and generous with his time, always hospitable... He was quietly radiant in old age."[113] Canon W. R. F. Browning, a biblical scholar and Canon Residentiary of Christ Church Cathedral, Oxford from 1965 to 1987, and so during the Macquarrie years at

Christ Church, said this of him: "John Macquarrie was an extraordinary gift to the Church: a profound and prolific theologian... a generous colleague, a preacher always sensitive to his congregation, and every inch a priest: modest, gentle, and devout."[14] This certainly was the Macquarrie I came to know and about whose theology this book has been written.

---

[1] John Macquarrie, *On Being a Theologian, Reflections at Eighty,* ed. John H. Morgan (London: SCM Press, 1999), 30.

[2] Rowan D. Williams, "Foreword," in Robert Morgan, ed., *In Search of Humanity and Deity: A Celebration of John Macquarrie's Theology* (London: SCM Press, 2006), xiii.

[3] Passages in italics are transcribed from taped interviews by the author with John Macquarrie in July, 1998.

[4] Eugene T. Long, *Existence, Being and God: An Introduction to the Philosophical Theology of John Macquarrie* (New York: Paragon House Publishers, 1985), 1-2.

[5] John Macquarrie, *On Being a Theologian,* 12.

[6] The M.A. is the first degree in the Faculty of Arts in the University of Glasgow.

[7] William Ian P. Hazlett, "Ebbs and Flows of Theology in Glasgow 1451-1843," in William Ian P. Hazlett, ed., *Traditions of Theology in Glasgow 1450-1990* (Edinburgh: Scottish Academic Press Ltd., 1993), 4. I am much indebted to this fine essay.

[8] William Ian P. Hazlett, "Ebbs and Flows in Theology," 5.

[9] Ibid., 7.

[10] Ibid., 19.

[11] Obituary of John Macquarrie, *The Daily Telegraph,* Wednesday, May 30, 2007.

[12] John Macquarrie, "Robert Burns: Poet, Prophet, Philosopher," *The Expository Times* 86 (1974-1975), 112-115.

[13] John Macquarrie, *Thinking About God* (London: SCM Press, 1975), 167.

[14] William Ian P. Hazlett, "Ebbs and Flows of Theology," 23.

[15] John Macquarrie, "Pilgrimage in Theology," in Alistair Kee and Eugene T. Long, ed., *Being and Truth: Essays in Honour of John Macquarrie* (London: SCM Press, 1986), xii.

[16] Second edition edited by F. L. Cross and E. A. Livingstone (London and New York: Oxford University Press, 1974), 194.

[17] In his *Twentieth Century Religious Thought: The Frontiers of Philosophy and Theology*, rev. ed. (Harrisburg, PA: Trinity Press International, 2002), 29.

[18] John Macquarrie, *Two Worlds Are Ours* (London: SCM Press, 2004), 21.

[19] F. H. Bradley, *The Principles of Logic*, 2ed., vol. II (London: Oxford University Press, 1922), 688-689.

[20] John Macquarrie, *Twentieth Century Religious Thought*, 29. See the brief but interesting description of Bradley in Timothy Bradshaw, "Macquarrie, John," in Alister E. McGrath, ed., *The SPCK Handbook of Anglican Theologians* (London: S.P.C.K., 1998), 167.

[21] John Macquarrie, *Twentieth Century Religious Thought*, 34-35.

[22] William B. Green, "Profile: John Macquarrie," *Epworth Review* 20 (1997), 13. I am much indebted to this fine article by Dr. Green.

[23] John Macquarrie, "Pilgrimage in Theology," in Alistair Kee and Eugene T. Long, ed., *Being and Truth: Essays in Honour of John Macquarrie* (London: SCM Press, 1986), xii.

[24] Ian Henderson, *Myth in the New Testament* (London: SCM Press, 1952).

[25] John Macquarrie, *An Existentialist Theology: A Comparison of Heidegger and Bultmann*, (London: SCM Press, 1955), xi.

[26] John Macquarrie, *Thinking About God* (London: SCM Press, 1975), 204.

[27] Georgina Morley, *John Macquarrie's Natural Theology: The Grace of Being* (Burlington, VT and Aldershot, UK, 2003), 2.

[28] Martin Buber, *I and Thou* (New York: Charles Scribner's Sons, 1958).

[29] John Macquarrie, *Twentieth Century Religious Thought*, new ed. (Harrisburg, PA: Trinity Press International, 2002), 428.

[30] Eugene T. Long, "Introduction," in Eugene T. Long, ed., *God, Secularization and History: Essays in Memory of Ronald Gregor Smith* (Columbia, SC: University of South Carolina Press, 1974), 4.

[31] Ibid., vii.

[32] Eugene T. Long, *Jaspers and Bultmann: A Dialogue Between Philosophy and Theology in the Existentialist Tradition* (Durham, NC: Duke University Press, 1968).

[33] See Eugene T. Long, "Self and Other," in Robert Morgan, ed., *In Search of Humanity and Deity*, 159-160.

[34] Eugene T. Long, ed., *God, Secularization and History: Essays in Memory of Ronald Gregor Smith* (Columbia, SC: University of South Carolina Press, 1974).

[35] Eugene T. Long, *Existence, Being and God: An Introduction to the Philosophical Theology of John Macquarrie* (New York: Paragon House Publishers, 1985).

[36] See also the intellectual biography of Long in Jeremiah Hackett and Jerald Wallulis, ed., *Philosophy of Religion for a New Century: Essays in Honor of Eugene Thomas Long* (Dordrecht, The Netherlands: Kluwer Academic Publishers, 2004), 349-352.

[37] Alasdair Heron, *A Century of Protestant Theology* (Philadelphia: The Westminster Press, 1980), 126.

[38] Ronald Gregor Smith, *The Doctrine of God*, edited by Allan D. Galloway (Philadelphia: The Westminster Press, 1970), 106.

[39] John Macquarrie, *Thinking About God*, 113-114; see also John Macquarrie, *God and Secularity* (Philadelphia: The Westminster Press, 1967), 23-25.

[40] Allan D. Galloway, "Introduction," to Ronald Gregor Smith, *The Doctrine of God*, 16.

[41] John Macquarrie, *Twentieth Century Religious Thought*, 429.

[42] Clive L. Rawlins, *William Barclay: The Authorized Biography* (Grand Rapids: Eerdmans, 1984).

[43] Robert P. Carroll, "Hebrew, Heresy and Hot Air: Biblical Studies in Glasgow Since 1900," in William Ian P. Hazlett, ed., *Traditions of Theology in Glasgow 1450-1990*, 95-96.

[44] Gerard Hughes, SJ, *God, Where Are You?* (London: Darton, Longman and Todd, 1997), 117-118.

[45] John Macquarrie, *On Being a Theologian*, 19. Baillie's brother, Donald M. Baillie (1887-1954) of the University of St. Andrews and who had an interest in continental European theology, had been one of Macquarrie's dissertation examiners.

[46] John Macquarrie, "How Is Theology Possible?" *Union Seminary Quarterly Review* 18 (1963); Martin Heidegger, *Being and Time*, translated by John Macquarrie and Edward Robinson (London: SCM Press, 1962).

[47] John Macquarrie, *Twentieth Century Religious Thought* (New York: Harper and Row, 1963), 13.

[48] Eugene T. Long, *Existence, Being and God*, 10.

[49] John Macquarrie, *On Being a Theologian*, 22.

[50] Thus, Georgina Morley, op. cit., 98

[51] John Macquarrie, *On Being a Theologian*, 35.

[52] John Webster, "Principles of Christian Theology," in Robert Morgan, ed., *In Search of Humanity and Deity*, 83, 92.

[53] See among John Webster's many Barthian publications the following: *Barth's Ethics of Reconciliation* (New York and Cambridge: Cambridge University Press, 1995); ed., *The*

Cambridge Companion to Karl Barth (New York and Cambridge: Cambridge University Press, 2000); *Barth (Outstanding Christian Thinkers Series)* (New York and Oxford: Oxford University Press 2004); *Barth's Moral Theology* (Grand Rapids: Eerdmans, 2004); *Barth's Earlier Theology* (New York and London: T. & T. Clark, 2005); *Eberhard Jüngel, An Introduction to His Theology* (New York and Cambridge: Cambridge University Press, 1986); *The Possibilities of Theology: Studies in the Theology of Eberhard Jüngel* (1995).

[54] John Webster, "Principles of Christian Theology," 85.

[55] Georgina Morley, op. cit., 58, 76.

[56] John Austin Baker, "Wrestling with the Divine Mystery," *Church Times,* May 4, 2007.

[57] John Macquarrie, "And it Came to Pass in Those Days," *Church Times,* December 19, 1997.

[58] John Macquarrie, review of Andrew Louth, *Discerning the Mystery* (New York and Oxford: Clarendon Press, 1983), in *Sobornost* 5 (1983), 86.

[59] John Macquarrie, "Process and Faith, An American Testimony," in his *Thinking About God* (London: SCM Press, 1975), 215. The book is dedicated to Williams.

[60] John Macquarrie, *In Search of Deity* (London: SCM Press, 1985), 146.

[61] Norman Pittenger, *Catholic Faith in a Process Perspective* (Maryknoll, NY: Orbis Books, 1981), 20.

[62] John Macquarrie, "Pilgrimage in Theology," xv.

[63] John Macquarrie, *On Being a Theologian,* 38-39.

[64] John Macquarrie, *On Being a Theologian,* 60.

[65] I owe this fact to the Rev. Dr. Arthur McCrystall who completed a D.Phil. on the Book of Daniel at Oxford during the latter years of Macquarrie's tenure.

[66] Robert Morgan, "John Macquarrie in Oxford," in Robert Morgan, ed., *In Search of Deity and Humanity,* 97.

[67] F. D. E. Schleiermacher, *The Christian Faith,* tr. H. R. Mackintosh and J. S. Stewart (Edinburgh: T. & T. Clark, 1928), 425, 428-429.

[68] John Macquarrie, *Jesus Christ in Modern Thought* (Philadelphia: Trinity Press International, 1990), 210.

[69] Robert Morgan, "John Macquarrie in Oxford," in Robert Morgan, ed., *In Search of Humanity and Deity,* 101.

[70] John Macquarrie, *On Being a Theologian,* 66. Arthur Cayley Headlam (1862-1947) had been an exceptional New Testament and patristic scholar at Oxford and later Bishop of Gloucester.

[71] John Macquarrie, "The Theological Legacy of Maurice Wiles," *Anglican Theological Review* 88 (2006), 597-616.

[72] Ibid., 599.

[73] Maurice Wiles, *The Making of Christian Doctrine*, cited in John Macquarrie, "The Theological Legacy of Maurice Wiles," 607.

[74] Karl Rahner, *Theological Investigations*, vol. 1 (London: Darton, Longman and Todd, 1961), 149, cited in John Macquarrie, "The Theological Legacy of Maurice Wiles," 608.

[75] John Macquarrie, "The Theological Legacy of Maurice Wiles," 613.

[76] William Green, op. cit., 15.

[77] From a letter to the author dated September 14, 1976.

[78] William Green, op. cit., 16.

[79] Robert Morgan, "Obituary: The Rev. John Macquarrie," *The Telegraph*, June 5, 2007.

[80] John Austin Baker, op. cit., ad loc.

[81] See, for example, Anthony Kenny, *What I Believe* (New York: Continuum, 2007).

[82] John Macquarrie, *On Being a Theologian*, 104.

[83] John Macquarrie, *Christology Revisited* (London: SCM Press, 1998), 7.

[84] Information from Norman MacLeod, lawyer and chairman of the London Gaelic Services.

[85] James J. Bacik, *Contemporary Theologians* (New York: Triumph Books, 1989), 77-78.

[86] In David F. Ford, ed., *The Modern Theologians*, 2nd ed. (Oxford: Blackwell, 1997), 252-285, with 261-265 on Macquarrie.

[87] James Bacik, op. cit., 87.

[88] James Bacik, *Apologetics and the Eclipse of Mystery: Mystagogy According to Karl Rahner* (Notre Dame and London: University of Notre Dame Press, 1980), xvi.

[89] Richard P. McBrien, *Catholicism* (Minneapolis: Winston Press, 1980), 19.

[90] Richard P. McBrien, "The Inspiration of John Macquarrie," the-tidings.com, July 13, 2007.

[91] Ibid.

[92] John Austin Baker, op. cit., ad loc.

[93] The point is also made by Timothy Bradshaw, "Macquarrie's Doctrine of God," *Tyndale Bulletin* 44 (1993), 2.

[94] The lecture was published in Robert Morgan, ed., *In Search of Humanity and Deity*, 76-82.

[95] Cited in Richard P. McBrien, "The Inspiration of John Macquarrie."

[96] Personal communication to the author in November 1983. Dulles's D'Arcy Lectures were published as *The Catholicity of the Church* (New York and Oxford: Oxford University Press, 1985). He speaks warmly of Macquarrie's ecumenical theology on pages 82, 141-142.

[97] Archbishop Williams' biographer writes: "Rowan felt that his teacher towered over everyone else in the Cambridge Divinity School, and displayed the genuine radicalism that most of his colleagues lacked." See Rupert Shortt, *Rowan's Rule: The Biography of the Archbishop of Canterbury* (Grand Rapids: Eerdmans, 2008), 63.

[98] Daniel W. Hardy, "Theology Through Philosophy," in David F. Ford, ed., *The Modern Theologians*, 2nd ed. (Oxford: Blackwell, 1997), 277.

[99] Frances M. Young, *Face to Face: A Narrative Essay in the Theology of Suffering* (Edinburgh: T. & T. Clark, 1990), 56-57. In the *Festschrift* for Frances Young, her former colleague David F. Ford, Regius Professor of Divinity at the University of Cambridge has this to say about Mackinnon as a teacher of Young: "Among her teachers was one of the most profound and rigorous British philosophers of religion, Donald MacKinnon, who drew his students into his own wrestling with Kant, contemporary British philosophy, theologians such as Barth and von Balthasar, and above all the problem of evil exemplified by Auschwitz. Her theology is therefore rooted in the early classics of Christian thought but has been through modernity without being contained by it." David F. Ford, "Wilderness Wisdom for the Twenty-First Century: Arthur, L'Arche and the Culmination of Christian History, in R. S. Sugitharajah, ed., *Wilderness: Essays in Honor of Frances Young* (New York and London: T. & T. Clark, 2005), 160.

[100] Cited from Humphrey Carpenter, *Robert Runcie, The Reluctant Archbishop*, (London: Hodder and Stoughton, 1996), 88.

[101] Nicholas Lash, *Theology on Dover Beach* (London: Darton, Longman and Todd, 1979), 4. In a Cambridge doctoral dissertation supervised by David F. Ford and in part by Nicholas Lash, Paul D. Murray provides a fine account of MacKinnon's theology. See Paul D. Murray, *Reason, Truth and Theology in Pragmatist Perspective* (Leuven-Paris-Dudley: Peeters, 2004), 163-189.

[102] Thus, Daniel W. Hardy, op. cit., 272.

[103] *Journal of Theological Studies* 18 (1967), 292. The entire review runs from pages 292-297.

[104] Fergus Kerr, O.P., "Idealism and Realism: An Old Controversy Dissolved," in Kenneth Surin, ed., *Christ, Ethics and Tragedy: Essays in Honour of Donald Mackinnon* (Cambridge: Cambridge University Press, 1989), 16.

[105] *Journal of Theological Studies* 29 (1978), 617.

[106] The letter was kindly provided by Professor Macquarrie, and is dated June 1, 1967.

[107] Guanghu He, "Professor Macquarrie in China," in Robert Morgan, ed., *In Search of Humanity and Deity: A Celebration of John Macquarrie's Theology*, 141.

[108] Ronald H. Stone, "John Macquarrie at Union Theological Seminary in New York City," in Robert Morgan, ed., *In Search of Humanity and Deity*, 71.

[109] Eugene T. Long, "Existential Anglican: Remembering John Macquarrie, 1919-2007," *The Weekly Standard*, June 18, 2007.

[110] David Tracy, *The Analogical Imagination* (New York: Crossroad, 1981).

[111] John Macquarrie, "Incarnation as Root of the Sacramental Principle," in David Brown and Ann Loades, ed., *The Sacramental Word* (London: S.P.C.K., 1996), 31.

[112] *Le Metier de theologien*, Entretiens avec G. Daix (Paris : Editions France-Empire, 1979), 156.

[113] Robert Morgan, "Obituary: The Rev. John Macquarrie," *The Guardian*, June 5, 2007.

[114] W. R. F. Browning, Obituary, The Rev. Professor John Macquarrie, *Church Times*, June 1, 2007.

2. THE EXISTENTIALIST WITHOUT ANGST

The whole point is that the value of any theology cannot be judged by the extent to which it is read at any given time.
John Macquarrie.[1]

The second edition of Existentialism became a best-seller with Penguin, read widely by non-theologians... Macquarrie's early interests persisted, and his early enthusiasms are not repudiated.
Robert Morgan.[2]

Existentialism and the Christian Tradition

In writing his autobiographical essay, "Pilgrimage in Theology," John Macquarrie describes his work from 1953 to the mid-1960s as "my existentialist phase."[3] "The existentialist without Angst" is the description that Ronald Gregor Smith gave to Macquarrie when they were colleagues at Glasgow.[4] Macquarrie never seems to have been surfeited with anxiety, with the excessive introspection that marks some of those typically regarded as existentialist in their thinking. His existentialism has been a quiet but confident absorption of Heidegger's philosophy as a meaningful way to understand and communicate the Christian faith. Thus, he is able to say, "I don't think I had ever been a thorough-going existentialist, for I feared that one might end up in a kind of subjectivism if one followed that path to the end."[5]

It is fair to say that Heidegger's thinking has so passed into Macquarrie's that the language of Heidegger has become for him the natural and spontaneous medium for the articulation of the Christian faith, though, it must also be said, not the *only* one. This has been the case since the days of his doctoral studies on Heidegger and Bultmann through his Hensley Henson lectures on "Heidegger and Christianity" at Oxford University in the Hilary Term, 1993. However, the primacy for Macquarrie — as for Aquinas with Aristotle — has always been the Christian faith. While that primacy of Christian faith remains throughout his theological thought, Macquarrie's approach develops into what might be called a mutually critical correlational methodology.[6]

When the Catholic priest-theologian, David Tracy (1939-), of the University of Chicago divinity school published his excellent book *Blessed Rage for Order* in 1976, many Christian theologians found in this text a much-needed map for negotiating the terrain of theology. Taking his title from a poem by the American poet Wallace Stevens, "The Idea of Order at Key West," Tracy set out to "order" the complex task of theology in a bewilderingly pluralistic context. Essentially, he points out that the Christian theologian attempting to do justice to the faith he has received and to the modern world in which he is situated is faced, one might say necessarily faced, with a correlationist methodology construed as mutually critical. On the one hand, the theologian is the interpreter of the multifaceted Christian tradition, beginning in the Scriptures. On the other hand, as interpreter the theologian seeks to render the tradition intelligible for the contemporary world. That rendering attempts to correlate common human experience with the texts, artifacts, monuments and various media expressive of the Christian tradition. That rendering also and necessarily "recognize(s) an exigence for metaphysical or transcendental reflection." Tracy is quite emphatic:

> If it is correct to state that the task of theology demands that the theologian first uncover the religious and theistic meanings in both our common human experience and language and in explicitly Christian texts, then I find it impossible not to affirm the need for metaphysical or transcendental reflection to investigate the cognitive claims of those religious and theistic meanings.[7]

The task described by Tracy is the task performed by Macquarrie throughout his theological career, but, especially at the beginning, in his engagement with existentialism and Martin Heidegger and Rudolf Bultmann.

Existentialist Theology

There is a perduring tendency in the academy to rubbish those approaches to one's subject or discipline that are not especially congruent with one's own approach. This has happened, at least in some measure and in some places, to "Existentialism." The quotation from John Macquarrie, however, at the beginning of the chapter stands as a refusal to rubbish any theology in principle. That is not to say that all theological perspectives are judged by him to be of equal value. That would be a performatory contradiction. But systematic and historical theologians, and one imagines any scholar with an historical interest as well as some degree of systematic orientation, constantly finds inspiration in texts and interpretations from the past. Human understandings never just die. They may lose center stage, perhaps for a very long time, but they often surface somewhat serendipitously as an invitation to reflection and contemplation for those who are willing to probe. This is the case with what may be described as classic theological existentialism.

David Law writes: "Existentialism has fallen out of fashion, and is generally no longer regarded as a significant way of doing theology."[8] Law's judgment — and he is very sympathetic to theological existentialism, as a specialist in the theology of Soren Kierkegaard — is accurate if the operative criterion is contemporary scholarly interest in existentialist theology.[9] "Existentialism" means different things to different people, as David Law remarks, "Assessment of existentialist approaches to theology is hampered by the difficulty of pinning down the meaning of the term 'existentialism'."[10] But we may take the following, again from David Law, as offering an entry point to its meaning: "Existentialism describes a diffuse group of thinkers who take the existence of the single, individual human being as the starting-point of their philosophizing and theologizing... In its broadest sense, the term 'existentialist' is used to identify writers and thinkers who show such interest in concrete human existence, particularly its crises."[11] In his essay in the Macquarrie Festschrift Law engages in this assessment of existentialist theology with theologian Gareth Jones. It is interesting, therefore, to acknowledge Jones's definition of existentialism since he too has specialized in existentialist thought, having written a book on

Bultmann's theology.[12] Jones defines existentialism as follows in an article for *The Blackwell Encyclopedia of Modern Christian Thought*:

> Existentialism is a form of philosophical inquiry which attaches primary importance to the immediate, lived experience of the individual. Unlike idealism, therefore, which concentrates upon ideas and how we know or understand them, and realism, which considers the world as a realm of objects, existentialism examines the ways in which the subject encounters other beings and events in a world dominated by the sense of its own finitude.[13]

Jones contrasts the lineaments of existentialism first with idealism. Macquarrie may certainly be considered as having made the transition from idealism in his undergraduate studies in philosophy at the University of Glasgow, and especially the thought of Bradley, through what might be regarded in his BD days as a version of Calvinist realism, to the emergence of his existentialist phase beginning with his doctoral research on Heidegger and Bultmann. However, it is most curious that while David Brown, another contributor to *The Blackwell Encyclopedia of Modern Christian Thought,* considers Macquarrie as the "most distinguished representative of the existentialist form of philosophical theology," Jones never formally considers Macquarrie in his article on existentialism.[14] To say the least, this seems something of an oversight. It is Jones's conviction that existentialism wants "to elevate the subject to autonomy," and he is clearly opposed for solid theological reasons to the notion of complete human autonomy. If this is part of the reason for his neglect of Macquarrie as an existentialist thinker, it is utterly misplaced. Macquarrie has always insisted upon the integral relation of Christian faith and reason in its existentialist mode, and has never been an advocate for autonomy *qua* autonomy.

Nevertheless as broad descriptions, the descriptions of existentialism found in Law and Jones essentially fit John Macquarrie's "existentialist phase," the years 1955 to 1972, from *An Existentialist Theology* to *Existentialism.* Macquarrie's work during this period is rooted in the individual human being as the starting-point for theological reflection. "What does this (text) mean for my existence? With what possibility of existence does it present me? Into what understanding of my own being does it bring me? Here we have the core of the existential approach to the New Testament, and to the questions of theology in general."[15] It is his attempt to root an understanding of the Scriptures and doctrinal tradition of Christianity in an understanding of the human person as well as in approaching God. Existentialist theology for Macquarrie has *never* been to the exclusion of God. However, his methodological starting-point in the human person, in concrete human existence, stands in contrast with Scottish theology of this time.

Macquarrie and Scottish Theology in the Mid-Twentieth Century

It would be fair to say that the prevailing theology of mid-twentieth century Scottish divinity schools was neo-orthodoxy mainly focused on the contributions of Karl Barth. The exceptions when Macquarrie's theological career was beginning were the Baillie brothers, John Baillie (1886-1960) --- described by Macquarrie as "probably the most outstanding Scottish theologian in the mid-century"[16] --- and Donald M. Baillie (1887-1954), both described as "sensible peacemakers who held back from Barthianism."[17] Donald Baillie had been one of the examiners of Macquarrie's doctoral dissertation, and John Baillie was to recommend Macquarrie to Union Theological Seminary in New York. The Baillies had a critical appreciation of Barth and his emphasis on the sheer transcendence of God, but they were not *sensu stricto* Barthians.[18] The Barthians at the time were the Torrance clan, and especially Thomas F. Torrance of the University of Edinburgh, described by Macquarrie as "the most eminent Scottish theologian since the Baillie brothers."[19] Macquarrie's own aversion in divinity school to systematic theology probably had less to do with Karl Barth as such than with a pervasive Calvinism, devoid as he saw it of living and critical contact with the post-war world.[20] There was a definite liberal side to Glasgow theology, exemplified in different ways by John Macquarrie and William Barclay, the former in systematic theology and the latter in New Testament studies and popular expositions of Christian doctrine. Iain Torrance, son of Thomas F. Torrance, has captured well the mood of theology in the Scottish universities during the 1960s, just as Macquarrie was leaving for New York. "During the 1960s, and when there were Faculties of Divinity at the four ancient universities of Scotland, the simplistic rule of thumb was that Glasgow was the liberal one, Edinburgh was the Barthian one, St. Andrews was the biblical one and Aberdeen the conservative one. What is interesting is that the open and questioning temper of Glasgow theology goes back a long way."[21] We have seen something of the long way in chapter one. Glasgow theology has indeed been open and questioning, yes, but not in an irresponsible direction.

Macquarrie's turn to existentialism coincided with his decision to pursue doctoral work in systematic theology under the supervision of the recently arrived Ian Henderson (1910-1969) in the University of Glasgow's divinity school. Henderson had studied under Karl Barth in Basle, and it was he along with the Irish Presbyterian theologian, James L. M. Haire, who had acted as Barth's translators when Barth came to Scotland to give his Gifford Lectures. Henderson had, however, become quite critical of Barthian theology, and his interests had turned to Bultmann and to an existentialist interpretation of Christian faith.[22] It is with Ian Henderson that Macquarrie's existentialist theological phase began. He had graduated with his BD from the University of Glasgow's Faculty of Divinity in 1943, five years before Ian Henderson came as Professor of Systematic Theology. Henderson was the pioneer of Bultmann studies in Britain, and it was through Henderson, as we have seen, that Macquarrie initially made contact with Heidegger's philosophy.[23] His doctoral dissertation under Henderson was published as *An Existentialist Theology: a Comparison of Heidegger and Bultmann* (1955). It was soon followed by his *The Scope of Demythologizing* 1960). The translation (with Edward Robinson) of *Being and Time* would come out in 1962, and *Studies in Christian Existentialism* in 1965. Rudolf Bultmann provided a very favorable foreword to *An Existentialist Theology* in which he said:

> I have seldom found so unprejudiced and penetrating an understanding of my intentions and my work as in this book. It also evidences a penetrating and, as I believe, an essentially correct understanding of Heidegger, as well as a rare capacity for unfolding simply and clearly this philosopher's ideas, which are often hard to understand. So I must give my opinion that the author's book is a distinguished performance. He shows himself to be a thinker of high rank, with outstanding power of exposition... I set great hope on the future work of the author.[24]

High praise indeed, and with a certain prescience about Macquarrie's future. High praise came also to the publishers of *Being and Time*, SCM Press of London, from Heidegger for the Macquarrie-Robinson translation.

Martin Heidegger and Macquarrie's *"Heidegger"*

Canadian philosopher Charles Taylor begins an insightful essay on Heidegger with these words: "Heidegger's importance lies partly in the fact that he is perhaps the leading figure among that small list of twentieth century philosophers who have helped us emerge, painfully and with difficulty, from the grip of modern rationalism."[25] From his perspective as a professional philosopher Taylor opens up the contribution of Heidegger. However, although the philosophy of Martin Heidegger (1889-1976) has had an enormous impact on continental European philosophy, and to a lesser extent on continental European Christian theology, its reception in the more pronounced empirical world of Anglo-Saxon philosophy has not been greatly significant. Furthermore, there continue to be various interpretations of Heidegger's thought, and that is the reason for speaking of Macquarrie's "Heidegger." While some aver in respect of Macquarrie that "we may not be getting the full Heidegger," the question emerges, "What would that mean?"[26] Especially when it comes to philosophical theology, Macquarrie's line, it is arguably impossible to get "the full Heidegger" without interpretation. This is what George Pattison means when he says that "every theologian who engages with Heidegger's thought is to some extent also engaged in translating him..."[27] Macquarrie's is but one reading of Heidegger, albeit a reading that has been warmly received. "Nobody in the English-speaking world has done more than John Macquarrie to open up Heidegger's work, both by lucid exposition of a formidably dark body of writing and by provocative exploration of its many ramifications."[28] In getting a sense of John Macquarrie's take on Heidegger it will be useful, indeed I really think it will be necessary to build the context in which to understand Macquarrie, to provide a brief sketch of Martin Heidegger's life and career.

Coming from a working-class background in Messkirch, Baden --- his father was the sexton of St. Martin's Church --- Heidegger studied at the Jesuit secondary school at Konstanz before moving on to three years at the Jesuit Bertholds-Gymnasium in Freiburg. Did he feel a call to ministry in the church, a call to the priesthood? One author comments: "Whether or not Heidegger felt a vocation to the priesthood, his best chance of higher education was through the clergy..."[29] Like others who followed the philosophical path before him but lacked the financial wherewithal, for example Hegel, the Christian Church opened doors to higher education.

Heidegger was under the considerable influence of the Austrian philosopher, Franz Brentano (1838-1917) as well, of course, of Edmund Husserl, Brentano's erstwhile pupil in Vienna, whose two volumes of *Logical Investigations* he was later to keep on his desk as a sort of "personal cult book."[30] Brentano was a former Catholic priest and had been schooled in Aristotle and scholasticism.[31] The young Heidegger had been given a copy of one of Brentano's books, *On the Several Senses of Being in Aristotle*, by the priest-rector of the seminary in Konstanz, Conrad Gröber. As Macquarrie puts it, "This book awakened in Heidegger the philosophical quest which kept him occupied for the rest of his life — the quest for the meaning of being."[32]

Heidegger entered in 1909 the novitiate of the German Province of the Jesuits at Feldkirch, Austria, but he was very soon sent away for reasons of health. Next, he entered the archdiocesan seminary at Freiburg, and studied theology and philosophy at the University of Freiburg until he left the seminary, giving up the notion of priesthood. Apparently on the advice of his superiors, and again due to poor health, he abandoned his seminary studies in 1911. Having to leave the Jesuits, and then having to leave the diocesan seminary, may have contributed to a certain kind of grudge that Heidegger harbored against Catholicism.

He maintained and furthered his philosophical studies at the University, completing in 1913 his doctoral dissertation, *The Doctrine of Judgment in Psychologism*. Two years later in 1915, Heidegger completed and presented his *Habilitationschrift, Duns Scotus' Doctrine of Categories and Meaning*, so that now he could lecture within the German university system. The dissertation set out "to lead the way to a contemporary appraisal of medieval philosophy, proving its enduring value and relevance."[33] This was to change by 1919 when his interests turn significantly in the direction of phenomenology, and away from medieval thought and traditional Catholicism. He remained teaching at Freiburg for most of the time until 1923. Heidegger's thought at this time stands in stark contrast with the Heidegger of *Being and Time*.

A friendly rivalry developed between Heidegger and the priest-theologian, Engelbert Krebs (1881-1950), over a chair in Catholic philosophy at Freiburg. Krebs was to have a quite distinguished career as a Catholic theologian, and was the supervisor of Romano Guardini's doctoral dissertation, and a defender of Judaism during the period of Nazi ascendancy.[34] As it turned out, neither Krebs nor Heidegger got the chair. In 1917 it was Krebs who witnessed Heidegger's marriage to Elfride Petri, from a northern German Protestant family and a student of economics. When the Heideggers' first son was born some eighteen months later, they decided not to have the child baptized and brought up in the Catholic faith. Heidegger informed Krebs early in 1919 of his decision and of his "departure" from Catholicism in a letter: "I believe I have an inner calling for philosophy, and that by answering the call through research and teaching I am doing everything in my power to further the spiritual life of man and work in the sight of God."[35] Both Rüdiger Safranski and John Macquarrie concur that, while this decision would have been looked upon askance by Krebs, and indeed by Heidegger's own family back in Messkirch, "He did not formally leave the church," but he was holding on to Christianity albeit in his own unique way.[36] Putting all of this in a wider context, one must recall that these were the years immediately consequent upon the Modernist crisis in Catholicism. Heidegger is one of many who experienced a degree of real alienation from Catholicism after Pope Pius X's moves against Modernism.[37] Thus, S. J. McGrath writes: "The young Heidegger's characterization of Catholicism as an ahistorical, pseudo-philosophical system must be situated: Heidegger is reacting to the anti-hermeneutical Catholicism of the Modernist crisis, a regimented, propositional Catholicism, which declared anything that appeared to contradict the dogmatic tradition 'anathema.'"[38]

The Safranski-Macquarrie judgment seems essentially correct, especially given Heidegger's statement much later in life to a confidant, "I never left the Catholic Church."[39] It is known, for example, that during the 1920s Heidegger spent periods of time at the Benedictine abbey of Beuron.[40] Stories abound about his genuflecting in church, about blessing himself with holy water in the various stoupes that he came across, and about reverencing wayside crucifixes. It must also be remembered that he wished to be buried at least as a Christian if not as a Catholic, but this is to anticipate.

In 1923, Heidegger was appointed professor of philosophy at Marburg, and here his colleagues included Rudolf Otto, Rudolf Bultmann and Paul Tillich. Rudolf Bultmann had preceded Heidegger to Marburg by two years, and the latter's philosophy was to be a major influence on him. His theology "is born of the spirit of Heidegger's philosophy" and "Heidegger and Bultmann soon became friends and would remain friends for life."[41] In 1924 Heidegger, along with Bultmann and Friedrich Gogarten (1887-1967), met regularly together to read the Gospel of St. John in Greek.[42] The shared thoughts and insights of this scholarly *lectio divina* must have made their way into Bultmann's great commentary on that gospel.

At the beginning of 1924, the eighteen-year-old Jewish Hannah Arendt arrived in Marburg to study under both Heidegger and Bultmann. Heidegger and Arendt soon became lovers. Naturally, Heidegger was very secretive about this for obvious reasons, but also because his wife Elfride was very anti-Semitic. During the Marburg years Heidegger wrote his major work, *Being and Time*, which was published in 1927. "(Hannah) becomes his muse for *Being and Time*. He will admit to her that without her he could not have written the work."[43] This major work, *Being and Time*, was an attempt to apply phenomenology to a study of the nature of being. John Macquarrie, along with Edward Robinson, was the first to translate *Being and Time* into English in 1962. Some philosophers compare *Being and Time* with such classics of Western European philosophy as Kant's *Critique of Pure Reason* and Hegel's *Phenomenology of Spirit*.[44] Others regard it as unnecessarily opaque in expression and even, in the words of Gilbert Ryle the Oxford analytic philosopher, something of a "windy mysticism."[45] Ryle was not unappreciative of Heidegger, and yet that term "windy mysticism" is something of a giveaway. Arguably, there is something of a mystical quality in Heidegger's understanding of Being, but to call it windy is but to reveal one's reductionist presuppositions, presuppositions that continue to prevail in analytic philosophy.

It is being and not merely human existence that is Heidegger's principal interest in *Being and Time*.[46] At the same time, it is the being of the human person, *Dasein*, that provides access to being in general. Through his phenomenology of human existence Heidegger opens up the question of being.

This phenomenological anthropology unfolds human existence as having a threefold structure. First, *Dasein* is constituted by possibility. *Dasein* is never complete. The essence of *Dasein* lies in his existence, as it opens up before him. "A *Dasein* can either choose itself or lose itself."[47] Second, *Dasein* is constituted by facticity. That is to say, he is constituted not by pure possibility, but rather finds himself limited by the facts of his situation, facts over which he has no control: his location historically, his natural abilities and talents, his ethnicity. "Man's situation as a finite entity thrown into a world where he must project his possibilities is not disclosed to him by theoretical reasoning but rather in his affective states, or moods, of which the basic one is *anxiety*."[48] Third, is fallenness. "Fallenness" describes the situation of *Dasein* when he "flees from the disclosure of anxiety to lose himself in absorption with his instrumental world, or to bury himself in the anonymous impersonal existence of the mass, where no one is responsible."[49] This is inauthentic existence, living "in the cave," living in darkness. "Falling takes place when *Dasein* flees from itself and from its possibilities and responsibilities. It does so by losing itself in the anonymity and irresponsibility of the 'they' and in its restless but tranquillizing concern with the things that surround it. This is the forgetting of Being, and in Heidegger's understanding of the matter, it is the way to nihilism."[50] The path to authenticity lies in the liberating awareness of death, where death is not understood simply as the biological term of life. "All possibilities are evaluated in the light of death as the capital possibility, and when one lives in the anticipation of death, one lives with a resoluteness which brings unity and wholeness to the scattered self... Only by living through the nothingness of death in anticipation does one attain an authentic existence."[51] Macquarrie comments on the appropriate section of *Being and Time* speaking of death as follows:

> Heidegger's long and subtle discussion of death and dying constitutes one of the most interesting chapters of *Being and Time*... Death marks off the *Dasein*, as Being-in-the-world, from the nothing into which he disappears when he ceases to be in the world; and to be marked off

from nothing in this way is precisely to stand out from it, that is to say, to 'ex-sist'. Moreover, it is to exist authentically...[52]

This movement towards authenticity awakens the wonder of being, either in the Leibnizian form, "Why is there anything rather than nothing?" or much more personally, "Why am I?" Now there is a clearing for Being to manifest itself to *Dasein.* "It is an inescapable question for man, who is confronted with the nothing in his own being. 'Each of us is grazed at least once, perhaps more than once, by the hidden power of this question.'"[53]

Freiburg, the Rectorate and Nazism

Heidegger returned to Freiburg in 1928 as successor to Husserl. "The retirement of his master (Husserl) brought a call back to the University where he had begun and would end his philosophical career."[54] In 1934, the young Karl Rahner, SJ came to Freiburg to begin a doctorate in philosophy.[55] We shall meet Rahner's theology and Macquarrie's appreciation of it in a later chapter. Reminiscing about this period many years later, Rahner was to write: "I studied mainly under Martin Heidegger, already known and becoming famous. He had just been the first rector of that University under the Nazi regime, and we two young priests, J. B. Lotz (a well-known Jesuit philosopher) and I, were not anxious to throw in our lot with him for good or for ill, and so we enrolled with the professor of Catholic Scholastic philosophy, Martin Honecker. Nonetheless, our encounter with Heidegger was the decisive, impressive experience."[56] In an autobiographical memoir Rahner adds:

> When we came to Freiburg, Martin Heidegger's rather odd and very short University chancellorship at the beginning of the Nazi period had just ended. As young chaplains in clerical black and not Nazi brown, we didn't exactly know how to cope with a Heidegger still linked in some way to Nazism, so we cautiously registered as doctoral students with Martin Honecker. But we were clearly interested in Heidegger's lectures and seminars, and if we had definitely known this right from the beginning, then we could have very easily done our doctoral studies with Heidegger, perhaps even better and more sympathetically as well.[57]

These reminiscences of Karl Rahner help us to situate Heidegger's time in Freiburg. It was a time of heady philosophical investigation and teaching. What was it that Heidegger contributed to someone like Rahner? Among other things, Rahner says:

> He taught us how to read texts in a new way, to ask what is behind the text, to see connections between a philosopher's individual texts and his statements that wouldn't immediately strike the ordinary person, and so on. In this way he developed an important philosophy of Being. That can and will always have a fascinating significance for a Catholic theologian, for whom God is and remains the inexpressible Mystery. In my manner of thinking, in the courage to question anew so much in the tradition considered self-evident, in the struggle to incorporate modern philosophy into today's Christian theology, here I have certainly learned something from Heidegger and will, therefore, always be thankful to him.[58]

Heidegger was later to visit his pupil Rahner in Innsbruck, and to pay tribute to his theological achievements.

Nonetheless, Heidegger's rectorship was a problem. His appointment as rector of the University in 1933 by the Nazis indicates some support of the party, though he resigned from the rectorship in 1934. John Macquarrie comments: "I do not think that Heidegger's conduct in that time can be excused or glossed over but it is also important that we see this episode of his career in its correct proportions."[59] What are these correct proportions? For a start, in the winter of 1931-1932 Heidegger's support for Nazism had to do with its being "a force of order amid the hardships of the economic slump and the chaos of the collapsing Weimar Republic, and above all as a bulwark against the danger of a communist revolution."[60] Many Germans, including many thoughtful Germans, thought like that. Nazism gave hope. Many Catholic leaders and thinkers, both in Germany and in the Vatican, were of a similar mind.[61] For such people the atheism of Marxism and of the U.S.S.R., as well as the growing attraction for Communism in various countries of Europe and elsewhere (Mexico, for example), was a far more serious menace and threat than Fascism. Heidegger was very strongly opposed to Communism. In those days, where would one look in order to avoid the Bolshevist menace? One would look to something that seemed to offer promise, and for many that something was National Socialism. As Heidegger's friend Karl Jaspers noted, "National Socialism had become an intoxication of the population." Heidegger too was intoxicated; indeed Safranski says he was "bewitched."[62] The denazification commission of Freiburg University, immediately after the war, summarized Heidegger's statements to them as follows: "He believed that Hitler would grow beyond the party and its doctrine, and that the movement could spiritually be guided onto other tracks, so that everything would come together on the basis of a renewal and concentration for a Western responsibility."[63] He thought at the beginning that the Nazi revolution was a "kairotic" moment, that is to say, a uniquely timed moment of opportunity, a moment of collective breaking out from "the cave" of inauthenticity.

While not for a moment detracting from the egregious horror of the Nazi era, it is important to recognize that for many good people the times were marked by a deep ambiguity. Take for example Conrad Gröber, the priest from Messkirch who had given a Brentano volume to the young Heidegger. Gröber was a friend of Monsignor Eugenio Pacelli, the nuncio of Pope Pius XI to Germany. In 1932, Gröber was appointed Archbishop of Freiburg. Initially, Archbishop Gröber attempted to find common ground between the church and Nazism. The priests of his diocese were counseled to adopt a conciliatory approach to the party and its philosophy so that they might be able to bring some Christian influence upon it. The church historian of the Nazi era, Klaus Scholder, reports that Gröber even donated personal monies to Nazi organizations.[64] These were difficult, complex and ambiguous days.

Heidegger's appointment as rector of the University on April 21, 1933 was something of a concession to the professors of Freiburg who had publicly opposed Hitler in 1933. Heidegger was supported for the rectorship among a significant number of his colleagues. However, two lectures in May and June of the same year by Heidegger indicate his sympathies at the time: "The Self-Assertion of the German University" and "The University in the New Reich." Macquarrie acknowledges that these lectures "while they certainly express support for the regime, they are not extreme or fanatical and — very importantly — they do not contain any anti-Semitic utterances."[65] While Heidegger dismissed professors who were either Jewish or politically dissident, historian Robert Krieg writes of the theological faculty: "The University's fifteen theologians and its instructors in theology taught approximately 320 seminarians in 1933. No theologian was a member of the Nazi party, and none of them joined the AKD, despite Archbishop Gröber's support for it."[66] The Catholic Archbishop, and his former pupil now University Rector were, at least in some respects, on one side, the Nazi side, while the theology faculty was on the other. But what about this question of Heidegger's anti-Semitism? Was he really anti-Semitic? Safranski is more nuanced than Macquarrie in this respect. Safranski writes: "Certainly not in the sense of the ideological lunacy of Nazism. It is significant that neither in his lectures and philosophical writings, nor in his political speeches and pamphlets are there any anti-Semitic or racist remarks."[67] While Macquarrie simply says that Heidegger's speeches at this time contain no anti-Semitic rhetoric, Safranski fills out the picture with some more detail. He refused permission to the Nazi student organization to display anti-Jewish posters within the University. He maintained this refusal even when visited by a senior official of the SA. It was after this visit, accompanied by a threat to close the University, that Heidegger joined the Nazi party. Evidently he thought he could best protect the institution of the University and higher education by being a party member. Heidegger attempted to protect several Jewish professors from dismissal, though this may have had more to do with their contribution to the University than with their Jewishness. He found a research fellowship at the University of Cambridge in England for his Jewish assistant, Werner Brock, who could not safely remain at the University. Brock, who was later to return to Freiburg as a professor, wrote important works on

Heidegger and maintained his friendship with Heidegger.[68] An examination of Nazi documents pertinent to higher education in Germany demonstrates a growing discomfort with Heidegger both as a party member and as University Rector. The tone of the documents is summarized by a commentator in these words: "The early documents reflect a guarded yet cordial relationship between Heidegger and the party functionaries, but it quickly becomes confused, and Heidegger is finally talked about as being 'dangerous.'"[69] Towards the end of 1933 and not yet a year in office, Heidegger began to realize that he was not being particularly effective in changing the climate of National Socialism. He wrote: "During several quiet days during Christmas vacation, it became clear to me that it was an error to think that my intellectual position, which had developed in long years of philosophical work, could exert an immediate influence to change the intellectual — non-intellectual — bases of the National Socialist movement. In early 1934, I decided to resign from the rectorate at the end of the semester."[70] He did so in February 1934. The Nazis prevented him from attending philosophical conferences, and he began lecturing on Friedrich Nietzsche in an attempt to disassociate Nietzsche from fascist theories. In the summer of 1944, when manpower was crucial throughout Germany and especially in the Armed Forces, Heidegger was judged by the Nazi authorities as "the least indispensable of the professors at the University," and he was drafted into the army reserves.[71]

And yet there is a cultural anti-Semitism in Heidegger, according to Rüdiger Safranski, a refusal to accept the assimilation of the Jews into German society at all levels. At a personal level, Heidegger ended his quotidian contacts with his Jewish friends and students. This included Edmund Husserl, his old teacher and friend, who, as a Jew, had become increasingly isolated. In the early 1940s, under some pressure from his publishers admittedly, Heidegger withdrew the dedication of his *Being and Time* to Husserl. In this respect he forms a contrast with his old friend and rival, Engelbert Krebs, who stood firm against the Nazis and suffered for it.[72]

Archbishop Conrad Gröber, though something of an enthusiast of Nazism at the outset and a broker of the Vatican's Concordat with Germany, later changed course and became an opponent of the system. In December 1945, Heidegger appealed to Gröber who had some influence with the allies for assistance in attempting to recover his professorship in philosophy at Freiburg. Gröber wrote on his behalf, but to no avail.[73]

When *Being and Time* was being translated by Macquarrie and Robinson, Heidegger suggested to the translators that, should they encounter specific difficulties, they ought to contact Hannah Arendt. This they did and Macquarrie continued to have contact with her after the translation had been finished. He tells us of his final meeting with her on May 19, 1973:

> Dr. Arendt was on her way to Europe for the summer vacation, and we agreed to meet at Heathrow Airport, where she had to change planes. Our conversation turned naturally to Heidegger and to the translation. There had been surprisingly large sales and several reprintings in the United States, and I said to her, 'Heidegger must be making a lot of money from the translation.' She replied, 'Oh no. He's not a business man, and most of the money goes to the publisher.' I took her up on this: 'Would you say then that it was because he is not a man of affairs that he became involved with the Nazis in 1933?' 'Yes,' she said, 'quite so.'[74]

In the spring of 1946, Heidegger had a physical and mental breakdown, but recovered, and went into a kind of exile, in part self-imposed. As Safranski puts it, "He had to answer for his commitment in 1933."[75] During this confusing and immensely complex period, it must be recalled that, without trying to excuse Heidegger, Elfride Heidegger had always been a much more convinced and active party member than her husband. The last thirty years of Heidegger's life were taken up with writing philosophy, giving occasional lectures, and preparing his *Collected Works.*

In January 1976, Heidegger asked his Messkirch compatriot, the Catholic priest-philosopher and professor of Christian philosophy at the University of Freiburg, Bernhard Welte, to visit him. During the visit, he told Welte that he wanted to be buried in the Messkirch Cemetery, with a Christian funeral and with

Welte speaking at his graveside. Heidegger died on May 20, 1976, and Welte honored Heidegger's request. "The funeral was conducted by Heidegger's nephew Heinrich, who used prayers specially composed for the occasion inside the chapel, but followed the prescribed Catholic rite at the burial itself... Both (Heinrich and Welte) did, of course, celebrate Mass that day for the repose of Heidegger's soul, but not as part of the funeral service."[76] In his words at the graveside Welte said:

> He traveled this path without ceasing. There were bends and turns along it, certainly there were stretches where he went astray. Heidegger always understood the path as one that was given to him, sent to him. He sought to understand his word as a response to an indication to which he listened without respite... Is it fitting to give Martin Heidegger Christian burial? Is it in keeping with the message of Christianity, with the path of Heidegger's thought? In any case he wanted it. Moreover, he had never broken his bond to the community of believers.[77]

In conversation Macquarrie told me that he found these words pleasing and found himself in complete agreement with them.

Heidegger and Mysticism

Of his early 1976 meeting with Heidegger Welte wrote: "Floating in the room was also Eckhart's idea that God equaled Nothingness." What an interesting statement! Welte had written about Heidegger's philosophy, and saw connections between Heidegger, Meister Eckhart and also St. Thomas Aquinas.[78] In a lecture given at Plater College, Oxford, in 1989 but published only in 2003, John Macquarrie treats of "Eckhart and Heidegger: Two Mystics."[79] He believes that both Eckhart and Heidegger stand historically within the broad stream of Neo-Platonism, and he notes that Neo-Platonism has a perduring mystical element, exemplified, for example, in the philosopher-mystic Plotinus. Both Eckhart and Heidegger in Macquarrie's judgment reflect this Neoplatonic mystical element, among other things. Macquarrie does not maintain that Eckhart and Heidegger share this element of mysticism in an equally Christian fashion. But he does think that a mystical "something" similar, indeed very similar, is to be found in both.

During the academic year 1910-1911, Heidegger took Joseph Sauer's course on the history of medieval mysticism at Freiburg. This course is described by S. J. McGrath as "the beginning of a lifelong interest in Meister Eckhart," and Heidegger spoke of mysticism in his dissertation on Duns Scotus as "the living heart of medieval scholasticism."[80] From some scattered notes on mysticism put together between 1917 and 1919, Heidegger showed himself interested in the following mystical topics: irrationality in Meister Eckhart; historical consciousness in Bernard of Clairvaux; Schleiermacher's notion of religion; and Rudolf Otto's 'noumenal experience.'[81]

The philosophical theologian, John D. Caputo, has investigated in depth *The Mystical Element in Heidegger's Thought* and sees a close analogy between Eckhart's "birth of God in the soul" and Heidegger's "the event of truth." Let us hear Eckhart's own words first:

> The Father gives birth to his Son in eternity, equal to himself.' The Word was with God, and God was the Word (John 1:1); it was the same in the same nature. Yet I say more: He has given birth to him in my soul. Not only is the soul with him, and she equal with it, but he is in it, and the Father gives his Son birth in the soul in the same way as he gives him birth in eternity, and not otherwise. He must do it whether he likes it or not. The Father gives birth to his Son without ceasing; and I say more: He gives me birth, me, his Son and the same Son.[82]

This is the doctrine of mystical union with God, essentially reflecting the intimate communion found in the Gospel of St. John. Something parallel to the Eckhartian understanding emerges in Heidegger's concept of *Dasein*. Let us hear Caputo's account of *Dasein*, and the parallel will emerge with some clarity:

> *Dasein* is not a term for anything psychological; it is not a 'faculty' of the 'mind', nor is it 'consciousness'. It is the process by which a 'world', and the things that are in the world, become manifest. *Dasein* is the ecstatic relationship of openness to Being in which and through which Being

reveals itself. *Dasein* comes to pass 'in' man, but it is not equitable with man. For man is a being, and *Dasein* is the process by which beings come to be manifest.[83]

The similarity is obvious, and Caputo goes to some length to establish it verbally and conceptually. Nonetheless, he is careful not to identify Heidegger as a mystic without remainder:

> One must be careful not to be fooled by Heidegger. He appropriates the talk of the mystic, and much of the structure of the 'mystical union' of the soul with God, but he makes these things over for his own purposes and to his own liking... The mystic for Heidegger is a kin and an ally, who says a great deal of what Heidegger himself wants to say: there is more to thinking than reasoning; true language depends upon silence. In *Gelassenheit* (serenity) a deeper truth reveals itself. And so Heidegger freely takes over and uses what he finds of service in the mystic, and particularly in Meister Eckhart. But Heidegger remains throughout his own man. The mystic is concerned with the eternal, the 'thinker' with time.[84]

The early Macquarrie appears to know nothing of this mystical link of Heidegger with Meister Eckhart even when Heidegger's understanding of "Being" and "Nothing" is so eloquently discussed and analyzed by him.[85] The later Macquarrie, however, knows of Caputo's work, but while he never adverts to Caputo by name on this mystical issue of Eckhart and Heidegger, the thrust of his understanding of Heidegger would indicate a very close measure of agreement. In a fundamental sense, Macquarrie does not believe that "theist" is an appropriate term for either Eckhart or Heidegger because in his judgment they would not have been able to endorse the traditional Western understanding of transcendence that trails Western theism. Both thinkers sought for a view of "God" that would be more expressive of God's immanence. This leads Macquarrie to conclude:

> Neither Eckhart nor Heidegger conceived of God in the traditional one-sidedly transcendent way, and this may account for the superficial and inaccurate opinions that Heidegger was an atheist and Eckhart a pantheist... I do not think they confused God and the creatures, but they could not conceive God without the creatures. In Heidegger's case, what could Being mean or how could we know anything of Being, were it not somehow manifested in the multiplicity of things? In Eckhart's case, could

we properly speak of God unless there were also souls into which God's word could be born?[86]

Both Eckhart and Heidegger have in common their desire to destroy "the representable God," the God *known*, the God *grasped*. Both, but each in his own way, prayed God to rid him of God.[87] Certainly, then, the later Macquarrie knows of this mystical link of Eckhart and Heidegger, but it is typical of his methodology not to let the link be stretched too far.

Conclusion

"Even if we accept that existentialism has been colored by the age in which the various existentialists were writing—and what philosophy or theology is not? -- the significance of existentialism is not dependent upon the age in which it came into existence."[88] Far from being only a context-conditioned and time-conditioned approach, a good case can be made for existentialism, and so for existentialist theology, as a basic type of thought that may be found throughout the history of Christian reflection, with greater and lesser degrees of intensity at different times. This is how Macquarrie puts it:

> Existentialism is not a philosophy but type of philosophy... The contemporary existentialists look back to Kierkegaard. But before him there were Pascal and Maine de Biran, who both showed marked affinities with existentialism. Father Copleston claims that there was a school of thought with resemblances to existentialism in the late Middle Ages. Brock (an authority on German philosophy) finds traces of existentialism in Augustine's reflections on 'the ceaseless unrest which marks the temporal life of the individual.' There were undoubted stirrings of the existentialist type of thought in ancient Greece, for example, in Socrates, though it was not the dominant trend in classical philosophy. Thus existentialism, it is claimed, is not merely a phenomenon of modern times. It appears rather to be one of the basic types of thought that has appeared from time to time in the history of philosophy.[89]

This appearance of existentialism from time to time as a "basic", that is, *fundamental* type of thought is ultimately rooted and founded in the actual human person who thinks, who philosophizes, who theologizes. "It is the acknowledgment that philosophizing is from the point of view of a finite human existence, and this cannot be exchanged for a divine eminence from which one might objectively survey all time and all existence... (Existentialism) is the *locus* in which all philosophizing takes place --- our own human existence."[90] In this basic-fundamental sense existentialism may be considered straightforwardly as the human person thinking about ultimate things.

Towards the end of his contribution in the 2006 Macquarrie Festschrift, David Law writes: "We need to find a balance between expecting too much and too little from existentialism. Existentialist theology is not the answer to all theological questions, but is a way of drawing out the significance of the Christian faith for the personal, individual existence of a human being. It is not the only valid way of doing theology, however, and needs to be supplemented by other theological approaches."[91] Law's words are not only accurate but they also accurately describe the theological course of John Macquarrie's thought. He has never been locked into existentialism as a comprehensive system. He has never regarded any system of thought concerning the things of God as final. He has always been open to different approaches and new or deepened interests, philosophically and theologically.

---

[1] John Macquarrie, *Studies in Christian Existentialism* (Montreal. McGill University Press, 1965), 55.

[2] Robert Morgan, "John Macquarrie in Oxford," in Robert Morgan, ed., *In Search of Humanity and Deity* (London: SCM Press, 2006), 98.

[3] Georgina Morley, *John Macquarrie's Natural Theology: The Grace of Being* (Burlington, VT and Aldershot, UK: Ashgate Publishing, 2003), 7.

[4] See George Newlands, "John Macquarrie in Scotland," in Robert Morgan, ed., *In Search of Humanity and Deity*, 23.

[5] John Macquarrie, *On Being a Theologian*, ed. John H. Morgan (London: SCM Press, 1999), 35.

[6] Consider David Fergusson's description, "For Macquarrie, the presence and knowledge of God are understood in a wider and more diffuse manner, thus enabling a positive correlation of Christian revelation with other faith traditions and religious experience more generally understood," in his "John Macquarrie as Interpreter of Bultmann," in Robert Morgan, ed., *In Search of Humanity and Deity*, 30.

[7] David Tracy, *Blessed Rage for Order*, rev. ed. (Chicago: University of Chicago Press, 1996), 53-56.

[8] David R. Law, "The Abiding Significance of Existentialist Theology," in Robert Morgan, ed., *In Search of Humanity and Deity*, 34.

[9] Law was awarded the D.Phil. of Oxford University for his 1989 dissertation, "Kierkegaard as Negative Theologian: An Analysis of the Hiddenness of God in the Pseudonymous Works of Soren Kierkegaard." His dissertation was supervised by John Macquarrie, and he has written widely on Kierkegaard's theology.

[10] David R. Law, "The Abiding Significance of Existentialist Theology," 34.

[11] David R. Law, "Existentialism," in Adrian Hastings and others, ed., *The Oxford Companion to Christian Thought* (New York and Oxford: Oxford University Press, 2000), 227.

[12] Gareth Jones, *Bultmann: Towards a Critical Theology* (Cambridge: Polity Press, 1991).

[13] Gareth Jones, "Existentialism," in Alister McGrath, ed., *The Blackwell Encyclopedia of Modern Christian Thought* (Oxford: Blackwell, 1993), 200.

[14] David Brown, "Philosophical Theology," in Alister McGrath, op. cit., 440.

[15] John Macquarrie, *Studies in Christian Existentialism*, 104.

[16] John Macquarrie, *Twentieth Century Religious Thought*, rev. ed. (Harrisburg, PA: Trinity Pres International, 2002), 340.

[17] Alistair Mason, "Scottish Christian Thought," in Adrian Hastings and others, ed., *The Oxford Companion to Christian Thought*, 652.

[18] Alasdair I. C. Heron, *A Century of Protestant Theology* (Philadelphia: The Westminster Press, 1980), 124-126; fine accounts of the Baillie brothers' theology may be found in David Fergusson, ed., *Christ, Church and Society: Essays on John Baillie and Donald Baillie* (Edinburgh: T. & T. Clark, 1993) and George Newlands, *John and Donald Baillie: Transatlantic Theology* (Bern: Peter Lang, 2002).

[19] John Macquarrie, *Twentieth Century Religious Thought*, 439.

[20] John Macquarrie, *Paths in Spirituality*, 2nd ed. (Harrisburg, PA: Morehouse Barlow, 1992), 155, and *On Being a Theologian* (London: SCM Press, 1999), 12-13.

[21] Iain Torrance, "A Long Tradition of Engagement: A Tribute to Trinity College, Glasgow, on its 150th Anniversary," in Paul Middleton, ed., *The God of Love and Human Dignity: Essays in Honour of George M. Newlands* (Edinburgh: T. & T. Clark, 2007), 5.

[22] John Macquarrie, "A Modern Scottish Theologian," in his *Thinking About God* (London: SCM Press, 1975), 204-212.

[23] See John Macquarrie, *On Being a Theologian* (London: SCM Press, 1999), 14-16, and "A Modern Scottish Theologian," in his *Thinking About God* (London: SCM Press, 1975), 204-212, especially 208.

[24] Rudolf Bultmann, "Foreword," in John Macquarrie, *An Existentialist Theology* (London: SCM Press, 1955), viii.

[25] Charles Taylor, "Engaged Agency and Background in Heidegger," in Charles Guignon, ed., *The Cambridge Companion to Heidegger* (Cambridge: Cambridge University Press, 1993), 317. See also Annemarie Gethmann-Siefert, "Martin Heidegger and Theology: 'Reciprocal Modification'," in Alistair Kee and Eugene Thomas Long, ed., *Being and Truth: Essays in Honour of John Macquarrie* (London: SCM Press, 1986), 18-42.

[26] See Thomas K. Carr, "Only a God Can Save Us: Heidegger and Christianity," *First Things* 55 (1995), 60.

[27] George Pattison, "Translating Heidegger," in Robert Morgan ed., *In Search of Humanity and Deity*, 65.

[28] Fergus Kerr, OP, Review: John Macquarrie, *Heidegger and Christianity* (London: SCM Press, 1994), in *Journal of Theological Studies* 46 (1995), 794.

[29] S. J. McGrath, *The Early Heidegger and Medieval Philosophy* (Washington, DC: The Catholic University of America Press, 2006), 26.

[30] Rüdiger Safranski, *Martin Heidegger, Between Good and Evil* (Cambridge, MA: Harvard University Press, 1998), 25.

[31] See John Macquarrie, *Twentieth Century Religious Thought*, 227-228.

[32] John Macquarrie, *Heidegger and Christianity* (London: SCM Press, 1994), 4.

[33] S. J. McGrath, op. cit., 42.

[34] Romano Guardini (1885-1968) was in many ways a precursor of Vatican II (1962-1965), arguably one of the most important Christian events of the twentieth century. Under the direction of Engelbert Krebs he chose for his dissertation not the theology of Aquinas, mandated for Catholics by Pope Leo XIII, but the thought of Aquinas's contemporary, Bonaventure of Bagnoreggio. The dissertation was entitled "The Teaching of St. Bonaventure on Salvation," and was awarded in 1915. It is curious that Guardini does not appear in any of the editions of John Macquarrie's *Twentieth Century Religious Thought*, both because of Guardini's connections with Karl Rahner, a serious influence on Macquarrie, and also because Guardini was a friend of Martin Heidegger. He was entirely opposed to the Nazi regime and would not compromise, unlike Heidegger. See Robert Krieg, *Romano Guardini, A Precursor of Vatican II* (Notre Dame, IN: University of Notre Dame Press, 1997), especially 1-22.

[35] Cited in Rüdiger Safranski, op. cit., 108.

[36] John Macquarrie, *Heidegger and Christianity*, 6; see Rüdiger Safranski, op. cit., 108.

[37] See Owen F. Cummings, *Prophets, Guardians and Saints: Shapers of Modern Catholic History* (New York-Mahwah, NJ: Paulist Press, 2007), 135-154.

[38] S. J. McGrath, op. cit., 45.

[39] Cited in Thomas Sheehan, "Reading a Life: Heidegger and Hard Times," in Charles Guignon, ed., *The Cambridge Companion to Heidegger* (Cambridge: Cambridge University Press, 1993), 72.

[40] Rüdiger Safranski, op. cit., 4. Safranski also points out that during the years 1945 through 1949, when Heidegger was forbidden to teach, Beuron Abbey "was the only place he appeared in public."

[41] Rüdiger Safranski, op. cit., 134.

[42] I owe this to the Rev. Dr. George Seidel, OSB, Professor of Philosophy at St. Martin's University/Abbey, Lacey, Washington. Gogarten is much less well known than Bultmann. For an introduction to his thought see John Macquarrie, *Twentieth Century Religious Thought*, 365-371.

[43] Rüdiger Safranski, op. cit., 140.

[44] For example, Dermot Moran, *Introduction to Phenomenology* (New York and London: Routledge, 2000), 192.

[45] Gilbert Ryle, "Heidegger's *Sein und Zeit*," in Michael Murray, ed., *Heidegger and Modern Philosophy* (New Haven: Yale University Press, 1978), 64.

[46] For a useful and lucid commentary on *Being and Time*, see the Macquarrie scholar Georgina Morley, *John Macquarrie's Natural Theology: The Grace of Being* (London and Burlington VT: Ashgate Publishing, 2003), 7-42.

[47] John Macquarrie, *Martin Heidegger* (Richmond: John Knox Press, 1968), 14.

[48] John Macquarrie, *Twentieth Century Religious Thought*, 354.

[49] Ibid.

[50] John Macquarrie, *Heidegger and Christianity*, 28.

[51] Ibid.

[52] John Macquarrie, *Martin Heidegger*, 30.

[53] John Macquarrie, *Twentieth Century Religious Thought*, 354. Macquarrie is citing Heidegger's post-*Being and Time* work, *An Introduction to Metaphysics*, 1.

[54] Thomas Sheehan, "Heidegger's Early Years: Fragments for a Philosophical Biography," in Thomas Sheehan, ed., *Heidegger the Man and the Thinker* (Chicago: Precedent Publishing, Inc., 1981), 15.

[55] In fact, Rahner had taught Latin to the Jesuit novices in the novitiate at Feldkirch, the same novitiate attended very briefly by Heidegger.

[56] Cited in Thomas F. O'Meara, OP, *God in the World: A Guide to Karl Rahner's Theology* (Collegeville: The Liturgical Press, 2007), 17.

[57] Karl Rahner, SJ, *I Remember* (London: SCM Press, 1985), 42.

[58] Cited in Herbert Vorgrimler, *Understanding Karl Rahner* (London: SCM Press, 1986), 59.

[59] Ibid., 112.

[60] Rüdiger Safranski, op. cit., 227.

[61] See, for example, Robert A. Krieg, *Catholic Theologians in Nazi Germany* (New York and London: Continuum, 2004), and Frank J. Coppa, *The Papacy, the Jews and the Holocaust* (Washington, DC: Catholic University of America Press, 2006), especially 142-218.

[62] Cited in Rüdiger Safranski, op. cit., 231.

[63] Cited in Rüdiger Safranski, op. cit., 232.

[64] See Robert A. Krieg, op. cit., 141, 201. For a sense of the Vatican and Pope Pius XII's position *vis-à-vis* Nazism see the relevant chapter in Owen F. Cummings, *The Popes of the Twentieth Century* (Lewiston, NY and Lampeter, UK: The Edwin Mellen Press, 2008).

[65] John Macquarrie, *Heidegger and Christianity*, 112.

[66] Ibid., 143.

[67] Rüdiger Safranski, op. cit., 254.

[68] I owe this reference to Fr. George Seidel, OSB, whose dissertation at Freiburg --- "Heidegger and the Presocratics" --- was done under the supervision of Werner Brock. Brock took Seidel to meet Heidegger, reaffirming the lasting friendship between the two men.

[69] Karl A. Moehling, "Heidegger and the Nazis," in Thomas Sheehan, ed., *Heidegger the Man and the Thinker*, 36.

[70] Cited in Karl A. Moehling, op. cit., 37.

[71] Ibid., 39.

[72] See Robert Krieg, op. cit., 131-151.

[73] Rüdiger Safranski, op. cit., 351.

[74] John Macquarrie, *Heidegger and Christianity*, 116-117. Thomas K. Carr, op cit., 58, 62, is critical of Macquarrie on this point.

[75] Ibid., 352.

[76] Fergus Kerr, OP, op. cit., 792.

[77] Bernhard Welte, "Seeking and Finding: The Speech at Heidegger's Burial," in Thomas Sheehan, ed., *Heidegger the Man and the Thinker*, 73-75.

[78] Bernhard Welte, "La Métaphysique de Saint Thomas d'Aquin et la pensée de l'histoire de l'être de Heidegger," *Revue des Sciences Philosophiques et Théologiques* 50 (1966), 601-614; "The Question of God in the Thought of Heidegger," *Philosophy Today* 26 (1982), 85-100.

[79] John Macquarrie, *Stubborn Theological Questions* (London: SCM Press, 2003), 184-195.

[80] S. J. McGrath, op. cit., 120.

[81] Ibid., 131.

[82] German Sermon 6, in Edmund Colledge, OSA and Bernard McGinn, trans. and intro., *Meister Eckhart: The Essential Sermons, Commentaries, Treatises, and Defense* (New York-Ramsey-Toronto: Paulist Press, 1981), 187.

[83] John D. Caputo, "Meister Eckhart and the Later Heidegger: the Mystical Elements in Heidegger's Thought," in Christopher Macann, ed., *Martin Heidegger, Critical Assessments*, vol. II (London and New York: Routledge, 1992), 148.

[84] Ibid., 171-172.

[85] See for example, *An Existentialist Theology* (*passim*), and especially his 1963 essay, "The Language of Being" in his *Studies in Christian Existentialism* (Montreal: McGill University Press, 1965), 79-96.

[86] John Macquarrie, "Eckhart and Heidegger: Two Mystics," in *Stubborn Theological Questions*, 185. See also his *Twentieth Century Religious Thought*, 355, and *Heidegger and Christianity*, 117-121.

[87] Emending words from Eckhart's sermon, "*Beati pauperes spiritu*," and following the line of the Eckhart scholar, Reiner Schürmann, *Wandering Joy: Meister Eckhart's Mystical Philosophy* (Great Barrington, MA: Lindisfarne Books, 2001), 209.

[88] David R. Law, "The Abiding Significance of Existentialist Theology," 39.

[89] John Macquarrie, *An Existentialist Theology* (London: SCM Press, 1955), 16-17.

[90] John Macquarrie, *Twentieth Century Religious Thought*, 371.

[91] David R. Law, op. cit., 54.

3. JOHN MACQUARRIE AMONG ANGLICANS AND CATHOLICS

Here we are dealing with a theologian who loves to stress the continuities rather than the discords of the realities he describes. An Anglican, Macquarrie can be seen as continuing a strong tradition within this denomination, that of liberal Catholicism ...
Timothy Bradshaw.[1]

There is a core ethos to Anglicanism: a balanced, modest, generous orthodoxy.
Alan Bartlett.[2]

Introducing the Anglican Tradition of Theology

"Theology may be defined as the study which, through participation in and reflection upon a religious faith, seeks to express the content of this faith in the clearest and most coherent language available"[3] or, more briefly "the attempt to state as clearly as possible the beliefs or doctrines that belong to the Christian way of life."[4] This is how John Macquarrie, describes theology. It is equally revealing of the man himself.

John Macquarrie was ordained as an Anglican priest in 1965 in New York. While he had experienced his own Presbyterian tradition as a "dreary evangelical Protestantism," he was attracted to the High Church movement in the Church of Scotland and to the Scottish Episcopal Church. Here are his words: "To begin with, the attraction was that of liturgy, forms of worship which through symbol and sacrament made real the presence of God in a way I had not experienced in services dominated by preaching."[5] Macquarrie was forty-five years old. It appears that he waited to make this transition until both his parents, devout Presbyterians, had died. Since 1965, his prominence and importance as an Anglican theologian has steadily grown. At the same time he is emphatic that this decision did not mean a simple abandonment of his Presbyterian tradition: "I should add that in becoming an Anglican, I did not feel that I was renouncing my past. Rather, I was taking it with me into something broader, richer, more fulfilling, more catholic."[6]

What is this Anglican tradition? There has been something of a sea change in the way that the English Reformation has been understood in recent decades. Suffice it to summarize for our purposes with Oxford theologian Mark Chapman: "Although different aspects moved at varying speeds, and it is probably better to talk of reformations in the plural, it is undeniable that in the 16th century England experienced a thoroughgoing Reformation."[7] A different direction was taken by the church in England. Under King Henry VIII it has been described as "Catholicism without the pope." Chapman writes: "The Church of England can be understood as perhaps the purest form of the late medieval church ideal surviving after the Reformation."[8] With the accession of Queen Elizabeth I in 1558 and the consequent revision of the Book of Common Prayer there emerged a fairly settled position for the Church of England between Roman Catholicism and "the more extreme varieties of Protestantism."[9] Thus, Chapman's description provides a good initial description of the Anglican Communion, though it is clearly the case that the Communion is global and that today and in the future perhaps the majority of Anglicans will worship and live in the southern hemisphere. Obviously changing demographics will have implications for Anglican theology and self understanding. That is not our concern here. What Chapman offers us in this description is an understanding of the Anglican tradition as both Catholic and Reformed that might be regarded as "classical." In this part of the chapter we shall examine John Macquarrie's theology within the context of "classical" Anglican theology. After his priestly ordination in 1965 "his writings during this period show an increased familiarity with and commitment to the distinctive character of Anglican theology."[10]

"Is there such a thing as an Anglican theological tradition?" This is the question with which John Macquarrie opened his reflection on Anglican theology in an essay published in 1984.[11] Macquarrie firmly believed that there was such a thing as the Anglican tradition of theology, but he believed equally that it was difficult to define. Anglicans have not unpacked their understanding of doctrine in quite the same way as other Reformation traditions. Macquarrie sees three reasons behind this failure, if failure it is. First, Anglicans have not understood themselves as other than the Catholic Church in England, albeit the reformed Catholic Church in England. This is how he puts it: "They have never thought of themselves as separating from the Catholic Church, and so it has been maintained that Anglican doctrine is simply the doctrine of the whole Church, not that of some particular tradition."[12] In precisely that sense he maintains that there is no such thing as "an Anglican theology."[13] What he means is that Anglicans do not understand the tradition of Christian doctrine to be significantly different for them. Rather, it is their way of doing theology that makes them distinctive. Second, what he calls "the somewhat empirical and pragmatic temper of the English people" seems to militate against the publishing of detailed doctrinal formulas and statements. Third, and related to the second, is that Anglicans traditionally have not been particularly interested in developing systematic theology. This may be due to their desire to cherish the mystery of God and the things of God and the consequent refusal to locate the mystery in systematic theological propositions and treatises. Thus understood, the Anglican tradition, arguably, is marked by "a pleasing combination of two principles: affirmation and restraint," and by an ethos that is reflective of both the Catholic and the Reformation traditions.[14]

The Commissions on Christian Doctrine

Macquarrie believes that a particularly fruitful moment occurred for Anglicans between the First and Second World Wars. In 1922 the archbishops of Canterbury and York set up a Commission on Christian Doctrine, which published its report in 1938. In line with this the Lambeth Conference of 1920 moved into the area of ecumenism, what Archbishop William Temple was later to call "the great new fact of our times." And then there were different theological perspectives on the Church of England as evidenced in the Anglo-Catholic Congress with its high ecclesiology and sacramental theology on the one hand, and the Modern Churchmen's Union with its tendency towards a low Christology on the other. This was the context in which the Commission on Christian Doctrine published its report in 1938, a report whose influence and importance are described by Macquarrie as follows: "More than fifty years after its appearance, one still finds it quoted by Anglican participants in ecumenical dialogues as representing the position of their communion."[15]

The report of 1938 acknowledges the central place of Holy Scripture for Christian doctrine, while refusing to accept what has become known as the verbal inerrancy of Scripture. The church also is a source of doctrine in its central role as mediator of the tradition. In describing the content of the report, which falls into three parts -- on the doctrine of God and redemption, on the doctrine of the Church and the sacraments, and on the doctrine of eschatology --- Macquarrie quips: "One can hardly fail to be struck by the disproportion in length of these three parts. The section on church, ministry and sacraments gets more space than the other two put together --- 102 pages, as against 58 for God and redemption and a mere 18 for eschatology!... We can see that it gives some support to the gibe that one can be a good Anglican if one believes in episcopacy, no matter how much else one disbelieves!"[16] No doubt Macquarrie is being humorous here, but the jest is somewhat unfair. These were the heady days of emergent ecumenical dialogue, and in dialogue with Reformation ecclesiological traditions it was surely important for the Anglican Communion to be very clear about its ecclesiology, not least about episcopacy. Macquarrie himself had a genuine concern for the episcopate, a concern that flowers in his treatment of bishops in his book on the sacraments. That is for a later chapter. At this point, it may be helpful to note that he saw in Michael Ramsey, Archbishop of Canterbury, perhaps the essence of episcopal leadership. In his magisterial biography of Ramsey, Owen Chadwick draws attention to Macquarrie's presence at the 1968 Lambeth Conference, over which Archbishop Ramsey presided, and offers the following remarks: "John Macquarrie was an Oxford theologian who attended the conference as an observer. He had a surprising observation about its members and its chairman. He said that he was astonished to find so many of the bishops being swept along among the fashions and the slogans of the popular thought of the sixties. And he felt in retrospect, that Ramsey's achievement, not only at this conference but throughout that unsettled age, was the intellectual stance --- not his books but his attitude --- open to new ideas but not being swept along by fashion, at once critical and respectful of tradition."[17] For Macquarrie a bishop had to be interested in theology, and to have a deep-rooted interest that prevented him being swayed simply by fashion. He saw that exemplified paradigmatically in Michael Ramsey.

The liturgy is clearly acknowledged as a *locus theologicus* in Anglican theology. Macquarrie cites several documents and then comments: "The liturgy and the way of doing it is seen as decisive. There may be no documents which spell out precisely the content of Anglican belief in the form of a confession of faith, but what people do is sometimes better evidence of their inward beliefs than what they say."[18] He makes the role of the liturgy more specific by adverting to the issue of the eucharistic gifts when the celebration of the Eucharist is over: "The practice of reverently consuming the consecrated gifts at the end of the Eucharist does imply some eucharistic theology, and although this too could be formulated in quite a number of ways, it is obviously a very different theology from that which prevails in those Protestant churches where any bread and wine left over is thrown in the trash-can or poured down the sink."[19] Liturgical practice expresses liturgical theology; Eucharistic actions express eucharistic belief.

In 1976 the Doctrine Commission, set in place a decade earlier by the Archbishops of Canterbury and York, published the report known as *Christian Believing*. In contrast to the earlier report of 1938, this was quite individualistic in terms of the members' contributions so that in Macquarrie's judgment it "is mainly concerned to stress the fluidity and pluralism which characterize contemporary theology."[20] There is a necessary place for pluralism of expression and understanding in the articulation of Christian doctrine, but where fluidity and pluralism are predominant in a report that is taken to be representative of the church's doctrinal position that surely becomes problematic. The description of the report offered by Bishop Stephen Sykes, while in part anecdotal, well captures its ethos:

The inner story of that Commission's work has yet to be told, but I am informed that it brought one of its distinguished members nearly to the point of resignation. A whole generation of Anglican scholars, including the Regius Professors of Divinity at both Oxford and Cambridge, plainly found the greatest difficulty in coming to a common mind about the significance of the creeds for the beliefs of modern Christians.[21]

To say the least, in an ecclesially commissioned report that is very problematic.

It is not surprising then that there was widespread disappointment with the report and it was soon left to one side. The then Archbishop of Canterbury, Donald Coggan, appointed a new commission with a quite different set of members, chaired by the Bishop of Winchester, John V. Taylor. The fruits of the commission's deliberations were published in 1981 as *Believing in the Church*, the very title seeking to combat the individualism that marked the 1976 report. The respected Anglican philosopher of religion, Basil Mitchell, has captured something of the tension between the individual and the corporate belonging and believing of the church, and has outlined the way forward:

> To belong to a church is to believe what the church believes. There is more to it, no doubt, than that, but there can scarcely be less... The individual is never as independent or autonomous as is often supposed, but depends for most of his fundamental beliefs on a continuing tradition or traditions; and any tradition depends for its vitality upon the free criticism of reflective individuals. Hence there is a tension between the two which is inevitable and, when properly understood and accepted, fruitful.[22]

Mitchell and Macquarrie, both members of the Oxford faculty of theology at the time, have quite precisely the same position in this regard. Moreover, Macquarrie has acknowledged that it was his reading of Basil Mitchell's writings that led him to a more affirmative appreciation of natural theology.[23]

Macquarrie aligns himself with the perspective of Bishop Stephen Sykes, in his 1978 book *The Integrity of Anglicanism*, the perspective that calls for a greater Anglican involvement with systematic theology. This interest in developing Anglican systematic theology was certainly part of the reason for Macquarrie being invited to take up the Lady Margaret Chair in Divinity at

Oxford. Some commentators, for example Peter Sedgwick, view the 1960s and the 1970s with a rather jaundiced eye when it comes to theology in England. Though he does not develop the point, Peter Sedgwick considers Macquarrie's advent in the 1960s into the Anglican Communion, and into the enterprise of teaching theology in England as marked by what he calls a "wholesale liberalism." This is what Sedgwick says: "When the later cultural challenges of the 1960s took place... the response of much English, Anglican theology was to embrace a wholesale liberalism (John Macquarrie, Peter Baelz, Ian Ramsey, Maurice Wiles, Dennis Nineham and Don Cupitt) which parallels other non-Anglicans like John Hick."[24] While Sedgwick's list of bedfellows is indeed Anglican, to describe them collectively as "wholesale liberals" is, quite frankly, nonsensical. Each has his own distinctive way. We have seen something of Maurice Wiles, Macquarrie's Oxford colleague in chapter one, but to illustrate with just a couple of examples, Cupitt and Ramsey. Certainly, Don Cupitt of Emmanuel College, Cambridge developed a very distinctive radical approach to theology that might be deemed agnostic with regard to the reality of God. Cupitt, however, is not representative. Ian Ramsey (1915-1972), professor of theology at Oxford and later Bishop of Durham, was prominent in promoting a philosophical theology that would speak, or at least be intelligible to the tradition of analytic philosophy, and in establishing a greater relationship between theology and science.[25] Admittedly all the theologians in Sedgwick's list are marked by an openness to modernity, but not wholesale liberalism --- however that is to be defined --- and surely the pattern of liturgy and personal devotion, certainly instanced in Macquarrie and even in Maurice Wiles, is not simply outwith their theological methodology. Further, an awareness of Macquarrie's similarity to Richard Hooker, a classic exemplar of Anglican theology, will show Sedgwick's judgment, without qualification, to be wide of the mark.

John Macquarrie and Richard Hooker

All theology is done in a particular tradition, and no theology can be done well without the constant recognition of what Alastair MacIntyre has called "tradition-constituted enquiry."[26] Needless to say, Anglican theology goes back to the foundations of the New Testament and patristic authors, as well as to the legacy of the Middle Ages. At the same time, Anglican theology also has its own community of the heart. Thus, Anglican theologian, Paul Avis, has written: "Anglican theologians will only have (faith in their tradition) if they are steeped in the writings of the great formative theologians of Anglicanism, among whom Richard Hooker is, by common consent, supreme."[27] Macquarrie had been well schooled in philosophy and theology long before becoming an Anglican in 1965. However, he offers us insight into his Anglican "tradition-constituted enquiry" in his 1984 essay on the Anglican theological tradition. In this essay, Macquarrie provides a brief theological genealogy --- Thomas Cranmer, John Jewel, Richard Hooker, the Caroline divines and members of the Oxford Movement. He was acquainted with them all. Nevertheless, all things considered, Macquarrie seems closer to Richard Hooker in theological methodology than to the others.

"Richard Hooker, the true father of Anglicanism much more than Cranmer or Henry VIII, was a humble country parson, but vastly erudite." Thus, Louis Bouyer on Richard Hooker.[28] What might be described as essential Anglicanism owes much to what was achieved during the reign of Queen Elizabeth I, daughter of Henry VIII and Anne Boleyn. The Queen was interested in theological matters. Thus, she read her New Testament in Greek regularly, her private book of devotions was full of prayers for "Thy Church my care," she saw to the elimination of the so-called Black Rubric forbidding kneeling at Holy Communion --- from the Book of Common Prayer, and believed in the eucharistic presence of Christ. She was a strong supporter of episcopacy though her own preference was also for a celibate clergy, and she consistently refused to receive at court the wives of her married bishops, nor did she allow the wives of clergy to live in colleges or in cathedral closes. At a time when the Puritans were vociferously denouncing episcopacy as a Romish creation far from the New Testament, Elizabeth described their position as "newfangledness." As she said once to the Spanish ambassador de Silva, "We only differ from other Catholics in things of small importance."[29]

Ordained a priest in the Church of England probably about 1581, Hooker remained in academic life at Oxford until his arrival in London in 1585. In that year he was appointed Master of the Temple by the Archbishop of Canterbury, John Whitgift. This was an important appointment. The Temple Church was at the Inns of Court, the very heart of the legal system, and the Master was the principal clergyman. It was here that Hooker began to develop his theology against the attacks of the Puritan divine, Walter Travers, a radical Calvinist who viewed the episcopal ordination of the Church of England as contrary to the New Testament. As one commentator has it, "It was the grit of Puritanism that brought out of the oyster the pearl which consists of the theological writings of Richard Hooker,"[30] while another says of the morning and afternoon sermons at the Temple Church, "the forenoon sermon spake Canterbury; and the afternoon Geneva."[31] It was here that Hooker laid the systematic groundwork of the Elizabethan Settlement of Religion.

Louis Bouyer compares Hooker's great work *The Laws of Ecclesiastical Polity,* begun at the Temple, with St. Thomas Aquinas's *Summa Theologiae,* although Bouyer would see Hooker more as a moralist and Aquinas more as a metaphysician.[32] *The Laws of Ecclesiastical Polity* is his basic response to the fundamental tenets of Puritanism. The first four books of the *Laws* were published in 1593, aided by his former pupil Edwin Sandys. In 1595 Hooker moved to the parish of Bishopsbourne near Canterbury. It was at Bishopsbourne that he published Book V of the *Laws* in 1597. Izaak Walton describes Hooker's death at forty-six years of age: "'Are my books and written papers safe? Then it matters not; for no other loss can trouble me'... and then the doctor (his confessor, Saravia) gave him and some of those friends which were with him, the blessed Sacrament of the body and blood of our Jesus."[33] When he died in 1600, three further books were readied for posthumous publication in 1648 and 1662. How is Hooker's theological style to be described?

Hooker's theology gets labeled in different ways by different scholars, and yet it has a universal appeal. Let us turn to three interpreters of Hooker to get an overall sense of his theology. The Irish Anglican, Archbishop Henry McAdoo, offers the following description of Hooker and it seems right on the mark: "If 'liberal' means 'an openness in the search for truth' rather than an accommodating and over-hospitable mind; if a 'conservative' is one who respects continuity, treasuring tradition's best and most durable gifts from the past, rather than being neurotically resistant to change, then, with some caution, one might say... that Hooker is a liberal conservative."[34] Here then is a theologian not easily pigeonholed, not easily put into a specific category. The distinguished American Hooker scholar of over thirty years, John Booty, describes his subject in these fine words: "Through the years the conviction has grown in me that here is a man who understood."[35] "Here is a man who understood" suggests suasively a "liberal conservative," for the terms "liberal" and "conservative" on their own in theology are seldom accurate and dialogically barren. Finally, the popular apologist, C. S. Lewis, could write of Hooker: "Every system offers us a model of the universe; Hooker's model has unsurpassed grace and majesty... Few model universes are more filled --- one might say, more drenched --- with Deity than his."[36] To say that someone's model of the universe is drenched with God is perhaps the ultimate accolade for a Christian.

For Hooker there are three ways of knowing: through our senses, through reason and through what he calls "prophetical revelation" or Holy Scripture.[37] Knowing through Scripture is superior, but it may not stand on its own apart from reason. Scripture itself presupposes reason --- how else could we know Scripture *as* Scripture --- and the God of Scripture gifts us with reason in order the better to know him as he draws humankind to communion with himself. In this fashion he opposes any view of *sola Scriptura*.

He certainly had a strong reverence for tradition: "Neither may we in this case lightly esteem what hath been allowed as fit in the judgment of antiquity, and by the long continued practice of the whole Church; from which unnecessarily to swerve, experience hath never as yet found it safe."[38] There can be for him no jettisoning of tradition coming from antiquity that has served the church well. At the same time, that which comes from tradition cannot be reverenced and clung onto for its own sake: "Lest therefore the name of tradition should be offensive to any, considering how far by some it hath been and is abused, we mean by traditions, ordinances made in the prime of Christian religion, established with that authority which Christ hath left to his Church for matters indifferent, and in that consideration requisite to be observed, till like authority see just and reasonable cause to alter them."[39]

Hooker is referring to things that can be changed, that is to say matters of order, but never of doctrine:

> The Church hath authority to establish that for an order at one time, which at another time it may abolish, and in both it may do well. But that which in doctrine the Church doth now deliver rightly as a truth, no man will say that it may hereafter recall, and as rightly avouch the contrary. Laws touching matter of order are changeable, by the power of the Church; articles concerning doctrine not so.[40]

That which enables the alteration of tradition is the right exercise of human reason. Reason in that sense interprets Scripture. It is "an instrument which God doth use unto such purposes."[41] The primacy belongs to Scripture, but while this is so, Scripture is never to be separated from tradition. Access to this Scripture-in-tradition comes through the exercise of our God-given human reason. Bishop N. T. Wright describes Hooker's approach to Scripture as follows: "Part of the legacy of Hooker, making some of the riches of mediaeval thought reaccessible within a Reformation framework, was precisely that holistic worldview which insists, not that Scripture should be judged at the bar of reason and found wanting, but that in reading and interpreting Scripture we must not do so arbitrarily, but with clear thinking and informed historical judgment."[42] Hooker, therefore, accepts Holy Scripture as foundational, cherishes tradition, but sees reason as God's gift at work in both. In other words, one might say that human reason is to be exercised with modesty, that is to say, a restrained self-awareness that takes "as many bearings as possible."[43]

Finally, something should be said about the mystical side of Richard Hooker. Returning again to the words cited from C. S. Lewis above, he described Hooker as follows: "Few model universes are more filled – one might say, drenched – with Deity than his. 'All things that are of God,' and only sin is not, 'have God in them and they in himself likewise, and yet their substances and his are wholly different.' God is unspeakably transcendent; but also unspeakably immanent."[44] This awareness of God's unspeakable immanence in his creation is reiterated by the contemporary Anglican theologian Donald Allchin who writes: "To speak of man's participation in God, still more to speak of his deification, otherwise than in the context of a whole world which participates in God is to speak a non-sense."[45] A transforming awareness of God's immanence in creation, and *par excellence* in the human person inviting him to transformation, is the very center of mysticism. Take for example this sentence from Hooker's *Laws*: "Although we be men, yet by being unto God united, we live as it were the life of God."[46] Or think of this purple passage to do with receiving the Eucharist from Book 5 of the *Laws*:

> The very letter of the word of Christ giveth plain security that these mysteries do as nails fasten us to his very cross, that by them we draw out, as touching efficacy force and virtue, even the blood of his goared side, in the wounds of our redeemer we there dip our tongues, we are dyed red both within and without, our hunger is satisfied and our thirst forever quenched, they are things wonderful which he feeleth, great which he seeth and unheard of which he uttereth whose soul is possessed of this Paschal Lamb and made joyful in the strength of this new wine, this bread hath in it more than the substance which our eyes behold, this cup hallowed with solemn benediction availeth to the endless life and welfare both of soul and body, in that it serveth as well for medicine to heal our infirmities and purge our sins as for a sacrifice of thanksgiving, with touching it sanctifieth, it enlighteneth with belief, it truly conformeth us unto the image of Jesus Christ.[47]

Historical theologian Egil Grislis comments on this passage: "In other words, in the Eucharist, as in prayer, Hooker did not remain the calm, analytical theologian, but at times could even record the ecstasy which he had personally experienced."[48] Those are most interesting words, "the ecstasy which he had personally experienced." It is clear that Hooker had this mystical awareness of God and of all creation participant in God, and yet, while he has this mystical understanding of all reality, nonetheless he consistently strove to present his theological thought as clearly and as reasonably as possible. The question may be asked with Egil Grislis: "Is Hooker a genuine mystic – or is he merely using traditional mystical expressions without a personal mystical orientation and experience?"[49] It is an excellent question and it may be asked also of John Macquarrie. Macquarrie consistently denied that he was a mystic, and that denial should be understood in terms of "personal mystical experience," probably accompanied by unusual expressions. But, of course, "personal mystical experience" is a loaded term. What exactly is "personal mystical experience"? Is a hard and fast distinction to be made between "a personal mystical orientation" and "personal mystical experience"? Arguably, a "personal mystical orientation" is best construed as living with a regular and constant sense of God's enveloping presence. Both Richard Hooker and John Macquarrie in terms of how they write about God and about creation's relationship to God certainly seem to have had that. Grislis describes this as "a corporate mysticism, placed in an ecclesial context," highlighting its traditional and perhaps especially Pauline expression --- "being in Christ." This is true of Macquarrie --- but with the addition of an "innate" Celtic sense of God about which more will be said in the chapter on prayer and mysticism.

Hooker as Model for Macquarrie

Macquarrie writes of Hooker in his 1984 essay on the Anglican theological tradition: "With admirable judgment, he held together on most matters the Anglican 'troika' of Scripture, tradition and reason."[50] However, he was fully aware of Hooker's theological skills well before 1984. In his *Principles of Christian Theology*, both editions, he had already said of Hooker: "The great historical exemplar of a multiform authority in applied theology is Richard Hooker... In Hooker's synthesis, scripture, tradition, and reason all had their place."[51] This is balance. This balance is one of the great characteristics of the Anglican way of doing theology. Indeed, the Anglican theologian Alan Bartlett talks about Anglicanism as "passionate balancing." He describes this passionate balancing in these words: "Alongside the passionate advocacy and embodiment of our own theological convictions, I have discovered that we must pay careful attention to others."[52] For Bartlett, the three stranded chord of Anglicanism --- Macquarrie's troika --- both in theology and in spirituality is Holy Scripture, human reason and tradition. These three strands for Bartlett are inextricably linked together, and find a classic expression in Richard Hooker. They find a contemporary classic expression, as it were, in John Macquarrie. Macquarrie, even before his conversion to the Anglican Communion, held together on most matters the 'troika' of Scripture, tradition and reason. If the troika of Scripture, tradition and reason are held inextricably together, albeit at times tensively, imbalance in theology and spirituality is avoided. It may even be said that the practice of this three corded strand will reduce the dangers too obviously present in the theological world, dangers well described by Archbishop Rowan Williams in our times, "an age when the theological debate so readily polarizes between one or other variety of positivism (biblically fundamentalist, ecclesiastically authoritarian, or whatever) and a liberalism without critical or self-critical edge."[53]

The Oxford Movement

The nineteenth century editor of the works of Richard Hooker was John Keble, and Keble, of course, was closely associated with the Oxford Movement. Indeed, John Henry Newman considered Keble's Assize Sermon (the sermon in the University Church of Oxford that opened the assizes or the annual session of the law courts for the County of Oxfordshire) as the beginning of the Oxford Movement. For John Macquarrie Keble was "an archetypal Anglican."[54] Although he expresses himself cautiously, Macquarrie sees a point of contact between the Oxford Movement and the theology of Friedrich Schleiermacher:

> One (could) see as a parallel to the Oxford Movement the new style of German theology associated with Schleiermacher, who stressed feeling and intuition. The comparison would hold only up to a point, for there is in Schleiermacher a streak of subjectivism, not found in the Oxford Movement, and Schleiermacher also lacked the Oxford apostles' veneration for antiquity.[55]

The parallel between the Oxford Movement and Schleiermacher is quite revealing. It is revealing because Schleiermacher is a favored author for Macquarrie, and also because "the young Pusey had discovered Schleiermacher, and had apparently found some things in him that excited his sympathy."[56] He realized that for Schleiermacher "feeling" had a cognitive dimension and, indeed, that it was "a kind of mystical vision, arising from a drive toward the whole or the infinite, a drive that is already within us and motivating our thought."[57] He uses the words "mystical vision" of Schleiermacher, and mystical vision for Macquarrie is the high point of Christian spirituality. He understood that for the Oxford Movement theologians theology stood in very close connection to spirituality not least because faith was thought to be a matter of the whole person an intellectual assent to a series of propositions. This kind of thinking has a very strong family resemblance to the theology of Friedrich Schleiermacher, especially when one considers his Pietist background.

If Tractarian theology was a protest against "the dry propositional theology of the eighteenth century, whether that took the form of deistic rationalism, Protestant biblicism or Roman Catholic scholasticism," and entered into a greater appreciation of feeling and intuition, there was also the principle of reserve. For the Tractarians the principle of reserve had a fairly wide range of meaning. It could mean, for example, not trying to be too explicit in the articulation of Christian doctrine because such doctrine is sacred and ought to be reverenced. The principle of reserve then could also be seen as opposed to "overdefinitions of doctrine." Thus, the principle moves in the direction of apophatism, of reverence before the unfathomable mystery of God, the recognition that "there can be no glib or easy talk of spiritual realities."[58]

There are obvious differences between John Macquarrie and the theologians of the Oxford Movement. Macquarrie has nothing like the Tractarian grasp of the complexities of patristic theology. While he is aware of the Caroline divines, his own thinking is not steeped in them, as it was for many in the Oxford Movement. While his appreciation of liturgical theology is very fine, he has no interest in the ritualism that arguably characterized later Tractarian thinking and practice, or was part of the Tractarian legacy. Nonetheless, an appreciation for feeling and intuition in the mode of Schleiermacher and a certain apophatism consequent upon the principle of reserve suggests strongly that, just as Macquarrie's way of doing theology has roots in Richard Hooker, it also has roots in the Oxford Movement.

John Macquarrie and Catholic Theology: Karl Rahner, SJ [1904-1984] and Hans Urs von Balthasar [1905-1988]

Though clearly and deeply influenced by Bultmann and Heidegger, and earlier by F. H. Bradley, Macquarrie "consciously broadened the base of his theology through his examination of the range of modern religious thought, and through the influence of such people as Karl Rahner and Hans Urs von Balthasar."[59] In point of fact, John Macquarrie had been reading Karl Rahner and Hans Urs von Balthasar well before they became household theological names among Catholics, and so it is useful to situate him not only in relation to Anglican theology but also Catholic theology, and most especially Rahner. Karl Rahner and Hans Urs von Balthasar are the two most significant figures of twentieth century Roman Catholic theology. "Each had periods in the ascendancy and periods when they were, one might say, in the doghouse, and it is probably still too soon to say which will be taken as the more important thinker in the long run."[60]

It is well known that Macquarrie had a very high regard for the theology of Karl Rahner, SJ. It is surely significant that both theologians took with great seriousness in both their writings and in their many public engagements their duty to communicate theologically to the wider Church, and not simply to the academy.[61] On John Macquarrie's desk in his Oxford home there was a framed photograph of himself and Karl Rahner, S.J. taken on the grounds of Christ Church, the University of Oxford, not long before Rahner died. In the first edition of his *Principles of Christian Theology* published in 1966 Macquarrie wrote: "Among contemporary theologians I have found Karl Rahner the most helpful. In saying this, I am acknowledging that the leadership in theology, which even ten years ago lay with such Protestant giants as Barth, Brunner, and Tillich, has now passed to Roman Catholic thinkers. Among them, Karl Rahner (himself a penetrating student of Heidegger) is outstanding. He handles in a masterly way those tensions which constitute the peculiar dialectic of theology..."[62] In his earlier *Twentieth Century Religious Thought*, Macquarrie acknowledged his interest in and awareness of Rahner's work.[63] He judged his discovery of Rahner more important to him than Paul Tillich, and that discovery was of a Rahner "untranslated and virtually unknown in Britain."[64] In 1984, for his eightieth birthday, Macquarrie gave a lecture in his presence at a symposium honoring him at Heythrop College, the University of London on February 17 1984, weeks before Rahner's death, and in Rahner's presence, entitled "The Anthropological Approach to Theology."[65] Soon afterwards, Rahner visited Macquarrie at Oxford, and that was the occasion when the photograph referred to above was taken.

Less well known is Macquarrie's interest in Hans Urs von Balthasar, whom he had wanted to meet while visiting Basel where Balthasar was resident, but due to some disagreement between Balthasar and Macquarrie's host, this proved impossible.[66] There is a brief, two page summary of Balthasar in Macquarrie's *Twentieth Century Religious Thought*, in which he writes: "Though he has much in common with Rahner and the transcendental Thomists, Balthasar brings along interests of his own, having written important studies of Barth and Buber, and having deep interest in both mysticism and aesthetics."[67] While he acknowledges the various volumes of Balthasar's *Herrlichkeit,* there is no evidence that he ever read them or the *Theodrama* or the *Theologik.* Almost unknown, however, is the substantial foreword Macquarrie wrote for Balthasar's *The God Question and Modern Man,* translated by Hilda Graef and published in the United States in 1967.[68] The mid 1960s were the years of the death of God theology, and when Macquarrie wrote the Balthasar foreword, he was at work on his response to this movement in his *God and Secularity.*[69] Pointing to the journalistic quality of so much of the death of God theology, Macquarrie contrasts it with the analysis of Balthasar: "I know of no recent work by any English-speaking author that even approaches this book in the depth of its analysis or in its understanding of the infinitely complex factors --- philosophical, literary, and political --- that have gone into the fashioning of Western man." He praises Balthasar, but, at the same time, he is critical. His critique has to do with what he takes to be a certain narrowness of understanding in Balthasar's approach to non-Christian religions and various strands of philosophy.[70] He is more at home with Rahner than with Balthasar.

Many of the criticisms of Rahner need to be seen against the background of Vatican II. There are those who feel that the Council went much too far in surrendering tradition to modernity, and find Rahner a type, perhaps *the* type of this surrender.[71] Others are of the view that the implications of Vatican II are insufficiently implemented, and so view the current interest in Balthasar as expressive of a restorationist perspective. Though it is a caricature, Karl Barth is seen to Friedrich Schleiermacher as Balthasar is to Rahner. Both Schleiermacher and Rahner in their different ways sought to modernize Christian faith by rooting it anthropologically. Barth and Balthasar maintained the integrity of Christian faith by keeping the focus on God where it ought to be, and not on the human subject. Yet, it is utterly simplistic to associate Rahner with the progressive wing of Catholicism and Balthasar with its conservative wing without qualification. The Rahner scholar, Philip Endean, says of Rahner devotees: "His fans often present him as a figure who adapted Catholic tradition to the modern world. But friends like these only make his critics' case appear more plausible."[72] Could we adapt for Balthasar? "His fans often present him as a figure who saved Catholic tradition from the acids of the modern world. But friends like these only make his critics' case appear more plausible."

Karl Rahner was fond of describing himself as an "amateur theologian." This piece of self-effacing modesty on the part of probably the most influential and widely-read Catholic theologian of the twentieth century affords an illuminating perspective on his work. Rahner referred to himself as an amateur theologian in part to signal the unsystematic nature of his work.[73] Rahner much preferred the genre of the essay over large volumes of systematics. Many of his collected essays find their origin in practical issues that he was addressing in the life of the church. Interviewed for his seventieth birthday, Rahner said: "Behind everything I did stood a very immediate, pastoral and spiritual interest."[74]

Rahner's academic work, however, did not begin in theology but in philosophy, much like Macquarrie. Initially, his graduate work in philosophy was at the University of Freiburg, as noted in chapter two. He failed his doctorate directed by the scholastic theologian Martin Honecker, but out of it *Spirit in the World* was published. The book breathes not only the spirit of Aquinas, albeit an Aquinas mediated by his Belgian confrère Joseph Marechal, SJ, but also shows the influence of Hegel and Heidegger. After this his superiors invited him to turn his hand to theology, and he received a doctorate in theology from the University of Innsbrück, with a dissertation entitled *E Latere Christi*, "The Church Born from the Side of Christ." The first dissertation was an interpretation of Aquinas through the lens of modern philosophy, while the second was an interpretation of Scripture through the lens of the Fathers of the Church.[75] Unlike Balthasar, Rahner spent most of his life teaching in universities. Apart from brief spells at the Universities of Münster and Munich, he spent most of his academic life at the

University of Innsbrück. Throughout all his work, Rahner is concerned with a foundational aspect of human consciousness, that is, that our knowing and willing and the act of loving in self-gift are, *ipso facto*, a being drawn towards the transcendental horizon of absolute mystery, the Mystery we call "God." As John Macquarrie, puts it, "There is a humanistic philosophy underlying much of his theology, a view of man as destined for God and seeking God."[76] This is worth spelling out at some length.

Whether we are consciously aware of it or not, we are always already related to God. Rahner puts it like this:

> We shall call *transcendental experience* the subjective, unthematic, necessary and unfailing consciousness of the knowing subject that is co-present in every spiritual act of knowledge, and the subject's openness to the unlimited expanse of all possible reality. It is an *experience* because this knowledge, unthematic but ever-present, is a moment within and a condition of possibility for every concrete experience of any and every object. This experience is called *transcendental* experience because it belongs to the necessary and inalienable structures of the knowing subject itself, and because it consists precisely in the transcendence beyond any particular group of possible objects or categories... There is present in this transcendental experience an unthematic and anonymous, as it were, knowledge of God.[77]

This is difficult language. A concrete example may help, the experience of driving a car. Driving a car is a concrete experience, better, a concrete series of experiences: putting the key in the ignition, looking in the mirror, accelerating, braking, and so forth. At the same time, and indeed necessarily, the driver is aware of a horizon through which he is passing. The experience of driving necessitates a horizon. The awareness of the horizon through which one is passing does not necessarily have an intensity to it. But that does not make it unreal. It is real, but without absolute lucidity, without absolutely focused awareness. The routines of driving the car is *categorical* awareness in relation to the horizon, which is *transcendental* awareness.[78] Transcendental and categorical experience are not two different experiences, but rather two dimensions of every and all human experience.

In other words, in all our knowing and willing and loving we *are* a transcendent drive towards Mystery, even if Mystery is not formally and consciously named as such. It is necessarily known, if not necessarily named. Rahner's theology in this respect is like a long extended comment on the famous axiom of St. Augustine: "Thou hast made us for thyself, O Lord, and our hearts are restless until they find their rest in thee."[79]

While it may sound as if Rahner's position is that the human person is autonomously finding God unthematically in the inner reachings and dynamics of knowing and willing, that is not actually the case. The human person's experience of transcendent drive is already a being drawn by God, to God, who desires communion with everyone. Each person is a *graced* orientation towards Mystery. Thus, Rahner writes:

> Whenever man in his transcendence experiences himself as questioning, as disquieted by the appearance of being, as open to something ineffable, he cannot understand himself as subject in the sense of an *absolute* subject, but only in the sense of one who receives being, ultimately only in the sense of grace. In this context 'grace' means the freedom of the ground of being (God) which gives being to man, a freedom which man experiences in his finiteness and contingency...[80]

Thus, for Rahner, in our restless knowing and willing it is less the situation that we are reaching towards God than that God is reaching towards us, and so enabling our reaching towards God. In a word, grace is at work from beginning to end. The Anglican theologian, Mark McIntosh, has captured the nature of our reaching towards God nicely when he describes it as a "momentum" that God "sets loose" in us.[81] This "momentum," this gracious outreach of God to every human person is what Rahner called the "supernatural existential." All are offered this grace of Christ --- there is no other grace --- and all who respond to it without necessarily realizing it are in Rahner's famous phrase "anonymous Christians."

Throughout his work Rahner emphasized the sheer incomprehensibility of God. "The incomprehensible, inexhaustible, limitless reality of the presence we call 'God' is not a term we have not yet succeeded in understanding entirely, but rather an ultimate of intelligibility inviting us to accept and embrace it unconditionally."[82] Everything that is said and thought about God is the categorical expression of this real, primal, albeit unthematic consciousness of God, and is, therefore, always inadequate, necessarily falling short of the Mystery. The categorical expression is always secondary to transcendental consciousness. The prior, originating and transcendent experience is always primary. This has implications for all theological expression, for all theological categories without exception, even for the category "God." "God" is often inadequately considered as an object in the world of objects, even if the Supreme Object, "a member of the larger household of all reality."[83] God is Holy Mystery:

> Whether he is consciously aware of it or not, whether he is open to this truth or suppresses it, man's whole spiritual and intellectual existence is oriented towards a holy mystery which is the basis of his being. This mystery is the inexplicit and unexpressed horizon which always encircles and upholds the small area of our everyday experience of knowing and acting, our knowledge of reality and our free action... We call this God.[84]

Not inevitably, and more than likely due to his detailed studies of Ignatius of Loyola with his vision of all things in relation to God, Rahner's theological method leads in the direction of mysticism. John Macquarrie writes: "Since Rahner had a strongly mystical element in his make-up, he often speaks of God as the Nameless..."[85]

What does Rahner's approach then say about the particularity of Jesus Christ, the categorical expression that *is* Jesus Christ? Is Christ but one example, even the unsurpassably unique example, of this universal orientation to the divine? One could choose to interpret Rahner along such lines. Arguably, however, there is another way of reading Rahner on Christ, that is, as the Savior, "as the decisive moment internal to the unfolding of God's universal saving will within the history of the world."[86] He is simultaneously the absolute fullness of God's self-communication to humankind and the fullness of humankind's response to the divine gift. In the particular human being, Jesus of Nazareth, God and God's creation become one, without ceasing to be what they each are. In this way of understanding, the divinity of Christ does not stand in polar opposition to the humanity of Christ. "To be human is to transcend all things, to 'go beyond' all things towards God: when this transcendence, this 'going beyond,' is carried to its single, highest and most radical instance, then in that case to be human is to be God: 'The incarnation of God is... the unique, *supreme* case of the total actualization of human reality.'"[87]

This approach to Christology is very interesting. Jesus is, therefore, simultaneously the coincidence of God's gracious outreach to creation and especially his human creatures, and the 'upward' striving of creation and especially human creatures towards absolute transcendence, that is, God. Rahner's language and thought patterns suggest that the difference between Jesus and us is a matter of degree. If Jesus is the supreme case of total transcendent actualization, then we are minor examples of it. This is not a reductionist interpretation. Karen Kilby has it right when she says: "It is quite possible... to talk about a difference of degree which is nevertheless a radical difference, and one can talk about the fulfillment of a possibility built into human nature without automatically suggesting that any of us could achieve this fulfillment if only we tried a little harder."[88] A difference of degree may be such that for all practical differences it is a difference in kind. Macquarrie, as we shall see, is in agreement.

In a very real way, both Rahner and Balthasar are experientially grounded Rahner offers a narrative of the self, grounded in knowing, willing and loving, that finds not only its term but also its origin in God. Balthasar offers a narrative of the self, grounded in the cosmic Christ, whose identity becomes in grace our identity. Both recognize our native orientation to the Mystery of God, Rahner from the universal dynamic of human consciousness understood as God's gracious self-communication, and Balthasar from the concrete particularity of Jesus Christ in whom all things find both their origin and their *telos*. The Irish Balthasar commentator, Gerald O'Hanlon puts the difference, and we may say "tension" between the two theologians well when he says:

> Running right through (Balthasar's) thought is unease with the attempt to build the bridge between humans and God starting from the side of the human... Balthasar is afraid that this 'turn to the subject'... in modern theology, in whatever form, ends up measuring God in terms of humanity so that there ensues that neat synthesis which is untrue to the awkwardness of life and the conflict and surprise which are intrinsic to the Christian revelation... Instead of the *a priori* of human natural desire for God, he prefers to stress the *a posteriori* of the loving call of God.[89]

Thus, there is indeed a tension between Rahner and Balthasar. Tensions may be understood as signs of life, and, indeed, as signs of genuine respect for the thought of another. If such respect were lacking, one would not bother so to engage the other's thought in such a way as to engender such tension. There is enough in life with which to be concerned! Both Rahner and Balthasar have been accused of heresy.[90] Often, however, when people accuse others of heresy, their real complaint is that the theological understanding and expression of the other is not entirely isomorphic with their own, and, therefore, must be suspect. In reality, however, genuine heresy as a serious threat to the integrity of the faith is relatively rare. As John Macquarrie has pointed out, "in the long run, the only effective answer to heresy, near heresy and errors of other kinds is for the Church to show that she has a better theology than the person suspected of error."[91] Theologian Morwenna Ludlow points out that "Both Macquarrie and Rahner are too good historians to forget the role of heresy in the development of early Christian doctrine," and arguably in the development of Christian doctrine throughout the entirety of the Christian tradition.[92] Neither Rahner nor Balthasar was heretical, but they both demonstrate quite different ways of doing theology. Perhaps we could say that Balthasar represents a high-descending theological methodology, whereas Rahner offers a low-ascending one. Perhaps we could also say that Balthasar is a mystagogue for those captivated primarily by beauty, and Rahner is a mystagogue for those marked with a penchant for philosophical analysis. Even as I write these comments, however, I recognize how inadequate they really are. At best, both theologians offer the community of the faith different styles of theology that reflect different styles of living, and different styles of theological thinking and living that mark the post-conciliar era.

While Rahner and Balthasar are often these days played off against one another, with Rahner as the "progressive" and Balthasar as the "conservative," they both as young men had been rooted in Ignatian spirituality. Acknowledging this common root leads the Scottish Dominican philosophical-theologian Fergus Kerr to conclude that "they were never as far apart as they seem" and "each was far more complicated than the standard story allows."[93] Add to this the comment of the priest-psychologist and Franciscan author, Benedict Groeschel, who is of the opinion that many people demonstrate a strong attraction to one or another of the transcendentals. Thus, for example, the primary transcendental for Aquinas was truth, but for Francis of Assisi it was goodness. Perhaps it might be possible to say, but with the necessary and obvious qualifications, that for Balthasar the primary transcendental is beauty and for Rahner the primary transcendental is truth. They are best understood as complementary not contradictory.[94]

There is indeed a tension-in-complementarity between Rahner and Balthasar. In this tension, Macquarrie would be situated more on the Rahner side than the Balthasar side. Both Rahner and Macquarrie are fundamentally philosophical theologians, and Balthasar, though held in appreciation by Macquarrie, is not. Balthasar's patristic studies, his appreciation of Karl Barth's theology especially in emphasizing the transcendence of God stand in serious contrast, though not in my judgment in contradiction with Macquarrie's interest in philosophy and his consistent emphasis on divine immanence.

Macquarrie on Postmodernism

In the last few years of his life Macquarrie turned his attention to what has been called "postmodernism." "I do not think we should exaggerate the importance of postmodernism. We have seen that it calls for both criticism and appreciation. We have seen the problems re-emerge that have dogged religious thought for centuries, and see new and sometimes ingenious attempts to come to grips with these problems. We must not exaggerate the importance of postmodernism, but we must not ignore it."[95] Thus John Macquarrie on postmodernism – his typical, careful analysis followed by his balanced conclusion. Postmodernism, of course, can mean a variety of things ranging from some version of conceptual relativism to the acknowledgment of the end of the grand narrative, and so forth. It seems to me that Macquarrie was not well read in this particular literary genre, although he was certainly informed about and acquainted with it. In the final edition of his *Twentieth Century Religious Thought* he lays out ten contrasts with philosophical and theological views that dominated the twentieth century.[96] Macquarrie would be the first to say that these ten contrasts (or oppositions) do not pretend to an exhaustive analysis between modernism, as it were, and postmodernism. However, they do afford a segue into difficult and complex argumentation.

1. Postmodernism and Modernism.

Modernism, in respect of religion and theology, is thinking done within the "canons" derived from the Enlightenment, exemplified for Macquarrie in the person of Rudolf Bultmann and his program of demythologization. The Enlightenment stands for an exaltation of reason. Postmodernism, in different ways according to its various exemplars, calls this excessive faith in reason, as it were, into question. But calling reason into question is itself problematic. Macquarrie writes: "In challenging the Enlightenment's exaltation of reason, has not postmodernism cut itself off from all knowledge of God, whether dependent on reason and revelation?"

2. Objectivism and Subjectivism.

"It is often said that postmodernism has a strong tendency toward subjectivism, while modernism prizes the objective." Macquarrie acknowledges that there is good reason for accepting this as a broad general statement, but insists on careful assessment. He notes that many postmodernist philosophers are raising for our times the traditional philosophical problem of objectivity. "Whatever we perceive, it is already in some way and to some degree interpreted by our minds." However, if there is nothing objective in any degree, but only interpretations of interpretations, does that not lead inevitably to skepticism?

3. Fragmentation and Totalization.

One of the characteristics of postmodern thought is to take apart traditional unities of thought because such unities refuse recognition of difference. Nonetheless, if this line of thought is continued without limit, it leads to a certain performative contradiction. Is that characteristic itself not in its own way a projection of unity? Macquarrie writes:

> Postmodern thinkers believe that the realities that make up the cosmos (including the human realities) cannot be assembled in a neat unitary package. Of course, there is a problem here for the postmodernists. If they criticize the modernist attempts at synthesis and system-building as subjective projections onto a fragmented reality, how does this square with their contention that objective reality is beyond our reach?

To deny the metanarrative is to affirm a metanarrative. Yet, Macquarrie recognizes that while systematic theology seeks coherence, it should not be excessively ambitious.

4. Particular and Universal.

"Enlightenment thinkers sought general laws that would be universal in scope, and so they tried to eliminate difference as far as possible." Again, Macquarrie shows himself sympathetic to this point of view. There needs to be a genuine focus on "difference," on the particular. When it comes to theology, however, care needs to be exercised. If the "difference" that is revelation is overly emphasized, then the Christian believer has something of a problem: How is the believer to recognize the revelation unless "there is already some capacity for it in his or her mind"?

5. Self and Others.

A common postmodernist term is "alterity" or "otherness." At its best this notion of alterity draws attention especially to those persons and events that would easily be overlooked. Macquarrie picks up Buber's teaching that "every particular 'thou' is a glimpse through to the eternal 'Thou'." Attention to others may be attention to the Other.

    6. Relative and Absolute.

"There is a distinctly negative strain in postmodernism, though it would be going much too far to suggest that it leads to nihilism or skepticism, as perhaps the Pope feared and as seems to be believed by many people." The Pope to whom Macquarrie is referring is Pope John Paul II in his many allocutions and writings, but it is no less true of his successor Pope Benedict XVI. There is much talk of the tyranny of relativism. There is indeed a tyranny to do with thorough-going relativism, and, in point of fact, such relativism is a performative contradiction. But, while Macquarrie does not quite speak of the phenomenon in these terms, there may well also be a tyranny of the conventional, a tyranny that disallows or discourages people from thinking for themselves --- all the while remembering that thinking for oneself is not the same as thinking by oneself!

    7. Pluralism and Uniformity.

All major thinkers who would judge themselves "postmodernist," would agree in approving pluralism over "any enforced uniformity." In a real sense, this flows from the recognition of alterity, the other, whose thinking and acting appear to be in definite contrast to one's own. Macquarrie rightly points out that pluralism goes beyond mere tolerance, and urges "respect and understanding for various traditions, and believing that society is enriched by diversity." At the same time, there are at least logical and moral limits to an extreme pluralism that would be self-defeating.

    8. Passion and Intellect.

There has been a strain in modernism, stemming from the Enlightenment, to privilege intellect "to the extent of crushing out the passional side of human nature." In this sense postmodernism expands our understanding of the human person "beyond what is permitted by a narrow empiricism." Although, and obviously, human passions need to be held in check by careful rational reflection, "a better balance than was bequeathed by the Enlightenment" needs to be found.

9. Ambiguity and Clarity.

"The postmodernists seem almost to delight in the fallibilities of language and in the ambiguities to which it may give rise." At times some postmodernists introduce neologisms, almost for the sake of introducing them. The desire to deconstruct contains explicitly and methodologically the self-evident threat to the deconstructionist!

10. Opinion and Truth.

Typically Macquarrie recognizes "truth" as polysemous. "There are many kinds of truth, many definitions of truth, and consequently many tests that can be applied to ascertain whether something is true or doubtful." Apart from sheer questions of fact, for example, the distance between one place and another, questions of truth become exceedingly complex. Again, typically in line with Macquarrie's careful understanding of understanding, not all opinions may be judged as of equal value. Some are more probable than others. "It seems to me," maintains Macquarrie, "that as soon as we open our mouths to say anything, the very act of 'saying' contains an implicit assertion that what I am saying is true." This means in effect that the very use of language "implies an ambience of mutual trust... anterior to and implicit in every act of speaking and hearing."

Finally, after laying out these ten contrasts Macquarrie reaches the following conclusion: "Postmodernism's criticisms of modernism deserve to be heard, and the whole movement cannot be dismissed because of some excesses." The problems and challenges he finds in postmodernist thinkers ---

and he mentions in this chapter on postmodernism John Caputo, Jacques Derrida, Emmanuel Levinas, Kevin Hart, J. F. Lyotard, Mark Taylor, Graham Ward, and Jean-Luc Marion --- are ultimately the perennial problems and challenges found in the history of at least Western thought, even though they may be presented in different language and garb.

Conclusion

John Macquarrie is indeed a theologian within the canonical tradition of Anglicanism, represented especially by Richard Hooker. At the same time, he can embrace what he finds particularly significant in other traditions and theologians. While not unaware of Balthasar, Macquarrie found himself especially attracted to Karl Rahner, both methodologically and conceptually. Finally, his acquaintance with post-modern thinkers, while limited in terms of the output of this diverse group of thinkers, shows his ability to recognize points of continuity with the philosophical and theological tradition, as well as points of discontinuity. It would be true to say of Macquarrie that he was possessed of "the unrestricted desire to understand," a Lonerganian phrase and emphasis, even as he did so as an outstanding representative of his Anglican tradition.

---

[1] Timothy Bradshaw, "Macquarrie's Doctrine of God," *Tyndale Bulletin* 44 (1993), 2.

[2] Alan Bartlett, *A Passionate Balance: The Anglican Tradition* (Maryknoll, NY: Orbis Books, 2007), 26.

[3] John Macquarrie, *Principles of Christian Theology*, rev. ed. (London: SCM Press, 1977), 1.

[4] John Macquarrie, *The Faith of the People of God* (New York: Scribner's, 1972), 12.

[5] John Macquarrie, "Pilgrimage in Theology," in Alistair Kee and Eugene T. Long, ed., *Being and Truth: Essays in Honour of John Macquarrie* (London: SCM Press, 1986), xi.

[6] Ibid., xv.

[7] Mark Chapman, *Anglicanism* (New York and Oxford: Oxford University Press, 2006), 14.

[8] Ibid., 1.

[9] Ibid., 31.

[10] Georgina Morley, *John Macquarrie's Natural Theology: The Grace of Being* (Burlington, VT and Aldershot, UK: Ashgate Publishing, 2003), 82.

[11] The essay was first published in Richard Holloway, ed., *The Anglican Tradition* (Morehouse-Barlow, 1984). It was later republished in Macquarrie's *Theology, Church and Ministry* (London: SCM Press, 1986), 91-104, and it is to the latter that reference is made in this chapter.

[12] John Macquarrie, "The Anglican Theological Tradition," 91.

[13] John Macquarrie, *Stubborn Theological Questions* (London: SCM Press, 2003), 177.

[14] Paul Avis, *The Identity of Anglicanism: The Essentials of Anglican Ecclesiology* (New York and London: T. & T. Clark, 2007), 15.

[15] John Macquarrie, "The Anglican Theological Tradition," 94.

[16] Ibid., 95.

[17] Owen Chadwick, *Michael Ramsey, A Life* (New York and Oxford: Oxford University Press, 1990), 275.

[18] John Macquarrie, "The Anglican Theological Tradition," 96.

[19] Ibid.

[20] Ibid., 97.

[21] Stephen Sykes, "The Genius of Anglicanism," in Geoffrey Rowell, ed., *The English Religious Tradition and the Genius of Anglicanism* (Nashville: Abingdon Press, 1992), 232.

[22] Basil Mitchell, "I Believe: We Believe," in The Doctrine Commission of the Church of England, *Believing in the Church: The Corporate Nature of Faith* (Wilton, CT: Morehouse-Barlow, 1982), 9-10.

[23] John Macquarrie, "Pilgrimage in Theology," xvii.

[24] Peter Sedgwick, "Anglican Theology," in David F. Ford with Rachel Muers, ed., *The Modern Theologians* (Oxford: Blackwell Publishing, 2005), 178.

[25] See the brief account of Ramsey in John Macquarrie, *Twentieth Century Religious Thought*, rev. ed. (Harrisburg, PA: Trinity Press International, 2002), 312-317.

[26] Alastair MacIntyre, *After Virtue* (London: Duckworth, 1981).

[27] Paul Avis, op. cit., 6.

[28] Louis Bouyer, *Orthodox Spirituality and Protestant and Anglican Spirituality* (New York: Desclée, Inc., 1969), 109.

[29] Henry McAdoo, "Richard Hooker," in Geoffrey Rowell, ed., *The English Religious Tradition and the Genius of Anglicanism* (Nashville: Abingdon Press, 1992), 107-109.

[30] Aidan Nichols, OP, *The Panther and the Hind: A Theological History of Anglicanism* (Edinburgh: T. & T. Clark, 1993), 40, slightly adapted.

[31] An unnamed commentator, cited in Mark Chapman, op. cit., 41.

[32] Louis Bouyer, *Orthodox Spirituality and Protestant and Anglican Spirituality*, 109.

[33] Izaak Walton, *Life of Mr. Richard Hooker*, 1644.

[34] Henry McAdoo, "Richard Hooker," 111.

[35] John Booty, *Reflections on the Theology of Richard Hooker* (Sewanee, TN: The University of the South Press, 1998), 3.

[36] C. S. Lewis, *English Literature in the Sixteenth Century* (Oxford: Clarendon Press, 1954), 450.

[37] Richard Hooker, *Ecclesiastical Polity*, 1.15.4.

[38] Ibid., 5.7.1.

[39] Ibid., 5.65.2.

[40] Ibid., 5.8.2.

[41] Ibid., 3.8.14.

[42] N. T. Wright, *The Last Word* (New York: HarperCollins, 2005), 80-81.

[43] Ibid., 20.

[44] C. S. Lewis, op. cit., 450.

[45] A. M. Allchin, *Participation in God: A Forgotten Strand in Anglican Tradition* (Wilton, CT: Morehouse-Barlow, 1988), 8.

[46] Richard Hooker, *Ecclesiastical Polity*, 1.11.2; 1.112.12, 19-20.

[47] Ibid., 5.67.12; 2.343.6-21.

[48] Egil Grislis, "Richard Hooker and Mysticism," *Anglican Theological Review* 87 (2005), 270.

[49] Ibid., 256.

[50] John Macquarrie, "The Anglican Theological Tradition," 102.

[51] John Macquarrie, *Principles of Christian Theology*, rev. ed., (London: SCM Press, 1977), 381. Geoffrey Wainwright also draws attention to Hooker in his essay, "Subjectivity and Objectivity in Theology and Worship," in Robert Morgan ed., *In Search of Humanity and Deity* (London: SCM Press, 2006), 306.

[52] Alan Bartlett, op. cit., 16.

[53] Cited in Alan Bartlett, op. cit., 31.

[54] John Macquarrie, *Two Worlds Are Ours: An Introduction to Christian Mysticism* (London: SCM Press, 2004), 218.

[55] John Macquarrie, "The Oxford Movement and Theology," in his *Stubborn Theological Questions* (London: SCM Press, 2003), 165.

[56] Ibid.

[57] John Macquarrie, *Thinking About God* (London: SCM Press, 1975), 161.

[58] John Macquarrie, *Two Worlds Are Ours*, 222; see also "The Oxford Movement and Theology," 168-169.

[59] Daniel W. Hardy, "Theology through Philosophy," in David F. Ford, ed., *The Modern Theologians*, vol. II (Oxford: Blackwell, 1989), 48-49.

[60] Karen Kilby, "Balthasar and Karl Rahner," in Edward T. Oakes, SJ and David Moss, ed., *The Cambridge Companion to Hans Urs von Balthasar* (Cambridge: Cambridge University Press, 2004), 256.

[61] See Morwenna Ludlow, "'The Task of Theology Is Never Finished,': John Macquarrie and Karl Rahner on the Challenges and Limits of Doing Theology," in Robert Morgan, ed., *In Search of Humanity and Deity*, 125.

[62] *Principles of Christian Theology* (London: SCM Press, 1966), vii.

[63] (New York and Evanston: Harper and Row Publishers, 1963), 293-294.

[64] John Macquarrie, "Pilgrimage in Theology," xiv.

[65] John Macquarrie, "The Anthropological Approach to Theology," in his *Theology, Church and Ministry* (London: SCM Press, 1986), 48-68.

[66] John Macquarrie, *On Being a Theologian* (London: SCM Press, 1999), 62.

[67] John Macquarrie, *Twentieth Century Religious Thought*, rev. ed. (Harrisburg, PA: Trinity Press International, 2001), 382.

[68] It was first published in the United Kingdom by Burns and Oates in 1958, but Macquarrie's foreword dates from the 1967 edition, Hans Urs von Balthasar, *The God Question and Modern Man* (New York: The Seabury Press, 1967), ix-xvi.

[69] (London: Lutterworth Press, 1968).

110

[70] See especially *The God Question and Modern Man*, xvi.

[71] Declan Marmion, "Christian Identity in a Postmodern Age: A Perspective from Rahner," in Declan Marmion, ed., *Christian Identity in a Postmodern Age* (Dublin: Veritas Publications, 2005), 170-171.

[72] Philip Endean, "Spirituality and Religious Experience: A Perspective from Rahner," in Declan Marmion, ed., *Christian Identity in a Postmodern Age*, 201.

[73] Joseph A. DiNoia, "Karl Rahner," in David F. Ford, ed., *The Modern Theologians*, 2nd ed. (Oxford: Blackwell, 1997), 118-120.

[74] Cited in Leo J. O'Donovan, "Karl Rahner, SJ (1904-1984): A Theologian for the Twenty-first Century," *Theology Today* 62 (2005), 357.

[75] Robert Kress, "Karl Rahner: A New Father of the Church?" *Emmanuel* 110 (2004), 254.

[76] John Macquarrie, *Twentieth Century Religious Thought*, 382.

[77] Karl Rahner, *Foundations of Christian Faith* (New York: Crossroad, 1982), 20-21.

[78] I owe discussion of this car-driving analogy to many fine conversations with the Rahner scholar, Fr. Eamon P. Clarke, of the Archdiocese of Birmingham, England.

[79] Michael McCabe, "The Mystery of the Human: A Perspective from Rahner," in Declan Marmion, ed., *Christian Identity in a Postmodern Age* (Dublin: Veritas Publications, 2005), 47.

[80] Karl Rahner, *Foundations of Christian Faith*, 34.

[81] Mark McIntosh, *Mystical Theology* (Oxford: Blackwell, 1998), 98.

[82] Leo J. O'Donovan, SJ, op. cit., 353.

[83] Michael McCabe, op. cit., 52.

[84] Karl Rahner, "The Need for a Short Formula of Christian Faith," *Theological Investigations*, vol. 9 (New York: Crossroad, 1973), 122.

[85] John Macquarrie, "Ebb and Flow of Hope: Christian Theology at the End of the Second Millennium," *The Expository Times* 107 (1995-1996), 208.

[86] Dermot A. Lane, "Karl Rahner's Contribution to Interreligious Dialogue," in Declan Marmion, op. cit., 95.

[87] Rahner, cited in Karen Kilby, *Karl Rahner, A Brief Introduction* (New York: Crossroad, 2007), 20.

[88] Ibid., 21.

[89] Gerard O'Hanlon, SJ, "The Legacy of Hans Urs von Balthasar," *Doctrine and Life* 41 (1991), 401-402.

---

[90] One thinks of Alyssa L. Pitstick, *Hans Urs von Balthasar and the Catholic Doctrine of Christ's Descent into Hell* (Grand Rapids: Eerdmans, 2007).

[91] John Macquarrie, *Thinking about God* (London: SCM Press, 1975), 50-51.

[92] Morwenna Ludlow, op. cit., 122.

[93] Fergus Kerr, *Twentieth Century Catholic Theologians* (Oxford: Blackwell Publishing, 2007), 104.

[94] I owe this reference to Benedict Groeschel to Tracey Rowland, *Ratzinger's Faith* (New York and Oxford: Oxford University Press, 2008), 8. Rowland does not acknowledge her source for Groeschel.

[95] John Macquarrie, *Twentieth Century Religious Thought*, new ed. (Harrisburg, PA: Trinity Press International, 2002), 476.

[96] Ibid., 447-462.

4. IN SEARCH OF HUMANITY

What then is a personal human being? There is no quick inclusive answer, and we shall have to consider a great many aspects, one after the other.
John Macquarrie.[1]

The coherence of Macquarrie's evolving thought ... lies in his insistence that human existence points beyond itself to the ontological reality of God and the nature of the cosmos.
Georgina Morley.[2]

John Macquarrie begins a 1964 essay, "Selfhood and Temporality," with these words:

One of the most serious problems confronting philosophical theology today is that of finding an adequate conception of selfhood. There are many areas of dogmatic theology, such as the doctrines of salvation, of grace, of judgment, and of a life to come, which can assume that man has, or perhaps rather he is, a self or a soul, and that this self or soul is somehow unitary, responsible and abiding. The business of philosophical theology is to bring into the open such a hidden assumption, to set out in a philosophically intelligible language the idea of which dogmatic theology is already making implicit use, and to show, if possible, that this idea is a coherent and defensible one. The problem has become serious in the case of the self because the traditional philosophical description has broken down in the face of mounting criticism.[3]

I have cited him at some length here because there is a certain parallelism between how he thinks of the self and how he thinks of God, how he thinks of anthropology and how he thinks of deity. In both cases Macquarrie rejects substance metaphysics. The self is not to be understood primarily as a substance, especially if this substance is construed along dualist lines, some version of the Cartesian *res cogitans*, "thinking thing," or, in the fine words of philosophical theologian Janet Martin Soskice, that human beings are "brains on sticks."[4] For Macquarrie and many moderns we are not simply body *and* soul, *res extensa* and *res cogitans* for Descartes, but rather one living and dynamic reality. In a parallel fashion, Macquarrie finds it impossible to consider God as monarchical, separated from creation, without any real connection, with a much reduced sense of God's immanence. In this chapter we shall attend to his anthropology and in the next to his understanding of God.

The Human Person, a Synthesis

The Macquarrie scholar, Georgina Morley, asks the following questions: "Can we talk about being human in such a way that its sheer, delicious glory is celebrated? And in such a way that its maddening, shaming, soul-destroying difficulties are admitted and raged against, but without inducing persistent self-flagellation?"[5] The immediate answer to her question is provided in the opening comment from Macquarrie, a comment that seems to me exactly right.

Studying the human person is significantly different from studying inanimate objects or even the world of animals. It is significantly different because we are what we are studying, and so self understanding comes into play in our understanding of the person. That is why there is no quick and immediate inclusive answer to the question. That is also why Macquarrie offers a phenomenological-theological synthesis of what it means to be a human person in his *Principles of Christian Theology,* and has followed this up with a much longer study entitled *In Search of Humanity.* This topic is in fact the third chapter in the *Principles of Christian Theology,* and this is entirely deliberate. Before entering into the complexities and intricacies of Christian theology, Macquarrie wants to begin with a basic anthropology that will open up into theological exploration, but that also will be accessible and intelligible to the nonbeliever. "It is in the very constitution of human existence that the quest for God begins and is answered."[6] This is virtually identical to the way of Karl Rahner, briefly noted in the last chapter. Somehow or another the quest for God must be found in the very fabric and constitution of what it means to be human. If that is not the case, God will always seem extrinsic to what it means to be human, some kind of adjunct or add-on to what makes us human. Macquarrie recognizes the magnitude of the task. "Even the task of description here is fraught with possibilities of error. Human existence is not only variable, it is also ambiguous and polar, so that even what professes to be only the description of the phenomena is in danger of becoming one-sided."[7]

The human person is differentiated from everything else in the world in the fact that "only man is open to his being, in the sense that he not only is, but is aware *that* he is, and aware too in some degree, of *what* he is."[8] The human person may be referred to as "existence," and the rest of reality as "nature." Man "exists" in the sense of standing out from the rest of reality. The things that are simply are the things that are, that is to say, they have no choice or determination over their being. The human person, or selfhood is not like that, but is open to self-shaping. Thus, the human person can reach towards authentic selfhood/existence, or fall below it, however authentic selfhood or existence is thought of. This may be referred to as transcendence, or perhaps spirit, but whatever the expression used it intends an understanding of humankind as unfinished, as open to development. This openness to development on the part of the human person leads Macquarrie to suggest that it may be preferable to speak not so much of a "human being" as of a "human becoming." This would be very cumbersome linguistically, but it certainly underscores the characteristic of openness to development.

"There are in the human being these extraordinary juxtapositions of opposites, an apparently chaotic mingling of positives and negatives..."[9] Human existence contains a series of polarities or tensions: possibility and facticity; rationality and irrationality; responsibility and impotence; anxiety and hope; individuality and sociality.

The first is possibility and facticity. One of the most obvious things about the human person is that he/she is a being-on-the-way, is someone on the move, "taking to himself new powers and devising new ways of realizing his projects."[10] "Possibility" recognizes the various possible ways of being that are open to the human person. "Facticity" indicates that these possible ways of being are not infinite, but are limited. They include such givens in the human situation as intelligence, race, temperament, and other factors over which the person has strictly speaking no control. So, a human being is "a being of possibilities," who makes his way through deciding among these possibilities, but the range of possibilities is limited and finite. This presents a dynamic picture of the human person, and although Macquarrie does not find the substance metaphysics of Thomism persuasive, he recognizes that "Thomism too has moved toward a more dynamic understanding of man." Referring especially to what has come to be known as "transcendental Thomism" --- exemplified in thinkers like Bernard Lonergan and Karl Rahner among others --- he acknowledges that in this traditional philosophy flowing from Aquinas there is now a view that "human nature is 'open' so that man has the possibility of passing beyond himself."[11]

The second is rationality and irrationality. "Rationality" is our capacity to understand, to judge, and to interpret. "Irrationality" stands for those aspects of ourselves that seem opaque to rationality. "The researches of Freud in particular have made clear the almost frightening extent to which our lives are ruled by dark irrational forces. We never fully understand our own motives, and we do things sometimes in ignorance of why we do them, sometimes deceiving ourselves about why we do them."[12] This leads him to point out that "the tendency to exalt rationality and to see it in abstraction from its setting in the totality of human life can lead to a one-sided and eventually impoverished view."[13]

Third, is responsibility and impotence. "Responsibility" refers to our conscience, our inner voice directing us towards right action and the avoidance of wrong action. It contrasts with "impotence," the fact that "we cannot bring ourselves to do what is demanded."

The fourth polarity is anxiety and hope. "Anxiety" is generated by the sense of absurdity and negativity that attends all human life sometimes. "Hope," on the other hand, acknowledges that somehow it is all worthwhile. Macquarrie recognizes that anxiety and hope feature not only in the life of the individual, but also in the life of society:

> Both in the life of an individual and in the experience of a generation moods may come and go almost unpredictably. Hope and anxiety may alternate almost like the perceptions of an ambiguous figure in a textbook of psychology. The twentieth century has seen many oscillations between hope and anxiety – even between a brash unthinking optimism which lacks the humility of true hope to an apocalyptic despair that has nothing of the subtlety of ontological anxiety. And there are other moods, ranging from what Camus called 'metaphysical rebellion' to sheer boredom.[14]

The final polarity to which he draws attention is individuality and sociality. "Sociality" is constitutive of personhood. "It is not just something that gets added on when a number of individuals come together, as was supposed in, for instance, the old social contract theories. The existent emerges as already a social being." As with all these phenomenological characteristics, Macquarrie is indebted to Heidegger's *Being and Time*. This is how Georgina Morley describes the notion of sociality in Heidegger: "Certainly it is the case for Heidegger that the human person is never an isolated subject, but is always being-with-others (*Mitsein*) in a shared world (*Mitwelt*). This being-with-others gives the other the character of *Mitdasein*, and the relation of *Dasein* to *Mitdasein* is not *Besorgen*, which is appropriate to entities, but *Fürsorge*, solicitude."[15] There can be no self apart from other selves so that community or communion belongs to the very being of humankind.[16] Yet, the individual is irreplaceable and unrepeatable, so that "there is a privacy about each existence which cannot be quite penetrated even by the most sympathetic friend or companion."[17] Arguably, it is this particular polarity between egoity and sociality, between the individual and social poles of the person that is the "most fundamental" for Macquarrie's anthropology.[18]

The Disorder of Existence

By this term "disorder of existence" Macquarrie intends what has been traditionally called original sin. As far as I can see Macquarrie does not use the term "original sin" in his *Principles of Christian Theology*. Certainly it is not found in the section on human existence, nor is it found in the index. To some extent this is unfortunate because it is the most traditionally recognizable term for the disorder of human existence about which he is speaking. At the same time, one must equally recognize that the term "original sin" is not the most helpful one. This is how Joseph Ratzinger, for example, expresses a similar opinion about the term "original sin" arising out of the account in the Book of Genesis: "The account tells us that sin begets sin, and that, therefore, all the sins of history are interlinked. Theology refers to this state of affairs by the certainly misleading and imprecise term 'original sin.'"[19] "Original sin" and "disorder of existence" are synonymous.

Macquarrie describes it in these terms: "Yet perhaps no one would deny that when we do look at actual human existing, we perceive a massive disorder in existence, a pathology that seems to extend all through existence, whether we consider the community or the individual, and that stultifies it." The proper tension that ought to exist between the polarities becomes collapsed in one or other direction "so that the whole structure is thrown out of joint." While this disorder of existence cannot be considered total, as in a Calvinist notion of total depravity, nonetheless it can be judged to be universal. "From the beginning (the individual) is wrongly oriented, and whatever decisions he makes or policies he adopts relative to the disordered situation. So we can assert that the disorder is universal in human existence."[20] We may notice here that Macquarrie makes reference to "a Calvinist notion of total depravity," and his aversion to this kind of Calvinist thinking has already been commented on. It may well be that he dislikes using the term "original sin" because of what he sees as its too close connection with his inherited Calvinism.[21] Here too in

Macquarrie's description we may observe similarity of thought with Joseph Ratzinger:

> Sin is loss of relationship, disturbance of relationship, and therefore it is not restricted to the individual...Consequently sin is always an offense that touches others, that alters the world and damages it. To the extent that this is true, when the network of human relationships is damaged from the very beginning, then every human being enters into a world that is marked by relational damage.[22]

Since humanity is pervaded by disorder, help and support must come from outside humanity. The theological term for this support and help coming from the outside is "grace." Looking back at *In Search of Humanity* in 1999 Macquarrie writes: "I wonder whether I was too optimistic. I did include a chapter on alienation and sin, but I may have paid too little attention to what may be called the 'mean streak' that seems to be in everyone."[23] "Mean streak" does not seem to me to be a strong enough term for this anthropological reality of sin, but it is graphic, especially when one turns to the work of Ian Rankin.

Ian Rankin and John Macquarrie

Ian Rankin, the crime novelist and John Macquarrie never met. As far as I am aware, Macquarrie had never read any of Ian Rankin's novels. Yet, they have something in common. They are both Scots. Rankin was born in Cardenden, Fife, on the east coast of Scotland in 1960. After a degree in English Literature at the University of Edinburgh in 1982, he went on to research for a PhD the novels of Dame Muriel Spark (1918-2006), whom he describes as "the greatest Scottish novelist of modern times." It was never completed because he began to write novels and they have become very successful, not least the novels in which the Edinburgh policeman Inspector John Rebus figures. Muriel Spark wrote of the genteel Edinburgh, perhaps most famously in her *The Prime of Miss Jean Brodie* (originally published in

1961). Like John Macquarrie, Ian Rankin's work has been translated into many different languages.

What is it that the crime novelist, Ian Rankin, and the systematic theologian, John Macquarrie, have in common? First, they are both critical of what they see as the negative dimensions of Scottish Calvinism. We have noted how Macquarrie reacted very strongly against its theological shape when he was a student for the Presbyterian ministry at the University of Glasgow. Macquarrie's spirit is more expansive, more Celtic we might say. Rankin too appears to react negatively to aspects of Calvinism in his novels, especially centered around Edinburgh, a less genteel city than Muriel Spark's. Rankin says: "(Edinburgh is) a very repressed city, a very Calvinist, Presbyterian place. As opposed to Glasgow, which seems to very Celtic and open and brash and loud..."[24] Sometimes in the novels he contrasts what he takes to be this repressed side of Calvinism with a more open aspect of Catholicism. Of course, both Macquarrie and Rankin are pointing to a particular aspect of Calvinism, in particular to Calvinist anthropology.

Second, what Macquarrie offers as a phenomenology of the human person in his various anthropological polarities noted above, Rankin expresses in his flesh-and-blood narratives. Macquarrie's anthropological polarities --- possibility and facticity, rationality and irrationality, responsibility and impotence, anxiety and hope, individuality and sociality --- are all played out dramatically in the carefully observed human nature of Rankin's *dramatis personae*. For both commentators, literary and theological, there is a very definite pathology in human existence, an observable pathology, but it is not totalizing. The goodness of the human spirit emerges in Ian Rankin, what Macquarrie would call the working of God's grace. In that respect, despite the fact that Rankin's crime fiction delves into the deepest recesses of human evil, hope and love still flicker, and are never quite extinguished. One of Rankin's central characters is Detective Inspector John Rebus of the Edinburgh Police Force. Rebus is a heavy smoker, hard drinker, and is often cynical about life in general and on occasion about his colleagues. This rough diamond character, however, searches out Edinburgh's churches on Sundays for a theological ambience that relates to his experience of life. When traveling to London to assist in solving a series of murders, he brings his Bible in a suitcase. While he knows his Old Testament, he appears to regard the God of the New Testament as more compassionate and forgiving. At the same time, Inspector Rebus knows the depths to which humankind can so very easily sink Rebus reflects to himself: "He felt a chill run through him. Because he *knew* how events like Villefranche (a French village where massive Nazi reprisals occurred) could come to be. Because he *knew* how the world's continuing horrors could come to be perpetrated at the cusp of the twentieth century. He knew that mankind's instinct was raw, that every act of bravery and kindness was countered by so many acts of savagery."[25] Rankin knows how easily human beings slide into savagery, but, at the same time he recognizes that a severely negative anthropology does not do justice to the acts of bravery and kindness. As Macquarrie would put it, God's grace is always ahead, always primary.

Rankin says: "I'm trying to make sense of the world and I can do that by writing."[26] It may be that the sense Rankin continues to make of the world flows also from the sense made of it by Muriel Spark. Perhaps Rankin picked up something of a Catholic anthropology from his research on Muriel Spark. It was said of Spark by a contemporary and a novelist, Penelope Fitzgerald that "(She) had pointed out that it wasn't till she became a Roman Catholic... that she was able to see human existence as a whole, as a novelist needs to."[27]

The Anthropological Argument for the Existence of God

In the final chapter of his book *In Search of Humanity*, simply entitled "Being," Macquarrie sets out what may be called an anthropological argument for the existence of God. The argument develops in a cumulative fashion, and points towards God not as an absolute and transcendent monarch, as it were, but towards a God "working and suffering in and with his creation, leading and inspiring human transcendence rather than standing over it."[28] The argument consists of six steps.[29]

Step one: "Human life has brought to light more than anything else we know the astonishing potentialities latent in the physical universe." He views the human person as a microcosm in which the macrocosm of creation/cosmos becomes manifest. By this form of expression Macquarrie suggests that materialism is simply inadequate. He cites the first great philosophic influence on his life, F. H. Bradley: "I am the eye with which the Universe beholds itself, and knows itself divine."[30] Contemporary science has unearthed the mysterious complexity of matter in such a way that a crude and reductionist materialism is virtually impossible, thus reaching out towards "a sacramental conception of the universe."

Step two: "Some aspects of our humanity suggest a transhuman spiritual source." Following from step one, but depending for its suasiveness on all the steps, he believes that human experience of such realities as morality and love seem to point to a transcendent and spiritual source.

Step three: "The human being in certain respects transcends nature, in such a way as to provide an analogy of divine transcendence and to suggest that the goal of humanity is participation in the life of God." Human beings are "bridge-being(s), both immanent in the world and transcendent of it." This is the same with God.

Step four: "Human beings show a natural trust in the wider being within which their existence is set." Human beings for the most part have a fundamental faith in being, a sort of basic trust in being. While this may not be immediately equated with faith in God, it tends in that direction. Macquarrie writes:

> Even people who find it impossible to believe in God may nevertheless have a basic faith in certain values or in the worthwhileness of life. Though one does not question the sincerity of their atheism, it must be a question whether their basic faith is not closer to faith in God than they

realize, and that what they cannot accept are the often naïve and sometimes immoral concepts of God that are all too common among those who profess to be believers.[31]

Step five: "There are some negative factors in human existence which cannot be understood as limit-situations, impressing on us our own finitude and at the same time evoking the idea of absolute being." He instances as negative factors death and suffering, sin and guilt. This is the region of theodicy. While some contemporary thinkers speak about the end of theodicy, Macquarrie does not so speak. One thinks, for example, of theologians such as John Thiel, Terrence Tilley and Kenneth Surin, and to some extent, Paul Crowley.[32] Crowley points out that theodicies can represent:

a calculus about suffering that fails to take into consideration the actual suffering of human beings. As such, theodicies devalue practical issues surrounding evil: they silence the cries of victims and marginalize their suffering; tend to valorize some forms of evil and minimize others; and ultimately promote complicity in injustice because systemic evils such as racism and sexism are rendered invisible.[33]

Rather than simply eliminating theodicy, Crowley and Macquarrie tend to reach toward a theodicy that does not fall into these condemnations. Thus, Macquarrie writes: "I have no new wisdom to offer on these topics, and do not believe that human wisdom can find a solution. I have a more modest aim, namely, to reflect on the nature of suffering and its place in human life, and to show that in most of its forms it does not nullify the worth of life."[34] God takes a certain risk in creating as he lets creation be.[35] Yet, at the same time, God does not stand outside creation in a spectatorial fashion. Rather, on the principle that "the higher the level of personal being the greater the vulnerability to suffering," God must suffer more than anyone else and yet not be overwhelmed by such suffering. God transforms suffering in a way analogous to human experience. "This seems to be clearly implied in the Christian belief that God is made known in and through the crucified Christ, yet crucifixion is not the end of the story but leads on to resurrection."[36]

Step six: "Many of these strands come together in religion, in which men and women claim to experience in various ways the reality of God, and this claim has a *prima facie* case as one deeply rooted in the human condition and one which has never been disproved and perhaps never could be." He makes the point that many who are unable to believe in God and to find commitment within religion often find a substitute in art, where "the sublime has something in common with the holy and is a vehicle of transcendence." Behind these six summary steps lies the basic conviction that human beings are marked by transcendence, by an openness that goes beyond the physical and the material. Behind this basic conviction of transcendence lies the experienced immanence of God. Thus, Georgina Morley says: "The brilliance of Macquarrie's understanding of human being lies in his overcoming of the polarity of divine transcendence and divine immanence by viewing them through the experience of being human."[37] It is difficult, indeed, to see how it could be otherwise since we have only human experience to go on, albeit human experience reflected on throughout the generations of the Christian tradition.

Selfhood

"Existence fulfils itself in selfhood. An authentic self is a unitary, stable, and relatively abiding structure in which the polarities of existence are held in balance and its potentialities are brought to fulfillment."[38] This is John Macquarrie's version of what traditional theology has called "the soul." He dislikes the term because in his judgment, and he is probably right about this in terms of the popular understanding, the soul has been understood as a substance in a Platonic sense that indwells the body and gives it unity and stability. This is a dualist approach to the soul, and has come in for severe criticism in modern times:

> This whole doctrine of a substantial soul has... been subjected to destructive criticism in modern philosophy. The conception of a disembodied soul or self is very difficult, since it is precisely through being embodied that we are in a world and with other selves, and... there

can be no selfhood apart from a world and other selves... By a 'person,' we do not mean an invisible, intangible and immaterial soul-substance, but always an embodied self in the world. Not only is no purpose served by imagining a ghostly soul 'inhabiting' the body, but the very idea is superfluous and confusing.[39]

Many philosophers and theologians would find themselves in agreement with Macquarrie in rejecting this dualistic understanding of the person, with its ghost-in-the-machine view of the soul. Very briefly, perhaps all too briefly, Macquarrie acknowledges an Aristotelian view of the soul. For Aristotle, the soul is the form of the body. His understanding of this hylomorphic view finds expression in this sentence: "What is given at the outset is not a fixed entity but a potentiality for becoming a self." Nonetheless, his preferred model for understanding the self is temporality. "It is temporality, with its three dimensions of past, present, and future that makes the kind of being called 'existence' possible." He draws attention to the fact that human beings differ from the animals in being able to remember the past and to anticipate the future. Their awareness is not simply of the present moment.[40] This model of temporality is helpful, but one has to ask: What is "it" that is temporal? What is "it" that has this awareness of past, present and future? It seems to me that once this question is raised, we are required to fall back on something like the "soul," as a fundamental word that stands for that self marked by this awareness of time.

"Authentic selfhood implies the attaining of a unified existence, in which potentialities are actualized in an orderly manner and there are no loose ends or alienated areas. The attaining of selfhood is therefore a matter of degree."[41] There are degrees of selfhood. May we not also say, in the light of the above, that there are degrees of "soul-making"? This kind of expression, "soul making," does not seem to fall prey to the objections to a dualist anthropology, and arguably, it is consonant with an Aristotelian perspective.

Now it may be argued that Macquarrie simply has it wrong. His understanding of the self or soul is too much in the camp of Plato and the dualists, and too little in that of Aristotle and hylomorphism. It may be argued further that he lacks a thorough understanding of substance metaphysics, something that will be taken up in the next chapter. Even if this could objectively be demonstrated to be the case, however, there remains a question: If self or soul need not be construed along such dualist lines of thought, how does one explain that the dualist version has had such a long hold, one might even say a strangle-hold, on Christian popular faith and piety? In some ways, a dualist view is paradoxically aided and abetted by many who would not formally subscribe to it. While many would acknowledge readily that the Christian doctrine of the soul is not dualistic, many would also tend towards the viewpoint that God directly creates the soul with each human being's coming to exist.[42] The *Catechism of the Catholic Church*, for example, insists that "every spiritual soul is created immediately by God — it is not 'produced' by the parents..."[43] Nicholas Lash asks the pertinent question: "If parents do not give their children natural human life, what *is* it that parents procreate, what is it that the process of generation generates? The answer cannot be a human body, because a human body is matter formed by a human soul."[44] Behind shall we say this "quasi-dualist" thinking of the *Catechism* lies the entirely laudable desire to see the hand of God in the creation of every human life. Lash writes, "I think one could say that the notion of every human soul being created immediately by God is an attempt to express the sense of the preciousness and dignity of every individual human being," but then he goes on to add that "Unfortunately, I think that *also* at work is an almost Manichean underestimation of the body."[45] There is no need, therefore, to posit an "immediate" creation of the soul by God since in the very act of procreation God is already acting in the acting of the parents. God can never be absent from creation, and must be especially present to human beings, conscious-creative-collaborators with God.[46] It seems to me very clear that Macquarrie is responding to this strangle-hold, dualist view of the person in order to show that, if it falls devastatingly to modern critique, Christian anthropology does not necessarily fall with it. There is an authentic Christian view of selfhood which is both defensible in terms of the tradition and intelligible to modern people.

Aspects of Authentic Selfhood
Transcendence

"Transcendence" literally means going beyond, a going beyond limits. For Macquarrie, in human terms this transcendence has to do with "becoming more," a becoming more that reaches towards a "fuller, truer, humanizing of life."[47] He is aware of this transcendence, both human and divine, in various philosophical traditions, from Marxism through Thomism (especially Karl Rahner and Bernard Lonergan) to process thought. Human transcendence reaches up towards God, becoming ever more and more God-like, in terms of patristic theology "being deified." Divine transcendence reaches down towards creation and especially humankind, luring humankind towards greater and greater transcendence and so fulfillment. Macquarrie cites Charles Hartshorne to this effect:

> The higher forms of power are not those which inhibit the freedom of others, but rather those which inspire appropriate degrees and kinds of freedom in them, the power of artists, prophets, men of genius and true statesmen. God is the unsurpassable inspiring genius of all freedom, not the all-determining coercive tyrant.' Here we at least come in sight of a God 'whose service is perfect freedom', and thus in sight of an affirmative relation between human transcendence and divine transcendence.[48]

It would be fair to say at this point that Macquarrie virtually endorses Hartshorne's perspective on transcendence.

Cognition

Macquarrie is aligned with the common judgment since the time of Rene Descartes that Western philosophy has been preoccupied with epistemology. Epistemological questions, such as "What do we know?" "How can we know?" "How can we know that we know?" have dominated philosophy. Yet, maintains Macquarrie, we ought to remember a dictum of J. G. Hamann: "Do not forget the noble *sum* on account of the *cogito*."[49] The *sum* is composed of all the multifaceted aspects of the human person described by Macquarrie in his *In Search of Humanity*. However, he also does justice to the *cogito*.

"We must do justice to the whole cognitive aspect of the human being, but in order to do this, we must break out of a very narrow conception of knowledge that has become something like a dogma in the West."[50] The philosophical dogma to which Macquarrie takes exception is, of course, empiricism. He recognizes, of course, that the empirical methods employed by the sciences are self evidently valuable. What he rejects is the claim that there can be no genuine knowledge outside the scope of empirical investigation. He develops his own manifesto for a more adequate theory of cognition, a theory of wisdom, in seven propositions:

1. "That some knowledge does *not* begin from observation.

2. That conjectures and imaginative hypotheses (even, and perhaps especially, improbable ones!) may be more fruitful than inductive generalizations.

3. That in many subjects, and not least in the study of humanity itself, the ideal of attachment is a hindrance.

4. That knowledge is a function of an active self participating in a world rather than the data collected by an abstract thinking subject.

5. That there are various kinds of tacit knowledge, ranging all the way from the skills of craftsmen to the insights of artists and even the visions of mystics, and these cannot be put into propositions expressed in clear and distinct ideas.

6. That knowledge of facts expressed in propositions is one kind of knowledge among others, and has to be considered in the context of more

direct forms of knowledge by participation, including knowledge of things, knowledge of other people and knowledge of ourselves.

7. That finally the concept of knowledge is far broader and richer than the narrower type of empiricist epistemology is prepared to concede."[51]

Art

Macquarrie illustrates his non-empiricist epistemology through art. "What (the artist) shows us can be expressed only on his canvas and could never be fully put into words. But is it possible to deny that it is a form of knowledge, or to dismiss it as 'non-cognitive'?" The same cognitive, non-empiricist knowing comes into play in knowing a person, a kind of knowledge that involves participation and reciprocity, and a kind of knowledge that brings about self-knowledge.[52] Macquarrie situates the knowledge of the mystic in this category also, as in proposition five above.

In discussing art further, Macquarrie reveals his distaste for Calvinism and its work ethic in a somewhat humorous passage:

> Having grown up in Scotland, I was early exposed to a very serious view of life. Even before the gloomy shadow of John Calvin fell over Scotland, the harshness of the climate and the bleakness of the terrain had prepared the ground for the Protestant work ethic and for a God who was far from playful... I have never lost my respect for the busy little bee (of the Reformed tradition), but in course of time I have come to prefer butterflies.[53]

He does not disdain what might be described as the active life of the empirical scientist, but he lauds also the contemplative life of the poet or artist: "The being or reality of a butterfly is to be learned as much from the poet as from the entomologist. Prosaic explanations touch only some aspects of the butterfly, and leave untouched the understanding that this creature is part of the play of the cosmos in its superabundant energy, and that it adds to the grace and beauty of the whole and needs no justification or explanation beyond the fact that it exists."[54] So, "In its simplest forms, art is scarcely distinguishable from play. It too springs from a surplus of creative energy that goes beyond what is merely utilitarian."[55] He includes under the heading of art such different media as architecture, opera, the novel, music, painting, sculpture poetry, drama. He asks the question, "Could we say that the work of the artist is to enable us to perceive with a new depth and intensity the reality of that which he is representing in his art work?"[56] This leads Macquarrie to conclude that "The work of the artist is something like revelation. What is revealed has been there all the time, but it has gone unnoticed in our humdrum everyday experience. It needs the sensitivity of the artist to bring it into the light, so that we notice things for the first time."[57] The artist is a creator of meaning, inviting others to co-create meaning through music, sculpture, painting, or whatever the medium is. This creation and evocation of meaning for Macquarrie is a real, though indirect, experience of God. It is that because it is an attempt to articulate and express what the human really is, and that is the question of God. "God" is a religious codeword for meaning, in its final gracious ultimacy. Karl Rahner takes this insight even further:

> If and insofar as theology is man's reflexive self- expression about himself in the light of divine revelation, we could propose the thesis that theology cannot be complete until it appropriates (the) arts as an integral moment of theology itself. One could take the position that what comes to expression in a Rembrandt painting or a Bruckner symphony is so inspired and borne by divine revelation, by grace and by God's self-communication, that they communicate something about what the human really is in the eyes of God, which cannot be completely translated into verbal theology...[58]

This will not be the last occasion on which to recognize the closeness of Macquarrie's theology to Rahner's.

Death

In moving towards the attainment of authentic selfhood, awareness of death is central. "What has to be taken into consideration if there is to be anything like a complete acceptance of the factical situation of human existence is death. For it is death that more than anything else brings before us the radical finitude of our existence, and it is in the light of this that every possibility must be evaluated." It is the recognition and acceptance of death that brings about our responsibility and the seriousness to human living that it would not otherwise have. Macquarrie is too aware of existentialist thought to downplay the ambiguity and indeed the destructiveness of death. And yet at the same time, emergent from his understanding of Heidegger, there is a positive and creative awareness of death. "Death, in one sense destructive, is in another sense creative of unified, responsible selfhood, the concerns of which become ordered in the face of the end." Death in a sense compels the individual to seek for "the master concern that can create a stable and unified self." It relates to the saying of Jesus in the Gospel of Mark, "What does a man gain by winning the whole world at the cost of his true self (τήν ψυχήν ἀυτου)?" (Mark 8:36). [59]

Peace and the Human Person

Writing about peace in his *In Search of Humanity* Macquarrie cites some words of St. Augustine: "The peace of the celestial city is the perfectly ordered and harmonious enjoyment of God and of one another in God."[60] This Augustinian citation might well stand as a concise summary of Macquarrie's views on peace from his book, *The Concept of Peace*, published in 1972,[61] a book that he describes in these terms: "Though I had moved far beyond my youthful flirtations with pacifism, I was still deeply interested in the question of peace."[62] The corporate virtue of peace is "love transposed into social or global terms." This virtue's practice reaches out in healing to the *corpus* of the individual person and to the corporate nature of society. It serves to heal the fractures in both the person and society, fractures that emerge from the disorder of existence.

The healing of both personal and social fractures is something that demands immediate and practicable responses. Otherwise language about peace is nothing more than meaningless chit-chat. At the same time, the pursuit of the realization of peace also demands some consideration of "those ulterior implicates of peace, implicates which may fairly be called metaphysical or theological." He isolates three such ideas behind the Christian understanding of peace: grace, atonement, resurrection.[63] By "grace" Macquarrie means the sense of our finding our striving after a more authentically human life supported by a non-human "reality" beyond ourselves. This reality is named "God" by Christians, but even when not so named, Macquarrie believes that poets and novelists in their work are seeking after this graceful, non-human reality, a sense of being supported and connected by something "outside" ourselves, however difficult it may be to be more precise. The complex idea of atonement, literally at-one-ment, always includes reconciliation and sacrifice. Reconciliation is the bringing into unity of those who have been estranged. This bringing into unity, however, is costly. Where human unity has been disrupted "it can be renewed again only through some price being paid." This is sacrifice, not understood as some kind of arbitrary, external price, but as the internal, demanding working-out of reconciliation. Obviously for a Christian theologian sacrifice has to do with the costly atoning work of Jesus Christ, but Macquarrie does not view it as ending there. Since Jesus Christ is the very revelation of the unseen God, sacrifice/atonement must be built into the very reality of God, as it were. "There has been a cross in God from the beginning." Although he does not develop it along these lines as such, this "cross in God from the beginning" may be understood as the inner dynamics of love, an emptying out *vis-à-vis* another. The third idea is resurrection, "the basic idea... that life is stronger than death, that man never finds himself in a dead end but that always opens a new possibility." This is no rosy optimism for Macquarrie because resurrection finally intends a goal to history, a goal that will be brought about by God. Christ, and so the Christian in Christ, is the peace-filled one. Christ is the guarantor of peace, and the Christian community pledges itself to this fulfilled, peace-making view of humankind. Christ is our peace. This brings us to the theological disciplines of Christology and ecclesiology, the subject matter of the next chapters.

Before leaving Macquarrie's holistic understanding of peace, however, one very serious, practical matter must be attended to. While Macquarrie analyzes the dynamics of peace, violence and the issue of the just war, he never explicitly takes up a position on nuclear weapons, arguably one of the most important factors impinging on the reality of global peace. This fact stands in clear contrast with the position of theologian Donald M. Mackinnon, one of Macquarrie's sharpest critics, as noted in chapter one. In line with his theological methodology of paying close attention to the facts, to concrete reality, Mackinnon denounced nuclear weapons consistently.[64] The moral issues are well rehearsed and known in the literature and, at least to some extent, in the eye of the public. But Mackinnon, a member of the Labour Party, insisted that the policy of nuclear weapons as a deterrent was morally abhorrent, not just their use. Macquarrie certainly is in agreement with Mackinnon when the latter states that "discussion concerning the authority of the just war tradition is remote and idealistic in so far as it very largely neglects the sort of world in which decisions have to be taken and many of the principles on which they are made."[65] A nuclear world changes the register of moral discourse about war. When it comes to the argument that nuclear weapons are necessary as a deterrent, "the balance of terror," Mackinnon insists that it cannot be the case that "we *must* behave like fiends because the alternative is worse." Nor may we plead that, like the war criminals on trial at Nuremberg, we were simply following the party or the national line on nuclear deterrence. "The individual therefore has to ask himself whether he is ready. Whether he believes himself morally justified in acquiescing in the use of these things. If he says no, then he must himself find his own way of making his protest effective."[66] Again, it would be extremely difficult to imagine John Macquarrie saying something other. His theology of peace is admirable, yet it would have been even more admirable had a more explicit position on nuclear weaponry been taken.

Conclusion

Reading through Macquarrie's phenomenological anthropology one is struck by its comprehensiveness. It offers a very complete reading of the human person. One is also immediately struck by the sheer range of his reading and comprehension in both philosophy and theology, both past and present. First, the existentialist tradition is there, broadly construed to include J. P. Sartre, Gabriel Marcel, Karl Jaspers and, of course, the omnipresent Martin Heidegger, and from the nineteenth century Kierkegaard. One would expect this from Macquarrie. Second, it is also clear that the influence of process thought has made itself felt, especially Whitehead and Hartshorne, but also Daniel Day Williams, his former colleague at Union Theological Seminary, New York. Third, Catholic thinkers are prominently featured, especially Hans Küng, Karl Rahner, Bernard Lonergan, thinkers with whom he feels a strong philosophical kinship. Included also is Maurice Blondel's *L'Action* (as well as J. M. Somerville's important book on Blondel, *Total Commitment*). I find it entirely admirable that Macquarrie also reads and cites authors who may not have instantaneous recognition in the academic theological world, but who have made in their own way a significant contribution, for example, Martin Thornton, the Anglican mystical and pastoral theologian, and Peter Baelz, the Anglican moral theologian. There is no intellectual elitism in the thinking of John Macquarrie, no premier league thinkers and those judged to be so much less. This is true catholicity in thought.

His method may be described not only as phenomenological, thus inviting catholicity of assent, but more accurately, with the personalist Scottish philosopher John Macmurray, as a "personalist phenomenology."[67] "Perhaps" is one of Macquarrie's favorite words. By using it so regularly throughout his work he eschews arrogance, indicating that he is critically open to many points of view, and, while entirely convinced of the reality of Christian faith, its use recognizes what may be called "relative absoluteness," or "virtual absoluteness."

---

[1] John Macquarrie, *In Search of Humanity, A Theological and Philosophical Approach* (London: SCM Press, 1982), 9.

[2] Georgina Morley, *John Macquarrie's Natural Theology: The Grace of Being* (Burlington, VT and Aldershot, UK, 2003), 3.

[3] John Macquarrie, *Studies in Christian Existentialism* (Montreal: McGill University Press, 1965), 59.

[4] Janet Martin Soskice, *The Kindness of God: Metaphor, Gender and Religious Language* (New York and Oxford: Oxford University Press, 2007), 10.

[5] Georgina Morley, "Trailing Clouds of Glory: John Macquarrie on Being Human," in Robert Morgan, ed., *In Search of Humanity and Deity* (London: SCM Press, 2006), 170.

[6] Ibid.

[7] John Macquarrie, *Principles of Christian Theology*, rev. ed. (London: SCM Press, 1977), 60.

[8] Ibid.

[9] John Macquarrie, *In Search of Humanity*, 5.

[10] John Macquarrie, *Three Issues in Ethics* (New York-Evanston-London: Harper and Row, 1970), 46.

[11] Ibid., 50.

[12] John Macquarrie, *Principles of Christian Theology*, 63.

[13] John Macquarrie, *In Search of Humanity*, 6.

[14] John Macquarrie, *Principles of Christian Theology*, 65.

[15] Georgina Morley, *John Macquarrie's Natural Theology*, 62.

[16] John Macquarrie, *Three Issues in Ethics*, 61.

[17] John Macquarrie, *Principles of Christian Theology*, 66-67.

[18] Thus, Eugene T. Long, "Self and Other," in Robert Morgan, ed., *In Search of Humanity and Deity: A Celebration of John Macquarrie's Theology* (London: SCM Press, 2006), 161.

[19] Joseph Ratzinger, *'In the beginning...' A Catholic Understanding of the Story of Creation and the Fall* (Grand Rapids: Eerdmans, 1995), 72.

[20] John Macquarrie, *Principles of Christian Theology*, 69-71.

[21] Ibid., 245-246.

[22] Joseph Ratzinger, op. cit., 73.

[23] John Macquarrie, *On Being a Theologian* (London: SCM Press, 1999), 73-74.

[24] As quoted in J. Kingston Pierce, "Interview with Ian Rankin," in *January Magazine*, January 2000, on-line.

[25] Ian Rankin, *The Hanging Garden* (New York: St. Martin's Press, 1998), 280.

[26] Cited in Gillian Bowditch, "There's more to me than Rebus, insists novelist Rankin," in *Times On Line*, October 19, 2008.

[27] Cited in Hal Hager, "About Muriel Spark," Muriel Spark, *The Prime of Miss Jean Brodie* (New York: HarperPerennial, 1999), 141.

[28] John Macquarrie, *In Search of Humanity*, 256.

[29] See *In Search of Humanity*, 257.

[30] F. H. Bradley, *Appearance and Reality* (Oxford University Press, 1893), 396, cited in John Macquarrie, *In Search of Humanity*, 259.

[31] John Macquarrie, *In Search of Humanity*, 260.

[32] John Thiel, *God, Evil and Innocent Suffering* (New York: Crossroad, 2000), Terrence W. Tilley, *Evils of Theodicy* (Washington, DC: Georgetown University Press, 1991), and Kenneth Surin, *Theology and the Problem of Evil* (Oxford: Blackwell, 1986). Paul G. Crowley, SJ, *Unwanted Wisdom: Suffering, the Cross and Hope* (New York: Continuum, 2005).

[33] Paul G. Crowley, op. cit., 78-79.

[34] John Macquarrie, *In Search of Humanity*, 222.

[35] See the similar reflections of the philosopher John Cottingham, "Religion and Science: Theodicy in an Imperfect Universe," in his *The Spiritual Dimension: Religion, Philosophy and Human Value* (Cambridge: Cambridge University Press, 2005), 18-36.

[36] John Macquarrie, *In Search of Humanity*, 231.

[37] Georgina Morley, "Trailing Clouds of Glory," 177.

[38] John Macquarrie, *Principles of Christian Theology*, 74.

[39] Ibid., 75.

[40] Ibid., 76.

[41] Ibid., 77.

[42] See the splendid discussion in Nicholas Lash, "Are We Born and Do We Die?" *New Blackfriars* 90 (2009), 403-412.

[43] *Catechism of the Catholic Church* (Washington, DC: USCCB, 1997), # 366.

[44] Nicholas Lash, op. cit., 408.

[45] Personal communication from Professor Lash, dated July 1, 2009.

[46] See Gabriel Daly, *Creation and Redemption* (Dublin: Gill and Macmillan, 1988), 50-53.

[47] Ibid., 26.

[48] Ibid., 36-37.

[49] Cited in John Macquarrie, *In Search of Humanity*, 59.

[50] Ibid.

[51] Ibid., 67-68.

[52] Ibid., 68.

[53] Ibid., 188.

[54] Ibid., 189.

[55] Ibid., 192.

[56] Ibid., 194.

[57] Ibid., 195.

[58] Karl Rahner, SJ, "Theology and the Arts," *Thought* 57 (1982), 24-25.

[59] John Macquarrie, *Principles of Christian Theology*, 78-79.

[60] John Macquarrie, *In Search of Humanity*, 184. The citation is from St. Augustine, *The City of God*, xix.13.

[61] John Macquarrie, *The Concept of Peace* (New York: Harper and Row, 1973).

[62] John Macquarrie, *On Being a Theologian* (London: SCM Press, 1999), 68.

[63] Ibid., 70-75.

[64] See, for example, Donald M. Mackinnon, *Borderlands of Theology and Other Essays* (Philadelphia and New York: J. B. Lippincott Company, 1968), 175-203.

[65] Donald M. Mackinnon, op. cit., 180. See John Macquarrie, *The Concept of Peace*, 54-61.

---

[66] Donald M. Mackinnon, op. cit., 203.

[67] John Macquarrie, In *Search of Humanity*, 42.

5. SPEAKING OF DEITY

There is a bewildering variety of concepts of God among theists.
Huw Parri Owen.[1]

A dynamic theology... cannot rest content with a knowledge about God and it positively abhors a chattering about God. Knowledge of God, like knowledge of friends, must ultimately be a knowledge based on communing. The knowledge of God merges finally with the love of God.
Hugh Montefiore.[2]

The opening words from Anglican bishop and theologian, Hugh Montefiore (1920-2005), provide a suitable entry to Macquarrie's speaking of Deity. The doctrine of God is absolutely central in any Christian account of theology. John Macquarrie's work in theology has coincided with developments and challenges to the received doctrine of God, from the death of God theologians of the 1960s in reference to whom he wrote his *God and Secularity,* to those who are concerned with a critique of classical Christian theism, with which critique he has been engaged from his *Thinking About God* to *In Search of Deity.* This chapter will attend to Macquarrie's understanding of God, both exposition and evaluation, but will necessarily be incomplete until a consideration of his christology is provided in the following chapter.

God as Holy Being-Letting-Be

The most succinct summary of John Macquarrie's understanding of God is provided towards the end of an essay, "God and the World: Two Realities or One?":

> We may say that God and the world are not identical, but they are much more intimately related to each other than much traditional theology has allowed. If we know God at all, it is in and through worldly realities --- where else? He is prior to the world and transcendent, but the world is organic to him. We may call him the form of the world, the meaning of the world, the being of beings, though recognizing that none of these concepts is adequate to the reality.[3]

This passage was published in 1975, after the first edition of his *Principles of Christian Theology* and before his Gifford Lectures, *In Search of Deity*, but it encapsulates in nuclear form his consistent thought about God. The most important affirmation in the statement comes in the final clause, "none of these conceptions is adequate to the reality." Macquarrie is absolutely clear about that. While he espouses an organic model of God over what he calls the monarchical model of God emphasizing God's transcendence, he is always careful to point out that *no* model can be final, that God *always* exceeds our intellectual grasp. Macquarrie insists that while he espouses his organic model of God, he takes the transcendence and immanence of God with equal seriousness:

> No single model is in itself adequate, and neither is any theory. The organic model of theism is better understood as a corrective to the monarchical model than as a rival which seeks simply to supplant it... The organic model qualifies rather than abolishes the monarchical model.[4]

This insistence that God eludes any final way of human knowing is something upon which most Christian theologians would agree, and yet both historically and in terms of contemporary theology they do speak of God differently. Much, therefore, will depend on how adequacy is to be understood in relation to God. When it comes to this notion of adequacy, as noted by Paul Fiddes in respect of Macquarrie, "All God-talk has to be adequate to the practice of prayer."[5] Theology is a second-order activity, with spirituality and experience of God as primary in the religious life.

How do we speak of God? There is no neutral, no purely objective approach to understanding "God." Everyone pursuant of an understanding of God brings to that quest the story that she or he is. Quite simply, everyone *is* a story, or better, a story made up of countless other stories. Everyone brings to the theological task presuppositions that are emergent from familial, ecclesial and cultural contexts. In other words, everyone is traditioned. We *see* God differently. That is not to say that there is no overlap between one person's seeing and another's, nor that all seeing of God is of equal value. That form of thoroughgoing relativism is nothing short of performative contradiction. What attracts to one form of seeing over against others, what is appealing about one system of metaphysics rather than another, is that it brings one's reflected experience to a depth of richness and vitality not matched by any alternative. It yields what the Scottish Presbyterian theologian, Allan D. Galloway, has called *sanitas* or wholeness, "the enjoyment of an integrity of response."[6] Or, changing the philosophical climate in the direction of Bernard Lonergan's brand of transcendental Thomism, a reflected metaphysical position, a reflected seeing of God and God's relations with created reality, is a *virtually unconditioned*, that is to say, no other alternative has the capacity satisfactorily to answer all relevant questions with suasive satisfaction.[7]

A theistic system of thinking is very close to what the American Jesuit philosopher, W. Norris Clarke calls "a personal psychological predisposition towards metaphysical thinking, something like a *metaphysical bent of mind*."[8] This predisposition toward metaphysical thinking, according to Clarke, is marked by two qualities: "a passion for unity, for seeing the universe and all things in it fit together as a whole, a longing for integration of thought and life based on the integration of reality itself," and "a sense of some kind of overall hidden harmony of the universe, which could be picked up and possibly spelled out if one listened carefully enough." Although arguably a metaphysics is never complete, since completeness in any Christian interpretation is itself an eschatological condition, a "way of seeing" offers real and sustained nurture to one who wishes to see. Throughout all his writings, John Macquarrie has offered such an integrated, harmonious, theistic way of seeing.

There is another consideration in approaching a Christian understanding of God, and that has to do with the capacity of that understanding to relate to and to integrate with the entire symbol system of the fabric of Christian doctrine. David Tracy writes: "… the full Christian understanding of God occurs only in and through an entire systematic theology encompassing all the great symbols of the tradition."[9] In terms of this criterion Macquarrie has clearly been successful, not only in the systematic vision which he presents in *Principles of Christian Theology*, but also in the numerous essays and books since that publication in which he has taken further or refined various doctrinal elements of that systematic vision. In the light of this paragraph, how does John Macquarrie "see" God?

In attempting to answer this question it must be recognized at the outset that while Macquarrie stands clearly within the history of Christian reflection as shall be seen, he is also pushing out the boundaries of this tradition to reach towards what he considers a more adequate understanding of God. Writing in 1985, Eugene T. Long summarizes Macquarrie's approach to God:

> Macquarrie shares much with classical theists, yet he argues that we have passed beyond the God of classical theism, that is, beyond the idea of God as a personal being, albeit invisible, bodiless, intangible, who created the world, exercises governance over it, and intervenes on occasions. The need for positing such a God has diminished, he argues, as the scientific capacity to account for the events of the world has grown. Macquarrie has not yet provided a fully developed theory of God to replace the God of classical theism; but he has taken several significant steps in that direction...[10]

This summary of Long's is helpful, but requires further nuance. To say that Macquarrie maintains that we have passed beyond "the idea of a personal God" as an aspect of classical theism is somewhat ambiguous. There is no doubt that he does not think of God as *a* being, nor that he expresses concerns about understanding God exclusively in personal terms, yet the idea of God as personal remains central to Macquarrie's theology. God is never less than personal for him. Again, it is questionable whether Macquarrie feels it is in principle possible to produce, as Long puts it, "a fully developed theory of God." There is a constant concern throughout his *oeuvre* to cherish and reverence the transcendent mystery of God in an almost apophatic fashion. Nonetheless, Long seems quite right to say that Macquarrie has taken "several significant steps" to push beyond the God of classical theism.

For Macquarrie, God is "Holy Being," and in so describing God he is adopting and adapting the philosophical categories of Martin Heidegger. In using this term, "Holy Being," Macquarrie is expressing his existential-ontological concern. God is Being, but Being understood as gracious and responded to by humankind. He is no deist. "To know Being as God... requires a human attitude of trust... To call Being 'holy' has the existential connotations of valuation, faith, commitment and worship."[11] In order to understand more completely this concept of God it is necessary to ask more exactly what he means by the term "Being." Immediately, the very term "being" raises questions, perhaps most especially in the English-speaking world of Anglo-American analytical philosophy. As Fergus Kerr has put it so well: "In the English language you can't handle *being*. Now why is that? Of course, there's the Heideggerian story --- there's something wrong with the Anglo-Americans (not just the British). It's a defect that we can't talk about *Sein*; there's something wrong with the language."[12] Since at least the latter half of the twentieth century, with roots much earlier, the philosophical temperament of the Anglo-American philosophical world has been anti-metaphysical, and suspicious of "being-talk."

First, it is useful to say what Being is not. Being is not *a* being. Commenting on Heidegger's concept of being upon which Macquarrie is reliant, Eugene T. Long writes: "Being, according to Heidegger, is not an entity. It is that without which beings would not be and as such cannot itself be a being. It is nothing from the standpoint of existing entities."[13] Neither is it a property nor a quality, and the use of the very word "it" is a concession to the human need for some usable symbol. Being is that which properties and qualities presuppose, and does not as such add anything to an entity. Nor again is Being "substance," because this is static, modeled after thinghood. Finally, Being is not the absolute, if this is taken to mean "the all-inclusive being or as the totality of beings or as the sum of beings."[14]

Since Being is not an entity, nor a property, nor a substance, nor the absolute, it is, strictly speaking, ineffable and incomparable. It is best described in Heidegger's phrasing: "Being is the *transcendens* pure and simple."[15] Being transcends all the categories of our thinking. Does that then mean, as some analytic philosophers might suggest, that the word "Being" is meaningless? The answer for Macquarrie is, "No" because Being, or better Being-letting-be is the response to the question, "Why is there anything rather than nothing?" Of course, there is nothing particularly new in this formulation of the God question. Coming from the standpoint of what has been termed "classical theism", for example, the Dominican theologian, Herbert McCabe, using the philosophical theology of St. Thomas Aquinas, argues that "God" is the answer to the question, "Why is there anything rather than nothing?"[16] How McCabe and Macquarrie "see" God is, however, quite different in some respects, but they both share at least the notion that "God" is an heuristic symbol that responds to this basic question arising from the fact of existence.

Aquinas, Classical Theism and Macquarrie

This may be the place to say something about the relationship between Aquinas, classical theism and Macquarrie. To do this, let us call upon this passage from Georgina Morley:

> Space prohibits a full discussion on the relation between Macquarrie's 'new' natural theology and traditional Thomism, and in particular the grounds on which it might be argued that Macquarrie revitalizes Aquinas' work in a contemporary philosophical and theological context. Indeed, Macquarrie's writings display an ambiguity towards Aquinas that confuses this question... In any case, Macquarrie's argument is not dependent on the extent to which Aquinas represents classical theism; he is concerned with the monarchical characteristics of classical theism itself, and with satisfying his claim that it is possible to construct a natural theology which does *not* objectify God.[17]

Morley's statement raises three important points: first but implied, how Macquarrie understands Aquinas; second, whether Aquinas is a representative of classical theism; third, Macquarrie's position on the monarchical model of God.

First, how Macquarrie understands Aquinas. Pope Leo XIII (1878-1903) published in 1879 the encyclical letter, *Aeterni Patris,* in which he renewed and mandated the study of St. Thomas Aquinas for Catholics. "Aquinas was to replace the eclecticism that prevailed in (Catholic schools and seminaries) and to put an end to the abuse that allowed professors to choose the authors to be studied..."[18] The results of this neo-Thomist movement were richer and more complex than one might have envisaged. In the words of historian, John O'Malley: "Thomism, originally a club with which to beat modern philosophers beginning with Descartes, took on a life of its own, especially in France, Belgium, and Germany, and produced outstanding scholars."[19] Combined with what has been called "Jazz Age Catholicism," the continental European Catholicism of the post-World War I 1920s and 1930s, Thomism had the capacity to cross-fertilize with and to integrate other aspects of the human spirit, most especially art, music and painting.[20] Nonetheless, the imposition of Thomism brought its own problems, as any imposed system of thought must. The Irish theologian Gabriel Daly, for example, speaks for many Catholic thinkers when he describes what happened in these terms:

> Leo's act did a serious disservice not merely to his church but also to a great medieval Christian thinker. I belong to a generation many of whom were Thomist by conscription rather than by conviction. I now find myself psychologically, as distinct from intellectually, incapable of profiting from the genius of Aquinas. I suspect that other Catholic theologians of my generation find themselves similarly affected. One does not return to chains even if the chains are golden.[21]

Many would be able to identify with Daly here, and this has not only created something of a negative reaction to Thomism, but also it has opened the way to non-Thomist metaphysical perspectives, that of Macquarrie for example, or that of process thought. However, the golden chains of Aquinas were not simply negative.

The Thomist scholars produced different varieties of Thomism, but it would be fair to say that no variety of Thomism objectifies or reifies God. Aquinas simply does not think of God as an entity or an object in the ordinary sense of the word.[22] Thomists point out, and they are right to do so, that when Aquinas insists that while creation is really related to God but God is not really related to creation, the central conviction behind this language is that God is not in any way dependent upon creatures. The "logic" of "God" seems to demand this. Further for Thomists, Aquinas could not have not thought of God more immanently and dynamically present in everything that is since his judgment is that creation is actually more in God than God is in creation. Consider, for example, *Summa Theologiae* 1.8.3 ad 3. In this remarkable passage we read that God exists in everything: "God exists in everything; not indeed as part of their substance or as an accident, but as an agent is present to that in which its action is taking place... Now since it is God's nature to exist, he it must be who properly causes existence in creatures, just as it is fire itself sets other things on fire. And God is causing this effect in things not just when they begin to exist, but all the time they are maintained in existence, just as the sun is lighting up the atmosphere all the time the atmosphere remains lit. During the whole time of a thing's existence, therefore, God must be present to it, and present in a way in keeping with the way in which the things possesses its existence. Now existence is more intimately and profoundly interior to things than anything else... so God must exist and exist intimately in everything." Then we go on to read that even more so does everything exist in God, since God is necessarily ontologically prior: "It is of the nature of knowledge and volition that the known should exist in the knower and the thing willed in the one willing; and so, by his knowledge and will, things exist in God rather than God in things."[23]

A good case can be made for saying that Macquarrie simply does not adequately understand Aquinas on this issue, a point that has been made by the Dominican philosopher Brian Davies.[24] Indeed, in Macquarrie's *In Search of Deity* when he discusses classical theism and talks about Aquinas, it is interesting that he never adverts to the above passage from the *Summa*.[25] He does not seem to have an adequate appreciation of the dynamic nature of Aquinas's (and Aristotle's) understanding of substance, nor of Aquinas's understanding of divine immanence. To be fair, Thomism would not have featured significantly in Macquarrie's studies in philosophy at the University of Glasgow in the way that it holds central place in the formation of Dominican philosophers and theologians like Fergus Kerr and Brian Davies. Though I have not seen this in Macquarrie's corpus as such, I suspect that the rather relentless analytic methodology of St. Thomas would not greatly have appealed to him. In this respect Macquarrie shares company with Joseph Ratzinger, Pope Benedict XVI. Ratzinger did not find himself attracted to the philosophy and theology of St. Thomas Aquinas, a style of thinking that was, in his own words, "simply too far afield from my own questions,"[26] and he preferred St. Augustine's thought "as a counter-weight to Thomas Aquinas."[27]

Second is the issue whether Aquinas is a representative of classical theism. Much depends on how one construes classical theism. Theologian David Tracy trained in neo-Thomism at the Gregorian University in Rome in the late 1950s but later moved towards his own particular version of process thought, points out that "there are good reasons (*pace* Hartshorne, Tillich, and even Gilson!) to doubt whether Thomas Aquinas himself was a neo-Thomist classical theist..." Tracy draws attention to the neo-Platonic elements in Aquinas over against the empirico-Aristotelian version, but most prominently to Aquinas's apophatism. These features call into question the judgment that Aquinas is *tout court* a classical theist.[28] Add to Tracy's considerations Aquinas's dynamic divine immanence in creation, and the case is strengthened. Aquinas himself, as contrasted with the many manualist interpreters of his thought, does not easily fit the classical description of classical theism, with its criticism on an excessively transcendent view of God. The renaissance of Thomist studies in the wake of Pope Leo XIII's endorsement and encouragement was such that the world of Catholic philosophy and theology was virtually identified with the thought of Aquinas, or perhaps better with various versions/interpretations of Aquinas. The point is well made by Fergus Kerr, OP with reference to Pope Benedict XVI's rejection of Aquinas. Kerr convincingly shows that the rejection of the "textbooks that set out the Thomist 'system' ... the version of Thomism that Ratzinger rejects here is some kind of rationalism," rather than the thought of Aquinas himself.[29] It seems to me that this is the Thomist system that Macquarrie rejects as classical theism rather than Aquinas himself. There is no doubt that Macquarrie is opposed to what has been called "classical theism," but it is not unambiguously clear that he judges Aquinas to be, without significant qualification, a classical theist. I believe that Macquarrie would be in complete agreement with the position of his fellow-student in divinity at the University of Glasgow, Allan D. Galloway, who comments on classical/traditional theism in this vein:

> The fact is that there never has been such a thing as 'traditional theism.' In every age Christians have tried to express the glory, the majesty, the power, the transcendence of God in the language and the metaphysical apparatus available to them. The form of the theistic image has changed with every change in the dominant metaphysical scheme. Every phase of culture enters upon its own hermeneutical confrontation with the Holy Scriptures. The scriptural tradition is the only constant in the situation. But the matter of Scripture becomes a living word only when interpreted by actual people in their own situation. Their metaphysics --- the total frame of reference within which they interpret --- is part of their situation. There is no revealed metaphysics. There is no single metaphysics of theism.[30]

Third is Macquarrie's rejection of the monarchical view of God. Many people have a monarchical view of God that overstresses God's transcendence and understresses God's immanence in creation. That would never have been the position of Aquinas as we have indicated, but that is the position of many, and Macquarrie is taking issue with *this* "classical theism," even if with Allan Galloway it is affirmed that there is no such thing. "This one-sided monarchical concept is, Macquarrie suggests, no longer *intellectually credible* in an age concerned with the organic integrity of the cosmos and with questions of human scope and autonomy. And it is for these reasons that Macquarrie also rejects substance metaphysics. Fergus Kerr, acknowledging that it has become axiomatic for many that the traditional doctrine of God has become contaminated by "substance metaphysics," and that this state of affairs in the English-speaking world is due in no small measure to the widespread use of John Macquarrie's *Principles of Christian Theology*, is one of the better-known scholars attempting to defend "substance metaphysics."[31] Macquarrie, using Heidegger, opts to replace what he takes as the obsolete language of substance (or "inert thinghood") with the language of temporality and history. The problem with Macquarrie's view of substance, as Kerr sees it, is that it is "quite fanciful," that is to say, is simply fails to recognize the fact that for Aristotle and his medieval disciples it is not something inert and lifeless like a rock, but rather a living organism. A living organism can hardly be regarded as inert. Nevertheless, maintains Kerr, "thinkers about God almost all want to replace categories of substance and being with those of process and becoming." While Macquarrie may be one of the major disseminators of these anti-substance metaphysical positions, the shadow of Alfred North Whitehead lurks behind them. "Whitehead's *Process and Reality* ... authorizes the wholly mistaken belief that the Aristotelian (and so Thomist) notion of substance is identical with the Cartesian/Lockean notion, with its aura of intrinsic self-enclosedness and unrelatedness."[32] Let us concede that Macquarrie inadequately understands or appreciates the meaning of substance in Aristotle and Aquinas. That seems to me an issue, but not *the* issue. *The* issue is that a great number of people no longer relate to substance metaphysics or what they take to be classical theism. Classical theism with its attendant substance metaphysics is disconnected from their experience and understanding and is simply not *religiously satisfying*, "since the religious consciousness seeks a God corresponding to the sense of affinity and immanence, rather than one who represents the 'cosmic forces' and 'reality of a higher order' as wholly external and other."[33] These are the words of Macquarrie scholar Georgina Morley and it may be, especially from a Thomist perspective or a classical theist perspective, that she overstates her claim. But, in terms of intellectual credibility and religious satisfaction many find the Macquarrie viewpoint --- or some variant of it --- preferable to that of classical theism, and if it is agreed that Aquinas is no "classical theist," preferable to Aquinas.[34]

Macquarrie and Holy Being

Not everyone feels the need to ask this ultimate, radical question, "Why is there anything rather than nothing?" This leads to the issue of awareness of Being, a reflexive awareness of Being, or an awareness tending toward reflexion. Awareness of Being is not something of which human beings are ordinarily conscious. Frequently, a person has to come up against the nullity of existence in order to be opened to the wonder of Being. "We only notice this wonder when it is placed over against nothing, but then we see that overcoming nothing and standing out from it is Being, not as something else which exists, but in the sense of that wider being within which all particular beings have their being. Since Being is not another being but the *transcendens*, the incomparable and wholly other source and unity of all beings, it normally escapes our notice."[35]

A person becomes aware of the threat of non-being when the precariousness of existence is encountered, and it is death that brings perspective and points beyond being to Being. If one is at all concerned about personal development, growth and direction in life, it is impossible to avoid thinking about death. This experience is called the "wonder of Being," or the "wonder of wonders" in Heideggerian terminology, and seems to be similar to what is expressed in Wittgenstein's words in the *Tractatus Logico-Philosophicus*: "Not *how* the world is, is the mystical but *that* it is."[36]

Although Being is the *transcendens* pure and simple, Being is known only through the beings. In other words, "Being" is a symbol which signifies "that which permits the beings to be; that which explains the being of beings. Being lets-be all that is. It is the essence of Being to let-be. And so, all entities in virtue of their existence participate in Being."[37] The Barthian scholar, John B. Webster, finds Macquarrie's notion of "letting-be" "a curiously passive and disengaged term."[38] This seems misplaced as an understanding of what Macquarrie is about. If everything is emergent from Holy Being, it is difficult to see how "letting-be" is to be understood primarily as disengaged or passive. Letting-be seems very active. On the contrary, it seem to indicate that the creative letting-be of things and persons is an acknowledgment of the absolute priority of grace. It is Macquarrie's term for the Pseudo-Dionysian *Bonum est diffusivum sui* "Goodness is diffusive of itself," and that is supremely active. Another way of putting it is to say that God is the condition that anything may exist, and in so far as something exists, it exists in God. Reflecting on Macquarrie's notion of letting-be as empowering or bringing into being, Yeow Choo Lak puts it like this: "A being *is* in virtue of the fact that it is, but Being is not something that is but lets-be and therefore precedes any is-ness. So, Being is different from beings, yet it is the *spring* and *origin* of all beings; the beings are contingent on and originate from Being."[39] A corollary of this is that we only know God because he lets himself be known, that is, knowledge of God depends on God's letting-be of reality, for it is through things and in things that we are led to the *transcendens.*

Belief in God is faith in Being. "Belief in God is the faith that there is a context of meaning and value that transcends our human life, a context that we do not create and in which we already find ourselves."[40] God is the creative, mysterious ground of our existence and the existence of all reality. To believe in God is to accept reality as trustworthy at the deepest level, to have faith in the worthwhileness of existence even when existence seems absurd. Faith in Being may be for many the basic, implicit, intuitive grasp that life is worth living, or it may flourish in response to Being as holy, a response encountered and nurtured through the givenness of the Christian tradition.

There are three basic criteria for measuring the adequacy of concepts of God in Christian theology. The first is Scripture: Does the concept of God reflect the biblical concepts of God? Second is tradition: Does the concept of God faithfully reflect and represent the triunity of God, the central affirmation about Deity in the Christian tradition? Third is worship or communion with God: Does the concept of God assist and promote deepening awareness of the reality of God in prayer?

The model of God as "Holy Being" is verified in Scripture and throughout the Christian tradition, according to Macquarrie. The classical biblical passage for understanding God as being is Ex. 3:14. The controversy surrounding the precise interpretation of this verse continues, but two things are certain. The Hebrew verb *hyh*/to be --- in whatever grammatical form --- is the center of the verse, and in Hebrew the verb "to be" includes the verb "to become."[41] In some way, the verb is connected with the is-ness of God. The New Testament lends further corroboration. In St. John's Gospel the words *ego eimi*/"I am" occur like a refrain: Jn. 6:35; 8:12, 58; 11:25; 15:1. According to Macquarrie, these words are "an unmistakable echo of Exodus." This tradition was continued through the Fathers into the medieval period. Macquarrie quotes Aquinas in this respect: "Since the being of God is his very essence (which can be said of no other being) it is clear that among names this one (Being, *esse*) most properly names God; for everything is named according to its essence."[42] Finally, the precise ways in which the concept of God as Holy Being can nurture the spiritual life is developed to some extent by Macquarrie in that section of the *Principles of Christian Theology* entitled "Applied Theology," and also in his *Paths in Spirituality*.

The Incomprehensibility of God

Nonetheless, the meaning of "God" is no more exhausted by the language of being than it is by any human language. There is a tendency in human nature to take our ideas of God too literally, almost as if in these ideas we were able to reach God-in-himself. Clearly, Macquarrie considers it illuminating to think of God as Holy Being, that this language has a long and respected tradition behind it, that it is consonant with contemporary philosophies of being, and that it is fundamental or foundational in a way that no other language is. However, such language needs to be complemented by other ways of talking about God, because God is indefinable and incomprehensible. Nicholas Lash is emphatic throughout his work on this notion of God's incomprehensibility as a perduring conviction of Christian discourse. Thus, he writes in respect of continuity and discontinuity in the Christian understanding of God:

Where continuity is concerned, if I were asked to list those features of Christian discourse concerning God which have recurred most persistently in the course of the Church's history, in am impressive variety of social and cultural contexts, one which would come high on my list would be the conviction that it is impossible to understand God.[43]

Macquarrie would be in complete agreement with Lash, and so he takes to task theologians who have tended to speak of God almost exclusively in terms of the I-thou encounter. Personal language for God, for Holy Being, is arguably essential for the reason that it best enables relationship in and with God in worship and prayer, but, at the same time, it cannot be denied that like all analogous language for God, personal language is also finally inadequate for understanding the Divine Reality. All human language is finally inadequate because God is not a being but Holy Being. An exclusive personalism tends to make the reality of God no more than a dimension of human existence. The meaning of God is no more exhausted in the terms of personalist philosophy than it is in terms of existential-ontological theism. Macquarrie is, therefore, suitably appreciative of those mystical thinkers, like Pseudo-Dionysius who prefers to speak of a "thearchy" rather than of "God," or Meister Eckhart, who recognized a "Godhead" beyond "God."[44]

The Immanence of God

Macquarrie is convinced that a more immanentist concept of God is required in which God and the world will not be so sharply separated. Western theological thought has been too much under the dominance of what Macquarrie refers to as the "monarchical" model of God, that is, God understood as absolutely self-sufficient, absolutely transcendent, and for whom the world is external to his own being. Here we come close to the spectrum of views that fall under the heading "process theology," typified in such thinkers as Samuel Alexander, Alfred North Whitehead, Charles Hartshorne. While Macquarrie is not, *sensu stricto*, a process theologian, "he shares much in common with them."[45] Macquarrie's concept of Holy Being-letting-be achieves this degree of intimacy, this organic connection between God and the world.[46] The model of perfection that stands behind the monarchical concept of God is of an utterly transcendent and a-relational God, an invulnerable God, sheerly impassible. Much modern Christian theology finds such a model of perfection deeply flawed, perhaps owing more to Greek philosophy than anything else. It is one model of perfection, but there are others. For many modern persons, process, relationality, or vulnerability and freedom are key and central aspects of perfection. Thus, David Tracy describes an alternative model of perfection:

> The relational, affecting, and affected person of modern process, Hegelian, and dialogical philosophies does provide more helpful candidates for possible models of human 'perfection' than the ancient Greek models of the unaffected (*a-patheia*) person (e.g., of the Stoics) or the modern liberal model of the purely autonomous individual. A relational model of human perfection is clearly a more adequate one for understanding divine perfection than either an ancient individualist or modern autonomous one.[47]

Macquarrie's seeing of God falls broadly within Tracy's sketch of an alternative model of perfection. It is an approach to divine perfection premised not upon the monarchical model of God, stressing God's transcendence over creation, but upon the organic model, giving emphasis to God's immanence in creation. It is a way of understanding the relation between God and the world as both transcendent but also as immanent, "distinguishable but not separable within an organic whole which embraces both of them."[48] Arguably, this sense of God's immanence reflects also Macquarrie's Celtic background. "When I reflect on my life and how I have grown from childhood to manhood, I begin by taking full cognizance of my ethnic background. Not just my own family or the people of my hometown but of the Celtic peoples themselves. I am a Scot, and the product of hundreds of years of Scottish pride and Scottish culture."[49] He notes that the Celts were marked by "the profound sense of the immanence of God in the world... They remained very much aware of a divine presence in all nature, and it is this sense of an all pervading presence that is characteristic of their Christian piety."[50]

Needless to say, not all theologians share Macquarrie's *seeing* of the God-world relationship. Huw Parri Owen, writing out of a tradition of "classical theism", finds Macquarrie's approach "both ontologically and logically illicit," and it is, given the ontological presuppositions of classical theism with which Owen was working.[51] This is to beg the question philosophically. Surely, the more foundational question remains: If two (or more) theistic systems are internally and logically free of fundamental contradiction, are coherent and cohesive, then the criteria for judging which is the more (or most) adequate must go beyond the purely logical into something like the *sanitas* or wholeness of which Allan Galloway speaks.

Macquarrie and Panentheism

Macquarrie's understanding of God thus far is best understood as "panentheism," and indeed he has been called the "Grand Old Man" of British panentheism.[52] What is panentheism? While there are variations on the theme, it may be described with Eugene T. Long as "the belief that the Being of God includes and penetrates the whole universe, so that every part of it exists in him, but (as against pantheism) that this Being is more than, and is not exhausted by, the universe."[53] Turning to an avowedly panentheistic theologian, Philip Clayton, we find a similar perspective.

> Panentheism has been defined as the view that the world is within God, though God is also more than the world. Every event is located within God and expresses something of the divine nature; no event is a purely 'natural' event. Thus no separation of God from these events needs to be granted; God is as intimately involved in each as you are in the beating of your heart and the movements of your hands.[54]

Panentheistic theologians want to affirm that since the world does not lie outside of God, God can influence the world as a whole in a way similar to the mind influencing the body. God is necessarily in some way incarnate in the world. However, it cannot be emphasized enough that while the world is within God, God is so much more than the world. Panentheism is not pantheism.

Arguably in modern theology the doctrine of God falls into one of three patterns of thought: classical theism, pantheism and panentheism. Panentheism is a middle path between the other two. Philip Clayton believes that panentheism is not only useful in terms of philosophical theology, but that it is no less useful in respect of Christian doctrines. Clayton believes that his version of panentheism works well with the tradition of Christian doctrine.

> The major options within Christology all remain options here; indeed, the idea of incarnation is perhaps made easier to think by the notion of God's continual incarnation in/as the world. Room for a high Christology and the strong doctrine of the Spirit means room for panentheistic Trinitarianism. Ecclesiology remains unchanged (note that the idea of Christ's headship of the church already represents a sort of mind-body model). There can be a special presence of God to the church or manifestation of God within the church, just as the divine is differently manifest in the worlds of physics, biology and psychology. The theology of nature is probably strengthened by panentheism, in so far as the natural world comes to be understood as a continuing part of the being of God.[55]

In some ways this is precisely what John Macquarrie achieves, this panentheistic turn in the entire range of Christian doctrine.

Although the term is somewhat cumbersome and Macquarrie himself tends to avoid its use, for purposes of brevity and exposition it serves its purpose. Macquarrie recognizes that the term has come to have a certain currency in contemporary theology: "I believe that in the past fifty years or so there has been a movement among Christian theologians to lay more stress on the closeness and immanence of God, in various forms of panentheism."[56] Panentheism seems to maintain balance between divine transcendence and immanence, always acknowledging the utter priority of God. It is in this precise sense that Avery Dulles, SJ finds himself open to Macquarrie's version of panentheism.[57] It moves away from more infantile and severely anthropomorphic images of God, it invites a deep sense of perduring companionship with God, in whom everything lives and moves and has its being, and it looks forward in hope to the eschatological consummation of this companionship. Panentheism assists those who have struggled with images of God that no longer have the ability to hold together in harmony and challenge their ongoing multi-faceted experience of reality in the modern world to reach a point of maturation in their spiritual and theological pilgrimage.

Marcus J. Borg, a New Testament scholar involved in the renewed quest of the historical Jesus, reveals how panentheism "made it possible for (him) to be a Christian again. The story of my own Christian and spiritual journey... involves the movement from supernatural theism through doubt and disbelief to panentheism. The God I have met as an adult is the God I never knew growing up in the church." As Borg explores panentheism in relation to Scripture and the Christian tradition, he acknowledges the work of John Macquarrie as having been particularly helpful.[58] Another popular theologian, sympathetic to panentheism yet critical of it, is the Anglican priest-physicist, John Polkinghorne, in his many books. He admits its achievement of balance between divine transcendence and immanence, but has difficulty with it in its process-theology proponents such as Charles Hartshorne, in whom it fails to accept the true otherness of the world from God, the classical doctrine of creation, the freedom of creation to be itself. One of Macquarrie's colleagues at Oxford was the scientist and Anglican priest-theologian, Arthur Peacocke (1924-2006). Peacocke taught biochemistry and theology, with doctorates in both disciplines, and was an avowed panentheist. Peacocke, like Polkinghorne, exercised a careful critical correlation between science and theology, found considerable support for his views within the world of process thought, but shared the reservations of Polkinghorne.[59] "Peacocke suggested that 'process theology has tended to over emphasize God's *total* receptivity to all events in the world in a way that seems to allow God little discrimination.' By contrast, Peacocke asserted that, in his own usage of the panentheistic model, 'I have not wanted to imply an equally direct involvement with God in all events nor that all events equally and in the same sense affect God.'"[60] While it would be true to say that process philosophy and theology has more support in the United States than in the United Kingdom, nevertheless it was in the air Macquarrie breathed, so to speak, in both countries.

While there is a family resemblance between Macquarrie and process theologians, he would share Polkinghorne's criticisms of the process version of panentheism. Macquarrie writes:

> I am not myself intending to make much use of the term 'panentheism', though it must already be apparent that I have a good deal of sympathy with the position for which it stands... For my own part, I am content to call this position 'dialectical theism', thereby stressing that it is essentially a species of theism and closer to theism than to pantheism, while the adjective 'dialectical' makes it clear that I intend to avoid the one-sidedness of classical theism and the difficulties which it brought with it.[61]

It could be asserted that if what is described as "classical theism" had been more adequately understood and appropriated by its most eminent representatives, for example St. Thomas Aquinas and his latter-day exponents and commentators, then the desired balance between transcendence and immanence would have been achieved without resort to "panentheism," although Macquarrie himself would question this claim: "Within the total framework of St. Thomas' classical theism, the weight given to immanence is not great."[62] Whether Macquarrie's judgment about St. Thomas is accurate or not is a very large question as we have seen, but it seems to me that the fact remains that many people schooled and catechized in the classical tradition, have not found it to be the case, and reach out to something like panentheism as a conceptual tool that moves beyond what was seen as an absolute dualism, or a quasi-absolute dualism between God and reality, and best enables the integration of their religious experience. If we move beyond the understanding centrally expressed in *Principles of Christian Theology* to *In Search of Deity*, we may detect a further glossing of his panentheism in the direction of dialectical theism. Before doing so, however, it may be helpful briefly to consider Macquarrie in relation to Process Theology, because, as has been noted, clearly he has something in common with this way of thinking about God.

Macquarrie and Process Theology

Process theology is a contemporary theological movement which emphasizes the processive or evolutionary nature of humankind and the world, and holds that God is in process of development through his intercourse with the changing world. There is a very distinctive emphasis on the priority of "becoming" over "being." In terms of philosophical genealogy the name is derived from Alfred North Whitehead's (1861-1947) 1928-9 Gifford Lectures, *Process and Reality,* a way of thinking that Macquarrie characterizes as "a brilliant attempt" to think about God.[63] As a distinctive theological movement, it originated in America, especially at the University of Chicago during the 1920s and 1930s. A slightly different emphasis in process thought emerges in the work of Whitehead's pupil, Charles Hartshorne (1887-1996). Macquarrie writes: "I do not wish to identify myself with the version of theism, found in A. N. Whitehead, for my own approach to these questions is very different from his," and yet he does suggest that the dipolar approach to God of process thought is "a significant attempt to build a concept of God that will take account of both the monarchical and organic models of God."[64]

All process, natural, human, or divine, is regarded as social in nature, entailing inter-relationship, mutuality and participation. Notions of "substance" are rejected as outmoded relics of a static metaphysic. Their place is taken by the concept of "event." "Substance" as the unchanging core in things is a concept that has been dominant in the history of Western thought. For process thinkers science has disclosed that all reality is in the process of change. Each event/actual entity, including God, "prehends" (grasps or actively receives) from all other events. Each event prehends in one way or another the external pressures upon it, and so each event takes change into itself and thus into the larger processes of which it is part. Each event is a "concrescence" of the past, which it inherits and remembers, its present relations, and its "subjective aim" or future goal for self-fulfillment. Each event is given by God (in his "primordial" aspect) its initial aim, which by free decision it seeks to satisfy, thus actualizing its possibility. God is the ultimate recipient of all such realizations, which he harmonizes in accordance with his nature as Love and then uses for further "creative advance" in the cosmos. This affective nature of God is his "consequent aspect." Thus, the di-polarity of God, who is seen as Whitehead said, not as the "exception to" but as "chief exemplification of" the metaphysical principles required to describe all elements in "reality in process." One Roman Catholic theologian, Charles R. Meyer, has made the point been that the future relevance of theology will be determined by its ability to adopt process categories and thinking: "So if theology is to be relevant to coming generations it will have to cease to be a logical game played with pieces like substance and accident, end and means, matter and form, natural and supernatural; pieces freighted with fixed and permanent values and allowed to move only in definite preconceived patterns on the chessboard of reality. Theology itself will have to become process."[65] Meyer's advocacy of process patterns of thought flows from a concern to make theology speak to modern people. In this respect his intention is coincident with that of Macquarrie, and while Macquarrie does not advocate process theology as such, he comes close to it at times.

Thus, the conviction of process theologians is that classical theism --- the presentation of God as absolute, infinite, immutable --- does not do full justice to what religion really believes God to be. Religion talks of a real relationship existing between God and people, a mutual relationship describable in anthropomorphic terms.

It may be helpful briefly to look at the thinking of Charles Hartshorne as a contrast with Macquarrie.[66] In his *Twentieth Century Religious Thought* Macquarrie offers a very brief description of Hartshorne, insisting that "Traditional theism presented us with a supernatural God, but the notion of 'supernatural' is one that has been discredited and is no longer tenable."[67] Thus far, Macquarrie and Hartshorne/process thinkers are coincident. For both there is an unchanging essence to God --- the alternative would be a very crude form of pantheism --- but God "completes himself in an advancing experience."[68] Traditional theists, of course, disallow this idea in principle.

Charles Hartshorne maintains that religion is intuitive in origin, and the religious idea of God is an intuitive or pre-philosophical grasp of who God is. Religion must be allowed to speak for itself before philosophical expression plays a role. The essence of religion is worship, "devoted love for a being regarded as superlatively worthy of love."[69] At the same time, Hartshorne insists that man is but a fragment of reality, limited in every way. So there are two parts to the definition of religion as worship: one, total love for God; two, acceptance of human fragmentariness. "We are or can be loving 'fragments'. We are also loved, called upon to enter a particular relationship with God. Thus, worship is actually an enhancement of ourselves and of the universe."[70] This leads to the notion of all-inclusiveness: "This follows from the meaning of worship as total love... If God is loved or can be loved with all one's capacities, then he must in some sense coincide with being or reality itself... That is to say, our love for anything or anyone includes God. Only if God is all-inclusive can devotion to him be total. We can love God with all our being only if God is said to be in everything and everything to be in God."[71] And so "God" is understood by the major religions of the world as "the Worshipful One who is the object of all our love and attention, who is present in everything because God embraces all, but who is unique because unsurpassable in goodness, power and knowledge."[72] This notion of God as the Worshipful One, or we might say the Adorable One, rules out pantheism understood as the sum of everything. Macquarrie would agree: "If the world is God, it must be not only awesome and mysterious but also adorable; and this, surely, our ambiguous universe is not. The world is not itself divine... Whatever can be called God must be adorable."[73]

Santiago Sia, the process philosophical theologian and expert on the thought of Hartshorne, comments on Hartshorne as follows:

> Hartshorne takes the statement that 'God is love' to mean literally that God finds joy in our joys and sorrow in our sorrows. Love, as Hartshorne uses the word even in its application to God, means sympathetic dependence on

others. God, as the God of love, is one of understanding and sympathy and one to whom we can appeal. God is truly the all-loving and efficacious friend of all. This can only mean, in Hartshorne's way of thinking, that God is really affected by what we do or what we are. In this way we can indeed talk of being related to God and God to us.[74]

If God is love, God must be capable of identifying with our plight to the extent that he too suffers, although not in exactly the same way we do. Sia continues: "If God is unaffected by the acts of creatures, God would hardly be described as sympathetic. Hartshorne argues that an important feature of the religious idea of God is that God is one with whom we are able to enter into a personal relationship. And this is understood as mutual relationship. Mutual relationship means being moved by whatever happens to the other party. To love is to be really affected by what the other does."[75] In many respects Charles Hartshorne's understanding of God comes close to Macquarrie's version of dialectical theism. Yet, it seems to me that Macquarrie resists a metaphysics and an approach to God that are for him more intellectually restrictive and less religious satisfying than his own version of dialectical theism.[76]

Dialectical Theism

In chapter thirteen of *In Search of Deity* Macquarrie sets out the parameters of his "Dialectical Concept of God." In this book is to be found his most mature thinking about God, as he moves away from classical theism and moves beyond panentheism, a term which he finally finds "confusing and not particularly helpful."[77] However, as he proceeds to describe "dialectical theism," he recognizes the limitations of the exercise. He presents a series of dialectical oppositions within God, but with great care: "So far as possible, I must show that in every opposition, each side has its right and each side can and must be asserted. But I draw attention to the modifying expression, 'so far as possible', for there must be limitations to any finite being's understanding of God. A 'God" understood and neatly packaged in philosophical concepts would not be God."

There are six dialectical oppositions which "in their mutual tension... correct the deficiencies of each affirmation taken on its own."[78]

The first dialectical opposition is between being and nothing. Acknowledging the complexity of the language of being, and its distinguished position as applied to God in the Christian tradition, is his starting-point. But obviously, as already noted, God does not exist in quite the same way as other entities. God is "not an item within the world". Hence, one may say that God is nothing, that is, no-thing. This way of speaking is an attempt to emphasize that God is the source of existence, the One who lets be all that is.

The second dialectical opposition is between the one and the many. As one it may be said that "God is the unity holding all things together and without which there would be chaos". At the same time, this oneness of God is not "a barren undifferentiated unity." Macquarrie believes that there is an inner differentiation in God that follows from understanding God as Being. There is the *primordial* mode of God's being, the ineffable-incomprehensible superexistence which lets-be everything that is. There is the *expressive* mode of God's being, the eternal event of giving in and through which God has shared existence with others. There is the *unitive* mode of God's being, whereby the cosmos seeks to return to its source in a deeper and richer unity. One is reminded here of an aphorism of Hans Urs Von Balthasar, expressing the deep intimacy between God and creation: "We belong more to God than to ourselves; thus, we are also more in him than in ourselves. Ours is only the way leading to the eternal image of us that he bears within himself. This way is like a carpet rolled out from him to us, a scroll *prodiens ex ore Altissimi* --- 'coming forth from the mouth of the Most High' --- and we should, like children, learn how to copy it, how to trace the pre-scribed, pre-written characters that have been presented to us. The pre-scription, the law, is what Love has written out in advance, what Love presupposes and proposes to us that we might... become it."[79] Balthasar is affirming the close connection between God's being and our being, a connection understood as a going forth from God and a return to God. In quite different language, that seems to be exactly what Macquarrie is talking about. Although there is an obvious Trinitarian pattern in Macquarrie's language here, one notices that he has made no appeal to the data of Christian revelation. Rather, he is suggesting that "the doctrine of a triune God belongs to natural theology", and in earlier chapters of the book he has discerned this Trinitarian pattern in such philosophical figures as Plotinus, Dionysius, Eriugena, Cusanus, Leibniz, Hegel and Heidegger.

The third dialectical opposition is between God's knowability and his incomprehensibility. If God is expressive and unitive Being, and not exclusively primordial Being, "then he does not confront us as a pure unknown". Knowledge of God is reached in the world "as a presence or as its unity," but such knowledge can never be exhaustive.

The fourth dialectical opposition is between God's transcendence and immanence. Macquarrie prefers a dynamic sense of transcendence "as God's capacity to go out from and beyond himself," that is to say, God's transcendence is supremely his capacity to let-be. This is not to insist that creation is intrinsically necessary to God. It is to claim that God's very nature is to create, "to overflow himself in his generous bestowal of the gift of existence." Perhaps one might come close to Macquarrie's nuanced understanding here if one were to say that God had *almost* no choice but to create. On the other hand, God's immanence "refers to his indwelling of the creation, his presence and agency within the things and events of the world." In his judgment, classical theism emphasized the divine transcendence, the divine ontological otherness at the expense of the divine immanence. A favorite analogy of Macquarrie's for expressing God's immanent presence in creation is the analogy of the artist to his or her work. The analogy for him appears to originate in William Temple's Gifford Lectures, *Nature, Man and God*.[80] An artist puts something of himself into his work, so that to encounter the work is to encounter in a real sense the artist's presence. Macquarrie considers a hierarchy of truths expressive of God's immanent presence. First is the doctrine of creation itself, in which the goodness of matter is affirmed. Second is the doctrine of divine immanence within that creation. Third, in the emergence of human beings the divine presence reaches a new level of expression, with humankind created in the divine image. Finally, the Incarnation of the Son, of expressive Being in Jesus of Nazareth, brings the expression of immanence to completion "so far." The process remains incomplete until the Parousia.

The fifth dialectical opposition is between impassibility and passibility. In classical theism God is pure act, and while God can affect creation, creation cannot affect God. God is impassible. Given Macquarrie's understanding of God's immanent presence within creation, "then he must be deeply affected by everything that goes on in the world... the suffering of that world must in some way be also experienced by God." Says Macquarrie in our July 1998 conversation, *I would not be able to subscribe to the impassibility of God. God must be the most sensitive reality that there is. If we could say that there is a kind of hierarchy of suffering as one moves up the chain of being, then in some sense God must be the one who suffers most sensitively. I am aware of the patristic debate about whether God suffered, and so forth. But the Son could not have suffered without the Father suffering. I can't really think of God the Father as untouched by the suffering of the Son.* Macquarrie's espousal of suffering in God is, needless to say, something widespread in recent theology, both Protestant and Catholic. The interesting thing is that it cuts across different camps of theologians and is in no wise confined to one kind of thinker. Among Protestant theologians may be named, for example: Karl Barth and his interpreter Eberhard Jüngel, Richard Bauckham (the New Testament scholar and commentator on the theology of Jürgen Moltmann), James Cone, Paul Fiddes, Robert Jenson, Wolfhart Pannenberg, Richard Swinburne, Thomas F. Torrance, Keith Ward and Nicholas Wolsterstorff. All the major Reformed ecclesial traditions may be found in this representative list. Catholic examples are no less wide ranging: Raniero Cantalamessa (theologian to the papal household), Jean Galot SJ, Hans Urs von Balthasar, Roger Haight SJ, Elizabeth Johnson CSJ, Hans Küng, and Jon Sobrino SJ. Even a Thomist philosopher like W. Norris Clarke feels the need to revise his understanding of God. Clarke thinks that today we must speak of God as having a real relation to the world, requiring some qualification of God's immutability, including his impassibility.[81] The diverse kinds of theology found in these lists witnesses to the fact that this notion of impassibility is judged wanting by thinkers who would not entirely identify with one another's theological thought.[82] The suffering of God, but in different ways and in to different degrees, has won a very wide acceptance.

However, Macquarrie recognizes that if we acknowledge that God suffers without any kind of philosophical nuance or gloss then God becomes nothing more than "a puny godling... the hapless victim of a world that has got completely out of control." God's possibility is then united to God's impassibility. The traditional notion of impassibility underscores and philosophically expresses God's sheer transcendence, the conviction that God is Creator and not creation. It cannot be dispensed with. At the same time, possibility points up God's *choosing* to suffer with us out of love. God's choosing to make himself vulnerable out of love flows from his self-description as Love in 1 John 4:8. 16: "Whoever does not love does not know God, for God is love... God is love, and those who abide in love abide in God, and God abides in them." It is not that possibility is a necessary characteristic of God --- as it would be for many process theologians and philosophers --- but rather how God wishes to be with his creation, and most uniquely in the entire event of the Incarnation.[83] God willingly makes himself vulnerable to suffering out of love for his creation. God's suffering, therefore, must be thought of as different from the suffering of creatures. Macquarrie puts it like this:

> Whereas the suffering of a human being can overwhelm and eventually destroy the person concerned, this cannot happen in the case of God. He can accept the world's pain, and does in fact accept it because he is immanent in the world process, but he is never overwhelmed by it. He has an infinite capacity for absorbing suffering, and even for transforming it, though we cannot know how this transformation takes place.[84]

The note of transformation sounded here is of immense importance. Suffering, and so God's co-suffering, is never just there. For Macquarrie it is always paschal suffering, that is, real and always cruciform in some degree, but never ultimate. While one wishes to recognize that a too easy speaking of resurrection and eternal life in and with God may seem not to take horrendous suffering seriously, nevertheless resurrection is the ultimate and eschatological transformation of human suffering. There seems daring precedent for this perspective, for example, in the insight of the 16th-17th century mystic and spiritual author, Benedict of Canfield, O.F.M.Cap., who wrote: "Therefore, our own pains --- insofar as they are not ours but those of Christ --- must be deeply respected. How wonderful! And more: our pains are as much to be revered as those of Jesus Christ in His own passion. For if people correctly adore Him with so much devotion on the Good Friday Cross, why may we not then revere Him on the living cross that we ourselves are?"[85] Benedict would have inherited the traditional attribute of divine impassibility, the axiom of divine impassibility being in place from the classical Christianity of the patristic period. Nonetheless, in this text he recognizes through sacramental identification with Jesus Christ a way of making sense of divine passibility that does not collapse the logic of traditional God-talk. If we are in Christ, and if Christ is in us, then there is a mystical but real identification of his suffering with ours and of ours with his. God's choice so to identify with humankind in the Incarnation opens up an avenue of understanding in the dialectical opposition between divine impassibility and passibility.

Macquarrie's argument for God's passibility is not left only at the level of the divine, as it were, in classical theism. It emerges also out of his own experience. *I had a colleague at Union Theological Seminary, Daniel Day Williams. I was a great admirer of Williams. After I left Union the school went through terrible troubles. Students were rebelling against the faculty, the faculty were divided among themselves, and in that situation Dan was a great reconciler, trying to heal these wounds. When I returned to Union for a visit, Dan asked me, 'How long have you been away from Union?' 'Three years,' I replied. 'Well,' said he, you chose three good years to be away.' Within six months of that conversation he died of a heart attack. When I reflected on that, I couldn't help thinking 'Dan has been so grieved by what was going on, and he has been taking into himself so much of the anger and pain.' And it was then I thought that Dan was a godlike man. God takes the anger and pain of the world into himself, and because he is God can transmute it. I would find it very hard to accept that God remains God regardless. You could think of God in his infinity as not only able but ready to embrace the suffering of the world and to absorb it into his own being. If I'm preaching or ministering to a sick person, I must be absolutely honest. I remember as a young minister being in a parish in Brechin for only a few weeks and the father of a young family was hospitalized with an incurable and inoperable cancer. And almost simultaneously his wife was taken to hospital with a tumour in the brain. What really hit me was when one of the orderlies from the hospital was passing me on his bicycle and he said, 'I'm on my way up the hospital. Have you any message for Bruce?' I could not have felt more inadequate than at that moment. The answer, of course, is the Lord, the Word of God. Nowadays the first thing I'd do is take him Holy Communion. I'm not sure that classical metaphysical theism and Holy Scripture are entirely reconcilable on this point. A text that always impressed me from Isaiah is: 'In all their afflictions he was afflicted.' And a book I find very helpful in this regard is Moltmann's "The Crucified God." I regard it as one of the classics in theology of the twentieth century. I'm not sure that I accept all he has to say about Christ being rejected by God.* His many comments on the suffering of God establish how important this topic is to Macquarrie.

Finally, God is both eternal and temporal. If God is both passible and impassible, he has to be both temporal and eternal. Somehow, God is involved in the events of time, temporality, but is also immune from the ravages of time.

If one comes from a strictly Thomist standpoint, perhaps the clearest example of what has come to be called classical theism, then Macquarrie's dialectical theism will be found entirely wanting. The Dominican philosopher of religion, Brian Davies, an established Thomist scholar, finds Macquarrie's dialectical theism disappointing and very close to the di-polar theism of process thinkers, such as Whitehead and Hartshorne. For Davies Macquarrie's real failure is to preserve the distinction between Creator and creation. A doctrine of creation *ex nihilo*, out of nothing, means quite simply that God is not a creature and cannot, therefore, be marked by any of the creaturely characteristics such as passibility.[86] Another trenchant critic of dialectical theism or panentheism, or anything that smacks of what be termed a process philosophical outlook is the philosophical theologian, David Burrell. Burrell takes issue with caricatured versions of Aquinas's thought, as the paradigm of what is taken to be classical theism. Such caricatures fail to grasp the profoundly *responsive* nature of Aquinas's God: "In fact, once one takes *esse* to be the source of all perfections, one finds divine activity to be thoroughly 'intentional' in character, relating to itself and its creation with an understanding love which is the quintessence of responsiveness."[87] Another example presents itself in the person of the Thomist theologian Herbert McCabe, OP. On one occasion, McCabe found himself in an ecumenical discussion group with Anglicans reading for the first time Jürgen Moltmann's *The Crucified God.* McCabe simply could not accept Moltmann's premise that God shares in human suffering. McCabe had no difficulty in asserting that God suffers in the Incarnation and Passion, because Jesus of Nazareth was and is God incarnate. That is to say that God suffers as such was impossible. "He was amazed that theologians accepted what he regarded as grotesque caricatures of the classical doctrine of divine impassibility."[88] It is perfectly possible that those who are attracted to the passible God of Jürgen Moltmann do entertain grotesquely caricatured views of the classical doctrine of divine impassibility. That does not mean, however, that their point of view is *a priori* mistaken. This takes us really to the heart of the matter. If we operate with the principles of Thomist metaphysics as given, as axiomatic, as Davies and Burrell and McCabe do, then we have to rule out *a priori* Macquarrie's dialectical theism as unacceptable. Within that framework, Macquarrie simply does not understand the logic of "God." If that is Macquarrie's failure, then it is one widely shared. Many in the theological community have rejected scholastic philosophy for a variety of reasons, including its seeming relentless abstract rationalistic analysis "that is too tedious for modern man to appreciate."[89] If, however, allowance is made for various metaphysical systems, including an alternative model of perfection, then within the framework of the metaphysics of dialectical theism, Macquarrie's vision seems most acceptable. Moreover, if it yields *sanitas*, health and balance, then it stands as a viable theology within the pluralism of Christian theologies. A viable theology, not the *only* theology. Santiago Sia writes: "Believers, therefore, will have to judge for themselves whether they find in process thought (and the thought of John Macquarrie) a fuller and a more faithful expression of their basic insights compared to, say, classical theism... If process thinkers (and John Macquarrie) were to regard their concept of God as *the* religious experience of God, then they would be guilty of the same fault that they accuse classical theists of having committed."[90] That puts the issue fairly and squarely.

The Theology of the Trinity

The doctrine of the Trinity is the Christian doctrine of God. Any doctrine or expression which is not Trinitarian in character is not fully Christian. It is not the case that Christians have a basic belief in God which is common to other theists, and then they add on to this basic concept further Trinitarian specifications, as it were. The uni-personal God is not the Christian God. Cardinal Walter Kasper goes so far as to describe this uni-personal God as heresy: "From the theological standpoint we must speak more accurately of the heresy of theism. This theism with its unipersonal God is untenable..."[91] The doctrine of the Trinity is the "summary grammar" of the Christian account of God.

Nicholas Lash offers as a possible example of this heresy of theism a reference in the work of the Christian philosopher of religion, Richard Swinburne.[92] Swinburne defines a theist as "... (one) who believes that there is a God." So far so good, but then God is described as like "a person without a body (i.e., a spirit) who is eternal, free, able to do anything, knows everything, is perfectly good, is the proper object of human worship and obedience, the creator and sustainer of the universe." There are indeed elements in this description with which one would wish to be associated, that is, that God is eternal, free, perfectly good, the creator and sustainer of the universe. Unfortunately, this description lacks as a central aspect of Christian theism anything that is essentially Trinitarian. It is almost as if the doctrine of the Trinity is a matter of believing some additional things about God beyond this agreed central core. This is not to impugn Swinburne's personal commitment as a Christian, but to suggest that something absolutely fundamental is missing from this Christian description of God.

Yet, Trinitarian language has often obfuscated the mystery of God for many people. Traditional Trinitarian language speaks of God as "one substance" and "three persons." Macquarrie thinks, like Karl Rahner, Karl Barth and other theologians, that the word "person" has become unhelpful in articulating Trinitarian convictions: "The word 'persons' has become so misleading that perhaps we would do better to think of 'movements' of Being, or 'modes' of Being (provided it is not in the sense of temporary modes)..."[93] Macquarrie's language may sound surprising, and perhaps even shocking to one who has a sense of the history of Christian doctrine and the pitfalls of modalism. William J. Hill, O.P., for example, describes Macquarrie's Trinitarian theology as "neo-modalism."[94] Hill thinks that since for Macquarrie the language of Father, Son and Holy Spirit "is only the rendering of (divine Being in its absoluteness) in Christian language, the doctrine assumes the character of Neo-Modalism. Hill is doubtful if Macquarrie's language of primordial, expressive and unitive modes explains *real* distinctions in God. The real issue at stake in Hill's criticism has to do with theological method. If a theological method is correlational, as Macquarrie's clearly is in his existential-ontology, then the distinctiveness and the reality of the Christian revelation may seem to evaporate in a mere naming of what is already given. The method of existential-ontological analysis finds a correlation between human existence and the symbols/doctrines of Christian revelation and teaching. If that is what is behind Hill's criticism, then the ground should shift to a more wide-ranging analysis of method in theology, and especially how one judges a given methodology to be adequate. John Webster has a similar concern about modalism, but expresses himself in a more nuanced fashion: "(Macquarrie's) text could be rather easily manipulated towards some variety of modalism."[95] Macquarrie wishes to eschew modalism every bit as much as Hill or Webster. There is an irreducible threeness in God. However, this much at least may be said in support of Macquarrie's position, that it helps us to realize the inadequacy of all human language to speak God's reality. God is not a person, or three persons, in the same way that we are persons. In point of fact, Macquarrie is doing little more than St. Augustine when he affirmed that when we use the word "person" with regard to the Trinity, we mean by "person" whatever there are three of in the Trinity.[96]

If we think of "person" too literally, then we end up with tritheism, according to Macquarrie, and this is the reason why he regards the so-called "social analogy" for the Trinity as somewhat unsatisfactory. Those who advocate the social analogy think of "person" in the Trinity in relational terms, that is, that relationality is constitutive of personhood, that one person is no person, and they tend to distance themselves from the modern sense of person as a rational and autonomous subject. Needless to say, Macquarrie is not alone as a critic of the social analogy. To offer but one example, when Cornelius Plantinga speaks of the Trinity as "a zestful, wondrous community of divine light, love, joy, mutuality and verve," as a community in which there is "no isolation, no insulation, no secretiveness, no fear of being transparent to another,"[97] he is taken to task somewhat humorously by Karen Kilby: "Where exactly, one might wonder, did (he) acquire such a vivid feeling for the inner life of the deity?"[98] While the language Plantinga uses is not unattractive, Kilby maintains that it is too strongly projectionist, and not sufficiently respectful of the Mystery of God. She has a point. Given that we have no language other than human in which to speak of God, ineluctably there would seem to be an element of projection in all theology.

Perhaps the real issue is not, *per impossibile*, to avoid projection at all costs, but rather to recognize the limitations of our language. Macquarrie writes, balancing as it were Plantinga and Kilby: "Even when we make every allowance for the fact that a person is constituted through his relation to other persons, such a model goes too far in the direction of 'dividing the substance'... But the social analogy has value in reminding us that because of the inescapable social dimension in man, any analogy between God and man must have in view man-in-community."[99] This is underscored by the New Zealand theologian, Douglas Pratt, in his analytical contrast of Hartshorne and Macquarrie: "Now, although Macquarrie dismisses the 'social analogy' as appropriately descriptive for the Trinity to be unsatisfactory, he does concede its worth as a reminder of the necessary social dimension of human being, whereby analogous discourse in respect of deity must take this into account. In other words, analogous to the essential relationality of human being (of which God is the creative source), God is likewise to be understood in relational terms."[100] So, despite Macquarrie's dislike of the social analogy for the reasons given, it seems virtually impossible to find a better word, a term that will express relationship between God and humankind. Perhaps the best that can be done in a sane (that is, related to *sanitas*) use of theological language is to use various models as mutually corrective in the common acknowledgement that all human language is ultimately inadequate in speaking of God.[101]

God as Holy Being has let itself be known in the Christian community of faith under the Trinitarian symbolism of Father, Son and Holy Spirit. These three "persons" are not just three consecutive stages in the Christian community's experience, or three temporal phases in God's self-manifestation, but rather belong to the very substance of the God-head, Holy Being. Macquarrie proceeds to outline what he thinks of as his "dim conception" of the Blessed Trinity in terms that will be familiar from the consideration of his natural theology of the Trinity, in the consideration of his dialectical theism above.

"The Father may be called 'primordial' Being."[102] By this term he understands God the Father to be "the condition that there should be anything whatsoever, the source not only of whatever is but of all possibilities of being." The Father, as primordial Being, however, is never isolated, on his own, as it were. Rather, the very being of the Father is letting-be, "the source of outpouring" of being on others.

The Son may be called "expressive Being," because the energy of primordial Being "is poured out through expressive beings and gives rise to the world of particular beings... Being mediates itself to us through the beings." Although the description "expressive being" for the Son may seem strange, if we recall the wording of the Nicene Creed, we will see at once a similarity with Macquarrie's language for the Son. In the Creed, it is professed that "through (Christ) all things were made." Or, going earlier in the tradition to the prologue of St. John's Gospel, we read "All things came to be through (the Word), and without him nothing came to be" (John 1:3). Macquarrie is giving philosophical expression, stemming ultimately from the categories of Martin Heidegger, to this biblical and credal conviction that through Jesus Christ, the Son, all reality has come to be. "The primordial being of the Father, which would otherwise be entirely hidden, flows out through expressive Being to find its expression in the world of beings."[103]

The Holy Spirit may be called "unitive Being," and this term is intended to recall the Church's structure of prayer. The Church generally ascribes glory to the Father and the Son "in the *unity* of the Holy Spirit." The Holy Spirit as unitive Being maintains, strengthens, and where necessary restores the unity of the beings with Being. The action of the Holy Spirit is a unifying action because it relates the beings to Holy Being. Wherever beings are seen not as self-subsistent, but as part of an integrated and larger whole, wherever unity is sought and maintained among all the entities that form God's good creation, there unitive Being, the Holy Spirit is at work.

The feminist theologian, Elizabeth Johnson, provides a fine summary of Macquarrie's Trinitarian vision:

> In existential-ontological terms John Macquarrie works out the notion of Being as the energy of letting-be and self-spending. God who is Being itself is constituted by three persons, which are movements within the mystery of Being: primordial Being, deep overflowing source of all; expressive Being, mediating the dynamism outward; unitive Being, closing the circle to accomplish a rich unity in love.[104]

In some ways Johnson's expression in this summary improves upon Macquarrie's own expression, and provides a gloss on the remarks of Balthasar cited above about reality emerging from God and returning to God. God is the source of everything and the rich and fulfilling term of everything.

Not everyone will favor Macquarrie's "dim conception" (his own description) of the Trinity. Some will find this talk about Holy Being as primordial, expressive and unitive obscure and unhelpful. Macquarrie's response would be to insist that there is no unclear, unambiguous language for God. God is Other, and the only language we can use to talk about the Other is faulty and frail human language. He finds that this kind of language is both helpful and credible in articulating the Christian doctrine of God, but he would insist that all responsible Christian forms of God-talk act as mutual correctives, pointing up the deficiencies in all God-talk. It seems to me, however, that the singular advantage behind Macquarrie's Trinitarian language is that we as human beings get caught up in it. We are beings, individual beings, and therefore, have come to be through expressive Being, the Son. And, as Christians, that which maintains us in unity/union/communion with the primordial Being of the Father and the expressive being of the Son is unitive Being, the Holy Spirit. The doctrine of the Trinity in Macquarrie's form of expression is not extrinsic to us.

Conclusion

"The account of Trinitarian theology (in Macquarrie's *Principles*) is almost exclusively economic in orientation. There is no presentation of the sheer spontaneous plenitude of the triune life." Thus, John B. Webster in summarizing Macquarrie's theology of the Trinity. It is true that Macquarrie does not use such traditional language of the immanent Trinity as paternity, filiation, spiration. This seems to me no bad thing, not least because this language does not communicate readily and easily, even for those who are particularly receptive to Trinitarian language. Elizabeth Johnson, for example, writes: "Further analysis of the inner life of the Trinity apart from saving concern for the world is a distraction. Metaphysical claims about God's inner life, if such need to be made, must function correctly with respect to God's redemptive work."[105] Taking this further, it might be argued that saving concern for the world/God's redemptive work, or the spontaneous plenitude of the divine life, as Macquarrie would put it, is to be found in the church, the sacraments, *par excellence* the Eucharist, and finally in being drawn into mystical triune communion. "We see that, for Macquarrie, philosophical theology is essentially spiritual, even mystical."[106] Finding the plenitude of divine life in this fashion returns us to the words of Bishop Montefiore that opened the chapter: "Knowledge of God... must ultimately be a knowledge based on communing. The knowledge of God merges finally with the love of God."[107]

---

[1] H. P. Owen, *Concepts of Deity* (London: Macmillan, 1971), vii.

[2] Hugh Montefiore, *Credible Christianity: The Gospel in Contemporary Society* (Grand Rapids: Eerdmans, 1994), 274. This statement is followed by an endnote referring to Macquarrie's 1972 edition of *Paths in Spirituality*, 72.

[3] John Macquarrie, *Thinking About God* (London: SCM Press, 1975), 120.

[4] Ibid., 112.

[5] Paul Fiddes, "On God the Incomparable: Thinking about God with John Macquarrie," in Robert Morgan, ed., *In Search of Humanity and Deity* (London: SCM Press, 2006), 179.

[6] See Allan D. Galloway, *Faith in a Changing Culture* (London: Allen and Unwin, 1968), 51-63, especially 63.

[7] See Bernard J. F. Lonergan, *Insight* (London: Longmans Green, 1958), chapter ten, and *Method in Theology* (New York: Herder and Herder, 1972), 57-99.

[8] "Fifty Years of Metaphysical Reflection: The Universe As Journey," in Gerald A. McCool, ed., *The Universe As Journey: Conversations with W. Norris Clarke, S.J.* (New York: Fordham University Press, 1988), 50.

[9] "Approaching the Christian Understanding of God," in Francis Schüssler Fiorenza and John P. Galvin, ed., *Systematic Theology: Roman Catholic Perspectives,* vol. 1 (Minneapolis: Fortress Press, 1991), 134.

[10] *Existence, Being and God* (New York: Paragon House, 1985), 37-38.

[11] Paul Fiddes, op. cit., 181.

[12] Fergus Kerr, OP, "'A Thomist, but not a Medievalist,' An Interview with Fergus Kerr, OP," *The Leuven Philosophy Newsletter* 16 (2007), 17.

[13] Ibid., 39.

[14] John Macquarrie, *Principles of Christian Theology,* 110.

[15] *Being and Time,* (tr. J. Macquarrie and E. Robinson), (New York: Harper and Row, 1962), 62.

[16] Herbert McCabe, O.P., *God Matters* (London: Geoffrey Chapman, 1987), especially 2-9, 39-51. See also his *God Still Matters* (New York and London: Continuum, 2002), 3-12, 29-35.

[17] Georgina Morley, *John Macquarrie's Natural Theology: The Grace of Being* (London and Burlington, VT: Ashgate Publishing Company, 2003), 141, fn. 9.

[18] John W. O'Malley, SJ, *What Happened at Vatican II* (Cambridge, MA: The Belknap Press of Harvard University Press, 2008), 62.

[19] Ibid.

[20] See Stephen Schloesser, SJ, *Jazz Age Catholicism* (Toronto: University of Toronto Press, 2005), for a discussion of Thomism in relation to Jacques and Raissa Maritain, Georges Rouault, Georges Bernanos, among others.

[21] Gabriel Daly, "Catholicism and Modernity," *Journal of the American Academy of Religion* 53 (1985), 775.

[22] See the important essay by Fergus Kerr, OP, in Jeremiah Hackett and Jerald Wallulis, ed., *Philosophy of Religion for a New Century: Essays in Honour of Eugene Thomas Long* (Dordrecht, The Netherlands: Kluwer Academic Publishers, 2004), 63-80.

[23] St. Thomas Aquinas, *Summa Theologiae, vol. 2 Existence and Nature of God (Ia.2-11),* English translation by Timothy McDermott, OP (New York and London: McGraw-Hill Book Company and Eyre and Spottiswoode, 1963), ad loc.

[24] Brian Davies, OP, review of *In Search of Deity, New Blackfriars* 64 (1984), 439-440. Note Macquarrie's own rather unfair description of Thomism in his "Ebb and Flow of Hope in Christian Theology at the End of the Second Millennium," *The Expository Times* 107 (1995-1996), 208.

[25] See John Macquarrie, *In Search of Deity* (London: SCM Press, 1984), *especially* 36-42.

[26] Joseph Ratzinger, *Milestones* (San Francisco: Ignatius Press, 1998), 44.

[27] Joseph Ratzinger, *Salt of the Earth* (San Francisco: Ignatius Press, 1997), 60. George Weigel comments on this as follows: "His seminary experience with neo-scholasticism would also mark him permanently, and would later make him the first non-Thomist in centuries to head the Catholic Church's principal doctrinal office." See George Weigel, *God's Choice: Pope Benedict XVI and the Future of the Roman Catholic Church* (New York: HarperCollins Publishers, 2005), 164.

[28] See David Tracy, "Kenosis, Sunyata and Trinity: A Dialogue with Masao Abe," in John B. Cobb and Christopher Ives, ed., *The Emptying God* (Maryknoll, NY: Orbis Books, 1990), 137-138.

[29] See Fergus Kerr, OP, "Comment: Ratzinger's Thomism," *New Blackfriars* 89 (2008), 367-368.

[30] Allan D. Galloway, "A God I Can Talk To," in Eugene T. Long ed., *God, Secularization and History* (Columbia, SC: University of South Carolina Press, 1974), 114.

[31] See Fergus Kerr, OP, Review: *Coming to Be: Towards a Thomistic-Whiteheadian Metaphysics of Becoming* by James W. Felt (Albany, NY: State University of New York Press, 2001), in *Modern Theology* 18 (2002), 413.

[32] Ibid., 414.

[33] Georgina Morley, op. cit., 124.

[34] Criticism on the score of classical theism has come not only from Thomist quarters, but also from the Reformed camp. The most comprehensive critic --- comprehensive with regard to all theologians and philosophers deemed to be panentheist --- is probably John W. Cooper in his justly praised *Panentheism, The Other God of the Philosophers* (Grand Rapids, MI: Baker Academic, 2006). In a very even-handed way, from the perspective and presuppositions of Reformed theology and philosophy, Cooper shows his differences from panentheism.

[35] John Macquarrie, *God Talk*, 99-100.

[36] Cited in *God Talk*, 82.

[37] Ibid., 100; *Thinking About God*, 106.

[38] John B. Webster, "Principles of Christian Theology," in Robert Morgan, ed., *In Search of Humanity and Deity*, 88.

[39] Cited in Eugene T. Long, op. cit., 41.

[40] John Macquarrie, *God and Secularity*, 107.

[41] John Macquarrie, *Thinking About God*, 107.

[42] ST Ia, q. 13, art. 11. See *God Talk*, 100.

[43] *Theology on Dover Beach* (London: Darton, Longman and Todd, 1979), 30.

[44] John Macquarrie, "Dialogue Among the World Religions," *The Expository Times* 108 (1996-1997), 170.

[45] Eugene T. Long, op. cit., 49.

[46] See the positive comments of the Methodist liturgical and ecumenical theologian, Geoffrey Wainwright, in his *Doxology, A Systematic Theology* (New York and Oxford: Oxford University Press, 1980), 350-351, a book dedicated to Macquarrie.

[47] David Tracy, "Approaching the Christian Understanding of God," 145. In fact, in this essay, in the section dealing with this alternative model of perfection, Tracy refers to Macquarrie's *In Search of Deity* as "an important study."

[48] John Macquarrie, *Thinking About God*, 111.

[49] John Macquarrie, *On Being a Theologian*, ed. John H. Morgan (London: SCM Press, 1999), 11.

[50] John Macquarrie, "Celtic Spirituality," in Gordon S. Wakefield, ed., *A Dictionary of Christian Spirituality* (London: SCM Press, 1983), 83-84.

[51] See his *Concepts of Deity* (New York: Herder and Herder, 1971), especially 131-151. Similar critical remarks are made of Macquarrie by Illtyd Trethowan, O.S.B., *Absolute Value: A Study in Christian Theism* (London: Allen and Unwin, 1970), 170-177, and by the Irish philosopher Maurice Curtin, "God's Presence in the World: The Metaphysics of Aquinas and Some Recent Thinkers — Moltmann, Macquarrie, Rahner," in Fran O'Rourke, ed., *At the Heart of the Real* (Philosophical Essays in Honour of Desmond Connell), (Dublin: Irish Academic Press, 1992), 123-136.

[52] By Michael Brierley, in his review of Georgina Morley, *The Grace of Being* in *Modern Believing* 43 (2002), 63, and also in Philip Clayton and Arthur Peacocke, ed., *In Whom We Live and Move and Have Our Being: Panentheistic Reflections on God's Presence in a Scientific World* (Grand Rapids: Eerdmans, 2004), 275.

[53] Eugene T. Long, op. cit., 50.

[54] Philip Clayton, "God and World," in Kevin J. Vanhoozer, ed., *The Cambridge Companion to Postmodern Theology* (Cambridge: Cambridge University Press, 2003), 206.

[55] Ibid., 215.

[56] John Macquarrie, *Stubborn Theological Questions* (London: SCM Press, 2003), x.

[57] Avery Dulles, SJ, "A Roman Catholic Response to *Principles*," in Robert Morgan, ed., *In Search of Humanity and Deity*, 81.

[58] *The God We Never Knew* (San Francisco: Harper Collins, 1997), 12, 30-33.

[59] For a comprehensive account of Peacocke's panentheism, see Gloria L. Schaab, *The Creative Suffering of the Triune God* (New York and Oxford: Oxford University Press, 2007).

[60] Gloria L. Schaab, op. cit., 154.

[61] *In Search of Deity*, 54.

[62] John Macquarrie, "Incarnation as Root of the Sacramental Principle," in David Brown and Ann Loades, ed., *Christ: The Sacramental Word* (London: S.P.C.K., 1996), 31.

[63] John Macquarrie, "Dialogue Among the World Religions,' 171.

[64] John Macquarrie, *Thinking About God*, 113. While one acknowledges Macquarrie's desire to distance himself from various aspects of process theology, it seems to me clear that is a very real closeness. See the comment of Fergus Kerr, OP, reviewing the Macquarrie Festschrift *Being and Truth* and Macquarrie's own *Theology, Church and Ministry* in *New Blackfriars* 68 (1987), 420.

[65] Charles R. Meyer, *A Contemporary Theology of Grace* (Eugene, OR: Wipf and Stock Publishers, 2002), 113.

[66] My major guide in this exploration will be the philosophical theologian, Santiago Sia. Sia is an established authority on process thought, and especially the thought of Charles Hartshorne. Hartshorne was the subject of his doctoral thesis at the University of Dublin, Trinity College.

[67] John Macquarrie, *Twentieth Century Religious Thought*, new edition (Harrisburg, PA: Trinity Press International, 2002), 275.

[68] Ibid.

[69] Santiago Sia, *God in Process Thought* (Dordrecht-Boston-Lancaster: Martinus Nijhoff Publishers, 1985), 10. See also his "The Doctrine of God's Immutability: Introducing the Modern Debate," *New Blackfriars* 68 (1987), 220-232, in which he maps the process position in relation to a wide range of thinkers, both historical and contemporary.

[70] Santiago Sia, *God in Process Thought*, 11.

[71] Ibid., 13.

[72] Santiago Sia, *Religion, Reason and God: Essays in the Philosophies of Charles Hartshorne and A. N. Whitehead* (Frankfurt: Peter Lang, 2004), 28-29.

[73] John Macquarrie, *Thinking About God*, 110, 119.

[74] Santiago Sia, *Religion, Reason and God*, 16.

[75] Ibid., 31. This is essentially the same point made by David Tracy in his essay, "Kenosis, Sunyata, and Trinity: A Dialogue with Masao Abe," especially 139-140.

[76] Somewhat similar reservations are made of Hartshorne by Santiago Sia, "Charles Hartshorne on Describing God," *Modern Theology* 3 (1987), 193-203.

[77] *In Search of Deity*, 171.

[78] This is how it is put in his description of Macquarrie by the Irish systematic theologian, Denis Carroll, *A Pilgrim God for a Pilgrim People* (Dublin: Gill and Macmillan, 1988), 143.

[79] *The Grain of Wheat*, (tr. E. Leiva-Merikakis), (San Francisco: Ignatius Press, 1995), 2.

[80] (London: Macmillan, 1934), 478.

[81] "A New Look at the Immutability of God," in Robert Roth, ed., *God Knowable and Unknowable* (New York: Fordham University Press, 1973), 43-72.

[82] The list is taken in adapted form from Thomas G. Weinandy, OFMCap, "Does God Suffer?" *First Things* 117 (2001), 35.

[83] See Thomas G. Weinandy, *Does God Suffer?* (Notre Dame, IN: University of Notre Dame Press, 2000) for an admirable defense of impassibility traditionally understood. Weinandy acknowledges briefly Macquarrie's nuanced position that God does not *necessarily* suffer. See also Weinandy's fuller argument in his *Does God Suffer?* (Notre Dame, IN: University of Notre Dame Press, 2000).

[84] *In Search of Deity*, 181. The Irish systematic theologian, Gerard O'Hanlon, S.J., in his fine study, *The Immutability of God in the Theology of Hans Urs von Balthasar* (Cambridge: Cambridge University Press, 1990), 212, seems to misunderstand Macquarrie as positing an almost unqualified, univocal impassibility in God. O'Hanlon bases his judgment on his reading of Macquarrie's *The Humility of God*, but has not taken account of the later Gifford Lectures, *In Search of Deity*.

[85] Benedict of Canfield, O.F.M.Cap., *Rule of Perfection*, 1609.

[86] Review of *In Search of Deity*, in *New Blackfriars* 64 (1984), 439-440. For a perceptive and sensitive understanding of Macquarrie's own appreciation of Thomism, see his *Twentieth Century Religious Thought*, 278-300, and his essay on the premier Anglican Thomist of the last century, Eric L. Mascall, "Mascall and Thomism," *The Tufton Review* 1 (1998), 1-13.

[87] David Burrell, CSC, *Faith and Freedom, An Interfaith Perspective* (Oxford: Blackwell Publishing, 2004), 18. The entire chapter is relevant, "Distinguishing God from the World," 3-19. See also the very fine work of Fergus Kerr, OP, *After Aquinas: Versions of Thomism* (Oxford: Blackwell Publishing, 2002), especially 181-206.

[88] Fergus Kerr, OP, "Editorial," *New Blackfriars* 83 (2002), 382.

[89] Charles R. Meyer, *A Contemporary Theology of Grace* (Eugene, OR: Wipf and Stock, 2002), 2. Throughout this book, Meyer attempts to present his own version of a process theology.

[90] Santiago Sia, *Religion, Reason and God*, 35-36, with adaptation to include John Macquarrie.

[91] *The God of Jesus Christ*, (tr. M. J. O'Connell), (London: SCM Press, 1983), 295.

[92] Nicholas Lash, "Considering the Trinity," *Modern Theology* 2 (1986), 183, an essay to which I am much indebted. Lash refers to Swinburne's *The Coherence of Christian Theism*, Oxford: Clarendon Press, 1977 as exemplifying what Kasper calls the "heresy of Christian theism," but perhaps he overlooks Swinburne's very considerable contributions as a Christian apologist.

[93] *Principles of Christian Theology*, 193.

[94] *The Three Personed God: The Trinity as a Mystery of Salvation* (Washington, DC: The Catholic University of America Press, 1982), 146-147. The same criticism that Macquarrie is modalist is made by Timothy Bradshaw, "Macquarrie's Doctrine of God," *Tyndale Bulletin* 44 (1993), 29.

[95] John B. Webster, "Principles of Christian Theology," in Robert Morgan, ed., *In Search of Humanity and Deity*, 89.

[96] St. Augustine, *The Trinity*, V.10, (tr. E. Hill) (Brooklyn, NY: New City Press, 1991), 196.

[97] Cornelius Plantinga, "Social Trinity and Tritheism," in Ronald J. Feenstra and Cornelius Plantinga, ed., *Trinity, Incarnation and Atonement* (Notre Dame: University of Notre Dame Press, 1989), 28.

[98] Karen Kilby, "Perichoresis and Projection: Problems with Social Doctrines of the Trinity," *New Blackfriars* 81 (2001), 439.

[99] *Principles of Christian Theology*, 194.

[100] Douglas Pratt, *Relational Deity: Hartshorne and Macquarrie on God* (Lanham-New York-Oxford: University Press of America, 2002), 178. Pratt's book is the fruit of a PhD dissertation presented to the University of St. Andrews, Scotland, directed by D. W. D. Shaw, one of the few Scots systematic theologians to take an active interest in process thought.

[101] Owen F. Cummings, "The Trinity Today: Some Recent Views of the Social Doctrine of the Trinity," *The Priest* (June, 2003), 13-17. See also the brief but helpful comments on Macquarrie of Paul M. Collins, *Trinitarian Theology, East and West* (New York and Oxford: Oxford University Press, 2001), 113.

[102] *Principles of Christian Theology*, 198.

[103] Ibid., 199-200.

[104] Elizabeth Johnson, CSJ, *She Who Is: The Mystery of God in Feminist Theological Discourse* (New York: The Crossroad Publishing Company, 1992), 210. Note also her approving comments on Macquarrie on 239, 251. In her more recent *Quest for the Living God: Mapping Frontiers in the Theology of God* (New York: Continuum, 2007), 219, she reiterates her approval of Macquarrie's understanding and expression.

[105] Elizabeth A. Johnson, *Quest for the Living God: Mapping Frontiers in the Theology of God* (New York: Continuum, 2007), 215.

[106] Paul Fiddes, op. cit., 181.

[107] See endnote 2 above.

6. KNOWING JESUS CHRIST

*If Christianity is not rooted in things that actually happened in first century
Palestine, we might as well be Buddhists, Marxists or almost anything else. And if
Jesus never existed, or if he was quite different from what the Gospels and the
church's worship affirms him to have been, then we are indeed living in cloud-
cuckoo-land.*
N. T. Wright.[1]

This introductory statement from the pen of N. T. Wright, former Anglican
Bishop of Durham and New Testament scholar, provides an excellent starting place
for exploring the christology of John Macquarrie. It affirms essentially two principles:
that there must be a bedrock of historical truth for christology, and indeed for
Christianity, and that there must be some fundamental isomorphism between the
christological understanding of the New Testament and the liturgy and Jesus' own self
understanding. In my judgment in the light of these two principles --- what we might
call the grammar of christological orthodoxy --- there are some deficiencies in
Macquarrie's christology. The deficiencies arise, however, less from the heterodoxy
of Macquarrie's own vision than from ambiguity of expression. It seems to me that if
the cartographer of orthodoxy were to limit himself only to the systematic expressions
of Macquarrie's christology, the ambiguity may have the upper hand. However, if
that orthodoxy is also mapped through his liturgical, sacramental and ecclesial
understanding, the ambiguity evaporates. It is to the systematic expressions that we
first turn our attention.

In conversation with me John Macquarrie said: *In my recent book on
christology I included a chapter, 'How do we know Jesus Christ?' I tried to say there
that you've got to introduce other ways of knowing besides the rational. You don't
know Jesus Christ, even if you have read John Meier's books on the historical Jesus,
as Meier himself really acknowledges. That's why my final chapter is actually called
'The Metaphysical Christ.' I'm not sure that it was a terribly good title for it, but it's*

Christ as the ultimate. There is also something about this in my book "In Search of Humanity", the chapter on "Cognition." Professor Gordon Stewart, Professor of Public Health at Glasgow University, read "In Search of Humanity", and he said the chapter he liked best was the one on cognition. To get a sense of what knowing besides the rational might mean, I like to quote St. Bonaventure: "First, therefore, I invite the reader to the groans of prayer through Christ crucified... so that he does not believe that reading is sufficient without unction, speculation without devotion, investigation without wonder, observation without joy, work without piety, knowledge without love, understanding without humility, endeavor without divine grace, reflection as a mirror without divine wisdom."

The best place to look for an up to date précis of Macquarrie's systematic christology is undoubtedly his Cardinal Meyer Memorial Lectures at the University of St. Mary of the Lake, Mundelein Seminary, the Archdiocese of Chicago, in 1998. The lectures were published as *Christology Revisited,* and they represent his most mature position.[2] In a perceptive but not uncritical review the Cambridge theologian, Lionel Wickham, has captured Macquarrie's christological tone: "John Macquarrie is an old hand at measured exposition. The clear language and serene tone of voice are welcome as ever."[3] The language is clear and the tone is serene in my judgment not least because Macquarrie is respectful of the history of tradition:

> To deny fundamental doctrines, like that of the Trinity; to reject the creeds; to set aside the beliefs of the early councils of the still undivided church – these may be actions to which individuals are impelled by their own thinking on these matters, but they cannot take place in Christian theology, for they amount to a rejection of the history and therefore of the continuing identity of the community within which Christian theologizing takes place.[4]

It is important to emphasize this because a number of critics believe that Macquarrie has drifted some distance from orthodox christology. At the same time, he recognizes the pastoral necessity of appropriating the doctrinal language of the tradition and then making it speak in language intelligible to our contemporaries. The objective is "to penetrate behind the possibly quaint and even alien language of the dogma to the existential issues that agitated the church at the time of the dogma's formulation, and appropriate for our own time and in our own language the essential insight which the dogma sought to express."[5] This is where the danger lies, when one attempts to put old faith convictions into new language, as it were.

He is quite clear in the "Introduction" that his intention is to pay particular attention to the christological issues and difficulties that have been felt since the Enlightenment. Obviously, it is possible to advocate a christology marked by the exemplarity of its patristic matrix or some other period in the two millennia of Christian tradition. But the value of Macquarrie's starting-point is that it is where we are, that is to say, for better or worse we are living in a world strongly influenced by the Enlightenment. He characterizes the period since the Enlightenment as "an unprecedented era of theological renewal and creativity."[6] People's questions and concerns about Jesus Christ are shaped by that tradition in many respects. To neglect it in favour of an earlier period in the tradition seems pastorally misguided. One might wish to take people to a richer appreciation of the pre-Enlightenment tradition of christological reflection, but first one must begin where people in fact are. This does not mean for him, however, accepting all the presuppositions of modernity without critique. In that sense Macquarrie is no modernist, but while he is aware of the pitfalls and the biases of the Enlightenment, he is unwilling to trash modernity.

So, while acknowledging that "the christology worked out in patristic times attained a classic status, and is indeed still the norm today," Macquarrie is insistent upon the need to do christology *for today*. More precisely, the need is to reflect upon "the fundamental paradox, that Jesus Christ is both human and divine."[7] Accepting this paradox as the faith of the Church, every intellectual effort must be made to understand something of it without avoiding the paradox through taking a short cut. Docetists take a short cut through Christ's humanity, Adoptionists through his divinity. Both avoid what needs to be done: "We have rather to stretch our minds as far as they will go to show that this is indeed a paradox and by no means nonsense or mere contradiction."[8]

Starting from Below

Christology finds its first textual expression in the documents of the New Testament. Prior to the texts was the worshipping Christian community, and in that sense, liturgy precedes text. When it comes to an examination of those texts, especially the texts in the Gospels, of necessity for post-Enlightenment people the question of the historical veracity comes into play, and this is enormously complex, as noted by the New Testament scholar Raymond E. Brown: "Judgments about details of Jesus' life in the first third of the first century require painstaking scholarship; and when properly phrased, those judgments use the language of 'possibly' or 'probably' - -- rarely 'certainly.'"[9] Macquarrie has certainly read the contributions of the questers of the historical Jesus in the last twenty years or so, and is best understood as moderately liberal in his position.

However, one can see a certain line of development. In *The Scope of Demythologizing* from his existentialist phase Macquarrie acknowledges the necessity of establishing a minimal core of historical factuality concerning Jesus of Nazareth. That minimal core is "that there was someone who once exhibited in history the possibility of existence which the *kerygma* proclaims."[10] That was 1960. By 1990 he has gone considerably further with this historical core, citing from the work of Ed P. Sanders quite an expanded list of "the basic facts" about the historical Jesus, facts about which according to Macquarrie "we can have reasonable certainty."[11] However, it seems to me that Macquarrie has gone even further than this when he says, "(Jesus) did manifest the self-giving that the tradition ascribes to him."[12] This form of expression is considerably more generous, and comes close to identifying the christological understanding of the community with the self understanding of Jesus.

Starting from below, the humanity of Jesus is fully affirmed, with reference to the texts of the New Testament. There are many unequivocal testimonies to his humanity: he is tempted by Satan, he prayed to the Father, he was baptized by John, he experienced deep human emotions. Nonetheless, "from the very beginning or very near it, the disciples were discovering that there is something 'more' in Jesus that distinguishes him from the rest of the human race."[13] The Scottish Presbyterian theologian, John McIntyre, a distinguished contributor to christology with his *The Shape of Christology*, has well described Macquarrie's "something more" as "transcendental characteristics beyond the human... cognized by spiritual discernment, or quite simply faith."[14] McIntyre insists against those who question the orthodoxy of Macquarrie's christology from below that it is also and necessarily complemented in him by a christology from above. "Chronological priority may lie with the approach to Christology from the human life of Jesus upon earth ('from below'), but logical priority must lie with the approach which moves in the opposite direction of the incarnation of the Divine Logos, with the descent of the Logos 'from above,' as Macquarrie points out. It is clear that... for Macquarrie there is full commitment to both approaches to Christology and that these approaches answer to what older Christologies called 'the two natures of Jesus Christ.'"[15]

This is what Macquarrie means by the "something more." That something 'more' is engaged in five issues: the virginal conception, the miracles, the knowledge of Jesus, the sinlessness of Jesus, the resurrection of Jesus. The difficulty, as Macquarrie sees it, is that these issues have often been understood in such a fashion that they appear to compromise Jesus' full humanity, and so he seeks an understanding of them that will not fatally compromise that humanity.

The Something More

First, the virginal conception. The standard issues are raised, that Paul and Mark know nothing of it, and that the account of it in Matthew is somewhat different from the account in Luke. Eschewing a purely biological approach, Macquarrie fixes on a theological interpretation as primary: "(Matthew) and (Luke) were saying that the life that had been implanted in Mary had come from God. Jesus Christ is not simply the product of natural evolution nor even of human procreation --- there is something 'more' in Jesus..."[16] For the Gospel of St. John that something more is that

Jesus comes from God, and Macquarrie points to the words from the Prologue found in John 1:12-13: "But to all who received him, he gave power to become children of God; who were born, not of blood nor of the will of the flesh nor of the will of man, but of God." While the latter part of the verse sounds as though it might be referring to a virginal conception/birth, in fact the words are applied to those who actually received him, to his followers. Macquarrie summarizes this point as follows:

> Here the theological interpretation of the virgin birth is extended to those who have believed in Jesus. The individual Jesus is surrounded by a community which he has called into being, and together they constitute a new humanity, a new creation deriving from a new Adam, Jesus Christ, who realizes the intention of God where the old Adam had failed.[17]

If the virgin birth is interpreted in this fashion, then for Macquarrie it does not infringe the full humanity of Christ. The value of the position is the ontological link that is clearly established between Jesus and the Church, christology and ecclesiology, a traditional affirmation of the broad Catholic tradition, and something of a *leitmotif* in Macquarrie's theology. Nonetheless, the question of the historicity of the virginal conception of Jesus, that is the biological sense, remains an issue. In his book on Mary he adumbrates the theological interpretation given here, but in his *Jesus Christ in Modern Thought* he appears not to accept the historicity of the virgin birth.[18] When asked about this in the taped interview of July 1998, Macquarrie said that he remained agnostic about this issue. "Agnostic" is a very precise word here. Macquarrie's use of it reveals not only his difficulties with the doctrine of the virginal conception, but also his methodological caution. Where the evidence is found wanting, he refuses to make a definitive judgment. To some extent, Macquarrie's position finds an echo in some remarks by the Catholic biblical scholar, Raymond E. Brown:

> My judgment, in conclusion, is that the totality of the *scientifically controllable* evidence leaves an unresolved problem -- a conclusion that should not disappoint since I used the word 'problem' in my title ("the Problem of the Virginal Conception of Jesus") -- and that is why I want to induce an honest, ecumenical discussion of it. Part of the difficulty is that past discussions have often been conducted by people who were interpreting

ambiguous evidence to favor positions already taken. I would urge, however, that this discussion be pursued in an atmosphere of pastoral responsibility... It must be with an awareness of what the virginal conception has meant to Christianity that we theologians and church historians and exegetes begin our ecumenical discussion of it. Discuss it we must, for Christianity can never seek refuge in anything except the truth, painful as it may be. But as we discuss Mary's virginity, we must assure all those ordinary people in our churches, the 'little people' who happen to be God's people, that in our quest we 'experts' have not forgotten that we too must obey the biblical injunction (Luke 1:48) that all generations, even this 'nosey' generation, shall call her blessed.[19]

Macquarrie could readily identify with Brown's position, but, while Brown as a Catholic accepts the doctrine because it is taught by the church, Macquarrie feels unable to do that. He remains in that sense "agnostic." This may be the philosophical Macquarrie having the upper hand here. Other Anglican theologians, equally recognizing the challenges posed by the virginal conception, nonetheless show themselves more open to receive it. Take, for example, Bishop N. T. Wright:

No one can prove, historically, that Mary was a virgin when Jesus was conceived. No one can prove, historically, that she wasn't. Science studies the repeatable; history bumps its nose against the unrepeatable. If the first two chapters of Matthew and the first two of Luke had never existed, I do not suppose that my own Christian faith, or that of the church to which I belong, would have been different. But since they do, and since for quite other reasons I have come to believe that the God of Israel, the world's creator, was personally and fully revealed in and as Jesus of Nazareth, I hold open my historical judgment and say: If that is what God deemed appropriate, who am I to object?[20]

The Miracles of Jesus

Second, the miracles of Jesus. If all the miracles attributed to Jesus in the gospel narratives are accepted at face value historically, does this not mean that we have another version of docetism? Is this not an image of Christ as a supernatural being sweeping across the stage of history, and does this not infringe his true humanity, and in fact render him incredible to modern people? Macquarrie has no difficulty acknowledging that Jesus healed people, though this ought not to be understood as a demonstration of divinity, nor as an unqualified intrusion of divine power. He concludes: "The relations of body and mind are still not understood, though they are obviously relations of a most intimate kind. Perhaps such healings will be much better understood in the future, but neither then nor now does it seem necessary to suppose that the agent or instrument of such healings possesses magical or supernatural powers, though the gift which he or she exercises comes ultimately from God."[21] Some will read Macquarrie here to be denying divine agency in miracle. However, the underlying issue is what model of divine agency is being presupposed. What is the relation between God and creation? Now Macquarrie's understanding of the relation is dialectical, or panentheistic, as we have seen in the last chapter, so that God is never absent from his creation, but may be understood as present with varying degrees of intensity, in given persons or places. Healings emerge when the intensity of the divine presence manifests itself in a particular context, in particular circumstances. What Macquarrie wishes to avoid is an invasive sense of divine presence, and so of divine agency. If healing happens, then that is God's gift, whoever the instrument of that healing. He judges that "there are good reasons for doubting whether any nature miracles were ever performed by Jesus." His doubt is not merely symptomatic of the skeptical temper of the modern age, "but because Jesus himself rejected such actions and because they are incompatible with his true humanity." The refusal of Jesus in the temptation narratives (Matt. 4:5-7, Luke 4:9-12) to impress the people through the performance of spectacular deeds is noted, as well as the docetist implications of the nature miracles. He offers two examples of a non-docetic interpretation of the nature miracles, Jesus walking on the Sea of Galilee, and the feeding of the multitude (especially in John 6). Walking on water, far from being a description of his supernatural divine power is rather "a perfect description of the human condition." For Macquarrie the term conjures up all the insecurities and invulnerabilities of this life, and demonstrates Jesus' full humanity with its insecurity and vulnerability. The stories of feeding the multitudes are essentially to be understood as eucharistic allegories.

The Knowledge and Sinlessness of Jesus

The same mode of interpretation is followed through with regard to the knowledge of Jesus. He would not align himself with Bultmann and others who judge the predictions of Jesus' passion to be *vaticinia ex eventu* --- "that is perhaps going too far."[22] Jesus, with ordinary human knowledge, would have known the risks he was taking, and what the possible/probable outcome could have been. But a detailed knowledge of the future and of his final *denouement* would not have been his.

What about Jesus' sinlessness? The Letter to the Hebrews affirms the sinlessness of Jesus in these words: "We have not a high priest who is unable to sympathize with our weaknesses, but one who in every respect has been tempted as we are, yet without sin" (Heb. 4:15). This does not detract one iota from Jesus' humanity for Macquarrie because "sin is not part of human nature but a violation of human nature."

In all of this Macquarrie is aware of the response that suggests that this is to reduce Jesus to the merely human. He dislikes the term "merely human" because humanity has a marvelous destiny that is not captured in that description. Human beings are made in God's own image and likeness, and so to speak of "merely human" is insufficiently appreciative of this dimension. Furthermore, to claim that Jesus is fully human is not necessarily to affirm that he is *only* human. "His humanity is not abolished by the presence of God in him but is transfigured into a true humanity. For the first time we are shown what the potentiality of humanity really is."

The Resurrection of Jesus

There has been no major development in Macquarrie's thinking on the resurrection of Christ since his *Principles of Christian Theology*. Even his *Jesus*

Christ in Modern Thought does not carry a very extensive treatment of the resurrection.

For the writers of the New Testament the resurrection is always the work of God, the work of the Father, who raised up Christ from the dead. The resurrection thus tells us something about God, that his working never comes to a dead end, for he can always open up "a new possibility."[23] The resurrection reveals God, showing that his creative act is not limited, not even by the apparent *impasse* of death.

For Macquarrie, resurrection is not so much a clearly defined concept as a symbol or image "pointing to something which lies at the very limits of our understanding."[24] There are two basic ways of trying to understand and evaluate belief in the resurrection of Jesus: to begin with the reports of the New Testament, or to begin from our present human experience.

The biblical accounts of the resurrection of Jesus are of two kinds, the empty tomb stories and the stories of Jesus' appearances to his followers. Although there are certain discrepancies in the gospel accounts of the discovery of the empty tomb, they all agree that certain women went to the tomb of Jesus to anoint his body, but found the tomb empty. Similarly, there is disagreement among the witnesses about the details of Jesus' post-resurrection appearances, but they are unanimous in insisting that some of Jesus' followers, both as individuals and in groups, experienced visions of Jesus which they understood to mean he was alive.

With respect to the veracity of the empty tomb stories, Macquarrie insists that Jesus' disciples were not in any way expecting his resurrection, so that there is little substance in the explanation "either that they had contrived the empty tomb or that they jumped to the conclusion that Jesus must have risen from the dead because his tomb was found empty."[25] He cites with approval the judgment of his Oxford colleague and authority on Second Temple Judaism, Geza Vermes: "When every argument has been considered and weighed, the only conclusion acceptable to the historian must be that the opinions of the orthodox, the liberal sympathizer and the critical agnostic alike --- and even perhaps of the disciples themselves --- are simply interpretations of one disconcerting fact: namely, that the women who set out to pay their last respects to Jesus found, to their consternation, not a body, but an empty tomb." However, while the empty tomb tradition must be taken seriously, "there is no straightforward route from the empirical fact of an empty tomb to the raising of the dead by God."[26]

Just as the empty tomb stories are susceptible of various natural interpretations (e.g., secret removal of the body, going to the wrong tomb), so the reports of the appearances may be thought of in terms of psychological explanations (e.g., individual or mass hallucinations). The major negative factor in this type of naturalistic or psychological explanation --- as in the case of the empty tomb tradition --- is the fact, upon which there is general scholarly agreement, that the disciples of Jesus were not expecting his resurrection, and so there was no motive force present as the ground for hallucination in the post-resurrection appearances. There is one other point that militates against a hallucination theory, and that is the existence of the Church. Macquarrie observes that "It is hard to believe that a community founded on hallucination could have survived for long, let alone have shown the unparalleled creative power of the Christian people of God."[27]

The historical fact of the Church has to be taken into account in any serious discussion of the resurrection. No one disputes that the Christian community is and was an historical fact capable of verification. Yet, the fact that there is a Church at all is dependent upon the transforming event or experience of the resurrection of Jesus. Macquarrie asserts the continuity between the earliest Christians' experience and contemporary Christian experience, drawing upon the principle of analogy as it has been developed by Ernst Troeltsch: "The principle states that the report of an event will be more or less probable to the extent that we can point to analogous events in present experience."[28] In other words, it is only on the analogy of our own experience that historical understanding is possible at all. Gerald O'Collins implicitly accuses Macquarrie of affirming "a democracy of experience vis-à-vis the risen Christ."[29] However, O'Collins has not come to terms with the necessary epistemological base for affirming any historical judgment, that is, some fundamental continuity in our contemporary experience with the recorded experience of the past. There is no denial by Macquarrie of the recognition of the ontological novelty of the resurrection and, therefore, of the disciples' experience of this in the Scriptures. But the Christ experienced in Christian liturgy and witness today cannot be a different Christ. As Macquarrie puts it, "The report of a resurrection would be very difficult to accept unless we could point to some present experience."[30]

Noting the hazards of speculation about the resurrection, Macquarrie thinks that in 1 Cor. 15 St. Paul provides "a substantial piece of theological reflection" on the resurrection. The resurrection is not the reanimation of a corpse, but has to do with a "spiritual body" (1 Cor. 15:44). Macquarrie interprets this as meaning "a new mode of existence in which the person is incorporated into the life of God." For Paul, this new mode of existence is every man's destiny, though Jesus Christ is the first to attain it. Jesus in the resurrection remains alive, and not just in and with his community, but with God, "no longer bounded with the particularities of a human existence in space and time."[31] Jesus has fulfilled the potentialities of human existence and indeed raised that existence to a new level, and he has revealed its potentiality for an eternal life in God; he has "abolished death and brought life and immortality to light" (2 Tim. 1:10).

What is meant by this fulfillment of the potentialities of human existence? It means essentially that Christ has brought to light a true humanity, showing what human beings have it in them to become. In Jesus we see the qualities that are essential to a true humanity, such qualities as love, freedom, integrity, creativity, moral sensitivity, and resurrection, because resurrection has as "an important part of its meaning, precisely the emergence of a new level of human and personal existence."[32] This new level of human and personal existence will elude our understanding so long as "we are seeing it only from below." If Jesus is the fulfillment of the potentialities of human existence, the resurrection is necessarily part of this fulfillment, because in the resurrection "he now lives as one sharing in the eternal life of God."[33]

Adoptionism

In stressing, or in attempting to give due weight to the humanity of Jesus, there often lurks in the background the suspicion that one might be an adoptionist in respect of his divinity. The issued is raised for Macquarrie by Georgina Morley: "Macquarrie accepts adoptionism as a model of Christology which must be retained. However, since this is only 'half the story,' and since adoptionism must be completed in incarnationism, it is important to ensure that this is indeed the case in his own Christology. Certainly, in places his terminology is unfortunate." She goes on to ask quite pointedly, "Does Macquarrie verge too close to adoptionism in his commitment to rid Christology of its docetic tendencies?"[34] Morley's question and her points are well taken. "Adoptionism" as a christological term does not fit well in the grammar of christological orthodoxy, and so Macquarrie's use of it demands some closer examination. Adoptionism is something of a slippery term, but Macquarrie provides a broad definition of it: "... the type of christological theory which, it is usually believed, so emphasizes the humanity of Christ that it rules out any special ontological or metaphysical relation between him and the Father."[35] He notes further that the term gets used rather loosely today to describe those theologians who may criticize some or other elements of the Christology consequent upon the Council of Chalcedon (451) that have so shaped the Christian tradition.

A key, if not the key issue in adoptionism is the pre-existence of Jesus Christ. Did Jesus Christ *qua* Jesus Christ pre-exist his incarnation in the womb of Mary? Macquarrie had articulated his position as early as 1966 in an article entitled "The Pre-Existence of Jesus Christ." In that article he had said: "The idea of pre-existence, like so many other ideas in the New Testament, does have a value that lies obscured beneath its mythological associations, and it would be wrong to reject pre-existence in favour of a thorough-going adoptionism. Rather, we ought to look more closely at the idea of pre-existence, and see whether we can restate its essential meaning in a language that would be intelligible to our time."[36] If pre-existence in the mind and purpose of God may be equated with real pre-existence, then Macquarrie has no particular difficulty with it. If the Logos is co-eternal with the Father, and if the Logos became flesh in our Lady's womb as Jesus of Nazareth, then some intelligibility can be made out of pre-existence. However, this seems different from a personal pre-existence, in some way an "embodied" pre-existence of Jesus Christ as such. In *Jesus Christ in Modern Thought* this is how he expresses himself: "... I have consistently argued that if there is some *nisus* or goal-seeking striving in the evolutionary process, it is better understood in immanental terms than as imposed from outside by a transcendent 'watchmaker'. But I am saying that --- however one may interpret the matter --- this earth, the human race, yes, Jesus Christ himself were already latent, already predestined, in the primaeval swirling cloud of particles."[37]

There remains a fear that the language and expression of Macquarrie about pre-existence somehow detracts from the tradition of christological orthodoxy. Perhaps this fear is founded on a failure to recognize that all language about Christ and God limps, and no language is perfect. However, one may go further and ask about the function and role of the language of pre-existence. Gerald O'Collins, S.J. has suggested a possible way forward here. "Pre-existence means... that Christ personally belongs to an order of being other than the created, temporal one. His personal, divine existence transcends temporal (and spatial) categories; it might be better expressed as trans-existence, meta-existence, or, quite simply, eternal existence." Furthermore, O'Collins takes Macquarrie to task in suggesting that "he fails to see that personal pre-existence does not mean that Jesus eternally pre-existed *qua Jesus*. His humanity first came into existence as such around 5 BC. The human consciousness of Jesus did not pre-exist 'in heaven.'"[38] Essentially the same criticism is made of Macquarrie by the New Testament scholar, Simon Gathercole. He judges against Macquarrie's position that preexistence for Christ means just preexistence in the mind or plan of God, "that from the beginning Christ the incarnate Word was there in the counsels of God."[39] For Gathercole, this language at least, if not Macquarrie's entire meaning, is "far too attenuated."[40]

Macquarrie writes: "Incarnationism teaches the priority of God, and that the event of Jesus Christ is not just an arbitrary or natural evolution; adoptionism guards against a docetic distortion of Christ by insisting on his humanity and on the need for human obedience and co-operation in fulfilling the potentialities of God's creation."[41] Macquarrie believes that three criteria may be posited for distinguishing an incarnational christology from various kinds of reductionist christologies: the initiative comes from God; God is deeply and intimately involved in creation; the center of this initiative and involvement is Jesus Christ. If these three criteria may be shown to be present in a given christology then it may not be judged adoptionist, or reductionist.

The three criteria fit his understanding of the incarnation: "… the unitary person, leading edge, or *hypostasis* of Jesus was not the *hypostasis* of the divine Logos displacing the human *hypostasis* and using the body of Jesus as a mere instrument, nor was it a composite *hypostasis* constituting Jesus a new species distinct from *homo sapiens*, but was the human *hypostasis* transfigured by a constant immersion in the divine Spirit." Jesus Christ, constantly immersed in the divine Spirit, is different from the rest of humanity in degree rather than in kind.

Christological Critics: Hefling, Molnar, McCready, Purdy

This has led some critics of Macquarrie's christology, in particular Charles Hefling, Paul Molnar and Douglas McCready, to accuse him of heterodoxy. Hefling charges Macquarrie with being doctrinally imprecise, insisting that he does not go far enough in this talk of "degree" rather than "kind."[42] Hefling is right --- there is a certain imprecision here, but it seems unavoidable given Macquarrie's theological methodology.

Molnar, in my judgment, strays very far from any accurate understanding of Macquarrie's christology in the context of his entire *oeuvre*.[43] Molnar accuses Macquarrie of Adoptionism, Pelagianism, soteriological pluralism, and at least implicitly, of pantheism, believing that "panentheism always collapses back into pantheism."[44] This is certainly a real danger, arguably an ever present challenge in any persuasive approach to God that treats seriously and consistently of God's immanence in creation, but it is far from clear that Macquarrie has succumbed. Molnar's extreme dissatisfaction with Macquarrie's christology seems to flow from a significantly different theological horizon and methodology, that of Karl Barth and Thomas F. Torrance, perhaps Molnar's two ideal theologians. He seems to disallow even in principle that, given a quite different starting-point and methodology, it may still be possible to discern, albeit in quite different terminology and concepts, a very real degree of christological coincidence.

Douglas McCready judges that, while Macquarrie, "a fascinating theologian," "labors mightily to be both modern and orthodox," "in the end he is unsuccessful at holding the two together."[45] He acknowledges that Macquarrie rejects modern adoptionist tendencies. However, in attempting to strip away what he sees as mythological forms of expression concerning the pre-existence of Christ, Macquarrie's existentialist presuppositions prevent him from developing a fully orthodox alternative. He appreciates Macquarrie's attempt to retrieve an incarnational christology through: first, acknowledging that the christological initiative comes from God and not from humankind; second, showing that God is deeply involved in creation; and third, recognizing that the focus of God's initiative and involvement is Jesus Christ. For McCready, Macquarrie is much clearer in articulating the first two than the third. For McCready, Macquarrie does not struggle enough with the so-called mythological language of pre-existence in the New Testament, and ultimately opts for an "indwelling Christology" that he finds does not match what the New Testament authors are up to. Thus for McCready Macquarrie is one of those theologians "whose spirituality exceeds what his theology permits."[46]

The posthumous publication of Vernon L. Purdy's *The Christology of John Macquarrie* is without doubt the most thorough study of Macquarrie's christology to date.[47] Originally a dissertation directed by Colin Brown of Fuller Theological Seminary, Purdy is always very even-handed in his analysis and critique. Yet he too reaches a somewhat negative conclusion about Macquarrie's christology: "In the final analysis, Macquarrie's dialectical theism is very suggestive in its possibilities but unfortunately the potential of his project is aborted when it comes to Christology. A contemporary incarnational Christology could be based on Macquarrie's dialectical theism and his understanding of human persons as beings open to transcendence. This is probably his greatest contribution to contemporary Christological reflection rather than his own constructive proposals that are essentially adoptionistic without the balancing incarnational emphasis that he admits is needed."[48]

If Macquarrie's christology is mapped out in relation to his treatment of other Christian doctrines, and especially to his liturgical and sacramental positions, Molnar's accusation seems most incredible, but nowhere does he take account of these factors. Neither does McCready nor Purdy. Even if it were shown, and I remain unconvinced that it has been, that Macquarrie's christological views are not consonant with the thrust of the New Testament texts, ecclesiological-liturgical-sacramental considerations must be taken into account in assessing his christology. Otherwise, a verbal consonance with past formulations --- New Testament and conciliar --- would seem to establish christological orthodoxy, and it is doubtful if any of Macquarrie's critics would be happy with that position. Or, it may be that a latent but real principle of *sola scriptura* or *sola fides* is at work here, a principle that radically disallows the legitimacy of philosophical and rational analysis of christological tenets.

Macquarrie points out that a difference of degree "may be so great that for all practical purposes it counts as a difference of kind."[49] This is most important. In *Jesus Christ in Modern Thought*, this is how he understands incarnation: "... it is the progressive presencing and self-manifestation of the Logos in the physical and historical world. For the Christian, this process reaches its climax in Jesus Christ, but the Christ-event is not isolated from the whole series of events. That is why we can say that the difference between Christ and other agents of the Logos is one of degree, not of kind."[50] This is undoubtedly ambiguous language, moving in the direction of suggesting that Jesus simply has "more" of what we lave have, so to speak. That is not Macquarrie's position. He says: "A difference of degree can be quite decisive, and may be so great as to be virtually a difference in kind."[51] There is no sense of christological minimalism here. Ultimately, Macquarrie is searching for a christological coherence that will speak for our contemporaries. He thinks that too much christological speculation and expression has been too artificial and removed from the ordinary horizon of Christian understanding, and this is the primary reason for his christological perspective. He wants it to "speak" through an elimination of a docetic register of discourse. In the words of Georgina Morley, "Macquarrie's christological construction, whilst arguably balanced towards Christ's humanity, is an explicit attempt to rebalance christological tendencies by a re-emphasis of an under-valued aspect."[52]

Christ and Other Faiths

If the difference between Christ and other agents of the Logos is one of degree and not of kind, then we are led into this difficult and complex issue of understanding the relationship between him and other savior figures of the world's religions. A central theme in panentheistic theology, according to one of its most suasive contemporary exponents Michael Brierley, is a degree christology. "According to Brierley, to hold a panentheistic model of God is to regard Christ as distinctive by *degree* from other persons, rather than by kind... (If) God is in the cosmos and the cosmos is in God, then consistency demands that God's embodiment in Christ be continuous with that cosmic activity."[53] That cosmic activity surely has to do in some way, shape or form with other religions.

Since his days in graduate school, Macquarrie has shown an openness towards and an interest in other religious faiths. His way, as with others who work in this field, is the way of dialogue, "the rational, civilized way of resolving conflict, as opposed to the methods of violence and coercion." For dialogue to be successful, there must be a willingness to listen and to learn as well as to teach, and he has shown himself in his writing willing to enter fully into dialogue.[54]

In an essay responding to Paul Knitter, a Catholic theologian whose work is marked by a strong interest in this matter of the uniqueness of Jesus Christ, Macquarrie outlines his understanding of that uniqueness. The gist of it is given in his own words:

> I have urged the case for a combination of 'commitment' and 'openness' on the part of the religious believer, that is to say, a full commitment to one's own faith and to its mediator (in my own case, this would be to Christianity and Jesus Christ), yet at the same time an 'openness' towards other faiths and other mediators, in the sense of acknowledging that God has made himself known and has made salvation available through these other channels also.[55]

Starting with the New Testament, one can see that there are various christologies, sometimes in tension with one another, even within the same book. For example in the Acts of the Apostles 4:12 St. Peter preaches before the Jewish Sanhedrin that "There is no salvation through anyone else, nor is there any other name under heaven given to the human race by which we are to be saved." When we come to Acts 17 and St. Paul's speech to the Athenians, St. Paul appears to presuppose some common ground between Greek religiosity and himself. Turning to St. John's Gospel, the affirmation is found that "No one comes to the Father except through (Jesus)" (14:6), but at the same time the Logos "was the light of the human race," and the implication seems to be that this light somehow enlightens everyone (1:4). Finally, in the Letter to the Hebrews a unique priestly role is given to Jesus Christ, but within "a great cloud of witnesses" including Abel, Enoch and Noah, as well as Abraham and Moses (Heb. 11). In summary, there appear to be both exclusive and inclusive christologies in the New Testament, which perdure through the patristic period, and perhaps the inclusivist view "was never suppressed." Macquarrie comments on the basis of such texts and references that "from creation onward, God (or the Logos, if one prefers) has been incarnating itself in the world in many ways and in many degrees," and he cites (albeit without the precise reference) Teilhard de Chardin, "The prodigious expanses of time which preceded the first Christmas were not empty of Christ."[56] The incarnation is "the culminating point of what God has been doing in all history."[57] Macquarrie finds this approach exemplified in St. Athanasius: "The philosophers of the Greeks say the world is a great body; and rightly they say so, for we perceive it and its parts affecting our senses. If then the Word of God is in the world, which is a body, and he has passed into all and into every part of it, what is wonderful or what is unfitting in our saying that he came in a man?"[58]

It is of course one thing to say that God is immanent in the world, and something else entirely to say that he is equally immanent in everything. The latter would be a crude form of pantheism. The former provides Macquarrie with a way of maintaining the climactic expression of the divine immanence in the incarnation of Jesus Christ, "in whom God was signally present," but without denying other expressions of the divine immanence, or degrees of incarnation in other savior figures. If in fact the point of religion is to achieve union between the divine and the human, something like "incarnation" seems required: "... incarnation would seem to instantiate such a union in the most intimate way conceivable."[59] Thus, if incarnation is not associated exclusively and uniquely with Jesus Christ, it may not be an insuperable barrier to dialogue among the religions.

Given this approach dialogue among the religions becomes a moral imperative. This does not make mission or proclamation redundant for Macquarrie. He maintains that "There probably is still a place for the old-fashioned type of missionary proclamation, especially in the secularized nations of Europe and North America." However, dialogue does not go far enough for him. Using the example of the late Mother Teresa of Calcutta he suggests that service of others, while not taking the place of dialogue, speaks a more profound missionary message.

Christ is definitive for the Christian not only of the nature of God, but also of the nature of the human person. There cannot be "a *full* revelation of God, for the infinite cannot be fully comprehended in the finite" and this same acknowledgment of finitude "prevents us from embracing an unlimited pluralism."[60] It would be exceedingly difficult if not impossible for a person to become genuinely conversant with and fluent in other faiths, even one other faith. From the vantage point of the ordinary human being, the choice would seem to be between deepening one's own faith or becoming an easy-going relativist, or perhaps becoming indifferent. To maintain that Christianity is definitive for oneself, or for Christians, is a way of saying "that within my limited faith and experience, Jesus Christ is *sufficient*. Through him I think I have been brought into relation to God." A Christian, therefore, is committed to Jesus Christ, but at the same time is open to the truths to be found in other faiths.

Knowing Jesus Christ

Central to any and all discussion of christology is what constitutes "knowing Jesus Christ." Or, what constitutes knowledge? There are different ways of knowing, according to Macquarrie. If we turn to the chapter entitled "Cognition" in his *In Search of Humanity*, the chapter that the Glasgow physician Gordon Stewart (mentioned earlier) found so attractive, then we find the lineaments of Macquarrie's epistemology. In this chapter he discusses the theories of Karl Popper and Michael Polanyi to break open the widespread, common sense empiricism which characterizes so much of the western world. He sees Popper and Polanyi as "like a pincer movement threatening the core of conventional empiricism," and he proceeds to list seven principles that inform his work, the principles already noted in the chapter "In Search of Humanity."[61]

Each of these principles or statements could be defended, as Macquarrie in fact does, but the backdrop to them all is the permeative position of those who would claim that only objective empirical knowledge counts as real knowledge. This is hardly adequate when it comes to knowing art, another person, a spouse, or God. Nor does it get us very far in knowing Jesus Christ. Statements 5 and 6 are further articulated christologically in Macquarrie's *Christology Revisited*. Accumulating historical knowledge/data about Jesus is clearly legitimate, but such information would lack any sense of encounter, confrontation, engagement with him as anything more than a figure of the past. Macquarrie disallows too sharp a distinction between historical knowledge, the testimony of the past, and knowledge that comes through present experience, something already noted in his treatment of the resurrection of Jesus. Christians do not come to knowledge of Christ simply from the reading of the Scriptures, as though they were reading of some great historical figure. Such a view would entirely fail to realize the connection between Christ and the Church. "The church is the Body of Christ, continuing his presence on earth. To quote Michael Ramsey, 'The fact of Christ includes the fact of the Church.'"[62] This fact yields a knowledge of Christ that is "spiritually discerned", but is in no fashion arbitrary. It is like "seeing in depth," seeing the inward constitutive meaning of things. For that reason, he is also cautionary about a critical reading of the gospels: "If we read the Gospels primarily in a critical way, we are not likely to be encountered by Christ in them." Such an excessively critical reading of the Gospels almost presupposes a model of knowledge that Macquarrie is trying to expand, the model of neutral, systematic, objective knowledge.

There is knowledge born of love. "Love could be described as a way of knowing... All kinds of love have a cognitive component."[63] Using an example from ordinary human experience, he notes that one who "loves" his subject will notice and attend to things that someone who is indifferent might miss. The insight becomes enlarged when speaking of Christ. Here Macquarrie is approximating what can only be called the cognitive dimension of mysticism. In point of fact, he describes mystical knowing: "Perhaps the highest reach of faith is found in mysticism, which I take to be a kind of total immersion in the divine and therefore perhaps the highest level of knowledge possible for a human being on earth."[64]

The Christ known in the knowledge of love, by that special "spiritual discernment" that is consequent upon love, the Christ of mysticism is also the "metaphysical Christ." Following Dietrich Bonhoeffer's *Christ at the Center*, Macquarrie finds three focal points about this Christ: Christ as the center of human existence, as the center of history, as the mediator between God and nature. In other words, if Christ is at the center, at the center of everything, then what is outside the circumference is quite literally *nothing*. The metaphysical Christ is the all pervasive

Christ, in whom we live and move and have our being, so that 'reality' is Jesus Christ."[65]

Conclusion

Bishop N. T. Wright says of the pursuit of the historical Jesus:

I have argued that the historical quest for Jesus is necessary for the health of the church. I grieve that in the church both in England and America there seem to be so few -- among a church that is otherwise so well-educated in so many spheres, with more educational resources and helps than ever before -- who are prepared to give the time and attention to these questions that they deserve. I long for the day when seminarians will again take delight in the detailed and fascinated study of the first century. If that century was not the moment when history reached its great climax, the church is simply wasting its time.[66]

Macquarrie was not a New Testament scholar, but he certainly would have been in complete agreement with Bishop Wright in this regard. Systematic christology must be grounded in solid historical research.

In an interesting but tantalizingly brief comparison of the christologies of Macquarrie and Hans Urs Von Balthasar, Francesca Murphy seems to conclude that Balthasar's christology "from above" is realist, stemming from a realist metaphysic, while Macquarrie's christology from below is idealist, flowing from an idealist metaphysic.[67] Perhaps this in a sense gets us to the heart of the matter. Realism may be defined as a philosophical position affirming that reality exists independently of the human knowing subject, and idealism as a philosophical tradition originating with Plato which understands the mind, ideas, or spirit as fundamental and basic to reality. One must affirm that reality exists outside the knower, as it were. That seems to be plain common sense. At the same time, there can be no awareness of reality without the knowing subject. One may not be had without the other. If Macquarrie evinces a contemporary Platonic rendering of reality in terms of degrees of being, of christology in terms of degrees of divine immanence, and if that rendering engages many people in a fashion that satisfies the curiosity of the theological mind, and in a way that satisfies the linguistic and regulative conventions of Christian orthodoxy, may one ask for more? In terms used earlier, if Macquarrie's theological metaphysics yields a *sanitas* both theologically from within the Christian tradition, and metaphysically, then it stands.

---

[1] N. T. Wright, *The Challenge of Jesus* (Downers Grove, IL: InterVarsity Press, 1999), 18.

[2] John Macquarrie, *Christology Revisited* (London: SCM Press, 1998).

[3] Wickham's review of *Christology Revisited* is aptly entitled "Hold That Paradox," *Church Times*, November 7 (1998), 20.

[4] John Macquarrie, *Principles of Christian Theology*, rev. ed., (London: SCM Press, 1977), 12.

[5] Ibid., 181.

[6] In his *Mary for All Christians* (London: Collins, 1990), 120.

[7] John Macquarrie, *Christology Revisited*, 17.

[8] Ibid., 18. Macquarrie acknowledges that he has been described as an "adoptionist," though he believes it an unjust description. He does not tell us who his critics are, but the charge was leveled by Charles C. Hefling of Boston College in his article, "Reviving Adamic Adoptionism: The Example of John Macquarrie," *Theological Studies* 52 (1991), 476-494. In principle, the same criticism is made of Macquarrie by Thomas G. Weinandy, OFMCap, *Does God Suffer?* (Notre Dame, IN: University of Notre Dame Press, 2000), 199.

[9] Raymond E. Brown, S.S., *Reading the Gospels with the Church* (Cincinnati: St. Anthony Messenger Press, 1996), 18.

[10] John Macquarrie, *The Scope of Demythologizing* (London: SCM Press, 1960), 93.

[11] John Macquarrie, *Jesus Christ in Modern Thought* (Harrisburg, PA: Trinity Press International, 1990), 351. The book by Sanders is *Jesus and Judaism* (London: SCM Press, 1985), cited by Macquarrie, op. cit., 53-54.

[12] John Macquarrie, *Studies in Christian Existentialism* (Montreal: McGill University Press, 1965), 48.

[13] John Macquarrie, *Christology Revisited*, 32.

[14] John McIntyre, Review of John Macquarrie, *Christology Revisited* in *The Expository Times* 111 (1999), 265. There is an excellent and full critical account of Macquarrie's christology in McIntyre's *The Shape of Christology*, 2nd ed. (Edinburgh: T. & T. Clark, 1996), 259-282.

[15] John McIntyre, "The Christology of Donald Baillie in Perspective," in David Fergusson, ed., *Christ,*

Church and Society (Edinburgh: T. & T. Clark, 1993), 113.

[16] John Macquarrie, *Christology Revisited*, 34.

[17] Ibid., 35.

[18] John Macquarrie, *Jesus Christ in Modern Thought*, 393-394

[19] Raymond E. Brown, SS, *The Virginal Conception and Bodily Resurrection of Jesus* (New York-Paramus-Toronto: Paulist Press, 1973), 66-68. For a fuller, more contextual treatment see his *The Birth of the Messiah* (New York: Doubleday, 1977), 517-534.

[20] N. T. Wright, "God's Way of Acting," *The Christian Century* December 16 (1998), 1215-1217.

[21] John Macquarrie, *Christology Revisited*, 37.

[22] Ibid., 40.

[23] John Macquarrie, *Principles of Christian Theology*, 289.

[24] John Macquarrie, *Christian Hope* (New York: The Seabury Press, 1979), 74.

[25] Ibid., 72; see also *Principles of Christian Theology*, 288.

[26] Ibid.

[27] John Macquarrie, *The Faith of the People of God* (London: SCM Press, 1972), 63.

[28] John Macquarrie, *Christian Hope*, 76.

[29] Gerald O'Collins, SJ, *Jesus Risen* (London: Darton, Longman and Todd, 1987), 27.

[30] John Macquarrie, *Christian Hope*, 76.

[31] John Macquarrie, *The Humility of God* (London: SCM Press, 1978), 79.

[32] John Macquarrie, *Principles of Christian Theology*, 305.

[33] John Macquarrie, *Christian Hope*, 80-81.

[34] Georgina Morley, *John Macquarrie's Natural Theology: The Grace of Being* (Burlington, VT and Aldershot, UK: Ashgate Publishing, 2003), 154.

[35] John Macquarrie, *Christology Revisited*, 62.

[36] *The Expository Times* 77 (1966), 199-200. There is an excellent discussion of Macquarrie's use of the findings of New Testament scholarship on the pre-existence of Christ in Pauline and Johannine texts in Niall Coll, *Some Anglican Interpretations of Christ's pre-Existence: A Study of L. S. Thornton, E. L. Mascall, J. A. T. Robinson and J. Macquarrie* (Rome: Gregorian University Press, 1995), 190-208. A revised version has been published as *Christ in Eternity and Time: Modern Anglican Perspectives*

(Dublin: Four Courts Press, 2001).

[37] John Macquarrie, *Jesus Christ in Modern Thought*, 391-392.

[38] Gerald O'Collins, SJ, *Christology* (Oxford and New York: Oxford University Press, 1995), 238.

[39] John Macquarrie, *Christology Revisited*, 114.

[40] Simon J. Gathercole, *The Pre-Existent Son* (Grand Rapids: Eerdmans, 2006), 287.

[41] John Macquarrie, "The Pre-existence of Jesus Christ," *The Expository Times* 77 (1966), 199-202, 202.

[42] Charles Hefling, "Reviving Adamic Adoptionism: The Example of John Macquarrie," *Theological Studies* 52 (1991), 489. Macquarrie is defended against this charge by Marion Lars Hendrickson, *Behold the Man! An Anthropological Comparison of the Christologies of John Macquarrie and of Wolfhart Pannenberg* (Lanham-New York-Oxford: University Press of America, 1998), 31-32, but the defense is more on the grounds of the limitations of language than of christology as such. Another defense of Macquarrie comes from Stephen W. Need, "Macquarrie, John," in J. Leslie Houlden, ed., *Jesus in History, Thought and Culture* (Santa Barbara, CA and Oxford, UK: ABC-CLIO, 2003), 586.

[43] Paul D. Molnar, *Incarnation and Resurrection, Toward a Contemporary Understanding* (Grand Rapids: Eerdmans, 2007), especially 157-171.

[44] Ibid., 363.

[45] Douglas McCready, *He Came Down From Heaven* (Downers Grove, IL: InterVarsity Press, 2005), 267.

[46] Ibid.

[47] Vernon L. Purdy, *The Christology of John Macquarrie* (New York: Peter Lang, 2009).

[48] Ibid., 250.

[49] John Macquarrie, *Christology Revisited*, 59.

[50] John Macquarrie, *Jesus Christ in Modern Thought*, 392.

[51] Ibid., 361.

[52] Georgina Morley, op. cit., 159.

[53] Cited in Gloria L. Schaab, *The Creative Suffering of the Triune God* (New York and Oxford: Oxford University Press, 2007), 94. See especially Michael Brierley's comprehensive essay, "Naming a Quiet Revolution: The Panentheistic Turn in Modern Theology," in Philip Clayton and Arthur Peacocke, ed., *In Whom We Live and Move and Have Our Being: Panentheistic Reflections on God's Presence in a Scientific World* (Grand Rapids: Eerdmans, 2004), 1-15.

[54] John Macquarrie, "Dialogue Among the World Religions," *The Expository Times* 108 (1996-1997), 167.

[55] John Macquarrie, "Revisiting the Christological Dimensions of Uniqueness," in Leonard Swidler and Paul Mojzes, ed., *The Uniqueness of Jesus: A Dialogue with Paul Knitter* (Maryknoll, NY: Orbis Books, 1997), 94. Here Macquarrie's position is presented without specific reference to Knitter.

[56] Ibid., 96.

[57] John Macquarrie, *Mediators Between Human and Divine, From Moses to Muhammad* (New York: The Continuum Publishing Company, 1996), 148.

[58] The quotation is from *De Incarnatione*, 41, cited in *Mediators Between Human and Divine*, 148. St. Athanasius has remained a special interest of Macquarrie's, as Alistair Kee points out in his *The Way of Transcendence* (Harmondsworth: Penguin Books, 1971), 55. See also John Macquarrie, *Studies in Christian Existentialism* (London: SCM Press, 1965), 221ff, and *God-Talk* (London: SCM Press, 1967), 123-146.

[59] John Macquarrie, "Incarnation," in Alister E. McGrath, ed., *The Blackwell Encyclopedia of Modern Christian Thought* (Oxford: Basil Blackwell, 1993), 269.

[60] John Macquarrie, "Revisiting the Christological Dimensions of Uniqueness," 97-98.

[61] John Macquarrie, *In Search of Humanity* (London: SCM Press, 1982), 67.

[62] John Macquarrie, *Christology Revisited*, 86, 95-97.

[63] Ibid., 91.

[64] Ibid., 92. He goes on to add, "I hasten to say that I myself am not a mystic. I have admired the river from the banks and dabbled in the shallows, but I have never had the courage to plunge into the depths." It seems to me that this is the characteristic of the man, because his sense of God's presence is so complete that it is not adequately described in anything less than mystical terms.

[65] Ibid., 106.

[66] N. T. Wright, op. cit., 30-31.

[67] Francesca A. Murphy, *Christ the Form of Beauty* (Edinburgh: T. & T. Clark, 1995), 176-178, 180-183.

7. CHURCH AND ECUMENISM

Anglicans consistently define themselves as both Catholic and reformed.
Paul Avis.[1]

Today what is at issue is, quite simply, the catholicity of Anglicanism. Are we to be part of the church catholic, or are we to devolve in North America, to two more sects, only with vestments?
George Sumner.[2]

Century of the Church

While the opening comment of Paul Avis speaks to Anglican ecclesial self-understanding, that of George Sumner, principal of Wycliffe College Toronto, is speaking directly to the somewhat polarized situation of the Episcopal Church in the United States. Sumner is right – the catholicity of Anglicanism in the United States is at issue, but it is equally important not to forget the amazing advances in ecclesiology across the ecumenical frontiers in this century. This century has been described by Otto Dibelius as the "century of the Church."[3] Behind this remark lies the ecumenical movement which got under way after the Edinburgh Missionary Conference in 1910, paving the way for the establishment of the World Council of Churches in Amsterdam in 1948. The renewal of ecclesiology in the Catholic Church is another factor in the making of this ecclesial century, a renewal fueled by Vatican Council II, especially its "Constitution on the Church" and "Decree on Ecumenism." With the publication of these documents the Catholic Church moved into the ecumenical movement, and has remained committed to it ever since.

As Vatican II moved to its conclusion in 1965, John Macquarrie moved from the Presbyterianism in which he had been brought up and in which he had ministered to the Anglican Communion. This took place while he was teaching at Union Theological Seminary in New York. He had felt the attraction of the Episcopal Church, as the Anglican Communion is known in Scotland, from his youth, and he tells us that "Back in Scotland, and for family reasons, it was difficult for me to break away from the prevailing Presbyterianism and I had been a Presbyterian minister since 1944."[4] In 1965 he was ordained a priest in the Anglican Communion. During this New York period he had also readied his *Principles of Christian Theology* in which he provides an account of his ecclesiology, an ecclesiology that obviously reflected his new ecclesial allegiance. In 1975 he followed this with *Christian Unity and Christian Diversity*, in which he treated of ecumenism and ecumenical theology. Using these books as our primary sources we shall present an account of Macquarrie's ecclesiology. The one thing that is immediately noticeable about Macquarrie's ecclesiology is that it does not indulge in "narcissism," an introversion of the church upon itself that can all too easily slide into place. Macquarrie has no time for that kind of ecclesiology. His ecclesiology describes a church that is connected with the world, that is not self-seeking, and that attempts to engage with difficult questions honestly. For these reasons, it is particularly difficult to understand why the ecclesiological work of John Macquarrie has not featured significantly in contemporary Anglican expressions. For example, neither Daniel W. Hardy in his *Finding the Church* (2001)[5], nor Paul Avis in his *The Identity of Anglicanism: Essentials of Anglican Ecclesiology* (2007)[6], adverts to the work of Macquarrie.[7] Of course, it is not necessary that they should consider his contribution, but both his prominence in Anglican systematic theology generally and his particular contributions to ecclesiology and to ecumenism seem to warrant some mention.

It is not easy to define with precision what the late Anglican philosophical theologian Daniel W. Hardy (1930-2007) is up to in his essay, "John Macquarrie's Ecclesiology."[8] Hardy always had a real concern for the doing of theology and for the doing of theology in and for the church. In this essay, he points out the Cinderella status of ecclesiology (along with liturgy and ethics) in British universities. However, he notes even in Macquarrie's earliest work on Bultmann and Heidegger, *An Existentialist Theology*, that Macquarrie critiques Bultmann for the decided lack of an ecclesial perspective, and as he moved to

New York and then to Oxford, he acknowledges that Macquarrie grew in awareness of ecclesiological issues. But these issues were always understood as elements of *practical* theology, as, for example, in the treatment of the church in *Principles of Christian Theology.* Hardy writes: "All these institutional settings (in Macquarrie's case Glasgow, New York, Oxford) have one thing in common: they make ecclesiology a matter for practical, rarely doctrinal, concern." What would it mean to make ecclesiology a matter of doctrinal concern? Reading between Hardy's lines it seems to be the case for him that ecclesiology should flow out of Christian doctrine --- and although he is not explicit he seems to intend such doctrines as Trinity and Incarnation --- and thus be treated on a par with them, entirely integrated with them, rather than be regarded as a practical consequence of them. On this particular point Hardy is in line with the best and longest of the Christian tradition of theological reflection. His criticism of Macquarrie, similar to his criticism noted in chapter one, is that Macquarrie starts from human experience in general, not specifically Christian experience. This being so, Macquarrie's starting-point for theology cannot explicitly be ecclesiological. Macquarrie's approach to theology is experiential-reflective and Hardy finds the experiential-reflective starting-point problematic, probably (but not explicitly) in line with George Lindbeck's critique of experiential-expressivism in theology.[9] Hardy writes: "Furthermore, as widespread as it is in theology and theological education, there is a problem with the experiential-reflective mode of theological reasoning. Reflection is always *posterior* to experience, and *prior* to further experience. It is a 'moment' after and before experience when experience is correlated with theological reflection, which... is usually so generalized as to be disconnected from experience. In other words, even the best theological reflection loses touch with the particularities of experience."[10] Does Hardy have reflection right here? As the human person develops, she develops always in an environment that is already interpreted, or reflected, in some tradition or another. However, she always reflects as the inheritor of a tradition and as the contributor, in some fashion, to that tradition. To speak of reflection as a moment after and before experience does not seem to be the case, and certainly does not seem to reflect adequately the position behind Macquarrie's theology and ecclesiology.

The Church in Relation to Other Christian Doctrines

All of Christian doctrine is inter-connected, so that to engage with one doctrine is inevitably to find oneself engaged with another, and ultimately with the entire fabric of Christian teaching. In this vein Macquarrie sees the church knit into other doctrines, and arguably deals with ecclesiology in terms of doctrinal concern, *pace* Hardy. First, the church must be understood in relation to the doctrine of creation. "... The Church is already implicit in creation."[11] The church is there in the beginning, from the beginning. There has always been a community of faith in the world, "as far back as we can go," well captured in Hebrews 11:4-7. In that sense the entire human race constitutes the people of God, but "this does not detract from the need for a special group, a special people whose destiny and service it is to realize and to represent an authentic existence for all... (The church) is the spearhead of what is going on in the creation as a whole."[12]

Moving towards the doctrine of the incarnation the church finds its most distinctive title as the "body of Christ" (1 Cor. 12:27; Eph. 1:23; Col. 1:18). The church, those "in Christ," are being "conformed to christhood, as they participate in the Paschal Mystery. The church is those who are re-created in Christ, so that it becomes in John Knox's words "the historical embodiment of the new humanity."[13] In this light one may speak of the church legitimately as the "extension" of the incarnation, though care must be taken not to mistake the church in its complete and final condition. "The incarnation which reached its completion in (Christ) is in process in the Church. Our hope is indeed that it is moving toward completion in the Church too, but at any given time, the Church is a mixed body. It is not free from sin, and there may even be times when it slips back."[14]

The doctrine of "the last things" comes next. The Church is not be identified with the kingdom of God without qualification, but nor can it be simply distinguished from the kingdom. "We may think of the kingdom as the entelechy of the Church, the perfect unfolding of the potentialities that are already manifesting themselves in the Church."[15] The church is the anticipation of the kingdom, *the* sacrament of the kingdom.

The Marks of the Church

The four traditional marks of the Church are unity, holiness, catholicity and apostolicity. "The Christian hope is that these notes will come through more and more clearly as the Church moves towards its consummation."[16] The first note of the church is unity, the center of which is Jesus Christ himself. Since Christ is the head of the body, the church, he is the source of that body's unity. The unity of the body, however, is not to be identified with uniformity. Macquarrie underscores the insight of St. Paul that unity and diversity go together, as in that wonderful passage of 1 Cor. 12. The challenge is to maintain unity and diversity in a fine balance, eschewing both uniformity and autonomy, and the key is the doctrine of the holy Trinity. In the Trinity the unity of God is expressed in the three persons of the Trinity: "The ultimate model for the Church's unity is therefore the unity of the triune God, a unity embracing the richest diversity and thus one in which there is neither stifling absorption nor damaging division."[17]

Perhaps we can see here an ecclesiology of communion in Macquarrie, communion being a central ecclesiological concept in contemporary theology. "Communion" clearly does not have the developed place in Macquarrie's ecclesiology that it enjoys in today's ecumenical reflection on the church. One thinks, for example, of the influential work of the Greek Orthodox theologian, Metropolitan John D. Zizioulas and the Catholic Jean M. R. Tillard, O.P. In both of these authors communion is a key category for understanding the church.[18] This is missing in Macquarrie, at least as an explicit, ecumenical, ecclesiological, category. However, insofar as communion is seen to be ecclesial participation in the life of the Trinity --- and one recognizes that it is more nuanced than this bald statement would lead to believe --- then this is reflected in Macquarrie's thought.

The second note of the church is holiness. Holiness means "being an agent of the incarnation, letting Christ be formed in the Church and in the world."[19] This formation of Christ that is both ecclesial and cosmic in scope is always partial and unfulfilled before the Parousia. The church is always the church *in via*, on the way. It is a church in the pellucid phrase of Aidan Nichols, O.P., echoing an Augustinian emphasis, in which sinners "are hospitalized... with a view to being made well, and made saints."[20]

Catholicity is the third note of the church, and it includes two distinct but related ideas. First, is the notion of "universality." The church is for all people everywhere, transcending all cultures. "It is this inclusive unity-in-diversity that constitutes the catholicity of the church as universality."[21] Secondly, catholicity also means authenticity, "authenticity of belief and practice in the church." The authentic faith is learned from the church as a whole, from the universal church, and so this second sense of catholicity is related to the first. Councils of the church, expressive of the consensus of the faithful, is a primary measure of catholicity, for example, in giving rise to the creeds of Christianity, formulated under the guidance of the Holy Spirit. The catholicity of the church in this double sense preserves the church from the dangers of insularity and even ethnocentrism on the one hand, and from loss of identity on the other.

The final mark of the church is apostolicity. It consists in "the church's own living continuity with the apostles."[22] Macquarrie draws a helpful analogy for apostolicity with the development of the self: "As the commitment of faith plays an important part in unifying a self, so that we can recognize it as the same self as it moves through time, so too the community of faith is united by the same faith that has spanned the centuries. The formulations of that faith have changed and will change, but the existential attitude which constitutes the core of the faith, has remained constant."[23] The obvious question now is, "How is apostolicity maintained in practice?" The answer is for Macquarrie that the episcopate is the institutional form that protects apostolicity. "This office, publicly transmitted by the apostles to their successors and then on through the generations, is the overt, institutional vehicle for ensuring the continuity of that heritage of faith and practice which was likewise transmitted by the apostles."[24] Macquarrie finds himself in agreement with his Union Theological Seminary colleague, John Knox, when he says, "I for one have no hesitancy in ascribing the same status to episcopacy as to canon and creed."[25] Historically the church exhibits these four marks in a "more or less" fashion until it reaches its completion in the kingdom of God.

The Petrine Ministry

Macquarrie's views of the Petrine Ministry have undergone considerable development over the course of his theological career. Writing an Anglican reply in 1970 to the question, "What Still Separates Us from the Catholic Church?" Macquarrie insists along with most members of the Anglican Communion that the Anglican Communion does not consider itself *separate* from the Catholic Church: "Anglicanism has never considered itself to be a sect or denomination originating in the sixteenth century. It continues without a break the *Ecclesia Anglicana* founded by St. Augustine thirteen centuries and more ago, though nowadays that branch of the church has spread far beyond the borders of England." The question is better formulated in this way: "What still separates Anglicans and Romans *within* the Catholic Church to which they so visibly and manifestly belong?"[26] Responding to the question thus phrased, Macquarrie went on to give his attention to the papacy and it has remained a published interest of his.

> At the very least, we have to affirm that any vision of a reunited church, one, holy, catholic and apostolic, must envisage it in communion with the most illustrious of the apostolic sees. Anything short of this can be regarded only as an interim step; and anything that might make this ultimate consummation more difficult should be scrupulously avoided.[27]

Thus does Macquarrie begin his first treatment of the papacy in his *Principles*.

The New Testament in his judgment makes clear the special status, the primacy of St. Peter among the apostles: his recognition of Jesus as Messiah (Mark 8:29); Christ's declaration that he was the rock on which he will build the church (Matt. 16:18); he was the first of the apostles to see the risen Christ (1 Cor. 15:5, etc.); and it is to Peter that the risen Christ commends the care of the church in the Gospel of John (John 21:15-19); in the Acts of the Apostles Peter acts as a spokesman for the church; Peter is the first to open the church to the Gentiles; even when Paul has a disagreement with Peter, he makes it abundantly clear that he acknowledges the special place Peter has in the church.[28] Though there are historical obscurities in the post-apostolic church about the development of the Petrine ministry, Macquarrie does not see this as a significant problem. Rather, the same kind of obscurity obtains in respect of the rise of the New Testament canon, the development of the sacraments, and the emergence of the threefold shape of ministry (diaconate, presbyterate, episcopate). "If we are to call the latter three apostolic, should we deny the title to the papacy?"[29] Just as these have been instrumental in nurturing the unity and integrity if the church, so has the papacy.

The central problematic issue for Macquarrie is infallibility. He admits a basic meaning to the doctrine, a freedom from error, the quality of indefectibility: "For what is freedom from error if it is not penetration into truth? Could we say that just as a compass needle, when distracting influences have been removed, turns unfailingly toward the north, so the mind of the church, when fully open to the Holy Spirit, turns unfailingly toward the truth?"[30] Indefectibility, thus understood, is not infallibility. Indefectibility is for him an eschatological idea, "but when we talk of 'infallibility', we are asking about the kind of guidance available to the church *in via*."[31] The doctrine of infallibility implies that "given certain carefully specified conditions... on a particular occasion and on a particular matter one can assert that the Pope (or the church) has made a pronouncement that is guaranteed to be free from error."

Writing in 1975, Macquarrie judged this doctrine to be such a formidable obstacle that "(he did) not see any way in which this doctrine could ever become acceptable to Anglicans and Protestants."[32] This description is in his own words "in very negative terms."[33] In his later essay, "The Papacy in a Unified Church," Macquarrie comes to a more positive judgment on infallibility, based on the insights of the late Bishop Christopher Butler, two insights in particular.[34] First, Butler maintained that any verbal expression is necessarily involved in the fallibilities of language, so that, as a result, it may be "inadequate, misleading, and even trailing clouds (of culturally derived error)." This allays some of Macquarrie's anxiety about any linguistic formula being utterly free of error. Butler emphasized that one ought to look at the governing intention behind the term. The actual term "infallibility" is a negative term, that is to say, "it seems to stress the negative notion of inerrancy, whereas what is really at stake is guaranteed truth --- a positive notion." Macquarrie still has some difficulty with the expression "guaranteed truth", but recognizes behind it the pneumatological conviction that the Holy Spirit will lead the church into the fullness of truth, using his analogy of the magnetic needle. At the same time, he also accepts that this infallibility, a gift to the whole church, may be exercised in a special way by "the one who leads the church." This leadership, however, must be seen in a corporate or collegial context.[35] Understood in this fashion the dogma of papal infallibility may make sense to Christians not in full communion with Rome.

Invited to comment on Macquarrie's essay, "The Papacy in a Unified Church," the Irish systematic theologian, Eamonn Conway, rightly suggests that the Catholic understanding of infallibility, though very close to his point of view, actually goes further than Macquarrie. He also uses the analogy of the magnetic needle to good effect to establish his point: "... the doctrine of papal infallibility claims that, at *particular* decisive moments on its journey the Christian community can be assured that the compass needle is not under any distracting influences and is, in fact, pointing north."[36] But, having said that, Conway insists that, given the stricture that all human language is conditioned by circumstances, noted by Butler and accepted by Macquarrie, "even a defined doctrine is open to development not just in terms of its formulation but also in terms of its content."

The indefectible relation to truth pertains to the whole church and its leadership. In this way Macquarrie sees the role and function of the papacy within the episcopate, as having a primacy within the episcopate: "a papacy truly integrated with the bishops and eventually with the whole people of God. The Pope is a sacramental person, an embodiment of the whole church, but he is nothing apart from the church."[37] This is Macquarrie's version of what Vatican Council II called "collegiality," a collegiality that he sees first expressed in the apostolic period: "… the scriptural record seems to visualize the leadership of Peter, but it is not a monarchical leadership, but one exercised in consultation with colleagues."[38]

Perhaps when all is said and done the nub of the issue is raised well by Bishop Mark Santer, formerly Bishop of Birmingham in England: "In what does the Petrine ministry essentially consist? How far does it entail a function of government?"[39] Macquarrie does not quite raise the question of the papacy in this way, but it is the practical issues implicit in Santer's question that proves particularly problematic. Santer acknowledges, just as Macquarrie would have, that "there is no problem about seeing the Petrine office as a focus for unity," but the issue is whether that ministry really entails the active involvement of the Pope in the government of other churches "such as is exercised today." He allies himself with the perspective of Cardinal Walter Kasper who argues that it is not so much the actual dogma of the First Vatican Council that is problematic as much as its "maximizing interpretation."[40] How is this maximizing interpretation to be avoided, especially in respect of those ecclesial traditions stemming from the sixteenth century Reformation, traditions that have *a priori* rejected this Petrine ministry? Bishop Santer rightly believes that the response to this question lies in the notion of reception. "Lurking here is the sensitive issue of reception and what has come to be called re-reception (a word I first learned from the late Fr. Jean Tillard). Anglicans have made it absolutely clear that for them the recognition of the infallibility, freedom from error or irreversibility of any authoritative statement of faith, whether conciliar or primatial, is inseparable from its reception by the church." He knows the formulas of the First Vatican Council, the *ex sese et non ex consensu ecclesiae*, and so he goes on to say: "This is not to say that reception by the faithful is in any way constitutive of the infallibility, freedom from error or irreversibility of a dogmatic statement, but that it is necessary for its recognition as such."[41] Needless to say, there are degrees of reception, but without reception authority is virtually meaningless. What would it take to achieve reception, to re-receive the Petrine Ministry for Anglicans, and equally what would it mean for Roman Catholics to "re-receive and re-conceive this office and ministry in order that other churches and communities could receive it not as a burden but as a gift?" Santer's splendid response to the question is that such re-reception on the part of both Anglicans (and indeed others in the Reformation traditions) and Roman Catholics would be enabled by "a shared re-reading of history leading to a sharing and purification of memories."[42] This is in fact what Pope John Paul II called for in his encyclical on ecumenism, *Ut Unum Sint* (par. 2), and indeed what John Macquarrie has called for when he speaks of the need for "an atmosphere of love and purgation."

Ecumenism

In 1999 Macquarrie wrote about ecumenism in this vein:

As far as ecumenism is concerned, I was, like many people of my generation, at one time an enthusiast. But in fact, as one looks back over what has happened in the twentieth century, the ecumenical movement seems to have run out of steam. The World Council of Churches, which seemed so important when it was founded in 1948, has been a disappointment. In the first place, it was never entitled to call itself a 'world council' for the largest of all the Christian churches and the only one which might be called a worldwide church, namely, the Roman Catholic Church, has never belonged to the WCC. In the second place, in its earlier years the WCC was very deeply under the influence of Barthian theology, which among other things meant that there could be no dialogue with non-Christian religions. Fortunately, that particular phase passed, but it was succeeded by one in which the WCC became intensely political and seemed to be more influenced by ideology than by theology.[43]

This is a rather bleak view of ecumenism and it may be challenged in different ways. For example, while it is true that the Roman Catholic Church has not belonged to the WCC, that has more to do with its own ecclesiological principles than it has with the WCC as such. And there is a Catholic theological conviction that its membership in the WCC would diminish and even damage its claim that the one Church of Christ "subsists" in the Roman Catholic Church.[44] Further, Macquarrie fails to note that since the late 1960s the Roman Catholic Church has been a full participant in the Faith and Order Department of the World Council of Churches. That is not full participation, but it is not nothing!

Providing the foreword to a recent book entitled *Rome and Canterbury, The Elusive Search for Unity,* Macquarrie gives us a bird's eye view of his "reading of church history since the sixteenth century and of the ecumenical movement: "The Reformation was, to some extent, a revolt against materialism and an attempt to establish the essential spirituality of the church, but it failed and produced in the end only a broken church." He goes on to note the fissiparous dimension of ecclesiology in the Reformation tradition and then ends the section with these remarkable words: "Then something like a miracle began to manifest itself. The so-called Ecumenical Movement was born. The many relatively small Christian groups began to seek unity among themselves, and *this is possible only in an atmosphere of love and purgation.*" One assumes that he means "love and purgation" not only on the part of the individual and within local congregations, but also at the widest and highest ecclesial levels. The challenge is obvious and Macquarrie entertains no romantic or optimistic view. Rather, he insists that: "There is a very long way to go, and much of it still lies ahead of us. The Protestant bodies will have to find the way to Rome and Rome will have to find an acceptable way of accepting them and whatever may have been valid in the character of each. Overarching these divisions of the West, attention must be given also to the difference between East and West."[45] This is his way of acknowledging that the ecumenical movement is dialectical and complex, and should not be understood in terms of its goal as simply unilateral. Consistently throughout his entire *oeuvre* Macquarrie insists on a legitimate pluralism in the church, provided that this pluralism does not lead to a basic lack of cohesion. Uniformity is not synonymous with unity.[46] He is, therefore, suspicious of a unity that would fail to acknowledge and respect the different Christian ecclesial traditions.

He sees a paradigm of a single Christian communion that combines both unity and pluralism exemplified in his own Anglican Communion. "Anglicans affirm the basic doctrines of Catholic faith, but allow latitude in the interpretation of these doctrines and believe that free but responsible theological discussion rather than appeal to a detailed *magisterium* is the best way of sifting truth from falsity."[47] Admittedly, in the run up to and in the wake of the 2008 Lambeth Conference the combination of unity and pluralism working effectively in genuine communion had become acutely problematic for Anglicans. Even acknowledging the present difficulties, however, the way in which Macquarrie understands the issue is still commendable, that is to say, when it comes to truth and falsity it is better not to have immediate recourse to a detailed *magisterium*.

Because of this panoramic vision of a united Christian communion, but not uniform in expression, Macquarrie is utterly opposed to schemes of Christian union, schemes based on national or geographical lines particularly. The various Christian traditions have their own integrity and, "like an art style, cannot be mixed with other traditions without loss of its distinctive appeals."[48] Avery Dulles provides a strong endorsement of Macquarrie's perspective here, and goes on to insist along with Macquarrie that the only really worthwhile unity between the churches is a unity that gathers up all their complementary and enriching diversity.[49] Macquarrie makes the further cogent point that "In the history of religions, syncretism has always proved to be a weakness and there is no reason to suppose that it would be any different in the context of Christian ecumenism."

For Macquarrie one of the most worrying concerns of the ecumenical movement is this failure to recognize the value of the various Christian traditions, and he is quite scathing in his criticism of a certain kind of ecumenist: "There has come into being a kind of ecclesiastical jet set, whose members seem always to be on the point of departing for conferences in Jakarta or Uppsala, or just getting back from other conferences in Accra or Caracas."[50]

Most schemes of union for Macquarrie seem to aim at the greatest degree of compromise and uniformity. The best existing model for Christian unity, as he explores it in his 1975 *Christian Unity and Christian Diversity*, is the uniate model, "which we find in the relation of the Roman Catholic Church and the so-called 'Uniate' churches of the East." His concern is not with the way that these unions came about historically, "some of them decidedly shady." The value is in the model itself which at the same time allows union with Rome, and a measure of autonomy for the individual churches, for example, in the areas of liturgy and canon law. The uniate model thus keeps together both values of unity and legitimate pluralism. Here also veteran ecumenical theologian Avery Dulles finds himself in agreement with Macquarrie, although he points out that uniatism often carries with it the negative sense of submission of one church to the doctrinal and ecclesiological principles of another, thus undermining the enriching complementarity already alluded to.[51]

Macquarrie's position has not been without its critics, most notably the late Lesslie Newbigin, Bishop of the Church of South India, an ecumenically united church. Newbigin immediately points out that whether one likes it or not, united churches have proliferated and that "millions of Christians are living in such united churches, daily thanking God for the blessing of unity."[52] Newbigin, as a life-long committed ecumenist, had a much clearer vision of the impact of such church unions than Macquarrie. His own experience in the united Church of South India bears witness to at least the value of that successful experiment in church union. "In 1965, after an absence of eighteen years," writes Bishop Newbigin, "I returned to Madras as bishop to serve the same churches which I had known two decades earlier as competing congregations. I did not find that they had become uniform: on the contrary I found a rich variety of styles in worship and practice. What I found was congregations less concerned about their own affairs and more ready to think in terms of God's will for the life of the city as a whole, less like competing clubs each trying to enlarge itself and a little more recognizable as sign and foretaste of God's kingdom."[53] Where church unions function in this way, the problems to which Macquarrie was drawing attention are diminished.

It is also difficult to avoid the conclusion that Macquarrie's antipathy toward pragmatic ecumenical solutions is much colored by the theology of his Glasgow doctoral supervisor, Ian Henderson. Henderson deeply distrusted what he took to be schemes of ecclesial union that neglected in principle the particularities of churches. "In (Henderson's) *Power Without Glory* the implied criticism of ecumenical theology is greatly developed. Here he makes the point that ecumenical language 'is designed not to describe but to conceal' and that it is 'a fiesta of double-think'... There is a language which conceals in order to evade, a language which does not explore open theological possibilities but rather manipulates the data in order to arrive at predetermined results."[54] Macquarrie does not share every aspect of Henderson's point of view as is established in his personal and published commitment to ecumenism, but there remains a lingering distrust of pragmatic bureaucracy that can seem to give short shrift to important theological presuppositions and convictions that have contributed to Christian disunity in the first place.

It would be most unfortunate to end this account of Macquarrie's approach to ecumenism on a negative note because that would certainly not be congruent with his perspective. In what must have been his very last published comment on ecumenism he says this: "Impossible, do we say? I don't think so, but it will need enormous patience, for which we should all be praying. The prayer itself produces the way to recovery."[55] That final comment recognizes both the priority of God's grace and initiative as well as hopeful realism, and underscores the absolute need for what has been termed "spiritual ecumenism."

Pride in the Church

Distancing himself from any kind of ecclesial triumphalism, Macquarrie nonetheless believes that there is a right kind of pride in the church, a pride in the church's history or activities. "Such pride becomes sinful and blameworthy only when it settles into a hardened attitude of superiority or when it becomes egocentric and issues in an exclusive and contemptuous attitude to others."[56] Yet again this attitude exemplifies John Macquarrie himself. There is no attitude of superiority in the man, no egocentricity, no contempt of others. His ecclesiology and sacramental theology establish this to a fine degree. He knows that "The church shows, even if only weakly and fitfully, a hidden glory that is striving to find expression and realization," but it does show this glory. In 1970 Macquarrie wrote: "My personal love and admiration for the Roman Catholic Church, and my great commitment to the Catholic form of Christianity are great... I rejoice that even now we are so close to each other, and look forward to our drawing still closer together in the decades ahead."[57] If this is true of his theology of church and of his ecumenical commitment, it is amply verified in his sacramental theology and to this we now turn.

---

[1] Paul Avis, *The Identity of Anglicanism: Essentials of Anglican Ecclesiology* (New York and London: T. & T. Clark, 2007), 66.

[2] George Sumner, "After Dromatine," *Anglican Theological Review* 87 (2005), 561.

[3] Cited in Paul McPartlan, *Sacrament of Salvation* (Edinburgh: T. & T. Clark, 1995), xiii.

[4] John Macquarrie, *On Being a Theologian, Reflections at Eighty* (London: SCM Press, 1999), 38.

[5] Daniel W. Hardy, *Finding the Church: The Dynamic Truth of Anglicanism* (London: SCM Press, 2001).

[6] Paul D. Avis, *The Identity of Anglicanism: Essentials of Anglican Ecclesiology* (New York and London: T. & T. Clark, 2007).

[7] In the case of Daniel Hardy the omission of Macquarrie is particularly striking. Hardy was thoroughly familiar with Macquarrie's theology. In the first edition of David F. Ford's *The Modern Theologians*, he offered a critical summary of Macquarrie's theology, noted in chapter 1 above.

[8] In the 2006 celebration of Macquarrie's theology, *In Search of Humanity and Deity* (pages 267-276) he wrote an essay entitled "John Macquarrie's Ecclesiology."

[9] See George Lindbeck, *The Nature of Doctrine* (London: SPCK, 1984), and the appreciative assessment of Lindbeck in Owen F. Cummings, "Toward a Postliberal Religious Education," *The Living Light* 28 (1992), 315-324. While I stand by much of what is written in this essay on Lindbeck, even then and much more now I feel that he is philosophically flawed when it comes to the role of philosophy in theology. It is no surprise that in Lindbeck's collection of essays *The Church in a Postliberal Age* (London: SCM Press, 2002), there is no reference to John Macquarrie.

[10] Daniel W. Hardy, "John Macquarrie's Ecclesiology," 275.

[11] John Macquarrie, *Principles of Christian Theology*, rev. ed. (London: SCM Press, 1977), 386.

[12] Ibid., 388, 407.

[13] As noted in chapter 1, John Knox was Macquarrie's friend and colleague at Union Theological Seminary in New York City. Macquarrie quotes this phrase from Knox's book, *The Church and the Reality of Christ*, 104.

[14] John Macquarrie, *Principles of Christian Theology*, 389.

[15] Ibid., 390.

[16] Ibid., 402.

[17] Ibid., 403. The same point is made in John Macquarrie, *Christian Unity and Christian Diversity* (London: SCM Press, 1975), 47.

[18] John D. Zizioulas, *Being as Communion, Studies in Personhood and the Church* (London: Darton, Longman and Todd, 1985), Jean-Marie R. Tillard, O.P., *Church of Churches* (Collegeville: The Liturgical Press, 1992).

[19] John Macquarrie, *Principles of Christian Theology*, 405.

[20] Aidan Nichols, OP, *Epiphany, A Theological Introduction to Catholicism* (Collegeville: The Liturgical Press, 1996), 237.

[21] John Macquarrie, *Principles of Christian Theology*, 407.

[22] Ibid., 409.

[23] Ibid., 410.

[24] Ibid.

[25] Ibid., 411.

[26] Macquarrie's essay may be found in Hans Küng, ed., *Post-Ecumenical Christianity* (New York: Herder and Herder, 1970), here 45-46.

[27] John Macquarrie, *Principles of Christian Theology*, 416.

[28] These last three notes about Peter come from Macquarrie's essay, "The Papacy in a Unified Church," in his *On Being a Theologian, Reflections at Eighty*, 163-164.

[29] John Macquarrie, *Principles of Christian Theology*, 413.

[30] Ibid., 415. This is a favorite analogy for Macquarrie. He returns to it again in his essay, "The Papacy in a Unified Church," *On Being a Theologian*, 170.

[31] John Macquarrie, "Structures of Unity," in Mark Santer, ed., *Their Lord and Ours: Approaches to Authority, Community and the Unity of the Church* (London: S.P.C.K., 1982), 126.

[32] John Macquarrie, *Christian Unity and Christian Diversity*, 99-100.

[33] John Macquarrie, *On Being a Theologian*, 169.

[34] Macquarrie finds particularly helpful Bishop Christopher Butler's "Roman Requirements," *The Tablet* (July 5, 1975), 99-100.

[35] John Macquarrie, *On Being a Theologian*, 170-171.

[36] Eamonn Conway, "The Papacy in a Pilgrim Church: Response to Prof. John Macquarrie," in John Macquarrie, *On Being a Theologian*, 175.

[37] John Macquarrie, *Christian Unity and Christian Diversity*, 99.

[38] John Macquarrie, *On Being a Theologian*, 164. Macquarrie's positive comments on the papacy are mentioned by J. Michael Miller, C.S.B., *The Divine Right of the Papacy in Recent Ecumenical Theology* (Rome: Gregorian University Press, 1980), 125, 127, 133-134.

[39] Mark Santer, "Communion, Unity and Primacy: An Anglican Response to *Ut Unum Sint*," *Ecclesiology* 3 (2007), 290.

[40] Walter Kasper, *That They May All Be One* (New York: Continuum, 2005), 146.

[41] Mark Santer, op. cit., 292-293.

[42] Ibid., 295.

[43] John Macquarrie, *On Being a Theologian* (London: SCM Press, 1999), 64.

[44] See Vatican II's *Lumen Gentium/Constitution on the Church*, paragraph 8.

[45] John Macquarrie, "Foreword," in Mary Reath, *Rome and Canterbury, The Elusive Search for Unity* (Lanham-Boulder-New York-Toronto-Plymouth, UK: Rowman and Littlefield Publishers, Inc., 2007), VIII, my emphasis.

[46] See his "Structures of Unity," in Mark Santer, ed., *Their Lord and Ours: Approaches to Authority, Community and the Unity of the Church* (London: SPCK, 1982), 113-128.

[47] Ibid., 119.

[48] John Macquarrie, *Christian Unity and Christian Diversity*, 17.

[49] Avery Dulles, SJ "Ecumenical Strategies for a Pluralistic Age," in his *The Resilient Church* (Garden City, NY: Doubleday, 1977), 186.

[50] John Macquarrie, *Christian Unity and Christian Diversity*, 19.

[51] Avery Dulles, SJ, op. cit., 188. See also the helpful comments of Geoffrey Wainwright, *Doxology, a Systematic Theology* (New York and Oxford: Oxford University Press 1984), 319-322, as well as the ecclesiological comments and glosses found throughout his *Lesslie Newbigin, a Theological Life* (New York and Oxford: Oxford University Press, 2000).

[52] Lesslie Newbigin, "All in One Place or All of One Sort? On Unity and Diversity in the Church," Richard W. A. McKinney, ed., *Creation, Christ and Culture: Studies in Honour of T. F. Torrance* (Edinburgh: T. & T. Clark, 1976), 293.

[53] Ibid., 299.

[54] John Macquarrie, "A Modern Scottish Theologian," in his collection *Thinking About God* (London: SCM Press, 1975), 210-211.

[55] In Mary Reath, op. cit., VIII.

[56] John Macquarrie, *Theology, Church and Ministry* (London: SCM Press, 1986), 107.

[57] John Macquarrie, "What Still Separates us from the Catholic Church?" in Hans Küng, op. cit., 53.

8. THE SACRAMENTAL LIFE

My aim is to maintain the general mystery of the sacraments as means by which divine grace is mediated to us in this world of space and time and matter, but at the same time to get away from all magical and superstitious ideas about them.
John Macquarrie.[1]

The Renewal of Anglicanism

Sacramental theology has always been a strong focus of concern in Catholic circles as any acquaintance with a seminary theological curriculum would immediately show. However, a constant complaint of Bishop Stephen Sykes about Anglican theology in the latter half of the twentieth century was the apparent lack of interest in sacramental or liturgical theology. In his Foreword to Alister E. McGrath's *The Renewal of Anglicanism*, John Macquarrie writes that "There are few things, if any, that I long more to see than the renewal of Anglicanism."[2] There can be little doubt that Macquarrie has contributed to this renewal in his clear articulation of sacramental theology. In his *A Guide to the Sacraments* he has provided a worthy successor to Oliver Chase Quick's excellent *The Christian Sacraments*, first published in 1927.[3] However, as will be evident from the survey in this chapter, he speaks not only to the renewal of Canterbury, but to the renewal of the entire *oikumene*, including Rome, and that is why Aidan Nichols, O.P. can say of him that "the orthodox Roman Catholic can recognize in him with but little effort a 'separated doctor' of the Catholic Church."[4] His sacramental theology, especially as found in his *A Guide to the Sacraments* is, in the words of Fr. David Forrester, a former Roman Catholic chaplain at Eton College, "Extremely informative, and obviously the product of deep faith and wide reading; it is a joy to read, written in a clear, concise, indeed lapidary style, and there is something in it for everyone."[5]

Word and Sacrament

Taking his point of departure from the broad understanding of the Word of God in the Christian tradition, Macquarrie is mindful that the Word of God meets us in a threefold form. First, the living Word is Jesus Christ himself, he who in himself is the fullness of divine revelation. Second, the written Word of the Bible, which witnesses to the living Word, Jesus Christ. Third, the proclaimed Word of the church, "the living voice of the church... in its preaching and teaching." He brings the threefold shape of the Word into synthesis in these terms: "The living Word, or incarnate Lord, has priority and gives birth to the other two forms of the word; but it is only through the mediation of the written word and the proclaimed word that we have access to Christ, the revealed Word."[6] A strong sense of the incarnation permeates Macquarrie's christology and his theology of the Word. At the same time, and as a result of the incarnation, one recognizes what might be called the intertextuality of the Bible and Christian tradition in and with the living Word, Jesus Christ. "The Christian revelation comes in a person, not in a book."[7]

Typically, Macquarrie roots this interrelation of Christ, as incarnate Word, and of Scripture as written word, and of preaching and teaching as proclaimed word in human reason. Language has a threefold function: it expresses, it refers and it communicates. This threefold function is true of any word, but it has a further nuance for Macquarrie, a further nuance that is christological. He understands the second Person of the Trinity as Expressive Being, and, of course, Expressive Being is necessarily eternal. Expressive Being finds its perfect expression in "the particular being of Jesus Christ." The language might be slightly odd, but it is a perfectly acceptable rendition of the *Homoousios* formula of classical christology, from Nicaea I (325) to Chalcedon (451). The Holy Scriptures in turn refer to Jesus Christ as their very center, and finally the proclamation of the word, its perpetual traditioning in the church communicates the revelation. The work of the Word, if we may so put it, in this threefold way, is not in the first instance to be understood as a human action, but rather as the action of God as Holy Spirit in us. The characteristic mode of the Spirit's work in

Macquarrie's theology is to unite. "It is this unitive action of the Spirit that brings into one the spoken word of the Church's proclamation, the written word of her scriptures, and the incarnate Word in and through whom Being has made itself known." The Holy Spirit *is* the uniting of these three wordings of the Word. That means, therefore, that "Whenever a human word is heard as a divine word, something takes place that is analogous to what has been described in the analyses of revelation, of miracle, of the incarnation itself."[8]

Macquarrie notes the phenomenological commonplace that the major religions all have their Scriptures. One thinks, for example, of the phenomenological analysis of Ninian Smart, who sees Scriptures as one of his seven dimensions of religion.[9] Typically eschewing any form of positivism, Macquarrie provides a reason for this. "Just as the brain provides storage cells on which the memory of the individual depends, so scriptures or written accounts provide for the community a kind of memory by which it can reach back and recall its past."[10] The past of the Scriptures is that disclosure of the holy that is termed "primordial revelation." This primordial revelation is kept alive in and by the community of faith.

This keeping alive of the primordial revelation in the church ensures for Christian experience a stable objectivity "over against the vagaries of individual experiences in the community... a safeguard against subjectivist excesses."[11] Perhaps it might be said that the Scriptures-in-community provide a *regula fidei*, a "rule of faith," both to measure the authenticity of individual experience and also to challenge what are taken to be deviant forms. He is opposed to any absolutizing of the Bible or to viewing it as the exclusive formative factor in Christian theology. Nonetheless, while he affirms that the Bible comes out of the community of the faith, and so is that community's foundational document, "it also retains an independence over against the community." The Bible constantly has the power to judge, and to summon the community to renewal, to conversion.[12] This certainly what is intended by Vatican II's "Constitution on

Divine Revelation" when it says of the church's teaching office: "Yet this Magisterium is not superior to the Word of God, but is its servant."[13]

In the preface to his 1997 *A Guide to the Sacraments* Macquarrie states the aim of the book very clearly: "My aim is to maintain the genuine mystery of the sacraments as means by which divine grace is mediated to us in this world of space and time and matter, but at the same time to get away from all magical and superstitious ideas about them."[14] As well as this, he has an ecumenical aim "in the book's insistence that word and sacrament are inseparable or certainly ought to be."[15] This takes him beyond the traditional, and indeed superficial Reformation divide: Catholic emphasis on sacrament, Protestant emphasis on word. For Macquarrie, indeed as for the Great Tradition, one may not be had without the other.

The Anglican priest-poet, George Herbert, is cited as summing up a natural theology of sacramentality: "Teach me, my God and King, in all things Thee to see." The goal of sacramental theology is to enable the experience of God's transparency and grace through created reality. This is a pervasive theme in Macquarrie. In the first edition of his *Paths in Spirituality* he points up the connection between "natural theology, the Incarnation, the Eucharist and the sacramental principle generally."[16] His conviction is that there must be some revelational consistency in the movement of God from creation through the Parousia. Protology and eschatology have an intrinsic teleological relationship. The Incarnation is the center point, revealing the direction and meaning of this process, and anticipating its final fruition. Nor is this to be thought of as some pelagian and necessary working out of the dynamics of nature and history apart from God: "(God) comes to us before we think of seeking him."[17] God's graceful and prior initiative demands not only a sense of his transcendence as the origin of all creation, but also a sense of his immanence in creation, his active dwelling within his world. God's immanent presence in creation may be fruitfully compared to Archbishop William Temple's analogy of the relation of an artist to his or her work, an analogy of which Macquarrie is quite fond. It occurs not only here in his *A Guide to the Sacraments*, but also in *The Humility of God*.[18] "The artist certainly transcends the work, for it is the artist who has created it. But the artist is bound to the work so created and has poured something of his own self into it so that from the work or through the work we can have a relation to the artist. Something of the artist is present in the work and revealed in the work." Thus, the universal presence of God yields "a sacramental potentiality in virtually everything."[19] This does not mean, of course, that God is to be thought of as equally present or present with equal clarity in everything. The sacramental system of the church gives us the grace "to see God in some very dark phenomena." Although Macquarrie does not develop his thought immediately in this direction, perhaps we might say that the God who is encountered as omnipresent is the God most fully manifest in the person of our Lord Jesus Christ, and the shape of that supreme manifestation is cruciform. Christology (and soteriology) would then be a link between theology and sacramentality. Macquarrie wishes to avoid, at this point, a narrower Christocentric construal of sacrament because of his explicit desire to secure the sacramental sense "in the very constitution of humanity." At the same time, since all creation without exception comes to be through Expressive Being, the Being of the Word that became enfleshed in Jesus, the potential of anything to be sacramental and the actuality of any sacrament is already to that extent Christocentric.

Sacramental Anthropology

Macquarrie will not let go of this universal religious sense in humankind, doing theology through anthropology. In the contemporary debates about non-foundationalism, Macquarrie's position, in which is rooted the universal sacramental sense, is to acknowledge a general awareness of transcendence co-extensive with human existence, and within this to recognize its supreme and unique expression in Jesus Christ and in the tradition of Christianity. If this universal religious experience is not to be dissolved, then we must not proceed too quickly or too immediately to Christian faith. This is not the place to argue

Macquarrie's views over the non-foundationalists, but simply to note how this universal sacramental consciousness is rooted.

Since we have access to the physical world both through our various senses and our rational minds, there is an appropriate fusion in the church's sacraments of the verbal and the non-verbal, of word and sign/symbol. If the verbal may be seen historically as more characteristic of the Reformation tradition, and the symbolic of the Catholic tradition, Macquarrie, as already noted, welcomes the narrowing of the ecumenical gap in recent times between these two ecclesial emphases.

Christ-Church-Sacrament

In respect of the institution of the sacraments by Jesus Christ Macquarrie notes approvingly the position of the *Catechism of the Catholic Church:* "As she has done for the canon of Sacred Scripture and for the doctrine of the faith, the Church, by the power of the Spirit who guides her 'into all truth,' has gradually recognized this treasure received from Christ and, as the faithful steward of God's mysteries, has determined its 'dispensation.'"[20] He distinguishes this position from what he sees as the more radical grounding of the sacraments in the person of Christ understood as the "primordial sacrament," a view associated with the influential Flemish Dominican theologian, Edward Schillebeeckx, O.P. Schillebeeckx's views have the merit of bringing together the entire sacramental sensibility, Christological-ecclesial and natural, in a certain hierarchy. "Christ is the sacrament of God; the church is the sacrament (body) of Christ; the seven sacraments are the sacraments of the church; the natural sacraments scattered around the world are, from a Christian point of view, approximations or pointers which find fulfillment in the sacraments of the gospel."[21] Here one may detect some advance over his earlier views on Christ as sacrament. In his book, *The Faith of the People of God: a Lay Theology*, Macquarrie distances himself somewhat from understanding Christ as sacrament or the church as sacrament.[22] Although curiously he does not make use of the idea of Christ as sacrament in his work *Jesus Christ in Modern Thought,* it is after this large work in Christology that he seems more favorably disposed to it.[23]

Macquarrie points out that the idea of Christ as the primordial sacrament at the center of the sacramental nexus is no new discovery, but "was obviously implicit from the beginning, and was occasionally made explicit." Perhaps it is first rendered explicit in Justin Martyr's *Logos Spermatikos,* but Macquarrie finds it clearly represented in the twentieth century Anglican theologian, Oliver Chase Quick (1885-1944), who wrote some fifty years before Schillebeeckx: "The life of Jesus Christ is seen as the perfect sacrament."[24] As the primordial sacrament, Christ may be seen as the true minister of the sacraments and, indeed, as their content. He is the Baptized One, whose faith is the ideal for every Christian; the Confirmed One, who expresses what it means to live out that baptismal vocation in deep and dedicated commitment; the Reconciler; the Really Present One; the Healer; the Priest; the Lover.

To engage with his sacramental theology the sequence of thought in Macquarrie's *A Guide to the Sacraments* will be followed but within the context of his entire *oeuvre,* and then a fuller appreciation of his eucharistic theology will be developed in the next chapter. Macquarrie presents five chapters each on sacramental theology in general and on the Eucharist, four on Holy Orders, two on Baptism, and one each on Confirmation, Penance/Reconciliation, Unction and Marriage. It is difficult, given his table of contents in the book, to avoid the suggestion that Macquarrie's principal ecumenical dialogue partner is contemporary Catholicism.

A Common Ordinal

In touching upon the validity of the sacraments, Macquarrie notes the common insistence of both Anglicans and Catholics on episcopally ordained priests for the celebration of the Eucharist. He does not spend much time in dealing with Pope Leo XIII's papal bull, *Apostolicae Curae* (1896), condemning Anglican orders as "absolutely null and utterly void." Nor does he spend time treating the Anglican response, the response of the archbishops of Canterbury and York, *Saepius Officio*. While this papal bull remains officially in place from the Roman Catholic point of view, the fact of the matter is that the tone of ecumenical discourse since the Second Vatican Council is now very different. Thus, Paul Avis says: "Courtesy, charity and genuine respect and friendship between Anglican and Roman Catholic church leaders have replaced the hostile, defensive and admonitory style of a century ago."[25] Not only that, but the outstanding theological work of the Anglican and Roman Catholic International Commission, although it has not addressed as such and as yet Pope Leo XIII's position, has found in the fine words of Henry Chadwick "the unintended side-effect of destroying the central argument of *Apostolicae Curae*, viz., that Roman Catholics and Anglicans are committed to essentially different beliefs about the Eucharistic presence and sacrifice and consequently about the nature and offers of ministerial priesthood."[26]

This notion of sacramental validity has been a consistent concern for him, and yet at the same time, he is aware of the Reformation tradition. In 1975, he advocated the use of a common ordinal which might bring the two western ecclesial emphases together: "As more and more groups might be persuaded to use it, then there would gradually grow up a ministry universally recognized, though differentiated according to the customs of the various churches. Such an ordinal, I assumed, would provide for episcopal ordination, and one might hope that Roman Catholic bishops would eventually take part in the ordinations, so giving them a claim to wide recognition. In this way, the ordinal would be based on the Catholic substance of the doctrine of the ministry. But it would incorporate whatever might seem of value in the Protestant principle, as applied to that doctrine." Much has happened in ecumenism since then, but, if anything like the goals of classical ecumenism were regarded as desirable, it is difficult to see how they could be realized without proposals such as these. Macquarrie's theology will not dissolve or disallow the possibility of real and valid "doors to the sacred" in other churches. In his perspective, "validity" enables us to affirm that "grace is here." It does not entitle us to state absolutely where it is not.

Baptism and Confirmation

His consideration of baptism is very fine, but his treatment of confirmation leaves much to be desired. There are various aspects to the meaning of the sacrament of baptism: "forgiveness, repentance, conversion, justification, election to the common ministry of all the baptized, and the gift of the Holy Spirit to make the new life possible." We can see in this list of the theological marks of baptism characteristic emphases of the Catholic and Reformation traditions. With his persistent sense of balance and concern for catholicity of presentation Macquarrie states that "If we omit any of these items, then we have mutilated the Christian sacrament of baptism and made it less than it was intended."[27]

While there is some truth to the observation that confirmation remains a sacrament in search of a theology, much work has been done in recent years on the history and theology of this sacrament, for example, by the Anglican scholar, J. D. C. Fisher and by the Catholics Aidan Kavanagh, Gerard Austin and Paul Turner. Macquarrie shows no real awareness of such contributions, so that his understanding remains essentially what it was years before.[28] Though he admits to "puzzling over the question of what is distinctive in confirmation or of what it confers that is not given in baptism," essentially confirmation is for him the sacramental ratification of what took place in baptism, "a particularly solemn renewal in the presence of the Church."[29] From a Catholic or Orthodox point of view, this is very helpful, but not quite enough. To be more satisfactory, the account would need to move in the direction of something like "The Effects of Confirmation," as we have them in the *Catechism of the Catholic Church*: "Confirmation brings an increase and deepening of baptismal grace: it roots us more deeply in the divine filiation which makes us cry, 'Abba! Father'; it unites us more firmly to Christ; it increases the gifts of the Holy Spirit in us; it renders our bond with the Church more perfect; it gives us a special strength of the Holy

Spirit to spread and defend the faith by word and action as true witnesses of Christ, to confess the name of Christ boldly, and never to be ashamed of the Cross."[30] If this description from the *Catechism* meets Macquarrie's meaning, and a good case could be made for that, to describe confirmation as "a particularly solemn renewal (of baptism) in the presence of the Church" is to place the sacrament too much on the Reformation side of the divide, giving emphasis to the sacrament as a personal profession of the faith that was made on behalf of a child baptized in infancy. It fails adequately to recognize and emphasize confirmation as the second stage of sacramental initiation to be completed by Eucharist. This seems to me the weakest part of Macquarrie's sacramental theology. In 2002 he wrote to me: "I fully accept your point that my treatment of confirmation is inadequate. But, and here I think Rahner expresses the same difficulty, just what does confirmation confer that makes it distinct from baptism? Certainly, because it comes (usually) at a later stage in life, confirmation is remembered in a way that baptism is not, and may therefore be more influential in the life of the candidate, but this has to do with human psychology rather than with the nature of the sacrament."[31]

Kathryn Tanner, in a lecture to the American House of Bishops on the sacrament of confirmation, provides an Anglican account of what may be missing in John Macquarrie, at least up to a point. Tanner speaks of confirmation "in terms of a shift from actuality to manifestation or epiphany" with reference to baptism.[32] What has happened in terms of sheer gift in baptism "despite our sinful lives and beyond created capacities" comes to manifestation or to light in our lives as a whole way of living for which we now take a measure of responsibility in the sacrament of confirmation. Tanner draws attention to analogous thinking in her own expression of, and yet very traditional christology: "In Christ, humanity becomes the Word's own – that is what Incarnation means – for the purpose of making the power of the Word humanity's own and thereby transforming, healing and deifying it. In much the same way we are made Christ's own in virtue of our baptism (parallel to the Incarnation in which humanity is made the Word's own).

Then in confirmation, Christ becomes our own, as a visibly manifest transformative force determining the character of our whole lives (parallel to the way Jesus' humanity is elevated to a new form – literally raised from the dead – as a consequence of Incarnation)."[33] Thus, confirmation looks ahead to what living a Christ shaped life in witness and in service is like. "Simply stated, in confirmation one shows oneself ready to do what one has promised to do in baptism." It is a new sort of public rite of accountability. "Confirmation is for those who are already Christians, while baptism makes Christians out of those who are not."[34]

This makes sense of confirmation when it is chronologically separated from baptism. However, does it really help when baptism, confirmation and the Eucharist are celebrated as an integral whole, as, for example, at the Easter Vigil? The sacrament of confirmation, it seems to me, will continue to remain something of "a sacrament in search of a meaning" until the various ecclesial traditions can find mutual agreement more than they have, and, indeed, until the Catholic Church finds a more uniform, ritual understanding of its meaning.[35] If the sacraments of baptism-confirmation-Eucharist were more thoroughly understood as initiatory, with the Eucharist as the terminal sacrament of Christian initiation, as was the understanding substantially of the first millennium, then perhaps confirmation might cease to be so ambiguous. It would be a point of graceful growth between baptism and Eucharist, and would not be required to bear the burden of autonomy, so to speak. This is the practice of the Orthodox Churches and has much to commend it. If, however, confirmation remains in its present range of various theological meanings, then the ambiguity surrounding the sacrament will continue.

Penance and Reconciliation

Macquarrie was invited by the Doctrine Commission of the Church of England to prepare a report on the sacrament of penance.[36] The report is vintage Macquarrie, as he moves from general considerations of penance and reconciliation, through a brief history of the tradition to some practical conclusions. Undoubtedly, one of the reasons for the invitation in the first place had to do with the clear articulation of the theology of the sacrament of penance in the revised edition of his *Principles of Christian Theology*.[37] One of his major concerns in both publications has been to emphasize the ecclesial and corporate nature of the sacrament. He thinks that the sacrament is seen as so private and secret that it seems "to contradict the communal character which would appear to be needed in the sacraments of the Church."[38] He is convinced that "The Church of today would appear less indulgent and more worthy of respect if it had a little more of the spirit of discipline --- not indeed so harsh as at some times in the past, but with some more bite than there is at present, when virtually anything seems to be acceptable."[39] There is something in this, but Macquarrie's point might be better made by attending to the fruitful pastoral distinction in one and the same sacramental rite between "penance" and "reconciliation," a distinction made particularly well by the liturgical theologian, M. Francis Mannion.[40] While all Christians require ongoing penance as they are further conformed to the mind of Christ ("a little more of the spirit of discipline" in Macquarrie's words), fewer may require reconciliation, which presupposes that they have put themselves out of the communion of the Church by their aware, free and deliberate action.

Anointing and Marriage

Macquarrie recognizes that "unction" or the anointing of the sick goes beyond those who seem to be on the threshold of death, in line with the revised rite in the Catholic Church. Unction is about healing, and it is important to be clear about the distinction between curing and healing. While curing has to do with "relieving or removing the physical illness," healing "means to 'make whole'."[41] The distinction is a key one because while unction aims at the healing, the making whole of the entire person, "that could mean that although the physical condition is not cured, the sick person is enabled to integrate even his or her suffering into the personality and to become a better person in the process."[42]

A cursory perusal of the General Introduction to the Catholic *Pastoral Care of the Sick*, would easily establish the concord between Macquarrie's sentiments and the teaching of the Catholic Church.[43] In line with Catholic teaching, Macquarrie sees that the sacrament is particularly apposite in the context of dying: "Death belongs to the finitude of our existence, and this sacrament of unction can be understood as the bringing of the grace in which to face death... It has its communal character, for it brings to the individual... the assurance that he is one with the whole body of Christ. He is therefore incorporated through Christ into the very structure of Being, and the destiny that awaits him is to be given a still fuller share in the life of Being."[44] When it is recalled that Macquarrie means by Being the Blessed Trinity --- the Father as Primordial Being, the Son as Expressive Being and the Holy Spirit as Unitive Being --- the sacrament of unction has a profound trinitarian character.

In treating of marriage Macquarrie remains consistent in his methodology, as he writes: "Marriage, of course, is a 'natural' institution as well as being a Christian sacrament, and as a natural institution, it is a far wider phenomenon. We must recognize the continuity between the natural institution and the Christian sacrament."[45] This is the revelational consistency mentioned earlier between the realms of nature and grace. In terms of the natural institution of marriage, there is first of all the ontological marriage bond, the *vinculum coniugale*, which is permanent and which comes to expression in the marriage vows by which partners pledge themselves to each other.[46] "A person is shaped by his decisions and by the way he stands by them. They enter into his being and make him the person he is. In a person of any depth and integrity, we find that there is a core of abiding commitments that gives to his whole life its set and character, making him a unified person rather than a bundle of loosely connected instincts, opinions, likes and dislikes."[47] Such decisions and commitments, essential to the development and flourishing of personhood, may justly be called ontological. "Any moral bond," maintains Macquarrie, "when explored in depth, is found to have ontological foundations."[48] Christian marriage adds to this sacramental character of natural marriage the belief that God ratifies the marriage, strengthens the couple who now may be considered to constitute "a Christian community, a tiny church, as it were, which, like the whole church, is the bride of Christ and the recipient of his faithful love."[49] All of these themes of Macquarrie's, described briefly, find a clear echo in the *Catechism of the Catholic Church*, as it talks about the ontological/indissoluble bond, the permanence of the marriage pledge, marriage and the family as a domestic church.[50]

Holy Orders

The four chapters of *A Guide to the Sacraments* devoted to "Orders/Ordination" cover not only the sacramental rites as such, but also the theology of episcopacy and the Petrine ministry. The latter has already been commented on, and here we shall briefly outline some of what Macquarrie has to offer on bishops and priests.

Historical perspective establishes that there have been in the West "two sharply distinguished ways of thinking about the ordained ministry," the Catholic emphasis on apostolic succession and episcopacy, and the Protestant view which "has not hesitated to speak of discontinuity in the ministry, when the Protestant principle of renewal seemed to call for a critique of the established order."[51] The Catholic emphasis has been on the sacraments, especially the Eucharist, while Protestants have stressed the ministry of the Word. In Macquarrie's ecclesiology, both emphases are equally necessary.

His thoughts on the episcopate reflect the emphases found in Vatican Council II's *Decree on the Pastoral Office of Bishops in the Church*. For Macquarrie the bishop is a teacher, a pastor, a sacramental figure and the leader of a diocese. He shows himself aware of the many demands made on a bishop in the contemporary church, but two comments stand out as of paramount importance. The first has to do with the bishop as teacher: "In modern times, it would be unrealistic to expect a bishop to be able to devote all his energies to theology, but he certainly should be aware of what is going on in theology if he is to fulfil his duty of maintaining and interpreting the apostolic faith."[52] The second comment notes how difficult it is in a large modern diocese for a bishop to fulfil his role as pastor. The bishop's pastoring of the pastors may be the best way for him to fulfil this role: "To whom can the purveyor of pastoral care turn, when he himself needs such care? Even in large dioceses, the bishop can still be a pastor to the pastors, so that he is still a pastor to the diocese, though indirectly."[53] The profound ecclesial wisdom in these sentences needs no further comment.

He connects ordained ministry to baptism when he writes: "All have a ministry in the Church of Christ, but not all have the same ministry." He then emphasizes the permanent character of ordained ministry. The ministry of word and sacrament, embodied in ordination, is "the high point in a process that has already begun with that person's calling to the sacred ministry, and that will continue for a lifetime. Ordination is a lifelong vocation and commitment, and indeed, it takes a lifetime for the full flourishing of a priestly character."[54] The character of ordination is given in the grace of the sacrament. The formation and flourishing of that character remains the responsibility of a lifetime.

Macquarrie attends to the distinction between the general priesthood of the baptized, and the special priesthood of the ordained. It is an important distinction for Catholics, enunciated in Vatican Council II's *Constitution on the Church*: "Though they differ essentially and not only in degree, the common priesthood of the faithful and the ministerial or hierarchical priesthood are none the less ordered one to another; each in its own proper way shares in the one priesthood of Christ."[55] There is no aspect of this distinction with which Macquarrie would find fault. First, there is only one priesthood, that of Christ, in which all share, as Macquarrie puts it: "All Christian ministry is derived from Christ, and all Christian priesthood is participation in his one priesthood."[56] Second, the difference between the ordained priesthood and the common priesthood is not to be understood at the functional level. For Macquarrie, "It is not just a specialized function within the general priesthood, a function for which some people are set apart by their fellows to represent them."[57] The apostles received a distinctive ministry from Christ, according to the New Testament, and this was not a delegation from the Church at large. "The truth is... that from the beginning the Christian church was an ordered people. Its order is constitutive, and so equiprimordial with its existence."[58] There is also a common sense argument. "The church, from the beginning was a community, not just a crowd. A community is not a mere aggregate of persons, but a structured body in which there are organs for oversight and other essential functions."[59] Of course, it is possible to interpret these matters in a congregationalist fashion, but it is not and never has been the Catholic way, nor is it Macquarrie's. Nevertheless, even accepting Macquarrie's point of view, concordant with Vatican Council II, more work needs to be done in an attempt to tease out the relationship between ordained and unordained ministry, all part of the one priesthood of Christ.[60] Perhaps the key is to eschew any Nietszchean model of competition between the priesthood of the baptized and that of the ordained, and then to recognize that the purpose of the latter is better to enable the flourishing of the former. This is especially the case with the sacrament of the Eucharist. The ordained preside over the Eucharist so that the baptized may become "eucharistized", as it were, and then be sent out to the world as sacrament of salvation. This said, it is now to the Eucharist that we turn.

---

[1] John Macquarrie, *A Guide to the Sacraments* (New York: Continuum, 1997), vii.

[2] John Macquarrie, "Foreword," in Alister E. McGrath, *The Renewal of Anglicanism* (Harrisburg, PA: Morehouse Publishing, 1993), 1.

[3] For a brief account of Quick's sacramental theology, especially the Eucharist, see Owen F. Cummings, *Canterbury Cousins: The Eucharist in Contemporary Anglican Theology* (New York-Mahwah, NJ: Paulist Press, 2007), 24-37.

[4] Aidan Nichols, OP, *The Panther and the Hind* (Edinburgh: T. & T. Clark, 1993), 128.

[5] David Forrester, Review of John Macquarrie, *A Guide to the Sacraments*, *The Tablet*, 20 September (1997), 1197.

[6] John Macquarrie, *Principles of Christian Theology*, rev. ed. (New York: Charles Scribner's Sons, 1977), 454.

[7] Ibid., 10.

[8] Ibid., 455-456.

[9] For example, see Ninian Smart, *The Religious Experience of Mankind* (London: Collins, 1969).

[10] John Macquarrie, *Principles of Christian Theology*, 9.

[11] Ibid., 10.

[12] Ibid., 457.

[13] Vatican II, "Constitution on Divine Revelation," par. 10.

[14] John Macquarrie, *A Guide to the Sacraments*, vii.

[15] Ibid., viii.

[16] John Macquarrie, *Paths in Spirituality* (London: SCM Press, 1972), 98-99.

[17] John Macquarrie, *A Guide to the Sacraments*, 6.

[18] John Macquarrie, *The Humility of God* (London: SCM Press, 1978), 3-5.

[19] John Macquarrie, *A Guide to the Sacraments*, 8.

[20] *Catechism of the Catholic Church* (New York: Catholic Book Publishing Co., 1994), # 1117.

[21] John Macquarrie, *A Guide to the Sacraments*, 37.

[22] John Macquarrie, *The Faith of the People of God* (New York: Charles Scribner's Sons, 1972), 127-128.

[23] See John Macquarrie, *Invitation to Faith* (Harrisburg, PA: Morehouse Publishing, 1995), 61.

[24] Oliver C. Quick, *The Christian Sacraments* (London: Nisbet, 1927), 105. In the entry under his name in *The Oxford Dictionary of the Christian Church* Quick is described in this fashion: "His approach to doctrinal issues was systematic and synthetic rather than historical, and essentially modern in expression" (2nd ed., Oxford: Oxford University Press, 1974, p. 1151.) Though he is arguably more historically sensitive and aware than Quick, this could stand as a description of Macquarrie himself.

[25] Paul Avis, *The Identity of Anglicanism: Essentials of Anglican Ecclesiology* (New York and London: T. & T. Clark, 2007), 139.

[26] Henry Chadwick, *Tradition and Exploration* (Norwich: The Canterbury Press, 1994), 92.

[27] John Macquarrie, "Baptism, Confirmation, Eucharist," in J. Greenhalgh and E. Russell, ed., *Faith, Hope and Love* (London: St. Mary's, Bourne St., 1987), 61-62; *The Faith of the People of God*, 128-131; *Principles of Christian Theology*, 460-466.

[28] John Macquarrie, "Baptism, Confirmation, Eucharist," 57-70.

[29] Ibid., 65; John Macquarrie, *A Guide to the Sacraments*, 84.

[30] *Catechism of the Catholic Church,* # 1303.

[31] Letter to the author dated August 18, 2002.

[32] Kathryn Tanner, "Towards a New Theology of Confirmation," *Anglican Theology Review* 88 (2006), 86.

[33] Ibid., 87.

[34] Ibid., 88-92.

[35] The various books by Paul Turner are especially helpful in showing how different models of confirmation continue to exist in the Catholic tradition and how difficult it is, as a result, to develop an integral understanding of the sacrament. See, for example, *Ages of Initiation* (Collegeville: Liturgical Press, 2001), *Confirmation: The Baby in Solomon's Court,* rev. ed. (Chicago: Liturgy Training Publications, 2006).

[36] John Macquarrie, *The Reconciliation of a Penitent* (London: General Synod of the Church of England, 1987).

[37] John Macquarrie, *Principles of Christian Theology,* 483-485.

[38] John Macquarrie, *A Guide to the Sacraments,* 98.

[39] Ibid., 93.

[40] See M. Francis Mannion, "Penance and Reconciliation: A Systemic Analysis," *Worship* 60 (1986), 98-118, republished in his *Masterworks of God: Essays in Liturgical Theory and Practice* (Chicago: Hillenbrand Books, 2007), 22-41.

[41] John Macquarrie, *A Guide to the Sacraments,* 165.

[42] Ibid., 166.

[43] See especially pages 10-12 in *Pastoral Care of the Sick* (Collegeville: The Liturgical Press, 1983).

[44] John Macquarrie, *Principles of Christian Theology,* 485-486.

[45] Ibid., 513.

[46] John Macquarrie, *Christian Unity and Christian Diversity* (London: SCM Press, 1975), 82-83.

[47] Ibid., 85.

[48] John Macquarrie, *A Guide to the Sacraments,* 221.

[49] John Macquarrie, *Christian Unity and Christian Diversity,* 88.

[50] Op. cit., nos. 1601-1666.

[51] John Macquarrie, *A Guide to the Sacraments,* 197.

[52] Ibid., 200.

[53] Ibid., 280.

[54] John Macquarrie, *A Guide to the Sacraments*, 169.

[55] Vatican II, *Constitution on the Church*, par. 10.

[56] John Macquarrie, *Christian Unity and Christian Diversity*, 57.

[57] Ibid., 59.

[58] Ibid., 60.

[59] John Macquarrie, *A Guide to the Sacraments*, 176.

[60] This is emphasized by Kenan Osborne, *Priesthood: A History of the Ordained Ministry in the Roman Catholic Church* (New York-Mahwah: Paulist Press, 1988), 341. Osborne provides a wealth of background to the issue in his monumental *Ministry: Lay Ministry in the Roman Catholic Church* (New York-Mahwah: Paulist Press, 1993).

9. THE EUCHARIST

It is hardly disputed that modern Anglicanism has a rich and full doctrine of the Eucharist, one with a strong sense of the real presence of Christ and with a proper understanding of the Eucharistic sacrifice.
Paul Avis.[1]

The Eucharist in Recent Anglican Discussion

In 1998, the Catholic Episcopal conferences of Britain and Ireland issued a statement on the Eucharist entitled *One Bread One Body*.[2] Partly in response to this document – Paul Avis would say "provoked" by it – came the statement of the bishops of the Church of England, *The Eucharist: Sacrament of Unity*.[3] The Catholic document reiterates a fine exposition of eucharistic theology in the Catholic tradition, as one would expect. The same holds true broadly speaking of the Anglican document. While the Catholic document points out quite strongly the church's rules concerning eucharistic sharing, the Anglican document takes issue with some of these restrictions, and objects, in the words of Paul Avis "to some of the assumptions made about Anglicanism... They did not dissent from the theology, but they disputed the consequences drawn from it."[4]

Thus, the Anglican document endorses the five major emphases of the Catholic document.[5] First, the sacramental identification of the Eucharist with the one full and complete sacrifice of Christ is affirmed. The one sacrifice of Christ on Calvary is not repeated but re-presented. Second is the teaching that Christians are united through the Holy Spirit in the celebration of the Eucharist with this sacrifice of Christ, so that they enter into it. Third, sacraments are efficacious signs of grace, effecting what they signify, and are not to be understood in some reductionist sense of symbol. Fourth, in the Eucharist there is a true, real and personal communion of the Christian with Christ, so that Christians are one-d with Christ in and through the celebration. Fifth, since this communion with Christ is corporate and not only individual, Christians are, therefore, also in communion with the saints and with the faithful departed. The contentious issues in the sixteenth century of eucharistic presence and eucharistic sacrifice are now overcome. The Anglican bishops, however, naturally find themselves at odds with *One Bread, One Body*'s judgment that their orders are deficient, that is to say, that they lack validity. Furthermore, they see this judgment as perhaps the primary factor in disallowing Catholics from receiving Holy Communion in Anglican celebrations: "It is scarcely surprising that, given the repudiation of the Roman Catholic rejection of the validity of Anglican orders, they should find the ban on Roman Catholics receiving communion at Anglican Eucharists, even in the most exceptional circumstances, an ecumenical, theological and pastoral affront. They hope that mutual ecclesial recognition will become possible in due course, in acknowledgement of the ecclesial authenticity of Anglican ordinations. They long for the Roman Catholic prohibition on mutual Eucharistic hospitality to be lifted."[6] The eucharistic theology of John Macquarrie was well in place long before either of these documents was published. It is, therefore, very pleasing to recognize the degree to which his theology harmonizes with Catholic eucharistic theology.

The Jewel in the Crown

The Eucharist is for John Macquarrie "the jewel in the crown," the "queen of the sacraments."[7] He was ordained a priest of the Anglican Communion on June 15, 1965. He presided at the Anglican Eucharist for the first time the following day in the Church of St. Mary the Virgin, New York City. During his first week of ordination, Macquarrie also celebrated Benediction of the Blessed Sacrament in the Lady Chapel of this church.[8] His first week as an Anglican priest witnesses to the centrality of the Eucharist in his life. There is a purple passage in *Paths in Spirituality* which reveals the comprehensiveness, the depth and the richness of Macquarrie's eucharistic theology, and which deserves to be quoted in full: "The Eucharist sums up in itself Christian worship, experience and theology in an amazing richness. It seems to include everything. It combines Word and Sacrament; its appeal is to spirit and to sense; it brings together the sacrifice of

Calvary and the presence of the risen Christ; it is communion with God and communion with man; it covers the whole gamut of religious moods and emotions. Again, it teaches the doctrine of creation, as the bread, the wine and ourselves are brought to God; the doctrine of atonement, for these gifts have to be broken in order that they may be perfected; the doctrine of salvation, for the Eucharist has to do with incorporation into Christ and the sanctification of human life; above all, the doctrine of incarnation, for it is no distant God whom Christians worship but one who has made himself accessible in the world. The Eucharist also gathers up in itself the meaning of the Church; its whole action implies and sets forth our mutual interdependence in the body of Christ; it unites us with the Church of the past and even, through its paschal overtones, with the first people of God, as an anticipation of the heavenly banquet. Comprehensive though this description is, it is likely that I have missed something out, for the Eucharist seems to be inexhaustible."[9] If ever a statement were needed, demonstrating clearly the integration of eucharistic belief and theology with the entire fabric of Christian doctrine, this is it. The Eucharist is related to all of life and theology. At the same time, he notes that in the history of the Christian tradition there have been different emphases on various aspects of the Eucharist. This is almost impossible to avoid, but "it is only wrong when one aspect is stressed to the exclusion of others, and this has sometimes happened."[10] To avoid such forms of exclusion Macquarrie deliberately sets out to articulate eucharistic theology in a way that would be acceptable to "most of the major communions of the Christian Church."[11]

This interpretation of the sacrament, consonant with his systematic theology as a whole, is in existential-ontological terms. This way of proceeding is typically expressive of the *via media anglicana*. As existential, the eucharistic reality cannot be understood in purely objective terms, and cannot be an event that takes place *extra nos*. As ontological, the eucharistic reality cannot be founded on any merely subjective appreciation of the sacrament. "The Eucharist is decidedly not a mere memorial or a way of helping us to remember what Christ did a long time ago. It is a genuine re-presenting of Christ's work. In this sacrament, as in the others, the initiative is with God; it is he who acts in the sacrament and makes himself present."[12] From a traditional Catholic point of view, Macquarrie's perspective tensively holds together the *ex opere operato* and the *ex opere operantis* dimensions of the sacrament.

The Eucharistic Sacrifice

While he obviously distances himself from viewing the Eucharist as a memorial of Christ in a subjectivist sense, curiously there seems to be in his earlier theology a degree of ambivalence in Macquarrie's handling of the notion of memorial/*anamnesis*. On the one hand, he seems to fault the Anglican-Roman Catholic International Commission's *Windsor Statement on the Eucharist* of 1971: "... for some reason ARCIC was very biblicist in its treatment of the eucharist. Thus the difficult notions of eucharistic sacrifice and eucharistic presence were made to rest very largely on a highly dynamic exegesis of the Greek word *anamnesis*, 'memorial.' The exegesis may be correct, but there are scholars who contest it, and *by itself* it provides an insecure base for what ARCIC wanted to say."[13] This is an unnecessarily harsh interpretation of ARCIC's use of *anamnesis*, which is not faulted by the formal 'Responses' of the Church of England or of the Catholic Bishops of England and Wales. In fact, the only dissenting scholar that Macquarrie presents is the Evangelical Anglican, Philip E. Hughes.

On the other hand, in his more recent *Jesus Christ in Modern Thought* he develops a much more favorable reaction to *anamnesis*, this time relying especially upon the contribution of Joachim Jeremias: "A further point made by Jeremias and again commonly accepted by liturgical scholars, is that *anamnesis* does not mean just a remembering of the past, 'God's remembrance is never a simple remembering of something, but always an effecting and creating event.'"[14] Thus Macquarrie ends up with an interpretation of *anamnesis* more consistent with his existential-ontological methodology. The Christian assembly remembers, that is, represents, the unique saving action of Christ in the Eucharist, but the foundation of the assembly's remembering is the efficacious, creative 'remembrance' of God. Macquarrie's understanding here is entirely consonant with the expression and meaning of ARCIC's *Windsor Statement*, paragraph 5: "The notion of *memorial* as understood in the Passover celebration at the time of Christ --- i.e., the making effective in the present of an event in the past --- has opened the way to a clear understanding of the relationship between Christ's sacrifice and the Eucharist. The eucharistic memorial is no mere calling to mind of a past event or its significance, but the Church's effectual proclamation of God's mighty acts."

Macquarrie's treatment of eucharistic sacrifice is quite brief in contrast to his consideration of the real presence of Christ. With respect to eucharistic sacrifice, Macquarrie sees its origins immediately in the events of the Last Supper and the death of Christ. Ultimately, however, sacrifice means self-giving, and self-giving is characteristic of the very life and existence of God: "He is the God who is always coming out from himself in love and sharing and self-giving, and the commitment that he makes to his creation already points forward to the fuller involvement of the incarnation and the passion."[15] The people of God realizes itself to the extent that it takes into and is formed by this divine self-giving, that is, by Eucharist. This sacrificial self-giving is simultaneously the ultimate realization of human potential, not in a pelagian sense, but in the sense of surrender to and conformity with the very being of God. The sacrifice of the Eucharist is the ritual focus that unites protology and eschatology, christology and ecclesiology, and each one of these doctrines is but comment on the Self-Giving that the mystery of the Trinity is.

Within the eucharistic rite itself two moments especially touch on the ideal of sacrifice: the offertory (the offering of the bread and wine before the consecration), and the oblation (the offering of those elements after the consecration). In the offertory the bread and wine stand for the people of the assembly themselves as they co-operate with and submit to God in response to the initiative of God's self-giving, proclaimed in the Liturgy of the Word. In contrast, the oblation "is done by the priest alone, for in this he is acting in Christ's place, and this means that it is Christ who makes the oblation."[16] This affirmation that the priest is acting in Christ's place takes Macquarrie into a consideration of ordained ministry through the notion of "character", but in a particularly nuanced fashion.

As recognized in chapter eight, Macquarrie eschews a purely functionalist approach to ordination. He insists that the ordained ministers are not simply persons authorized to perform specific functions within the church, that there is an ontological dimension to ordination, traditionally designated by the word "character."[17] "Character" is best understood as a formation and pattern of personal being. "It is through the doing of acts that character is formed, then character in turn informs the acts." The character of baptism and confirmation is not instantly injected into the person, as if in some magical way. Christians grow into the character of their baptism and confirmation, initiated on the day of ritual celebration. The character of ordination is to be understood similarly. "Priesthood is a lifetime commitment and a lifelong vocation, and indeed takes the best part of a lifetime for the full flowering of priestly character."[18] What has been referred to traditionally as the indelibility of the character expresses primarily God's faithfulness to his enabling grace and consequently, the irreversibility of the process initiated by ordination. The fact that the process may be arrested or not exercised by some of the ordained cannot detract from the self-giving faithfulness of God in the act of ordination. While, however, the ministry of the ordained remains distinctive within the church, it is integrated into and is continuous with the general ministry of all the baptized.

Nowhere in Macquarrie's *corpus* can one find any very detailed account of Anglican debate about eucharistic sacrifice such as that of the late Bishop Richard P. C. Hanson and (now Archbishop of Canterbury) Rowan Williams.[19] Hanson, an acknowledged expert in patristic theology, combed the patristic period with reference to eucharistic sacrifice. His views reflect the Reformed perspective of evangelical Anglicanism: "I do not see how the primitive and central doctrine of the collective priesthood of all believers (or of all the baptized) can seriously be thought to be consistent with the doctrine of a priestly class empowered to control eucharistic sacrifice."[20] Williams, in his response to Hanson's "impeccably documented survey" is complementary rather than contradictory, but represents an Anglo-Catholic position.[21] He emphasizes the uniqueness of Christ's sacrifice on the cross, the role of the priest "in the person of Christ," and the re-presentational act of the Eucharist. Hanson and Williams are a contemporary expression of the ongoing tension on eucharistic sacrifice that made itself present in Anglicanism in the sixteenth century. Macquarrie is aware of the tension, but does not enter into the *minutiae* of patristic and medieval theology. The only reasonable conclusion is that he viewed the matter sufficiently explored and resolved within the frame of his own theology and, therefore, that it required no further comment. Unlike Hanson and Williams, Macquarrie seems to have little time for the nuances and subtleties of historical theology on this particular issue. His methodological bias is avowedly philosophical, but careful, even if brief attention to the historical evolution of the doctrine of eucharistic sacrifice would both enhance and strengthen his already solid judgment. In a private communication, Macquarrie indicated to me that he had considered in some detail historical dimensions of eucharistic sacrifice and a sacrificing priesthood in the second edition of *Paths in Spirituality* and *A Guide to the Sacraments*.[22] This is absolutely true, but the point is, however, that his historical reflections deal almost exclusively with the Reformation period debate concerning eucharistic sacrifice. A more penetrating patristic and medieval study, like Hanson-Williams, would have made his already very fine position even more suasive. The brilliance of his rooting of eucharistic sacrifice in the reality of God as Self-Gift, reaching its climactic expression in Christ's sacrifice, re-presented in the Eucharist, could be anchored in historical narrative that would push the question back long before the Reformation made it a singularly divisive issue. But perhaps this is asking Macquarrie to be omni-competent!

Eucharistic Presence

God is acknowledged in the Christian tradition to be universally present to his creation, and Jesus Christ as the divine Logos/Word is, therefore, also universally present.[23] How is this acknowledgment of the universal presence of the Triune God to be reconciled with the idea of a particular presence, for example, in the incarnation, in the church, in the sacraments? Macquarrie's response is to affirm that it would be virtually impossible to recognize the universal presence if there were no particular presences: "It is very important not to let particular presences be simply swallowed up in a universal presence. I doubt very much whether such a universal presence could ever be detected or recognized unless we were pointed to it by particular presences, moments of intensity, of meeting or encounter. It is part of our human nature to seek those particular occasions."[24] Thus, in the Old Testament, the Ark of the Covenant, the tabernacle, the temple, the *Shekinah*, are to be understood as centers which focused with intensity God's universal presence for the ancient Hebrews.

In respect of the Eucharist, just as the entire celebration falls into two distinct parts, the Liturgy of the Word and the Liturgy of the Eucharist, so the recognition of Christ's presence takes this twofold shape. In the Liturgy of the Word, the climax of this recognition is the proclamation of the Gospel. In the Liturgy of the Eucharist the climax occurs in the consecrated elements.[25] Secondly, Macquarrie sees the congregation's response to the presence in the word coming in the communal affirmation of the creed, and the presence in the consecrated elements in the reception of Holy Communion. Finally, two ritual gestures express in a parallel fashion this dual mode of Christ's presence: the elevation of the book of the gospels and the elevation of the eucharistic gifts.[26]

In speaking of the body of Christ care must be taken to note the three-fold significance of the term. Literally, the term applies to the "actual personal being-in-the-world" of the historical Jesus of Nazareth, the body he took from the womb of the Virgin Mary. The body of Christ is also the sacramental host, representing

Christ and received in Holy Communion. The body of Christ is at the same time the worshiping assembly, incorporated into Christ through baptism and confirmation, "and now being steadily conformed to him through participation in the Eucharist."[27] One might say that Christ has three bodies and these three are one.

After commenting on the eucharistic presence of Christ as temporal and as spiritual, Macquarrie opts for the category of "personal presence" as the most appropriate. Personal presence is not, however, to be construed as synonymous with purely "spiritual" presence, because "a person is embodied and includes a physical presence."[28] His notion of personal presence transcends the typical representation of the subject-object pattern. Personal presence is objective-ontological because it entirely depends on the initiative of Holy Being epiphanied in particular beings, the eucharistic elements of bread and wine. At the same time, the presence is just as much subjective-existential, insofar as this particular manifestation of Holy Being occurs only in the context of the body of Christ, understood in the polyvalent sense noted above. Here again is seen the continuous application of Macquarrie's existential-ontological theism.

As with all personal presence, the personal presence of Christ is the eucharist is multi-dimensional. Christ is present in his body, the community, the presiding minister, the word as well as in the consecrated elements. "Christ is present *par excellence* in the consecrated bread and wine."[29] Macquarrie warns about trying to fix a "moment of consecration" too precisely, insisting that "the whole prayer of consecration consecrates."

This multi-dimensional personal presence of Christ in the Eucharist has been expounded in various theories employing philosophical categories such as "substance," "significance," "value." The central issue is belief in a real, abiding eucharistic presence, but a degree of theological pluralism in articulating this belief is both permissible and desirable. Macquarrie gives attention to substance/transubstantiation and significance/transsignification. He does not give the same degree of exposure to "transvaluation," a eucharistic theory that enjoyed some success in the Church of England. The Anglican lay theologian, Sir Will Spens, seems to have been the first to advance a view of eucharistic presence in terms of value-philosophy, but he was overshadowed by the more famous Archbishop William Temple in his illuminating *Christus Veritas*.[30] Macquarrie notes that the doctrine of transubstantiation has been dominant in the western church for a long time. He considers it historically important as "the official eucharistic theology of the Roman Catholic Church... even if it is no longer held to be explanatory," though he does not subscribe to it himself.[31] Distancing himself from Protestant polemicists, Macquarrie affirms that transubstantiation has absolutely nothing to do with a magical approach to the Eucharist and, in fact, is best regarded as one of the solid defenses against such a position. According to this theory of eucharistic presence, there is no sensible difference whatsoever in the eucharistic elements before and after consecration. "Physics and chemistry have got nothing to do with what happens in consecration; or, to put it in different language, one could never get any empirical verification of the presence of Christ in the consecrated elements."[32] The presence of Christ is perceptible only to the eyes of faith, to a seeing "in depth", and Macquarrie is fond of citing the words of St. Thomas Aquinas from the hymn *Tantum ergo*: "Faith, our outward sense befriending" enables us to perceive the divine eucharistic presence.[33]

While St. Thomas may be the architect of transubstantiation, it does not originate with him.[34] While the term had been used occasionally, it was first officially sanctioned by the Fourth Lateran Council in 1215: "The body and blood (of Jesus Christ) are truly contained in the sacrament of the altar, under the appearances of bread and wine, the bread being transubstantiated into the body by the divine power and the wine into the blood...."[35] The statement of the council, in Macquarrie's judgment, is careful, especially the emphasis that the transformation comes about "by divine power." It was St. Thomas, however, who was to flesh out the details of the meaning of "substance." For St. Thomas, "substance" is a metaphysical term, not to be identified with physical matter. For him the accidents of bread and wine remain unchanged. "Substance" language, therefore, affirms a doctrine of eucharistic presence that is realistic without being materialistic or physicalist. When, however, the austere language of the Lateran Council and of St. Thomas is set alongside the statement about transubstantiation from the Council of Constance in 1417, against the opinions of Wyclif and Hus, there have occurred some significant changes. In the decrees of Constance we read: "After the consecration of the priest in the sacrament of the altar under the covering of bread and wine there is not material bread and material wine but Christ himself…"[36] As Macquarrie interprets this language, there is reference here not to a metaphysical change of substance, but rather substance has been identified with physical matter. Material bread and wine have been "replaced" by the body and blood of Christ. Furthermore, the transformation is not effected "by divine power" but "after the consecration of the priest." The originally austere doctrine of transubstantiation had degenerated into "the semi-magical teaching which the Reformers knew as transubstantiation and which they rejected, as in Article 28 of the *Book of Common Prayer.*"[37] The real defect of the eucharistic language of Constance in Macquarrie's judgment is the denial of the sacramental-incarnational principle whereby material realities become ontologically the presence of the divine, but without ceasing to be material realities. The Reformers latched on to the defective or corrupt form of transubstantiation but failed to advert to the earlier, more positive forms of the doctrine.

The Council of Trent is more in harmony with the earlier form of transubstantiation than the Council of Constance. While Trent affirms a real or substantial change in the eucharistic elements, this is never teased out precisely. The "how" of Christ's presence in the Eucharist is not explained and "it is simply claimed that the word (transubstantiation) is one that may be suitably used, and has been so used by the church."[38] Macquarrie rightly sees this approach to transubstantiation reflected in the ARCIC Agreed Statement on the Eucharist.

While genuinely appreciative of transubstantiation, Macquarrie is also critical of the term. He takes notice of Edward Schillebeeckx, O.P.'s interpretation of Trent: "At Trent the word 'transubstantiation' explained nothing, but simply stood for the Catholic as against the Protestant understanding of the Eucharist."[39] This is firstly an oversimplification because there is no one Protestant way of understanding the Eucharist. Secondly, however, if the word simply affirms a "real presence" of Christ in the Eucharist without any explanatory theory (the "how" of that presence), then the term is quite misleading. It is misleading because it suggests the entire Aristotelian-Thomist philosophical apparatus of hylomorphism, and "this philosophical apparatus is not one that readily recommends itself today."[40] His own existential-ontological view understands the world not as "an aggregate of substances, but as a structure of meaning."[41] Finally, Macquarrie considers the language of hylomorphism inappropriate because it is impersonal language, whereas the language of eucharistic presence is best understood in personal terms.

Another theological theory which is just as capable as transubstantiation of sustaining a deep and rich eucharistic faith and practice, is transsignification. The philosophical backdrop of this theory is the phenomenological and existentialist categories of Husserl, Merleau-Ponty and Heidegger. In this philosophical tradition reality is not constituted by "thinghood" or, we might say "substance," but by "a personally structured totality of meanings."[42] This does not render reality the construal of the subject, finally expressed as some form of idealism. Rather, the linguistic and significant community, of which the individual is part and to which he contributes, determines meaning and reality. This is central to Macquarrie's existential-ontological theism, and seems to bear a family resemblance to the post-liberal theology of George A. Lindbeck. The linguistic-cultural perspective of the individual is established through and by a linguistic-cultural community, in this instance the church.[43] Macquarrie writes: "The effect of the language (of the eucharistic action) is to shift the elements out of the one region of signification into another — from the everyday world into the setting of the eucharistic community. This is not a subjective view of presence, if one accepts that significance enters into the ontological constitution of a thing; but neither is it an objective view, as if the body and blood of Christ existed outside the context of he eucharistic community, which is also his body."[44]

Macquarrie does not maintain that his version of existential-ontological theism applied to eucharistic presence is identical with transsignification as understood by Catholic scholars, but only that it is "close to" it, and is preferable to transubstantiation. For Macquarrie, "no theory of eucharistic presence can ever be more than an approximation,"[45] which could well stand as a twentieth century paraphrase of what the Anglican divine Lancelot Andrewes said to Cardinal Robert Bellarmine: "We believe no less than you that the presence is real, but concerning the mode of that presence we define nothing rashly."[46]

Eucharistic Reservation

"What happens to the consecrated elements at the end of the Eucharist? What people do with them is often a good guide to what theology of presence they hold."[47] If this axiom is applied to John Macquarrie, then what emerges is a very high theology of presence indeed. He maintains that the primary aim of reservation is the communion of the sick and of those unable to attend the Eucharist, and he is aware that this practice may be traced back to Justin Martyr and the *Apostolic Tradition*.[48] Yet, reservation for the sick cannot be isolated and includes latent possibilities for devotion: "For the sacrament cannot be retained or reserved in a merely casual way, as if one could be resolved to take a precious gift to the sick and yet be also resolved to treat that gift lightly."[49] A proper reverence for the reserved Eucharist may issue in personal prayer and devotion, the kind of devotion that seeks to extend the Eucharist to all of life that it may be conformed to its living Lord. The key eucharistic devotional practice is Benediction, of which Macquarrie is a staunch advocate. "Psychologically speaking we need some concrete visible manifestation toward which to direct our devotion, while theologically speaking, this is already provided for us by our Lord's gracious manifestation of his presence in the Blessed Sacrament."[50] Macquarrie relates his first experience of the service of Benediction. He shares one interesting experience from this time. In London, in a transit center waiting to board a ship for Egypt after World War II, he tells of an experience that made a lasting impression on him, attending Benediction of the Blessed Sacrament in the Anglican church, St. Andrew's, Willesden Green: "The bell was summoning the people, and I went in. The first part of the service was familiar to me, for it was Evensong, with its splendid collects and canticles, its psalms and readings from Scripture. But then followed something new to me, though I had indeed read about it and was able to understand what was going on --- Benediction of the Blessed Sacrament. No doubt I was in an impressionable mood that night, but this service meant a great deal to me. Evensong had already meant much, but now, as it were, an additional dimension, was also opened up. I did not know what lay ahead of me or when I might come back to these shores again, but I had been assured of our Lord's presence and had received his sacramental blessing... Looking back, I do not think I am wrong in seeing in this incident a step on the way by which God, in his merciful providence, was calling me into the fullness of Christian faith and worship."[51] In the essay from which this extract has been taken, Macquarrie offers a most commendable apologia for Benediction.

There is more to be said of the service of Benediction. It is something for the ordinary worshiper, standing in clear contrast to theological analysis.[52] This is what he writes of Benediction: "Benediction is a popular service, that is to say a people's service. The clever and the sophisticated do not come much to Benediction, but the simple, the poor, those who acknowledge an emptiness in their lives that only God can fill. Even those who might not come to Holy Communion will sometimes come to Benediction where God reaches out to them though they think they are only on the fringes. I think of some of those with whom I have knelt at Benediction: harassed city-dwellers in New York, working-class people from the back streets of Dublin, soldiers serving in the deserts of North Africa, Indian Christians living as a tiny minority... They all have had the grace of humility."[53] It seems to me that Macquarrie has no intention of patronizing those who have "the grace of humility." Rather, he wishes to underscore the centrality of devotion over above as well as alongside the work of theology.

Comparison with Richard Hooker

The claim was made in chapter three that Macquarrie comes close in Anglican theological methodology to Richard Hooker's way. It will be interesting to compare Macquarrie's Eucharistic theology with that of Richard Hooker.[54] Book 5 of Hooker's *Laws of Ecclesiastical Polity* is the longest section in the collected work and has been described as "probably the first in-depth theological commentary on the Book of Common Prayer."[55] It is here that one finds his treatment of ecclesiology and of liturgical and sacramental issues, especially as he attends to Puritan objections. Booty writes of Hooker in terms that have a very contemporary ring: "He understood the Church as communion and community and that which makes it what it is meant to be: Word and sacraments administered by deacons, priests, and bishops in service to God and God's people."[56] Some citations will provide a sense of his ecclesiology. "Christ is whole with the whole Church and whole with every part of the Church, as touching his Person... It pleaseth him in mercy to account himself incomplete and maimed without us."[57] This is classical Pauline and patristic ecclesiology, but the phrase "maimed without us" is very interesting. "Maimed" means something like crippled or disfigured or mutilated. Hooker seems to suggest in these words that Christ cannot be Christ without us. That takes Augustine's *totus Christus* a stage further. His ecclesiology is never Gnostic, never an invisible church, but a church founded in the very crucified flesh of Christ: "Yea, by grace we are every one of us in Christ and in his Church, as by nature we are in those our first parents... and his Church he frameth out of the very flesh, the very wounded and bleeding side of the Son of Man."[58]

This very realist and high ecclesiology is not possible apart from the sacraments for Hooker. "This is, therefore, the necessity of sacraments. That saving grace which Christ originally is or hath for the general good of his whole

Church, by sacraments he severally deriveth into every member thereof...
(Sacraments are) not physical but moral instruments of salvation, nor bare
resemblances or memorials of things absent, neither for naked signs and
testimonies assuring us of grace received before but (as they are indeed and in
verity) for means effectual... of... that grace available unto eternal life."[59] In this
passage may be heard the debates about the meaning of the sacraments between
Catholics and Reformed. Against the Reformed tradition, Hooker insists that the
sacraments are not to be understood as "naked signs" assuring us of salvation, but
must be seen as "effectual" means of grace. Against the Catholics, he is unhappy
with the idea that the sacraments are physically instruments of salvation. Physics
has to do with what may be sensibly approached --- water, oil, bread, wine, laying
on of hands. The sacraments, therefore, must be morally instruments of salvation,
to do with the intellect and the will in the transformation of persons.
Fundamentally, the sacraments have to do with participation, with grace, with
deification in Christ through the Spirit. "Participation is that mutual inward hold
which Christ hath of us and we of him."[60] "Participation" is a word he uses
frequently for what the sacraments bring about. Christ binds us to himself through
the sacraments and becomes the ground of our binding unto him. "Participation,"
or "deification," or "union with Christ" is a leitmotif of Hooker's theology: "No
good is infinite, but only God: therefore, he is our felicity and bliss. Moreover
desire leadeth unto union with what it desireth. If then in him we are blessed, it is
by force of participation and conjunction with him. Again it is not possession of
any good thing that can make them happy which have it, unless they enjoy the
thing wherewith they are possessed. Then are we happy therefore when fully we
enjoy God, even as an object wherein the powers of our soul are satisfied, even
with everlasting delight; so that although we be men, yet being unto God united
we live as it were the life of God."[61] This is the Athanasian *dictum* in Elizabethan
language, "God became human that humans might be made divine." Hooker
recognized with the entirety of the patristic tradition that the incarnation was not
purely about Jesus *qua* Jesus, but also is "the ground for a renewing the entire

human race."[62] It is not accidental that before he comes to the church and the sacraments he deals with christological and soteriological matters. His is a truly incarnational approach to theology. He placed "his whole sacramental analysis within an incarnational and soteriological framework."[63] If Christ is not *Deus*, his action in and through the sacraments could never *deify*.

This deifying mutual inward hold is clearly true of the Eucharist, but it is true not only of the Eucharist. "The grace which we have by the holy Eucharist doth not begin but continue life." The grace of Christ comes first through Baptism, and this is the real life of the real God: "Our life begun in Christ is Christ..." But we need to grow, maintains Hooker, and graceful growth for him is not possible without the Eucharist. "Such as will live the life of God must eat the flesh and drink the blood of the Son of Man, because this is a part of that diet which if we want we cannot live."[64]

There are tensions in Hooker's eucharistic theology in chapters 67 and 68 of Book 5 of *Ecclesiastical Polity*, especially with regard to the eucharistic presence of Christ and in respect of eucharistic sacrifice. Hooker is silent about sacrifice. This is what Bishop Kenneth Stevenson has to say on the point: "He is content to contemplate the sacrifice of Christ, and to see Christ's presence in the eucharist in terms that border on the sacrificial... But when in a later chapter he discusses priesthood, he passes over in a somewhat embarrassed manner the fact that the early Fathers themselves used sacrificial language of the eucharist."[65] In all variants of the Reformation tradition at this time, sacrifice was something of a neuralgic term when applied to the Eucharist. It trailed clouds of Catholicism, and of unsolved doctrinal issues. Hooker did not wish to be embroiled in this problematic. In fact, he seems to want to affirm somewhat variant eucharistic perspectives at the same time. It is clear, in line with his entire *oeuvre*, that he wants to distance himself from the Puritans. "It greatly offendeth, that some, when they labour to show the use of the holy Sacraments, assign unto them no end but only to teach the mind, by other senses, that which the Word doth teach by hearing."[66] In similar fashion, the Eucharist may not be understood simply as a sort of visual aid, a pedagogical help to the message of the Scriptures and preaching, a Puritan emphasis. The Eucharist is "not a shadow, destitute, empty and void of Christ."[67] Yet, Hooker can go one to say the following: "The real participation of Christ's body and blood is not therefore to be sought for in the sacrament, but in the worthy receiver of the sacrament."[68] This is perilously close to a receptionist view of the sacrament.

But, if one thinks of him now as a receptionist, what is one to make of this passage? "Christ assisting this heavenly banquet with his personal and true presence doth by his own divine power add to the natural substance thereof supernatural efficacy, which addition to the nature of those consecrated elements changeth them and maketh them that unto us which otherwise they could not be; that to us they are thereby made such instruments as mystically yet truly, invisibly yet really work our communion or fellowship with the person of Jesus Christ as well as in that he is man as God, our participation also in the fruit, grace and efficacy of his body and blood, whereupon there ensueth a kind of transubstantiation in us, a true change both of soul and body, an alteration from death to life."[69] Perhaps we might paraphrase Hooker here to the effect that the transubstantiation in us, which is the *telos* of the Eucharist, necessarily depends on the transubstantiation of the eucharistic elements, even if that term is not used. This is a near rendition, if not an actual rendition of traditional Catholic eucharistic theology. Indeed, John Booty does not hesitate to say that "Hooker nevertheless taught essentially the *Catholic* doctrine of the Eucharist."[70]

The question emerges, "What are we to make of these eucharistic tensions in Hooker?" The question admits of no easy answer. If one views the tensions from a position of iron-clad logic, then one might agree, in the words of the Anglican liturgical theologian Bishop Kenneth Stevenson, that "It is as if Hooker were (if the image is not appropriate here) trying to have his eucharistic cake and eat it."[71] Might there be another way of responding to these tensions? Might Hooker be offering an ecumenical eucharistic perspective, an eirenic perspective, a perspective that acknowledges the basic integrity of the Catholic tradition while simultaneously acknowledging the Reformation? Hooker is clearly aware of the Reformation-era debates about the eucharistic presence of Christ. He knows of the Puritans who eschew any traditional view of eucharistic presence, of the Lutherans who *consubstantiate* and of the Catholics who *transubstantiate*.[72] Hooker prefers meditation with silence on the Eucharist to verbal disputation. "I wish that men would more give themselves to meditate with silence what we have by the sacrament, and less to dispute the manner how."[73] He wants no part of "curious and intricate speculations": "(The Apostles) had at that time a sea of comfort and joy to wade in, and we by that which they did are taught that this heavenly food is given for the satisfying of our empty souls, and not for the exercising of our curious and subtle wits."[74] The contemporary Anglican theologian, George Pattison comments on this passage: "As Hooker saw only too clearly in his own time, and as the following century of religious wars more than demonstrated, such 'exercising of our curious and subtle wits' can only too quickly bring us back into a cycle of destruction in which angry words turn to angry blows and theoretical disputes prepare the way of terror and counter-terror by insurgencies and states alike."[75] Macquarrie's eucharistic theology is probably much less polemical than Hooker's. Much has happened in ecumenical understanding since the sixteenth century. But the emphases of Hooker in eucharistic understanding seems to come close to those of Macquarrie.

Conclusion

Macquarrie writes of theologians: "Theologians can only too easily begin to think of themselves as the *teleoi* (the perfect), those who attained to a *gnosis* (knowledge) that is beyond the reach of the ordinary faithful."[76] This is not a temptation to which John Macquarrie himself has succumbed. John S. Bowden, Macquarrie's publisher and editor at the Student Christian Movement Press in London, has this to say about him: "He has proved a successful mediator between the academic world and the parishes in producing a believing form of academic theology."[77] It is fashionable today to speak of theology having three publics – the church, the academy, and society – but perhaps less fashionable to see theology in the academy serving the faith of the church. If Bowden is correct, then John Macquarrie has consistently tried to serve the faith of the church, and the church understood in the widest sense, in its catholicity, and not only his own Anglican Communion. His eucharistic theology serves well his own ecclesial tradition, but it speaks powerfully to Rome and Geneva as well as to Canterbury. He knows, respects, and loves the eucharistic tradition, and yet in his retrieval of it he is critical. The cause of ecumenism is advanced not only through official, ecclesial dialogues, but also through the creative, careful mediation of theology to worshipping communities by theologians like John Macquarrie.

---

[1] Paul Avis, *The Identity of Anglicanism: Essentials of Anglican Ecclesiology* (New York and London: T. & T. Clark, 2007), 87.

[2] *One Bread One Body* (London: Catholic Truth Society and Dublin: Veritas Publications, 1998).

[3] *The Eucharist: Sacrament of Unity* (London: Church House, 2001).

[4] Paul Avis, *The Identity of Anglicanism*, 94.

[5] Following the analysis of Paul Avis, op. cit., 94-96.

[6] Foreword to *The Eucharist: Sacrament of Unity*, 34.

[7] John Macquarrie, *A Guide to the Sacraments* (New York: The Continuum Publishing Company, 1997), 102.

[8] According to the testimony of Canon Robert Wright of General Theological Seminary, New York City.

[9] John Macquarrie, *Paths in Spirituality*, 2nd ed. (Harrisburg, PA: Morehouse Publishing, 1992), 73.

[10] John Macquarrie, *Christian Unity and Christian Diversity* (London: SCM Press, 1975), 66. In this respect it is helpful to note what Macquarrie has to say about heresy. See his *Thinking About God* (London: SCM Press, 1975), 44-51.

[11] John Macquarrie, *Principles of Christian Theology*, rev. ed. (London: SCM Press, 1977), 469. Most of Macquarrie's writing on the Eucharist, while it pre-dates the Lima Statement of the Faith and Order Commission of the World Council of Churches in 1982, (*Baptism, Eucharist and Ministry*) is perfectly consistent with the eucharistic theology to be found there.

[12] John Macquarrie, *Principles of Christian Theology*, 470.

[13] In his essay, "Structures for Unity," in Mark Santer, ed., *Their Lord and Ours* (London: S.P.C.K., 1982), 123.

[14] John Macquarrie, *Jesus Christ in Modern Thought* (London: SCM Press, 1990), 68. This is also the basis of his treatment, though with a gloss on traditional Anglican positions such as that of Cranmer, in his *A Guide to the Sacraments*, 135-145.

[15] John Macquarrie, *The Humility of God* (London: SCM Press, 1978), 5.

[16] Ibid.

[17] John Macquarrie, *Principles of Christian Theology*, 425-426.

[18] John Macquarrie, *Theology, Church and Ministry* (London: SCM Press, 1986), 176.

[19] Hanson provides a fine account of the traditional evangelical Anglican criticism of eucharistic sacrifice in his *Christian Priesthood Examined* (London: Lutterworth Press, 1979), and, more extensively, in his *Eucharistic Offering in the Early Church* (Bramcote, Notts.: Grove Books, 1979). Rowan Williams' equally fine reply to Hanson is his *Eucharistic Sacrifice: The Roots of a Metaphor* (Bramcote, Notts.: Grove Books, 1982), 24-33 are particularly outstanding. For an account of both Hanson's and Williams' Eucharistic theology, see Owen F. Cummings, *Canterbury Cousins: The Eucharist in Contemporary Anglican Theology* (New York-Mahwah, NJ: Paulist Press, 2007).

[20] Richard P. C. Hanson, *Eucharistic Offering in the Early Church*, 26.

[21] Rowan D. Williams, *Eucharistic Sacrifice, The Roots of a Metaphor*, 2.

[22] In a letter dated June 12, 1999.

[23] John Macquarrie, *Paths in Spirituality*, 83.

[24] Ibid.

[25] John Macquarrie, *Principles of Christian Theology*, 474.

[26] Ibid., 449-450.

[27] Ibid., 477.

[28] John Macquarrie, *Paths in Spirituality*, 85.

[29] Ibid., 86.

[30] (London: Macmillan, 1924). See *A Guide to the Sacraments*, 132-133. See the treatment of Will Spens in Owen F. Cummings, *Canterbury Cousins*, 24-28.

[31] John Macquarrie, *Christian Unity and Christian Diversity*, 72.

[32] John Macquarrie, *Paths in Spirituality*, 88.

[33] John Macquarrie, *Principles of Christian Theology*, 478.

[34] There is disagreement about the genealogy of transubstantiation. See Owen F. Cummings, *Eucharistic Doctors* (New York-Mahwah, NJ: Paulist Press, 2006), 116-122.

[35] John Macquarrie, *Christian Unity and Christian Diversity*, 75. Macquarrie's citation is in Latin, and the English translation here is taken from Joseph Neuner, S. J. and Jacques Dupuis, S. J., ed., *The Christian Faith in the Doctrinal Documents of the Catholic Church*, rev. ed. (London: Collins, 1983), 15.

[36] John Macquarrie, *Christian Unity and Christian Diversity*, 75-76. Again, Macquarrie cites the Latin. The translation here is my own.

[37] Ibid., 76.

[38] Ibid., 88.

[39] Ibid.

[40] Ibid.

[41] John Macquarrie, *Principles of Christian Theology*, 479.

[42] John Macquarrie, *Christian Unity and Christian Diversity*, 73.

[43] See George Lindbeck, *The Nature of Doctrine* (Philadelphia: Westminster Press, 1984).

[44] John Macquarrie, *Principles of Christian Theology*, 480.

[45] John Macquarrie, *Paths in Spirituality*, 87.

[46] F. L. Cross and P. E. More, *Anglicanism* (London: S.P.C.K., 1951), 464. See also Owen F. Cummings, "Bishop Lancelot Andrewes, Liturgist," in *Worship* 85 (2011), forthcoming.

[47] John Macquarrie, *Paths in Spirituality*, 92.

[48] John Macquarrie, *Christian Unity and Christian Diversity*, 68-69.

[49] Ibid., 71.

[50] Ibid. See also Nathan Mitchell, *Cult and Controversy: The Worship of the Eucharist Outside the Mass* (New York: Pueblo Publishing Company, 1982), 417.

[51] John Macquarrie, *Paths in Spirituality*, 2ed. (London: SCM Press, 1992), 107.

[52] See Peter Groves, "John Macquarrie on the Eucharist," in Robert Morgan, ed., *In Search of Humanity and Deity: A Celebration of John Macquarrie's Theology* (London: SCM Press, 2006), 293.

[53] John Macquarrie, *Benediction* (London: The Church Union, 1975), 1.

[54] See Owen F. Cummings, "The Eucharistic Richard Hooker (1554-1600)," *Emmanuel* 112 (2006), 218-228.

[55] Henry McAdoo, "Richard Hooker," in Geoffrey Rowell, ed., *The English Religious Tradition and the Genius of Anglicanism* (Nashville: Abingdon Press, 1992), 118.

[56] John Booty, *Reflections on the Theology of Richard Hooker*, 3.

[57] Richard Hooker, *Ecclesiastical Polity*, 5.56.10.

[58] Richard Hooker, *Ecclesiastical Polity*, 5.56.7.

[59] Richard Hooker, *Ecclesiastical Polity*, 5.57.1.

[60] Richard Hooker, *Ecclesiastical Polity*, 5.56.1.

[61] Richard Hooker, *Ecclesiastical Polity*, 2.11.2.

[62] Rowan D. Williams, "Richard Hooker: Contemplative Pragmatism," in his *Anglican Identities* (Cambridge, MA: Cowley Publications, 2003), 27.

[63] Christopher Cocksworth, *Evangelical Eucharistic Thought in the Church of England* (Cambridge: Cambridge University Press, 1993), 38.

[64] Richard Hooker, *Ecclesiastical Polity*, 5.67.1. For a complete account of Hooker's baptismal theology, see Kenneth Stevenson, *The Mystery of Baptism in the Anglican Tradition* (Harrisburg, PA: Morehouse Publishing, 1998), 37-53.

[65] Kenneth Stevenson, *Covenant of Grace Renewed: A Vision of the Eucharist in the Seventeenth Century* (London: Darton, Longman and Todd, 1994), 34.

[66] Richard Hooker, *Ecclesiastical Polity*, 5.57.1.

[67] Richard Hooker, *Ecclesiastical Polity*, 5.67.2.

[68] Richard Hooker, *Ecclesiastical Polity*, 5.67.6.

[69] Richard Hooker, *Ecclesiastical Polity*, 5.67.11.

[70] John Booty, *Reflections on the Theology of Richard Hooker*, (Sewanee, TN: University of the South Press, 1998), 122.

[71] Kenneth Stevenson, *Covenant of Grace Renewed*, 29.

[72] Richard Hooker, *Ecclesiastical Polity*, 5.67.2.

[73] Richard Hooker, *Ecclesiastical Polity*, 5.67.3.

[74] Richard Hooker, *Ecclesiastical Polity*, 5.67.4.

[75] George Pattison, *A Short Course in Christian Doctrine* (London: SCM Press, 2005), 101.

[76] John Macquarrie, *Theology Church and Ministry*, 185.

[77] John Bowden, *Who's Who in Theology?* (New York: Crossroad, 1992), 81.

10. MARY

The widespread assertion that the Reformers ignored the Virgin Mary and had no
Mariology is not tenable.
George Tavard.[1]

If Moltmann represents Protestant minimalism (in his The Way of Jesus Christ),
then Anglican theologian John Macquarrie represents a kind of Protestant
maximalism.
Beverly R. Gaventa.[2]

Mary and the Reformers

In *Civilization, a Personal View*, Kenneth Clark made the following observation: "And so Protestantism became destructive, and from the point of view of those who love what they see, was an unmitigated disaster...We all know about the destruction of images... how commissioners went round to even the humblest parish church and smashed everything of beauty it contained... You can see the results in almost every old church and cathedral in England, and a good many in France. For example, in the Lady Chapel at Ely, all the glass was smashed, and as the beautiful series of carvings of the life of the Virgin was in reach they knocked off every head --- made a thorough job of it. I suppose the motive wasn't so much religious as an instinct to destroy anything comely, anything that reflected a state of mind that an unevolved man could not share."[3]

On the one hand, the ecumenical theologian George Tavard points out that the Reformers did not ignore the Virgin Mary and that they had a Mariology. On the other hand, Lord Clark points up the devastating iconoclasm of the Reformation, perhaps with a degree of acerbity. It is something of a paradox that both are correct. Our concern, however, will be more with Tavard than with Clark.

"Much to the astonishment of many Protestants and Catholics, it is on the topic of the praise of and devotion to Mary that the reformers were most outspoken."[4] Martin Luther's understanding of Mary was very real, was expressed in hymns that he composed, albeit strongly theocentric and christocentric. She is for him the foremost example of the grace of God, and everyone is utterly dependent upon God's grace. "His aim is not to exalt Mary; it is precisely her humility that is emphasized, in order to praise the greatness of the act of God's mercy. It was through grace that she became the Mother of God, not through merit!"[5] "Luther's warmth towards Mary continued to be expressed in his preaching, which remained tied to the liturgical year, because he kept so much more of the calendar than other churches in the Protestant world. Free to choose which he would retain of the festivals associated with Mary, he kept those which could be seen as centering on Christ rather than Mary: the Annunciation, the Visitation, the Purification."[6] Luther also loved the Magnificat, and so the feast of the Visitation was especially important for him.

In somewhat similar fashion, John Calvin affirmed that everything must be understood in the light of the majesty and glory of God. Calvin was mariologically the minimalist among the Reformers. For Calvin, Rome had made an idol of Mary and so in Calvin's Geneva all festivals of Mary were suppressed. Nonetheless, he maintains that "the greatest devotion we can give to Mary is if we follow her in discipleship and acknowledge her as our example and teacher."[7]

The third of the classic trio of Reformers, Huldrych Zwingli's mariology has been thus described: "Mary is an instrument of salvation-history, and a *model* of Christian life, a *sign* and a *witness*, who points to the miracle and mystery of Christ... Zwingli also retains to the last the Marian festivals, but decisively opposes the religious veneration of Mary, and strictly forbids men to worship her, even to call upon her. True honor is done to Mary by caring for the poor."[8] To illustrate Zwingli's position, let us turn to the account of a Franciscan friar from Avignon in France, François Lambert, who had composed a popular devotional work with the title *La Couronne de Notre Seigneur Jésus Christ* about 1520.

Though patterned on the rosary, and containing prayers to Mary as well as the angels and saints for their intercession, Lambert had changed the focus from Mary to the mysteries of Christ's life. In 1522 Lambert was in the Fraumünster in Zürich preaching on the intersection of Mary and the Saints. During the sermon he was heckled by Huldrych Zwingli with the words, "Brüder, da irrest du" ("Brother, that's where you're wrong"). The next day he debated with Zwingli. The outcome was Lambert's abandonment of the Franciscan habit and the championing of the cause of the Reformation. The episode witnesses to Zwingli's anti-Marian sentiments, at least to her intercession.[9] At the same time, amongst the Reformers Zwingli was the one who was most socially and politically aware. So, when the question is raised about how properly to praise Mary, this is his response: "Not with candles, incense, hymns and the like. Mary is not poor. She does not need money. She is extremely rich in every respect; she does not need us. She does not need treasures, not even special Marian churches. But she needs to be honoured in the women and daughters of the earth. We praise her by spending the money we would otherwise spend on candles, to enhance the dignity of poor daughters and women whose beauty is endangered by poverty."[10] Having taken all of these qualifying comments into consideration, one may still say that, in summary, the Protestant contribution was to prune away excess, to eliminate the medieval mariological axiom "of Mary never enough can be said." That leaves a reduced mariology, but a mariology it still is. "'Mary' must be defended from becoming the product of our pious imagination... The most important fruit of a Protestant contribution might then well be, that behind the rank foliage of a mystical and uncontrolled 'Mariology', the real picture of our Lord's mother would be revealed in a new astringency, simplicity, beauty."[11]

While iconoclasm was associated especially with the Continental Reformation, it occurred also in England. To take but one example by way of illustration, in May 1549, Archbishop Thomas Cranmer was in St Paul's Cathedral, London, to preside over the trial of Anabaptist heretics. These

Anabaptists had denied the doctrine of the incarnation. The seat of Cranmer as judge at the trial was in fact upon the altar in the Lady Chapel of the cathedral!

In order to get a flavor of Marian theology, and something of its development among the Scots, we might contrast two Scotsmen who may be said to summarize, at least as a contrast, the place of our Blessed Lady in the Scottish Reformation tradition from the beginnings to the present day: John Knox and Edwin Muir. First, John Knox (c.1513-1572), the father of the Scottish Reformation. In August, 1547, one hundred and twenty prisoners sailed in French galleys for the coast of Normandy. Among the prisoners was John Knox, a captive for nineteen months and a galley slave. Knox describes how he and three of his companions were forced by their French captors to do reverence to a statue of our Lady: "Soon after the arrival at Nantes, their great *Salve* was sung, and a glorious painted Lady was brought in to be kissed and amongst others, was presented to one of the Scottishmen then chained. He gently said, 'Trouble me not; such an idol is accursed; and therefore I will not touch it.' The Patron and the Arguesyn (Lieutenant), with two officers, having the chief charge of all such matters, said, 'Thou shalt handle it'; and so they violently thrust it to his face, and put it betwixt his hands; who seeing the extremity, took the idol, and advisedly looking about, he cast it in the river, and said, 'Let our Lady now save herself: she is light enough; let her learn to swim.' After that was no Scottish man urged with that idolatry."[12] This episode in Knox's life demonstrates the firm rejection of the veneration of Mary in Calvinism/Presbyterianism.

Second is the poet Edwin Muir (1887-1959). Born and brought up in the Orkney Islands, Muir moved with his family to the slums of Glasgow. It was for him a shattering experience for all kinds of familial and environmental reasons. In his diary for 1939, he wrote: "Once long ago when I was sitting in a crowded tram-car in Glasgow, I was overcome by the feeling that all the people there were animals; a collection of animals all being borne along in a curious contrivance in a huge city where, far and wide, there was not an immortal soul. I did not believe in immortality at the time, and thought I was happy in my unbelief... But now I know that if you deny people immortality you deny them humanity."[13] Muir moved in a more "Catholic" direction in his appreciation of the Christian tradition, but it was for him a long and painful process of rediscovery. He knew well a certain reading of Calvinist theology/culture:

The Word made flesh here is made word again,

a word made word in flourish and arrogant crook,

See here King Calvin with his iron pen,

And God three angry letters in a book,

And there the logical hook

On which the Mystery is impaled and bent

Into an ideological instrument.[14]

While in Italy, he had been moved by an image of the Annunciation: "I remember stopping for a long time one day to look at a little plaque in the wall of a house in the Via degli Artisti, representing the Annunciation. An angel and a young girl, their bodies inclined towards each other, their knees bent as if they were overcome by love, '*tutto tremante*', gazed upon each other like Dante's pair; and that representation of a human love so intense that it could not reach further, seemed the perfect earthly symbol of the love that passes understanding."[15] This encounter led to his poem, "The Annunciation," which provides attractive mariological insight:

See, they have come together, see

While the destroying minutes flow

Each reflects the other's face

Till heaven in hers, and earth in his

Shine steady there...

Muir was not a theologian, but his time and his work represent a rediscovery of Mary. His rejection, if such it may be called, of Calvinism, is close to that of John Macquarrie, who also reacted against what he took to be the drab Calvinism of his background.

Mary and Vatican Council II

One of the contributing elements to an appropriation of the place of Mary in the Reformation tradition has been the treatment of Mary at the second Vatican Council and subsequently. Three factors have combined to shape mariological reflection in the thirty-five years since the end of Vatican Council II: *Lumen Gentium*, ecumenical dialogue, new theological movements. At the time of the council, there was some interest in developing a separate document on the Mother of God, but the majority of the council fathers wanted reflection on Mary to constitute an integral part of reflection on the church. Thus, the final chapter of *Lumen Gentium*, "The Constitution on the Church," is given over to "Our Lady."[16] Mary is hailed "as pre-eminent and as a wholly unique member of the Church, and as its type and outstanding model in faith and charity."[17] The Constitution goes on to describe the Virgin Mary's role in the history of salvation, and treats briefly of the Immaculate Conception and Assumption. It insists with the tradition that "there is but one mediator" and that "Mary's function as mother of men in no way obscures or diminishes this unique mediation of Christ, but rather shows its power."[18] Finally, after advocating the legitimate cult of the Blessed Virgin, "especially the liturgical cult," the Constitution ends with Mary as "sign of true hope and comfort for the pilgrim people of God."[19]

Since Vatican II the entry of the Catholic Church into the ecumenical movement has further contributed to a renewal of Mariology. Writing in 2000, the veteran ecumenical theologian, the Methodist scholar Geoffrey Wainwright, made the point that while "Mary has not so far been the subject of sustained treatment in any modern international bilateral or multilateral dialogue," that does not mean that there has been no ecumenical advance on the subject.[20] Since that time the international ecumenical dialogue between Anglicans and Roman Catholics has produced the Seattle Statement (2005), "Mary, Grace and Hope in Christ."[21] Much earlier on the celebrated ecumenical volume, *Mary in the New Testament*, was one of the best examples of this kind of cooperation.[22] The various contributors to this volume establish very clearly "the plurality and ambiguity of biblical portraits of Mary."[23] The *Ecumenical Society of the Blessed Virgin Mary*, founded by the late Martin Gillett, is another example of ecumenical progress. This society was born in Brussels in 1966 during celebrations of the fortieth anniversary of the completion of the Malines Conversations (1921-1926), unofficial ecumenical exchanges between Anglicans and Catholics. The society held its first official meeting in 1967 in London and has produced various anthologies of essays on Marian theology. The upshot of these ecumenical essays is to extend the understanding of Mary across the ecumenical divide.[24]

Third, various movements in theology have had their own impact on the development of Marian theology, for example, feminism, liberation theology. Macquarrie notes: "The new interest in the feminine and the belief that God has for too long been presented in exclusively masculine terms is also leading to a new awareness of Mary and a willingness to reconsider her place in theology..."[25] In the former category one might think of Elizabeth Johnson's recent work, especially her *Friends of God and Prophets, A Feminist Theological Reading of the Communion of Saints*,[26] or Maurice Hamington's book, *Hail Mary? The Struggle for Ultimate Womanhood in Catholicism*.[27] Such works challenge the received view of Mary informed by patriarchal presuppositions, and search for new, liberating understandings of Mary. For liberation theology Leonardo Boff's *The Maternal Face of God* is an example of a liberationist theology of Mary.[28] Liberation theologians try to see the potential of Mary, not least in the Magnificat, for a non-oppressive and more just approach to social issues in Latin America and Asia especially. John Macquarrie was no advocate of feminist or liberation theology, though he has acknowledged some of their values. Rather he tended to respond to more traditional doctrinal categories for Mary, and brought out of his treasury new things and old.

John Macquarrie and Mary

Macquarrie writes: "No ecumenical theology could afford to ignore (Mariology)."[29] A hymn to our Lady composed in 1966, published originally in *Holy Cross Magazine*, May 1966, "Mother of the Church" witnesses to his Marian devotion around the time of the publication of his *Principles of Christian Theology*. The content of the hymn is essentially this: "What we see in Mary, we ought to see in the Church."[30]

Hail, blest Mary! Church's Mother,
Virgin Mother, full of grace!
Mother of our elder brother,
Mother of our renewed race!

You, dear Lady, station keeping
At the Cross while Jesus died,
Heard his voice amid your weeping,
'These your children now!' he cried.

With apostles you were praying,
Saw the Church in finest hour,
Spirit-filled, to men displaying
God's regenerating power,

Blest at last in your dormition,
Jesus called you to his side.
All your labours find fruition,
You are crowned and glorified!

In his ecumenical Marian theology, Fr. George H. Tavard has a fine chapter entitled "Mary in Anglicanism," in which he traces the development of Marian teaching from Thomas Cranmer to the present. Tavard's essay is not intended to be comprehensive and so, while he maintains that it would be "an exaggeration to speak of a Marian movement in contemporary Anglicanism," nonetheless significant contributions have been made in recent times, for example, by Donald Allchin, Macquarrie and Norman Pittenger.[31] These three Anglican theologians make an interesting contrast. Allchin has a particularly strong ecumenical sense and an equally strong sense of the development of the Anglican tradition of theology and spirituality.[32] *The Joy of All Creation: An Anglican Meditation on the Place of Mary* is an outstanding example of Allchin's ability to read the Anglican tradition, drawing out its richness for today. He is at his best in this kind of fruitful historical probing. His mining of the seventeenth century Anglican divines' teaching about Mary stands on its own. This kind of historical investigation is not in the forefront of Macquarrie's theological strengths. He is best compared to someone like the process systematic theologian, Norman Pittenger, as we shall see.

In *Principles of Christian Theology* Macquarrie treats of Mary in the chapter devoted to ecclesiology. He recognizes right away that his inclusion of this topic in a book on systematics may stir a negative reaction among those of a Protestant background, and so immediately he reassures by saying that his treatment will be roundly based on Holy Scripture, respecting the *sola scriptura* emphasis of the Reformation tradition.[33] If one begins with Scripture one sees that the discovery of the "historical Mary" is even more fraught with problems and difficulties than the "historical Jesus." In the gospel records as we now have them the narrative is a mixture of historical and legendary material. The data presented offer us truths of faith, not raw historical fact, and perhaps are best designated as "mysteries."[34] Macquarrie considers three of these Marian mysteries: the annunciation, the visitation and the station at the cross. The annunciation, emphasizing the initiative of God, reveals the Incarnation taking place through the action of the Holy Spirit. It has also a contemporary meaning in that something similar happens in and to the church: "... for just as (Mary) was the bearer of the Christ, so the church, his body, brings christhood into the world... through the action of the Holy Spirit..."[35] The visitation of Mary to Elizabeth was the occasion for the great canticle of the Magnificat. The key word in the canticle is "Blessed." Blessed among women, according to Elizabeth's greeting and blessed by all generations, Mary is indeed the blessed one. Her blessedness, however, "adumbrates the blessedness of the church --- no earthly happiness, but a 'likeness to God' which means a participation in God's self-giving love..."[36] Mary's blessedness in the visitation mystery is a type also of the blessedness of the church. It expresses something of the church's vocation. The third mystery, Mary's station at the cross, too contains an ecclesial aspect. Relying on an insight of the Danish theologian-philosopher, Soren Kierkegaard, Macquarrie points out that Mary's suffering is not to be understood "as only a natural grief at the sight of Jesus' death, but as a sharing in his self-emptying, as if Mary were experiencing something of what Christ expressed in his cry of dereliction; and Mary's suffering is experienced in turn by every disciple..."[37] In these three mysteries Mary is closely linked to the church, and this is where, according to Macquarrie, she is best understood.

The best clue to the scriptural understanding of Mary is the title given to her by Pope Paul VI, "Mother of the Church," essentially the substance of Macquarrie's 1966 hymn to Mary. This title, Macquarrie believes, provides an opening on which Catholics, Orthodox, Anglicans and Protestants may agree. It is an ecumenically accessible title for Mary. Its scriptural basis may be found on the lips of Jesus on the cross, "Woman behold your son... Behold your mother!" (John 19:26). Behind the title there lie two meanings. First, it accords to Mary "a certain priority in the church, as one who played an indispensable role in the Christian drama of incarnation and salvation."[38] The second meaning behind the title is Mary as the prototype of the church: "What we see in Mary, we ought to see in the church."[39]

The Immaculate Conception and the Assumption of Mary

Macquarrie turns his attention in a particularly fruitful way to the two Marian dogmas of the Immaculate Conception and the Assumption of Mary into heaven. "When purged of mythological elements, (they) can be interpreted as implications of more central Christian teaching."[40] Here too for Macquarrie there is a connection between Mary and the church.

He finds the language of Pope Pius IX's 1854 constitution promulgating the Immaculate Conception, *Ineffabilis Deus,* unhelpful: "We declare... that the most blessed Virgin Mary in the first moment of her conception was, by the unique grace and privilege of God, in view of the merits of Jesus Christ the Saviour of the human race, preserved intact from all stain of original sin." The language is unhelpful in that the image of sin as "stain" is too impersonal, and the emphasis on Mary's being "preserved" from original sin is too negative.[41] A fresh approach to the dogma needs to be found. One might go beyond the quasi-physical understanding of sin as stain by suggesting sin as alienation or estrangement. A person "preserved" from original sin, then, would be one whose life "has not been stunted and distorted by the alienation of the race."[42] But there is more to it than that. The Immaculate Conception affirms that the "original righteousness" of humankind was not totally wiped out by "original sin." There is grace in creation, a grace nurtured and strengthened in Israel and reaching its high point in the receptivity of Mary to the gift of the incarnation. "The moment had come when alienation was at an end, when mankind had been brought to the condition of being *capax Dei,* capable of receiving God in the gift of the incarnation."[43]

The assumption into heaven shows Mary, "the perfect type of the church," taken up by Christ to share his heavenly existence.[44] Macquarrie indicates that the assumption of Mary is dependent upon the ascension of Christ, and not simply its parallel: "The assumption of the blessed Virgin is dependent upon the ascension of Jesus Christ; it is indeed a corollary of it because of the glorification of human nature in him."[45] Or, as put by Karl Rahner, S.J., "The (ascended Jesus Christ) did not go to a ready-made heaven that was awaiting him, rather he created heaven, understood as a nexus of personal relations."[46] Primary place in this heaven belongs to the woman whose assent became the vehicle for the consummation of God's graceful plan for humankind. The assumption is the transformation of Mary from her familiar earthly state to a new mode of being in which she enjoys a perfected and immediate relation to God. Since that perfected state is the hope of all Christians, what Mary enjoys through the assumption is the hope for each and every Christian: "It is not just a personal dogma about Mary (though it is that) but a dogma about the church, the whole body of the faithful of whom Mary is the type. Mary's glorious assumption, we may say, is the first moment in the glorious assumption of the church."[47]

As already noted, the Anglican-Roman Catholic International Commission in 2005 produced in Seattle an agreed statement on Mary, entitled *Mary: Grace and Hope in Christ*. The statement traverses well trodden ecumenical ground on the Blessed Virgin Mary, but it also engages the two Marian dogmas of the Immaculate Conception and the Assumption. This is what the agreed statement says about these dogmas: "That the teaching about Mary in the two definitions of the Assumption and the Immaculate Conception, understood within the biblical pattern of the economy of hope and grace, can be said to be consonant with the teaching of the Scriptures and the ancient common traditions."[48] It could be said in the light of the above that John Macquarrie had anticipated this statement.

Macquarrie consistently refuses to sever the connection between Mary and the church, so that virtually everything that is said of Mary may be said of the church, and, therefore, of the individuals who constitute the church. Mariology in that precise sense is not a discrete theological discipline, but interfaces with christology, anthropology, ecclesiology.

The Celtic Mary

The final theological reflections on Mary to come from the pen of John Macquarrie focus on the Celtic Mary. This may have at least in part been due to his son, Alan Macquarrie, a distinguished ecclesiastical historian, specializing in early Scottish church history.[49] Though Macquarrie's interest in Celtic spirituality and theology undoubtedly goes back a long way, it seems to be his son's interest and research that has further sparked the father's.

John Macquarrie finds in Celtic theology an anticipation of his own version of God's immanence, discussed in an earlier chapter. In reality, Macquarrie would see his theology of God and of God's presence on a continuum with his Celtic forebears. Thus, describing Celtic religious thought, he says: "God was conceived not so much as a distant power in the heavens as a circumambient and inescapable presence here on earth."[50] This circumambient and inescapable presence of God did not stand in contestation with God's transcendence. Rather, this fundamental conviction invited "a tremendous sense of intimacy with God," and an intimacy that found expression in poetry and daily prayers. One example will illustrate the theme:

With God will I lie down this night,
And God will be lying with me.
With Christ will I lie down this night,
And Christ will be lying with me.
With Spirit will I lie down this night,
The Spirit will lie down with me.
God, and Christ and Spirit. Three,
Be they all down-lying with me.[51]

This closeness to and intimacy with God extended also to the angels, the saints and especially to our Blessed Lady. The Celts had a very strong corporate sense of church. The communion of saints was a daily experiential reality for them. In the vernacular Gaelic poetry and prayers, Mary becomes a daily experiential reality, in line with the immanence of God. This is how Macquarrie expresses it: "Mary does not appear as she does in a church, in a statue, let us say, or in a stained-glass window. She is one of the community, sharing the home and the work-place... So Mary is in the kitchen, at the bedside of the sick, among the farm animals, comforting the dying.... The Celt spoke of her with an affectionate intimacy."[52] Macquarrie provides an illustration:

Who keeps the night-watch now and over mine?
Who but the Lord Christ of the poor is there,
And the milk-white Bride, the Maiden of the kine,
The milk-white Mary of the curling hair.[53]

Norman Pittenger and Mariology

A New York colleague of Macquarrie's was Norman Pittenger. Though their theological methodology is in some ways very close --- both, for example, find classical metaphysics no longer useful or helpful, and a processive type of metaphysics more intelligible to modern people --- Macquarrie is more thorough and consistent in acknowledging the connections between Mary and the church than Pittenger. John Macquarrie and Norman Pittenger, both Anglican priests and theologians, had been friends since their days in New York, Macquarrie at Union Theological Seminary and Pittenger at the Anglican General Theological Seminary. Pittenger's Mariology makes an interesting contrast with Macquarrie's.

Norman Pittenger, born in 1905 and who was in retirement and until his death in 1997 senior resident at King's College, the University of Cambridge, has been a prolific Anglican theologian. His ninetieth and last book was on Marian theology and devotion, *Our Lady: The Mother of Jesus in Christian Faith and Devotion.*[54] Like Macquarrie in his ability and commitment to mediate academic theology to the general public of the church, Pittenger had the same gift. Dean Lawrence Rose of General Theological Seminary, New York City, where Pittenger worked all his life, said of him: "Many of his writings have been 'popular' in the best possible sense of the word --- for people --- designed to bring the truth of Christianity out of the cloister or the study and give it currency in the living thought of men and women today."[55] While Macquarrie found the philosophical apparatus of Martin Heidegger offering him a conceptuality in which to articulate for modern people the Christian faith, Pittenger's project of making Christian theology accessible to people led him to a growing appreciation of process thought, especially to the writings of Alfred North Whitehead and Charles Hartshorne. He has presented over the years almost the entire fabric of Christian doctrine in process conceptual categories. His book on Mary also contains a very clear precis of process theology.[56] His theological portrait of Mary, however, is not substantially dependent upon process thought. He has a solid acquaintance with the entire sweep of the Christian tradition. Because of his lucidity and the suasive charm and style of his writing, his book on Mary is close to Macquarrie's. Macquarrie's mariology is intended to have a broad ecumenical appeal, and Pittenger advocates a "chastened" Mariology which he sees as typically Anglican, valuing both the Catholic-Orthodox and the Reformation emphases of the Christian tradition.

Commenting on the apocryphal literature about Mary (the Infancy Gospel of Thomas, the Arabic Gospel of the Childhood, the History of Joseph the Carpenter, the Protevangelium of James), Pittenger considers them the products "of a devout but highly fanciful imagination whose details are of no significance for Christian faith..."[57] Macquarrie would be in agreement with Pittenger when he sees such literature as the stuff of sheer legend. Pittenger distinguishes such legend from what he calls genuine myth and into this latter category he places Mary as the second Eve, the perpetual virginity of Mary, the Immaculate Conception and the assumption of Mary into heaven. These are all classified as "mariological mythology." The difference between myth and legend for him is that in the latter category the pious imagination seems "to have run riot."[58] While there are aspects of his judgement about the apocryphal literature that ring true, it is unfortunate that Pittenger categorizes the immaculate conception and the assumption without further ado as "mariological mythology." Apart from the somewhat misleading terminology he employs, there seems to be no awareness on his part, as there is in Macquarrie, of the profound anthropological and ecclesial insights in the Marian dogmas.

Furthermore, Pittenger actually provides, and from an angle missing in Macquarrie, a basis for the doctrine of the Immaculate Conception when he describes so finely the influence Mary had on her son, Jesus. He gives particular emphasis to her maternal role in the formation of her son: "... as a mother whose son himself was a man of faith, we can see that her attitude and her way of behaving was of the sort which follows when we recognize that a son is influenced and affected by his parents and *above all by his mother.*"[59] The question rises naturally, "What must she herself have been like to have nurtured a son like that?" Arguably, we find in such observations the seeds of the doctrine of the Immaculate Conception, an inductive approach to the doctrine, as it were. Such a point of view may be found in an earlier Cambridge Anglican theologian, Harry A. Williams, who wrote of the Immaculate Conception in this vein: "The Roman Church, in declaring our Lady to be born without taint of original sin, gave expression in a theological idiom to what Freud later discovered in his consulting-room --- the overwhelming influence for good or bad which a mother has upon her infant and child."[60]

Like Macquarrie Pittenger emphasizes that Mary is a type of the church and he sees this fully developed in the annunciation. He does not use Macquarrie's favored term "mystery" for the event, and, indeed, is explicitly quite skeptical of the historical details surrounding the annunciation. Nonetheless, the annunciation is replete with theological insights: "The annunciation story may be dubiously historical both in detail and in background, yet perhaps it is telling us something that within the Christian tradition of faith, worship and life is of quite enormous significance."[61] Given that in the process conceptuality all divine activity in creation is dependent upon creaturely responsiveness to the divine initiative or lure, Mary's fiat may be seen as "precisely a supreme symbolic instance of consent to the divine will."[62] Her entirely appropriate yet free response to the divine initiative made known to her through the angel Gabriel makes her "a model for all genuine Christian discipleship."[63] Mary typifies the faith-filled

Christian response for the individual and for the body corporate, the response of receptivity and openness.[64]

Alistair Kee and Mariology

In the 2006 festschrift, *In Search of Humanity and Deity*, Macquarrie's former student, Alistair Kee (1937-), takes a very different approach to the Blessed Virgin Mary than his teacher. It has been described in these terms: "It is a splendid bare knuckle attack on the doctrine of the Blessed Virgin Mary, which Macquarrie had defended in *Mary for All Christians*."[65] "Splendid" seems to me a rather strange adjective to use of Kee's essay, not least because he shows himself unaware of the progress that has been made in ecumenical discussion concerning the Blessed Virgin Mary.

Kee had been a student of Macquarrie's at Glasgow University where he had studied economics for his arts degree before moving on to graduate studies in theology. Economics, along with politics, has been a strong interest of his in relation to theology, and he has published/edited several works in the field of liberation theology. His other area of major interest is probably best thought of as the phenomenology of religion, beginning with his first book, *The Way of Transcendence*. It would be fair to say that he has never made systematic theology an area of special interest. It comes, then, as something of a surprise that his contribution to the 2006 Macquarrie Festschrift should be on the Blessed Virgin Mary, "Deconstructing the Blessed Virgin." It is best described in his own words: "John Macquarrie sees the Marian cult as always directed to the glory of God. If only that were the case. The evolution of the Marian cult is guided by religious assumptions that are contrary to the original catholic tradition. It comes to have a dynamic of its own, apart from and over against the glory of God as revealed in Jesus Christ." He takes the position that It is not Mary who inspires Marian devotion but rather "certain values, religious and psychological (e.g., vowed celibacy, the superiority of vowed virginity to the married state), which constructs the Blessed Virgin."[66] It must be readily admitted that there is something in Kee's critique of the Marian cult, there is, one suspects, an ideological element, though the degree to which it is conscious and aware is arguable. At the same time, it certainly does not present the whole picture. There is no awareness in Kee of historical-theological studies that have altered perceptions, nor of ecumenical *rapprochement* that attempts with integrity to get beyond the barriers created by the past. In fact, while Kee affirms that he is writing explicitly "from a Reformed perspective," he seems uninformed about how that perspective is both varied and developing. Let us note only three examples. First, Frère Max Thurian (1921-1996), a founder of the ecumenical Taizé community and a Reformed theologian, published in 1963 a comprehensive Mariology, that was both biblical and Reformed and Catholic in emphasis.[67] Second, consider the brief but sensitive treatment of Mary by Methodist theologian Geoffrey Wainwright in his monograph, *Is the Reformation Over?*[68] Wainwright has been engaged in ecumenical dialogue throughout his entire theological career. Wainwright acknowledges Protestant fears about Mariology, especially its excesses, but then proceeds to show clear examples of mariological appreciation, not least in his own Methodist tradition. Third, there is the 2002 symposium *Mary Mother of God*, sponsored by the Center for Catholic and Evangelical Theology by St. Olaf College, Minnesota, with contributions from distinguished theologians of various ecclesial traditions.[69] These few examples from contemporary ecumenical theology establish that the Reformed tradition has gone significantly beyond Kee's strictures, even as his questions in their own way may remain very much alive.

Conclusion

Even in a very obviously Catholic discipline like mariology, John Macquarrie shows a remarkable openness to the broad Catholic tradition. He evinces a concern to retrieve traditional Marian doctrines by presenting them in a fashion that makes them more intelligible to people today, and he has been very successful. Introducing Macquarrie's *Mary for All Christians*, his colleague in the

Ecumenical Society of the Blessed Virgin Mary, Dom Alberic Stacpoole, O.S.B., stated that "We have been blessed by all our members, not least Oxford's former Lady Margaret Professor."[70] This chapter establishes some of the reasons for Dom Alberic's accolade.

---

[1] George Tavard, *The Thousand Faces of the Blessed Virgin* (Collegeville: The Liturgical Press, 1996), 126.

[2] Beverly R. Gaventa, *Mary, Glimpses of the Mother of Jesus* (Columbia, SC: University of South Carolina Press, 1995), 18.

[3] Kenneth Clark, *Civilization, a Personal View* (New York and Evanston: Harper and Row, 1969), 159.

[4] Walter J. Hollenweger, "Ave Maria: Mary, the Reformers and the Protestants," *One in Christ* 13 (1977), 287.

[5] Gottfried Maron, "Mary in Protestant Theology," in Hans Küng and Jürgen Moltmann, ed., *Mary in the Churches* (New York: The Seabury Press, 1983), 41.

[6] Diarmaid MacCulloch, "Mary and Sixteenth Century Protestants," in R. N. Swanson, ed., *The Church and Mary* (Rochester, NY and Woodbridge, UK: The Boydell Press, 2004), 201.

[7] Walter J. Hollenweger, op. cit., 288.

[8] Gottfried Maron, op. cit., 41-42.

[9] Diarmaid MacCulloch, op. cit., 196.

[10] Zwingli is thus paraphrased in Walter J. Hollenweger, op. cit., 288.

[11] Gottfried Maron, op. cit., 46.

[12] P. Hume Brown, *John Knox, A Biography* (London: A. & C. Black, 1895), 84.

[13] Cited in Arthur M. Allchin, *The Joy of All Creation, An Anglican Meditation on the Place of Mary* (Cambridge, MA: Cowley Publications, 1984), 131.

[14] Edwin Muir, *Autobiography* (London: The Hogarth Press, 1954), 228.

[15] P. H. Butter, ed., *Selected Letters of Edwin Muir* (London: The Hogarth Press, 1974), 278.

[16] Austin Flannery, O.P., ed., *Vatican Council II: The Conciliar and Postconciliar Documents* (New York: Costello Publishing Company, 1975), 413-423.

[17] Ibid., par. 53, 414.

[18] Ibid., par. 60, 418.

[19] Ibid., par. 68, 422.

[20] Geoffrey Wainwright, *Is the Reformation Over? Catholics and Protestants at the Turn of the Millennia* (Milwaukee, WI: Marquette University Press, 2000), 53.

[21] Donald Bolen and Gregory Cameron, ed., *Mary, Grace and Hope in Christ* (New York: Continuum, 2006).

[22] Raymond E. Brown, S.S., and others, ed., *Mary in the New Testament* (New York: Paulist Press, 1978).

[23] The phrase is Elizabeth Johnson's in her article, "Mary, Contemporary Issues," in Wolfgang Beinert and Francis Schussler Fiorenza, ed., *Handbook of Catholic Theology* (New York: The Crossroad Publishing Company, 1995), 460.

[24] All of the chapters, with the exception of chapter 4, of Macquarrie's *Mary for All Christians* (London: Collins, 1990), began as papers for the Ecumenical Society of the Blessed Virgin Mary.

[25] John Macquarrie, *Christian Unity and Christian Diversity* (London: SCM Press, 1975), 90.

[26] (New York: The Crossroad Publishing Company, 1999).

[27] (New York: Routledge, 1995).

[28] (San Francisco: Harper and Row, 1979).

[29] John Macquarrie, *Principles of Christian Theology*, 2nd ed. (New York: Scribner's, 1977), 393. A helpful situating of Macquarrie on the map of ecumenical Mariology may be found in Donal Flanagan, "Mary and the Unremembered Past," *Doctrine and Life* 43 (1993), 259-266.

[30] John Macquarrie, *Principles of Christian Theology*, 395.

[31] George H. Tavard, op. cit., 134-152.

[32] See his *The Joy of All Creation, An Anglican Meditation on the Place of Mary* (Cambridge, MA: Cowley Publications, 1985).

[33] John Macquarrie, *Principles of Christian Theology*, 392.

[34] Ibid., 393. For an approach to the historical Mary, see Owen F. Cummings, "The Real Mary of Nazareth," *The Priest* 48 (1992), 14-17.

[35] John Macquarrie, *Principles of Christian Theology*, 395.

[36] Ibid., 396.

[37] Ibid., 397.

[38] Ibid., 394; John Macquarrie, *Mary for All Christians*, 46-47.

[39] John Macquarrie, *Principles of Christian Theology*, 395.

[40] Ibid., 397.

[41] John Macquarrie, *Christian Unity and Christian Diversity*, 93.

[42] Ibid.

[43] Ibid., 94; John Macquarrie, *Mary for All Christians*, 66-67.

[44] John Macquarrie, *Principles of Christian Theology*, 398.

[45] John Macquarrie, *Mary for All Christians*, 81-82.

[46] Ibid., 84.

[47] Ibid., 91.

[48] Donald Bolen and Gregory Cameron, op. cit., 85.

[49] See especially Alan Macquarrie, *The Saints of Scotland* (Edinburgh: John Donald, 1997).

[50] John Macquarrie, "Mary and the Saints in Early Scottish Poetry," in William McLoughlin and Jill Pinnock, ed., *Mary for Earth and Heaven, Essays on Mary and Ecumenism* (Leominster, UK: Gracewing, 2002), 380.

[51] Cited in John Macquarrie, "Mary and the Saints in Early Scottish Poetry," 382.

[52] Ibid., 385.

[53] Ibid.

[54] (London: SCM Press, 1996). Pittenger said of this book, "This is my last book...", op. cit., ix.

[55] R. A. Norris, ed., *Lux in Lumine: Essays to Honor W. Norman Pittenger* (New York: The Seabury Press, 1966), 2.

[56] Op. cit., 2-22.

[57] Ibid., 10.

[58] Ibid., 14.

[59] Ibid., 28, my emphasis.

[60] "Theology and Self-Awareness," in Alec R. Vidler, ed., *Soundings* (Cambridge: Cambridge University Press, 1963), 101.

[61] Norman Pittenger, op. cit., 25.

[62] Ibid.

[63] Ibid., 26.

[64] For a more detailed critical appreciation of Pittenger see Owen F. Cummings, "A Critical Note on Norman Pittenger's Mariology," *New Blackfriars* 78 (1997), 336-340.

[65] By Timothy Gorringe, Review: Robert Morgan, ed., *In Search of Humanity and Deity: A Celebration of John Macquarrie's Theology* (London: SCM Press, 2006), in *The Expository Times* 118 (2007), 562. Compare Kee's views with the far more ecumenically informed and sensitive position of Cyril S. Rodd, Review: John Macquarrie, *Mary for All Christians* (Edinburgh: T. & T. Clark, 2001), in *The Expository Times* 113 (2001), 73-74.

[66] Alistair Kee, "Deconstructing the Blessed Virgin," in Robert Morgan, ed., *In Search of Humanity and Deity, A Celebration of John Macquarrie's Theology* (London: SCM Press, 2006), 311-313, slightly adapted.

[67] Max Thurian, *Mary, Mother of the Lord, Figure of the Church* (London and Oxford: Mowbray, 1963).

[68] Geoffrey Wainwright, op. cit., especially 51-53.

[69] Carl E. Braaten and Robert W. Jenson, ed., *Mary Mother of God* (Grand Rapids: Eerdmans, 2004).

[70] John Macquarrie, *Mary for All Christians*, xi.

11. ESCHATOLOGY

Along with eternal wakefulness, Christian
eschatology holds out the promise of eternal rest
and unalloyed security... What is sought is not a
blinkered security, but the kind of security that
comes from entrusting oneself unreservedly to the
truth, who is the one being entirely worthy of trust.
Carol Zaleski.[1]

Eschatology is a notoriously difficult area of Christian theology that demands of the theologian a posture of reverent agnosticism concerning doctrinal details. It is much too easy for theologians and preachers to pretend to an ordnance scale eschatological cartography, producing the kind of detail that brings this branch of systematic theology into disrepute. At the same time, the theologian must be committed to as reasonable an exploration of eschatology as of any other element of Christian doctrine. Christian doctrine develops from the person of Jesus, how he was received and interpreted, the complex impact he had upon his immediate followers and the writers of the New Testament. Eschatology may be said to develop from the resurrection of Jesus. In the earlier chapter on christology we saw that for John Macquarrie the resurrection of Jesus is real. The human Jesus did not die into nothingness, but now lives sharing fully and completely in the life of God. This also is what awaits every individual, the hope of resurrection. The hope of resurrection flows from Jesus as the first fruits of the resurrection harvest.

While this is the hope of the individual, it is for Macquarrie no individualistic hope, but rather must be set within the larger eschatological perspective. This larger eschatological perspective is sketched by Macquarrie in some detail in his book, *Christian Hope*.[2] Stephen Travis, the New Testament scholar, is one of those who recognize Macquarrie as one of the few theologians writing about eschatology in the late 1970s and the early 1980s who was interested in harmonizing corporate or cosmic eschatology with individual eschatology, as opposed to treating one at the expense of the other.[3] Now we shall explore Macquarrie's broad panoramic eschatological perspective.

The Eschatological Perspective

Macquarrie notes the commonplace that, beginning about 1900 with the work of scholars such as Johannes Weiss and Albert Schweitzer, eschatological hope and expectation had more and more come to be seen as the originating perspective of the New Testament writers. The key ideas of the supernaturalistic eschatology that was typical of Jewish apocalyptic are all expressed in the New Testament, for example, the glorious advent of the Son of Man, the final judgment with the consequent heavenly reward and hellish punishment.

The major difficulty for the Christian theologian is to interpret this eschatological perspective in a meaningful way for modern people. Even at the earliest stages of Christianity, there was a growing need for interpreted, or perhaps re-interpreted eschatology over against what might be termed a positivist approach. The author of 2 Peter 3:4, for example, tells us that scoffers were raising such questions as, "Where is the promise of his coming? For ever since the fathers fell asleep all things have continued as they were from the beginning of creation." An expectation of an imminent Parousia, seemingly rendered false in the experience of these early Christians, compelled a re-interpretation of what this meant. Again by way of example, the Fourth Gospel begins to re-interpret eschatology in the light of the primitive community's disappointed expectations.[4]

At this point, various understandings of the term eschatology should be clarified. Eschatology may be distinguished as individual, community or cosmic. As individual, it is concerned with the fate and destiny of the individual person in and after death. As community, it focuses on the society of which this individual is part, the fate and destiny of the group. As cosmic, it reflects on the fate and destiny of the whole world.

There are three possible ways of interpreting the eschatological perspective for modern people in Macquarrie's judgment: to leave eschatology to "a remote and indefinite future"; in terms of realized eschatology; and in existential-ontological terms.[5] Needless to say, Macquarrie opts for the third form of interpretation in line with his theological method, but by way of commenting on and evaluating the other approaches. Eschatology in a remote and indefinite future seems to have been the original viewpoint of St. Paul. The first Letter to the Thessalonians, probably the earliest letter in the Pauline *corpus*, is a response by Paul to a question of the Thessalonians concerning the fate of those who might be alive when the Parousia occurred. Paul's viewpoint is that all shall be translated into glory, whether they pass through death and resurrection or not. Paul's eschatological outlook here is to be contrasted, for example, with his teaching in the Letter to the Romans, 11:13-15, 25-26. The import of the Romans passage appears to be that resurrection/the eschatological events will not occur until the conversion of Israel. Paul has moved from a belief in an imminent end (1 Thessalonians) to the belief that the end has been postponed until Israel has been saved also. He has moved the *eschaton* into the future. This futuristic type of eschatology is characteristic of the traditional teaching of the church: there will be an individual judgment at death, and a final judgment at the end. This approach to eschatology takes seriously both the communal and the cosmic dimensions reflected in the New Testament. It does not consider simply the individual. This is its central insight and contribution.

As Macquarrie interprets him, St. Paul adopts an eschatology which is relegated to a remote and indefinite future. But is it possible so to categorize Pauline eschatology without qualification? There is a strong element of realized eschatology in Pauline theology, that is, an eschatology which is the maturation of a process already begun. Paul, in his teaching about baptism, notes that in this sacrament we have died and risen spiritually with Christ: for example, Rom. 6:4; Col. 2:12), and so we ought to be directed towards the things of heaven because that is where Christ is (Col. 3:1; cf. Eph. 2:6). In 2 Cor. 4:13-5,10, Paul talks about the gradual transformation of our bodies here and now. For Paul, the "earthly tent" is being destroyed, and we are longing for our building from God, not made with hands. We have a guarantee or pledge of this in the Holy Spirit (2 Cor. 3:18). Macquarrie in his schematization has not paid sufficient attention to this dimension of realized eschatology in St. Paul. Or perhaps better, he has not sufficiently adverted to the *development* of eschatology in Pauline thought.

There are two problems with this futurist type of eschatology, as Macquarrie sees it. In the first place, it has retained the mythological framework --- God intervening to bring about the end of the world, and all the ideas associated with this intervention, for example, a final judgment and separation of the good and the wicked. These "myths" of the end do not communicate in his judgment to twentieth century people. Secondly, this future emphasis deprives eschatology of existential significance here and now for the individual. By making eschatology otherworldly it leaves it open to the serious Marxist and Freudian criticism that it provides a comfortable escape from the harsh realities and uncertainties of life.

In realized eschatology the future happenings of the *eschaton* have already occurred. This is certainly an emphasis of Johannine theology: "eternal life" is a present possession of the believer (e.g., Jn. 6:47); the judgment usually is conceived as present (Jn. 5:24; 9:39). Realized eschatology is the position of Rudolf Bultmann who interprets it in existentialist terms. Macquarrie suggests that Bultmann's interpretation of eschatology may be "the most thoroughgoing example of a realized eschatology."[6] Bultmann insists that eschatological ideas be interpreted along the lines of ultimate decision, or ultimate decisiveness in striving for authentic human existence here and now. In point of fact, according to Macquarrie, there is no clear indication in Bultmann's theology of a hope for the individual beyond death.[7]

With respect to Johannine eschatology, many commentators claim that there is a future reference in the Fourth Gospel which cannot simply be overlooked without distortion. Indeed, in the Synoptic Gospels there is a tension between the here and now of the Kingdom and the not yet of the Kingdom. The New Testament evidence cannot be interpreted solely in terms of realized eschatology. The realized eschatology of Bultmann takes us beyond the "mythology" of futuristic eschatology, but has no place for the communal and cosmic aspects of eschatology through its narrow concentration on the individual.

Macquarrie's existential-ontological approach to eschatology takes up the insights of realized *and* futuristic eschatology. By laying emphasis on the existential dimension it draws upon the resources of realized eschatology, and by insisting upon the ontological dimension it respects the contribution of futuristic eschatology. Macquarrie's existential-ontological eschatology will be developed in the remaining sections.

Cosmic and Individual Destinies

We can *know* nothing of the final destiny of either the world or the individual. The Christian hope is not a matter of empirical knowledge. Nevertheless, it is legitimate to attempt to articulate the meaning of this hope, to show that it is not in conflict with reason or with well-grounded convictions about humankind and the world. Articulating the meaning of Christian hope, however, demands a certain degree of speculation. For Macquarrie, "The speculation consists mainly in drawing an analogy between Being and the particular kind of being that belongs to man."[8] The analogy that Macquarrie is referring to is the analogy of being/*analogia entis*, whereby recognizable concepts relative to a known object are applied to an object not properly known, in virtue of a real similarity. Holy Being, God, is known only in and through the beings which it lets-be. Being is present and manifest in the beings. In all the complexity of the beings which are let-be, the human person stands as the highest being. So, we can say that it is in humankind, in the human existent, in the self that Being is most clearly and fully present and manifest.

"Existence fulfills itself in selfhood," and selfhood is unity-in-temporality.[9] There is an analogous structure in being: "Being needs time in which to expand

and express itself, just as the human existent needs temporality to realize selfhood."[10] The human existent establishes selfhood as unity in the flow of time, and the flow of time itself is *in* Being which lets it be. In the Christian tradition, as has been noted in the chapter on God, "Being" is not some divine monad more akin to Aristotle's *noesis noeseos*. Rather, the Christian experience of God is such that it can only be expressed as Triunity, as Three-in-oneness. Primordial being/the Father emerges through Expressive being/the Son in time and history, and continues to reach an ever-growing richness through Unitive being/the Holy Spirit. The process which Being in its tri-modal unity is, is a never ending process.[11] Even when everything appears to be brought to the fullness of being (in Being) there never will be a time when a new degree of perfection will not be possible. The destiny of the cosmos then is to reach out to ever more complex and richer degrees of perfection.

What about the final destiny of the individual? Macquarrie describes and evaluates two different ways of thinking about the individual's final destiny in terms of a future life, and then proceeds to outline his own model. The two major traditional models for expressing belief in a future life are the doctrine of an immaterial and immortal soul and the doctrine of the resurrection of the body. Macquarrie rejects the doctrine of an immaterial soul, the doctrine that the soul is a subsistent and persistent entity distinct from but associated with the body. He appreciates the rootedness of this theory in the history of western thought, from the Orphic mysteries through Plato to the very influential analysis of Descartes.[12] The rejection of a theory which has had an enormous influence throughout the history of Christian theology is based on modern and contemporary philosophical analysis, so much so that "the very idea (of a substantial soul) is superfluous and confusing."[13]

Although anthropological dualism continued to find supporters --- one thinks in an earlier generation of British theological writers such as Hywel Dewi Lewis ---- against the theory of the substantial soul the following objections may be made. It is an overly individualistic view of the self. It fails to take due regard of the fact that a soul/self only comes into existence through interaction with other selves.[14] Implicit in this view is the reification of the self, thinking of the self as a thing, as a "ready made entity." When the immortality of the substantial soul is considered, the problems become even more acute. How could a disembodied, immaterial soul have relationships with other persons since normally relationships are mediated through bodies? Again, at the base of this objection is the refusal to accept an overly individualistic understanding of the self. Could such a discarnate state be realistically described as fully human and personal? Perception, understanding, memory are all physiologically based --- Macquarrie does not say fully determined --- and without sense organs and brain cells would be impossible.[15]

It should be noted, however, in line with the chapter on his anthropology, that Macquarrie does not object to, and in fact uses, the term "soul" in his theology. John Hick's student, Paul Badham, whose early work was in eschatology, criticizes Macquarrie on this score.[16] However, Badham's criticism, as Macquarrie points out, stems from his failure to distinguish between a dualist understanding of soul-body exemplified in Plato and Descartes, and the hylomorphic understanding which has been a characteristic of the Aristotelian-Thomist tradition.[17] This is not to imply that Aquinas held exactly the same views as Aristotle, nor that Macquarrie identifies *simpliciter* with this tradition, though he makes the following remark, echoed in a number of places in his writings: "I would be quite happy to follow the Aristotelian and Thomistic fashion of calling the soul the 'form' of the body, but such a form is itself active and creative."[18]

The doctrine of the resurrection of the body comes in for criticism too, although Macquarrie regards his own position as closer to this than to the doctrine of an immaterial, substantial soul. First of all, he points out that any crude, literal understanding of it is unnecessary. Even the more sophisticated understanding of St. Paul's spiritual body in 1 Corinthians 15 is not free of difficulties. The very term "spiritual body" is difficult. Logic and the requirements of personal identity demand "at least some formal continuity with the physical body, so it might be better to use a term such as 'transformation body' which would avoid the immediate ambiguity and paradox of 'spiritual body.'"[19] For Macquarrie, however, the real weakness of the doctrine of the resurrection of the body stems from some of its contemporary expositors. He names especially John Hick and describes, in my judgment rightly, Hick's psychophysical replica theory as "far-fetched," "straining credibility," "bizarre."[20]

Macquarrie's own approach to the future life is grounded in his consideration of the temporality of the self, "the self as a pattern in time." This is entirely in harmony with his time-shaped anthropology. We have noted above that one of the differentiating factors between humans and other entities is their consciousness or awareness of temporality: the human person comes out of the past (facticity), stands in the present, and is open to the future (possibility). It is the human capacity to rise above mere transience that establishes selfhood, which matures and develops over the course of a person's life. This ability of the person to transcend temporal successiveness and to hold together past, present and future in a "span of time" is a clue to what is meant by eternity.[21] It is a taste of eternity in the midst of time. God's experience, Macquarrie speculates, is analogous in that in God all time is gathered up. The human person in achieving selfhood gathers up by memory, decision, and anticipation in a fragmentary fashion. God gathers up all time in all its fullness. This perspective shades into a process approach to eschatology, just as Macquarrie's understanding of God more than hints at times at process categories of interpretation.

The cogency of Macquarrie's viewpoint does not depend solely on its making sense in terms of our understanding of time. He believes that confirmation of the value of his position is available elsewhere, especially in the idea of time that has emerged in modern science.[22] But perhaps his most convincing argument is his final one: "If God is indeed the God of love revealed in Jesus Christ, then death will not wipe out his care for the persons he has created."[23] The finality of the human person in God, after death, is fundamentally a reflection of the Love that God is.

In describing explicitly his understanding of the future life grounded in this understanding of the self, Macquarrie maintains that the selfhood which the individual achieves in the personal unification of temporality, transcending mere successiveness, is taken up into the wider process of the unifying action of Being. We are "summed up or gathered up in the experience of God as the people we are or have been in our several segments of time and in our bodies."[24] This taking-up preserves the distinctiveness of individual existents in a transformed state in God. They participate in the ongoing life of God himself, but without losing their individuality. The taking-up of the individual existent does not have the quality of finality about it. Just as with the cosmos, there will never be a time for the individual when a further degree or stage of perfection will not be possible. Continual expansion within the expansion of Holy Being is the destiny of the individual.

Two implications seem to follow. First, is the doctrine of universalism. If "expansion" equals the possibility of greater perfection co-extensive with the expansion of Being, then it would follow that no individual existence would ever be finally lost. Macquarrie writes: "If God is indeed absolute letting-be, and if his letting-be has power to overcome the risks of dissolution, then perhaps in the end (so we must speak) no individual existence that has been called out of nothing will utterly return to nothing, but will move nearer to the fulfillment of its potentialities, as the horizons of time and history continually expand, and it is set in an ever wider reconciling context."[25] Notice the presence of one of Macquarrie's typically qualifying words in this sentence, "perhaps." No absolute judgment is being made that would render universalism factual. The function of "perhaps" in this sentence seems to me equivalent to the hope of Hans Urs von Balthasar that "hell" will be empty. In similar fashion, the second implication is that since the achievement of selfhood is always a matter of degree, and thus never comes to an end, one cannot easily mark off the righteous and the wicked. If no one is ever finally lost --- because there is no *finis* --- then no one is ever finally wicked. Everyone has the opportunity constantly to improve, and to strive, under the impulse of grace, for fullness of being. One of the consequences of Macquarrie's view and one which he has noted himself, is that prayers for the departed must change. Instead of praying for eternal rest, prayer should be for constant growth. He remarks that this latter type of prayer is evidenced in the current American edition of the Book of Common Prayer.[26]

Eternal Life

What is meant by eternal life? Selfhood develops in proportion with the unity established or the integration achieved of the temporal dimensions of existence, past, present and future. To the extent that one is able to transcend the series of "nows" and achieve a degree of selfhood, one has a taste of eternal life. Eternal life is then attainable here and now to the extent that one achieves selfhood. The full meaning of the idea goes beyond this experiencing of transcending temporal successiveness. "'Eternal life' is the limit toward which this transcendence of the instant points."[27] Eternal life is then the goal or limit of selfhood because it is inasmuch as mere temporal successiveness is transcended that selfhood is achieved. In fact, Christian theology sees christhood as the limit or goal, through grace, of selfhood. In Macquarrie's theology christhood is the goal "toward which created existence moves." Christ is the one who has realized and fulfilled "all the possibilities of selfhood."[28] If eternal life is the goal or limit of selfhood, and christhood is the goal or limit of selfhood, then eternal life and christhood coincide in their achievement. This is nothing other than the concept of deification which was common among patristic writers. For example, St. Athanasius, a patristic theologian in whom Macquarrie has shown much interest as already noted, says: "(The Logos) was made man that we might be God."[29] The destiny of Jesus Christ taken up and participating in the divine life through his resurrection is in hope and through grace the destiny of everyman in the general resurrection because Christ is its first fruits.[30]

Judgment

Judgment for Macquarrie is part of the providential activity of God. Providence is not God's action or series of actions subsequent to creation. Creation-providence-reconciliation-consummation are not so much separate, successive activities of God. They are rather moments in the one action of God, or distinguishable aspects of the one movement of God which is his love or letting-be. Providence is God's "constant creating and sustaining energy." To have faith in providence is to believe in the purposiveness of reality, in the fuller realization of the possibilities of creation and in the overcoming of distortion. To return more specifically to judgment, belief in a final judgment is a particular specification of the more general belief in God's providence: "... the hope that what is now ambiguous will resolve itself, and the advancement of good over evil will decisively prevail."[31] In line with his "universalist" outlook Macquarrie maintains that this belief in a final judgment has a very positive dimension to it, involving the final transformation of evil into good. The fundamental belief in the graciousness of Being is such that nothing will remain forever and finally unhealed or untransformed. God "is... healing the past."[32] It is not that the mere givenness, the happenedness of the past is being changed. What is past is past and cannot change or be changed. However, Macquarrie believes that the *value* of the facts can change. Appreciation of past facts can change as the person moves into broader contexts. These contexts can shed new light on the complex intricacies of the past, and by so doing transform the past. God, then, is transforming the past in the sense that he brings it into "an ever wider reconciling context."[33] The similarity with process theology is quite striking here, but Macquarrie refuses to dispose of the individuality of eternal life, precisely because of its christological rootedness.[34]

Heaven

The problems which beset this particular eschatological idea, "heaven," are the layers of mythological imagery which have grown up around it and also its egocentrism as it has been popularly interpreted, a rather simplistic and straightforward "reward" for good living on earth. Macquarrie interprets heaven as the working out of the life of faith, hope and love. Since love is "letting-be," that is, consenting to and facilitating the fullest realization of potentialities for being, "heaven" stands for fullness of being. It is the *telos* or goal of life. Heavenly beatitude is the outcome of a total life orientation. However, as was stated above, there is never a complete and utter finality to being, so that there will never be a time when a new degree of perfection will not be possible.[35]

Hell

Just as heaven is interpreted as the fullness of being, but not a final fullness so to speak, hell is the loss of being, but in harmony with his universalism, Macquarrie considers that it cannot mean final loss of being. Just as heaven is the working out of faith, hope and love, so hell is the working out of sin. It is not, therefore, an external punishment for an immoral life but the intrinsic development of a sinful life. The Christian tradition's belief in hell springs from a deep conviction that to be human is to be ultimately responsible for the outcome of one's own becoming. It is a way of insisting on the human reality of freedom.

In the logical order the Christian must maintain that the total loss of personal being which is hell is a real possibility for the person. This is demanded by the personal nature of salvation, involving free acceptance. But in the ontological order where universalism is a consequence of the graciousness of Holy Being-letting-be, there can never be any question of a sinner reaching a point which is beyond the reconciling activity of God. Macquarrie finds support for his interpretation when he notes that "even earthly penologists are more enlightened nowadays."[36]

Ultimately, it is the Christian doctrine of God which is at stake here. If God is the merciful and loving Father of Jesus, Holy-Being-letting-be, then there is a basic inconsistency with this belief and talking about hell as a state of *eternal* punishment. The issue can be reflected upon adequately only in the light of a particular or given concept of God. The God of Christian faith is defined supremely as Love. This is the foundation of trinitarian doctrine, and it is equally the foundation of Christian hope. In order to avoid this charge of vindictiveness, one is forced to adopt a position with some family resemblance to Macquarrie's distinction between logical and ontological ways of understanding hell.

Purgatory

The state of purgatory is not an unnecessary accretion to individual eschatology but in fact it is demanded by a universalist approach to salvation.[37] Heaven, hell, and purgatory are more properly viewed as a continuum through which personal beings may move, from the point of loss of being which is the working out of sin, through conversion, to the point of the most intimate union with God. Purgatory is the experience of conversion in this one movement or process of sanctification. Just as heaven should not be understood as an external reward, or hell as an external punishment but as the intrinsic working out of personal being, so the sufferings of purgatory must be understood as the pain which is an intrinsic part of conversion. The transformation of personal being is achieved to the extent that egocentrism yields to theocentrism/christocentrism. If universalism is the Christian outlook, in hope and grace, then all personal beings will ultimately be offered the opportunity to purge themselves in their movement towards authentic being in all its never-ending fullness. Purgatory is an essential element in God's reconciling activity.

Norman Pittenger on Eschatology

We have recognized both certain continuities and discontinuities between the theology of John Macquarrie and process theologians, most notably Norman Pittenger in the chapter on the Blessed Virgin Mary. It may be helpful to contrast Pittenger's understanding of eschatology with Macquarrie's.

Amid his many publications Norman Pittenger addressed himself to eschatology in two books, *The Last Things in a Process Perspective* and *After Death-Life in God*.[38] Although there are some ten years between the two books, Pittenger's understanding of the last things remains the same in both. Three characteristics underlie his theological perspective. First is his total confidence and trust in God as disclosed in the person and work of Jesus. Pittenger's theological style is passionate and nowhere more passionate than when he is talking of his total trust in God as Love: "My strong conviction is that this God is self-disclosed in the total event of Jesus of Nazareth and is there disclosed as nothing other than pure unbounded Love, as Love-in-Act, as (if you will) the cosmic Lover."[39] Second is his consciousness of maintaining continuity with the Christian tradition. He contrasts himself with those radical theologians who disclaim any responsibility for maintaining continuity with the tradition. He believes their positions to be pseudo-radical because they are in fact not getting at the *radices*, the roots, of the religious movement in which they have grown and share. Faithfulness to the tradition demands a respectful but critical stance. Third is his insistence on a fresh conceptualization of Christianity for the contemporary world. This must be "defensible, meaningful, and acceptable in the light of our knowledge of ourselves and the world."[40] Pittenger's objective, then, is to demythologize the last things in a way which is both loyal to the main drive of the Christian tradition and which communicates to modern people.

The initial thing to be faced is the finality of death. Mortality is the most obvious and ultimate fact of life: "(Death) is an inevitable *finis*; and no good purpose is served by denying that such is the case."[41] At the same time he notes a growing disbelief in life after death, a disbelief fuelled especially by "the increasing recognition that there is no such thing as a substantial self."[42] He deems such a view, with its long history in European thought, as both too individualistic and too atomistic. It does not take seriously either the fact that we are psychosomatic organisms on the one hand, or that our existence is thoroughly relational on the other. By this Pittenger means that we are in our individual existence necessarily tied to and intimately linked with the entire nexus of "actual occasions" which constitute reality in a process worldview. Thinking of the human person in terms of soul-body overlooks this basic fact, though Pittenger himself tends to over look other non-dualist ways of thinking and speaking such as one finds in classical Thomism.

Closely allied to this rejection of the substantial self is the unacceptability for the thoughtful person of any emphasis on individual or personal salvation ("glory for me") which is not inclusive of the rest of humankind. And finally, the idea of "eternal rest" is "hardly likely to make much appeal to men and women who have been convinced that life, as they know it, entails activity and doing things." [43]

Pittenger dislikes the term "judgment" because it smacks of legalism, of law-courts, and does not really express what the religious person means by it. He suggests using "appraisal" as a substitute. This appraisal is an ongoing critique. "We are appraised in terms of what we have or what we have not contributed to the realization of justice, goodness, and love in the world." [44] Christians believe that the ultimate value in the whole scheme of things is love, pure, unbounded love, enfleshed in Jesus of Nazareth. The Christian's obligation is to search, to judge, to appraise his or her life in terms of this ultimate love. This does not reduce appraisal or judgment simply to the self-examination of the individual person. God is the ground of the entire creative process from which he is nowhere absent. His appraisal is ongoing too. It is worked out "in terms of what is taken into, and what is rejected from the "consequent nature of God", God as he is affected by what occurs in the world..." [45] God's favorable appraisal is all that is positively prehended in the creative advance of reality; God's negative appraisal is all that is rejected in this creative advance. God and the self are together in appraisal/judgment. There are two aspects to appraisal: the daily, ongoing aspect, and at death the final appraisal "When everything is taken into consideration." [46]

Heaven and hell can now be seen in the light of appraisal. They represent the two possibilities for the human person: heaven as the realization of our potential humanness, and hell as the denial and final frustration of that realization through our own deliberate choice and decision. Insofar as a person has lived a heavenly life, a life orientated towards and directed by love, that life is taken into God, is remembered by God, is positively prehended by God in the ongoing creative advance of the world, and this eternally. But is there some conscious, subjective persistence? Pittenger believes that, while "it is legitimate to entertain the pious hope," this idea of personal persistence should not be seen as essential to Christian faith.[47]

Conclusion

Macquarrie's negative reaction to substance metaphysics and his predilection for something like the categories of process thought, like the categories of Norman Pittenger, is clear from his treatment of his eschatology. He is fairer than Pittenger to classical Christian positions involving the distinction of soul-body. Finally, what is clear in Macquarrie is his utter commitment to the realism of traditional Christian eschatological teachings, albeit not to their conceptual formulation, unlike Pittenger. Perhaps being remembered by God is enough to consider Pittenger's position to have a close-enough family resemblance to Christian realism, operating with process philosophical categories. Macquarrie is more emphatic about the realism of our finality in God as transformed persons than Pittenger. Constantly Macquarrie's exploration of Christian doctrine is fuelled by his concern to make it speak to contemporary people. When all is said and done, the ongoing generations of the Christian tradition will be the final judges of the adequacy of his approach.

---

[1] Carol Zaleski, *The Life of the World to Come* (New York and Oxford: Oxford University Press, 1996), 78.

[2] John Macquarrie, *Christian Hope* (New York: The Seabury Press, 1978).

[3] Stephen H. Travis, *Christian Hope and the Future of Man* (Leicester: Intervarsity Press, 1980), 15.

[4] John Macquarrie, *Principles of Christian Theology*, rev. ed. (New York: Charles Scribner's Sons, 1977), 353.

[5] Ibid.

[6] John Macquarrie, *Christian Hope*, 101.

[7] Ibid.

[8] John Macquarrie, *Principles of Christian Theology*, 358.

[9] Ibid., 74.

[10] Ibid., 358-359.

[11] As noted above in the chapter "In Search of Deity," Macquarrie eschews any version of modalism in respect of the Trinity. See especially his *Principles of Christian Theology*, 190-202; *Thinking About God*, 110-120; *In Search of Deity* (London: SCM Press, 1984), s.v. "God-triune," especially 174-175; Christopher B. Kaiser, *The Doctrine of God* (London: Marshall, Morgan and Scott, 1982), 124-128.

[12] See, for example, John Macquarrie, *Studies in Christian Existentialism* (Montreal: McGill University Press, 1963), 60, and *Three Issues in Ethics* (London: SCM Press, 1970), 54-55, as well as the earlier chapter on anthropology.

[13] John Macquarrie, *Principles of Christian Theology*, 74, and *Studies in Christian Existentialism*, 59-60.

[14] John Macquarrie, *Principles of Christian Theology*, 68, and *Christian Hope*, 114.

[15] John Macquarrie, *Christian Hope*, 113-114.

[16] Paul Badham, "Recent Thinking on Christian Beliefs: The Future Life," *The Expository Times* 88 (1976-1977), 197-198.

[17] John Macquarrie, "Death and Eternal Life," *The Expository Times* 89 (1977-1978), 47.

[18] John Macquarrie, *Christian Hope*, 117.

[19] Ibid., 116.

[20] Ibid., 117. See also John Macquarrie, "Death and Eternal Life," 47.

[21] John Macquarrie, *Christian Hope*, 23, 117.

[22] Ibid., 122-127.

[23] Ibid., 127, and John Macquarrie, "Death and Eternal Life," 47. See also Stephen H. Travis, op. cit., 109-110. Macquarrie's very wording here is very close to that of his good friend and colleague from Union Theological Seminary, New York City, John Knox, whom he followed into the priesthood in the Anglican Communion. See John Knox, *Never Far From Home* (Waco, TX: Word Books, 1975), 146.

[24] John Macquarrie, Principles *of Christian Theology*, 358.

[25] Ibid., 361.

[26] Ibid.

[27] John Macquarrie, *Principles of Christian Theology*, 363.

[28] Ibid., 300, 364.

[29] St. Athanasius, *De Incarnatione Verbi Dei*, 54.3. See, *inter alia*, John Macquarrie, *Studies in Christian Existentialism*, s.n. "Athanasius."

[30] John Macquarrie, *Christian Hope*, 119.

[31] John Macquarrie, *Principles of Christian Theology*, 239, 364.

[32] John Macquarrie, *Christian Hope*, 119.

[33] Ibid., 120.

[34] Brian Hebblethwaite notes the similarity with process thought in his *The Christian Hope* (Grand Rapids: Eerdmans, 1984), 197.

[35] See also Geoffrey Wainwright: "Although the definitive character of the world to come appears to be such that the kingdom will be incontestably established and salvation inadmissibly enjoyed, there is no reason to think that this means an end of open systems: the inexhaustible riches of God will allow for continuing growth in the relations between him and his perfected creatures" in his *Doxology* (New York and Oxford: Oxford University Press, 1980), 458. It is not easy to chart Macquarrie's influence on Wainwright, whose *Doxology* is dedicated to Macquarrie.

[36] John Macquarrie, *Principles of Christian Theology*, 376.

[37] Ibid.

[38] Norman Pittenger, *The Last Things in a Process Perspective* (London: Epworth Press, 1970), and *After Death-Life in God* (London: SCM Press, 1980).

[39] Norman Pittenger, *After Death*, xi.

[40] Ibid.

[41] Ibid., 4; Norman Pittenger, *The Last Things*, 31.

[42] Norman Pittenger, *After Death*, 16.

[43] Ibid., 13-14.

[44] Ibid., 52.

[45] Norman Pittenger, *The Last Things*, 58.

[46] Norman Pittenger, *After Death,* 52.

[47] Norman Pittenger, *The Last Things,* 80.

12. PRAYER AND MYSTICISM

Though not myself a mystic, I am not a thoroughgoing rationalist either. I can follow Russell in his admiration for logical inquiry, but I part company with him when he rules out mysticism; similarly, I can follow St. John of the Cross when he invites me to join him in the soul's search for God, but I part company with him when he tells me that I must abandon our God-given reason and intellect in the search.
John Macquarrie.[1]

Allan Douglas Galloway (1920-2006), a contemporary student with John Macquarrie in the Faculty of Divinity at the University of Glasgow, and later professor there, wrote: "Contemporary philosophy of religion has been obsessed with the question *How can we talk about God?* But for contemporary religion a more immediate and pressing question is *How can I talk to God?* The two questions are, of course, related. A God who cannot be spoken about cannot be known and therefore cannot be addressed."[2] Earlier chapters have discussed how we can speak of God, and now and arguably more importantly we turn to the question of prayer, "How can we talk to God?"

The Jesuit theologian, Philip Endean describes an occasion, on February 17 1984, on which John Macquarrie was lecturing at Heythrop College, London, on the occasion of Rahner's eightieth year, and in Rahner's presence. The lecture was entitled "The Anthropological Approach to Theology."[3] Rahner's grasp of oral English was not good, and so quite visibly during the lecture which, in fact, he had already seen, he took out his rosary and began quietly to pray. Endean writes of this incident: "Within Rahner's own way of thinking, his impatient gesture at one of his last public appearances is significantly symbolic. Rahner's 'spirituality', the experience of being drawn into a reality beyond our grasp, is central, rather than incidental, to his theological creativity; his creativity depends on his having taken the witness of the mystics, not as the object of some arcane and marginal specialism within practical theology, but as a stimulus to renew the whole range of theological disciplines."[4] "His creativity depends on his having taken the witness of the mystics" --- this interesting description of Rahner belongs also to the creativity of John Macquarrie. He is a mystic in the sense of being drawn into a reality beyond his grasp, the reality of Holy Being letting-be so that it perdures in and permeates his consciousness, and both invites and enables transformation. Words spoken of God by Archbishop Rowan Williams would apply without qualification to John Macquarrie's relationship with God: "God is first and foremost that depth around all things and beyond all things into which, when I pray, I try to sink. But God is also the activity that comes to me out of that depth, tells me I'm loved, that opens up a future for me, that offers transformations I can't imagine. Very much a mystery but also very much a presence. Very much a person."[5] Macquarrie's insistence on God's transcendence and immanence, never one at the expense of the other, enables him too to sink into the ever-present God, and to be found loved and invited to transformation.

Prayer as Thinking

Prayer is at the heart of all religion, not just as a general principle, but as a living existential reality. At good times and in bad, in sickness and in health, with a heart full of praise and gratitude, or with a heart broken with grief and sadness, prayer takes us into the heart of God, into the heart of the divine reality. At the same time, it needs to be acknowledged, says Macquarrie, that while "Prayer is at the heart of all religion ... for many Christians prayer has become something of an embarrassment. Is there a place for prayer in the kind of world in which we live? Is prayer a childish exercise which the adult must put from him?"[6] Prayer has become something of an embarrassment for many people because, while they have grown older and have matured in the life cycle, oftentimes their way of praying has not kept pace with their maturation in life. So, it simply has been abandoned, as something one abandons as one grows up. Macquarrie offers us what might be called a phenomenology of prayer.

Prayer has to do with communication with God. In prayer we open ourselves to the reality of God, consciously and with awareness. This means that prayer is a kind of thinking. This fits with traditional catechetical definitions of prayer, such as that found in the Roman Catechism: "Prayer is a raising up of the mind and heart to God." Prayer has to do with awareness of God, an awareness that is, in Simon Tugwell's words "so habitual that it permeates absolutely everything."[7] In other words, prayer is thinking. Or perhaps better, prayer is not less than thinking. We need to make differentiations about thinking. There are different kinds of thinking, for example, the kind of thinking that goes on in science or in economics. Clearly, prayer is not that kind of thinking. It is not the pragmatic, or the clinical, or the objective kind of thinking, the routine kind of thinking that is all-important and upon which so much in life depends. Prayer as thinking is different. Macquarrie contends that prayer is the kind of thinking that is passionate, compassionate, responsible and thankful.

By passionate thinking he means the kind of thinking that goes beyond mechanical and routine thinking. "There is a thinking that enters feelingly into the world and knows itself deeply involved in all that goes on there."[8] Passionate thinking is thinking about matters that really concern us. We feel strongly about things, and when we feel strongly about things we are thinking, then that thinking is passionate thinking. And thus, we are different as a result of this kind of thinking. The difference is felt. Passionate thinking is sometimes marked by joy, sometimes by gratitude, sometimes by a great sense of sorrow especially when we have been responsible for causing sorrow to others. Passionate thinking is knit into the very fabric of what it means to be a human being.

"Compassion" means opening one's heart with sensitivity to someone else. It means feeling what they are feeling out of a strong sense of solidarity. "We go out from ourselves, we stand alongside the other, we try to share his feelings and aspirations."[9] Compassionate thinking, then, is thinking with compassion about a particular person, or a particular event, or a particular set of circumstances. Compassionate thinking too is knit into the very fabric of what it means to be a human being. Then, there is a kind of thinking that is responsible thinking. This is thinking that requires some kind of practical response from us.

Responsibility is answerability. Responsible thinking makes a claim upon us, a claim that we feel we need to respond to, a demand made upon our persons. Responsible thinking issues in practical action on our part. Responsible thinking leads to *doing* something.

Finally, there is a kind of thinking that might be described as thankful thinking. This is thinking marked by a strong sense of gratitude. It may be gratitude as a result of a positive health outcome, or a thankful sense of well-being in general, perhaps as a result of looking at a beautiful sunset, being in a particularly lovely location. The context and circumstances elicit the thought, the words, "Thank you," perhaps addressed to no one in particular. So, for Macquarrie, there are four basic kinds of thinking that go beyond routine and mechanical thinking: passionate thinking, compassionate thinking, responsible thinking, and thankful thinking. Needless to say, not only Christians engage in the kind of thinking that is passionate, compassionate, responsible, and thankful. Many ordinary people think like this. Are they praying when they think passionately, compassionately, responsibly and thankfully? It would be arrogant, suggests Macquarrie, to say *tout court* that when people are thinking in these ways, even when they have no intention to pray, they are in fact praying. That would be a complete disregard of the integrity of such people. And yet, even if people are unaware of God when they think passionately, compassionately, responsibly and thankfully, they are engaged in what might be called "anonymous praying," though Macquarrie does not actually use this term. There is a fundamental acknowledgement on their part, through their thinking, of something more than the isolated ego. These four kinds of thinking seem to take the person out from the imprisoned confines of the ego to recognize and to acknowledge something more. For Christians that "something more" is the reality of God. Thinking in these four ways is acknowledging the reality of God, even if that God is not formally named as such. God may be known without being named. This leads Macquarrie to conclude: "Prayer is a fundamental style of thinking, passionate and compassionate, responsible and thankful, that is deeply rooted in our humanity and that manifests itself not only among believers but also among serious minded people who do not profess any religious faith. Yet it seems to me that if we follow out the instinct to pray that is in all of us, it will finally bring us to faith in God."[10] It is not in his view inevitable that passionate, compassionate, responsible and thankful thinking will end up in conscious relationship with God but it certainly becomes more likely. To think in these ways is anonymously to think about God and his ways with humankind. At the very least, thinking like this is very close to prayer.

The four ways of thinking – passionate, compassionate, responsible, and thankful – really are the correlate of the four traditional modes of Christian prayer: adoration, contrition, thanksgiving, and supplication. If passionate thinking moves the person out of the immediacy of self concern, if it moves one out of the routine of ordinary trivial daily round of living and thinking, this is close to what has traditionally been called "adoration." Adoration for Christians is sheer awareness of God, an awareness that trans-figures and transforms. We could say that it is a passionate awareness. "Adoration" comes from two Latin words that imply movement out of oneself: *ad*, meaning "towards," and *orare*, meaning "to pray." It is a cumulatively intense awareness of and concentration on God as sheerly present. Patristic theologian, Brian Daley, writes: "The heart of Christian prayer, both for the individual alone and in the gathered community, has always been worship, adoration, the disinterested and preoccupying acknowledgment that at the heart of our reality lies a good and loving and self-dispensing Mystery who is Truth itself."[11] The foundational passage in Holy Scripture in this regard is surely that passage attributed to St Paul in the Acts of the Apostles, when St Paul is in Athens. Acts 17:28: "In (God) we live and move and have our being." To be is to be presenced in God. Adoration is the graceful recognition that it is so, that one is so. Consequently, Macquarrie maintains that adoration changes a person: "The person who loses himself in the wondering contemplation of God begins to reflect something of the divine glory so that the image of God in which he was made becomes more manifest in his being."[12] Adoration is passionate thinking in a higher key.

Contrition is saying that one is sorry, and contrition is another form of passionate thinking. It is taking ownership of moral failure, sin before God, not in the direction of excessive guilt and anxiety so much as recognizing that in the enveloping presence of God whose best name is Love, one is so unlovely, and that one has been so unlovely to one's sisters and brothers. One author in the tradition of Benedictine spirituality comments helpfully here: "It is humbling to stand before God with our failures, wounds, chaos, vulnerability. I think we all know deep down that it is only by facing them that we can hope to enlighten the darkness. This means that we must start by grieving honestly and without pretence or excuse."[13] This is passionate thinking in a contrite mode. Contrition is passionate thinking in a higher key also.

Thanksgiving is the third of the Christian modes of prayer. It is surely no mere coincidence that "Thanksgiving" is the word used for the central Christian act of prayer and worship, the Eucharist, *Eucharistia*. To say, "Thanks," is to acknowledge a gift and a gift-giver, or in Herbert McCabe's words, "To say thank you for a gift (or as the Greeks would say, to make a eucharist of it) is to recognize it, to think of it, as a communication of love."[14] Thanksgiving is thankful thinking in a higher key.

Finally, there is supplication. This is the mode of prayer in which God is petitioned. It is a form of prayer that comes with the highest recommendation, that of Jesus in the Lord's Prayer. The faithful have a very strong sense of praying for one another, and with trust, of placing all their needs in God's providential hands. At the same time, there is surely some awareness that requests to God should not be superficially egocentric or obviously trivial. One Christian scientist, Chet Raymo, makes this very negative comment about supplication, or petitionary prayer: "For many people, the entire purpose of prayer is to invoke God's intervention in the course of their daily lives, to adjust the tilt of the universe in their personal favor, to redirect the stream of time ever so marginally so that benefices flow their way... I struggle to shed the shabby shawl of petitionary and formulaic prayer that I inherited as a child --- to reject the default syllables 'Me, Lord, Me' --- so that I might attend to *things* --- to swallows and auroras --- to the voice that whispers in *all* of creation, to the voice that *is* all of creation."[15] It is difficult not acknowledge the experiential reality in Raymo's words. However, Macquarrie retrieves an understanding of petitionary prayer that transcends the "shabby shawl." It is more a matter of acknowledging God's holy permeative presence in creation, human interconnectedness or communion, and the mysterious but powerful engagement of both. Macquarrie put is thus: "Basically, it seems to me that intercessory prayer provides, as it were, openings into the dense texture of the human situation through which can come the creative and healing power of the reality we call God; and because within that human situation our lives are all bound together in a mysterious solidarity, then God's power is able to operate far beyond the particular person who offers the prayer, though through him. Prayer, as petition and intercession, helps to make the human reality porous to the divine reality – the whole human reality, and not only that part of it actively engaged in prayer."[16] This seems to me to avoid any suggestion of magic or manipulation, and philosophically, to be about as far as one can go in terms of an intelligible account of petitionary prayer. To ask something from God, to ask a favor of God, really is to enter into the mystery that is God, consciously and with awareness, opening our minds and hearts to the transforming and transfiguring reality of his presence. Human need is laid before this God, always caring, always loving, never absent from the human situation. That is what is meant by making the human reality porous to the divine reality. Supplication, or petitionary prayer, or intercession are all forms of responsible thinking, responsible acting, in a higher key. What petition adds to responsible thinking is an acknowledgement of being in God, of living and moving in God, and of fundamentally knowing that all shall be well.

There are very definite benefits to prayer. Prayer promotes a sense of unity or wholeness in life. If prayer is thinking in the ways described earlier, then in

Macquarrie's terms: "To think of things in the presence of God and in the light of Christ is already to experience a meaning in life and to let our many separate acts be brought together in a connected unity... Prayer enables us to see things in perspective, to attain the vision of them in their unity and interrelatedness rather than as just so many separate items. Prayer changes our vision of the world, and so influences action in it."[17]

When our minds are not functioning discursively, we are not thinking. We are wordless. This can be difficult to imagine since silence is so seldom found, we are so seldom without words, without music, without sound. But perhaps this analogy might help: two people in love. To begin with they are probably silent in each other's presence, not knowing quite what to say. Then they reach a point of confidence with each other, a certain ease with each other that issues in lots of words. "They hear each other's history and plans over and over again, they spend endless hours in exchanging confidences and exploring each other's mind. But eventually silence returns. However, this is a new kind of silence. It is not the silence of the blank mind, the mind that has yet to speak. It is the silence of the full mind, when all has been spoken and summed up and understood, and a new level of communing has been established."[18] This is like contemplation, like the silence of contemplation. It is not empty but full. Yet there is no need for a lot of words, and indeed there may be no need for words at all. It is an experience in which the human mind, as Macquarrie has it, "overflows with the fullness of divine truth, and we are given a foretaste here and now of the vision of God, the vision that gathers up everything in itself."[19]

Prayer has to do with communication with God. This is the case even with what is called "silent prayer," because "like silence in music or a significant silence in conversation, (it) has meaning only in a context that can be heard and understood."[20] This communicative aspect of prayer is at its most obvious when a Christian prays verbally, speaks to God. In Macquarrie's understanding, and indeed here he represents the best of the Christian tradition, our human address to God in prayer is a situation in which God is already ahead of us, so to speak, taking the initiative: "... we must say of prayer... that God himself is its author. It is unitive Being (the Holy Spirit) that moves us to prayer, in response to the self-communication of Being, a communication that is possible because Being is immanent in every being."[21]

This takes us to the very heart of prayer. It is not something that we humans do in order to make God present to us. God is never absent. It is not something we do to make God aware of us and our needs. God is never unaware. Christian prayer, rather, is the mechanism in and through which God reaches out to creation, to the high point of creation in human persons, in order to give himself and to share his existence. There is an entelechy to human existence, to existence as such, and that consists in the divine transformation of what is begun in creation, definitively shaped in reconciliation, and is being brought to consummation, all in and through Jesus Christ, as expressive Being. Approached in this way prayer can never be understood as an entirely discrete action. It is not "some special department of life, but continuous with all our activities."[22]

Varieties of Spirituality

"The eucharist is the center of Christian prayer and worship, but it has become surrounded by many other acts of prayer and devotion. These are designed to extend the pattern of the eucharist into all of life."[23] Macquarrie's perspective here echoes that of Vatican Council II's "Constitution on the Sacred Liturgy." While the Eucharist is the source and summit of Christian life, it must be supported and surrounded by other forms of prayer and devotion.[24] The primary focus of this eucharistic extension into the whole of life is the Liturgy of the Hours, but it is not the only form of prayer and spirituality.

Since every person is in some degree unique, "there must be many patterns of spirituality to suit the many needs and temperaments."[25] Throughout the sweep of the Christian tradition different types of spirituality have come into being, meeting the different needs and temperaments. However, within this great and legitimate plurality, "the vision itself is one and exercises a control over the plurality of spiritual disciplines."[26] There is a classic pattern to the vision.

The Shape of Christian Worship

"For the fundamental shape of Christian worship, we turn again to the eucharist, as the norm of such worship."[27] Throughout the Christian Churches which celebrate the Eucharist as norm there is a certain ritual flexibility, but, at the same time, a definite threefold sequence is discernible: penitence, the ministry of the word, the Eucharist proper.

Penitence may involve, as in the Catholic Mass, a formal aspect as in the penitential part of the introductory rites. Confession of and sorrow for sin is made to God before the assembly moves on to the praise of God in the Gloria. Even in those churches whose liturgy is somewhat different, however, penitence ought to take place before participation in public worship in line with the Pauline recommendation in 1 Cor. 11 about self-examination before receiving Holy Communion. In terms of the classic description of the spiritual life in the Christian tradition, penitence corresponds to what has been called "the purgative way."

The ministry of the word is based on the appointed readings from Holy Scripture, the homily and the recitation of the creed. This corresponds to "the illuminative way," as the assembly hears the good news and renews and confirms its faith. The Eucharist proper, the consecration of the elements and the sharing in Holy Communion is best understood as "incorporation into the body of Christ." This corresponds in the classic schema to "the unitive way."

This classic eucharistic shape of Christian worship finds further expansion in the liturgical cycle of the Christian year. "The penitential seasons of Advent and Lent lead the worshippers along the purgative way. The remembering and proclaiming of God's mighty acts in Christ and the new life which they open to mankind is the illuminative way that instructs and confirms the worshippers in faith. And the so-called 'green Sundays' that follow the feasts of Whitsuntide and

Trinity Sunday are the period of growth and sanctification when the unitive action of the Spirit builds up the church, so that we can speak of the unitive way."[28]

This approach of Macquarrie's is most helpful and expressive of eucharistic ecclesiology. The first axiom of eucharistic ecclesiology is that "the Eucharist makes the church."[29] The Eucharist is the text that inscribes itself on the entire shape of the Christian's life. He puts it like this: "What we are saying then is that eucharistic worship compresses the Christian life into the action of the liturgy... Worship concentrates existence by creating selfhood and confirming the existent to Christ; and this process of conformation is promoted by the summing up in the act of worship of the form and order of the Christian life."[30] In some quarters today, even among Roman Catholic theologians, there is a suggestion that the Eucharist no longer ought to enjoy this normative character and place in Christian life. The centrality of the Eucharist is sometimes seen as an assumption of "northern hemisphere Catholicism," and to that extent as an imposition on the innate religiosity of non-northern hemisphere peoples and cultures.[31] This would negate the catholicity of the Eucharist, eliminating its power as trans-cultural gift of unity. Macquarrie's perspective not only sees the Eucharist as central and normative for Christianity as a whole, but, indeed, shapes the entirety of Christian prayer and life.

Comparison with Karl Rahner, SJ

On John Macquarrie's desk in his home there is a framed photograph of himself and Karl Rahner, SJ taken on the grounds of Christ Church, the University of Oxford, just weeks before Rahner died. The picture frames not just the images of the two theologians, but also Macquarrie's relationship with Rahner. Earlier in this book we have noted Macquarrie's relationship to contemporary Catholic theology by outlining the basics of theology exemplified in Karl Rahner and Hans Urs von Balthasar. Now we look at Rahner's approach to prayer, so as to see in both him and Macquarrie a concern with prayer and a theology of prayer that speaks to modern people. It makes sense to contrast Rahner's theology of prayer with Macquarrie's.

In an interview given on his seventy-fifth birthday, Rahner made these comments on his book, *On Prayer:* "The little book *On Prayer* is... for me just as important as those more scholarly matters --- even though it is 'only' a devotional book."[32] He writes: "Prayer is not easy. It is not the speaking of words or the hypnotic spell of the recited formula; it is the raising of the heart and mind to God in constantly renewed acts of love."[33] Our lives are lived out within a certain context of ambiguity, that is, the quality of having more than one meaning. The meaning of life is not immediately and transparently clear to us. Such final and unmistakable clarity is available only in heaven. "Only in heaven can (one) fully achieve the syntheses of all one's faculties, of all the energies of one's being, in the contemplation of the beatific vision. Here on earth, hedged in by the things of the senses, such synthesis is impossible...; and yet, in prayer, though 'through a glass in a dark manner' one looks upon God and comes as near as one can to that unity of action and purpose for which the heart has a deep and secret longing."[34]

"Prayer is the opening of the heart to God,"[35] the God who is simply present to us, but there are obstacles to this opening. Rahner points to two: escapism and despair. "Escapism" attempts to deal with the restlessness of the human heart by offering a way out, an exit from this restlessness, by saturating the heart in "debris." "Filling our lives in the same futility, frustration, monotony, chatter, and all that weary swirl of pointless striving we call human life."[36] "Despair," or what he terms "chronic despair," is settling for the apparent normalcy of self-control in life, self-direction, informed by societal expectations. "Those who have settled down to this chronic despair preserve their self-control, appear to be leading --- and regard themselves as leading --- a perfectly natural life. They behave reasonably, work conscientiously, observe standards of decency, marry, found a settled home, discuss the arts and sciences. Occasionally, they like to indulge in a little speculation about the meaning and value of human life, or to listen to such speculation."[37] It's all tantalizingly reasonable and normal and even desirable, but without prayer, this chronic despair is death-dealing. Behind it, says Rahner, lies "that wound from which the heart is bleeding to spiritual death."[38] Without the transforming awareness of God we die. So, we must "dig it out, so to speak, from under the refuse of the ordinary business of life."[39]

Both escapism and chronic despair fail because they are ultimately egocentric. The pulsing center is the self, the ego, and not God, and to that extent it is not only deficient but destructive. Instead of being ego-centric, the heart, to find genuine and lasting fulfillment must be ec-centric, that is, it must find its true center outside the self, in God. Rahner writes: "Yet, by a splendid paradox, it can be said that in ceasing to be himself the center of his life, (man) becomes more entirely one with himself; because God is more the true center of our being than we are ourselves. The sheer immensity of God urges us to realize our being to its fullest through transcending the limitations imposed by choosing to remain our own center."[40]

How then in practical terms is this eccentricity, this centeredness in God, achieved especially if one is unaccustomed to regular prayer? Rahner's answer is very straightforward, and amounts to saying, "Just do it!" Here are his words: "... (One) must take the initial step of laying aside... paralyzing anxiety. If (a person) feels incapable of praying, he must nevertheless kneel, join his hands, speak words of prayer even if he feels that these words come only from his lips and that his heart remains unmoved."[41] The very discipline of "just doing it" is an effective step toward the opening of the heart to God.

For Rahner there is a profound sense in which this opening up of the heart cannot fail. It cannot fail because the very doing of it demonstrates our personal acknowledgment, however limited, that our hearts are restless and God is the *terminus a quo* and the *terminus ad quem* of the restlessness. Citing especially those famous words of Augustine, Rahner concludes: "For deep in our hearts there is a profound restlessness, because God has given us a thirst for the infinite, for the incomprehensible, for himself: 'Thou hast made us for thyself, O Lord...

and our heart is restless until it rests in Thee.' Deep in our buried heart, we find this seed of the divine, this restless reaching out toward something infinitely beyond the things of this world..."[42] This restlessness in the human heart is not a human achievement. It is not a restlessness created by human beings. It is just there. It is given with our existence so that this restlessness for God is a gift from God: "A thirst for the infinite has been made part of the very essence of the human soul... The paradox here is that we must love God with a love implanted in us by God; for this love... is a free gift of God, beyond our power to achieve or to merit by our own unaided efforts... When, under the guidance of grace, we recognize this vague yearning as a thirst for infinity, for God, the love of God comes alive in our souls. Deeply implanted in human nature is a... longing for the God of his heart and the God who is his portion for ever."[43]

Reaching into (being reached into?) this deeply implanted longing for God brings the Christian to the brink of mystical experience. This is not mystical experience accompanied by all manner of special psycho-physical manifestations. These for Rahner are secondary. "If we want to describe as 'mysticism' this experience of transcendence in which man in the midst of ordinary life is always beyond himself and beyond the particular object with which he is concerned, we might say that mysticism always occurs, concealed and namelessly, in the midst of ordinary life and is the condition of the possibility for the most down-to-earth and most secular experience or ordinary life."[44]

This description of prayer by Rahner is not far removed from Macquarrie's. For both of them God is the author of prayer. God is the final satisfaction and fulfillment of the restlessness of the human heart. Prayer has absolutely nothing to do with magic or manipulation. Rather, it pulls the human person from within into deep alignment with God. For both the need of prayer is an anthropological constant that is ignored to the detriment of the human person. Prayer is awareness of and in that awareness responsiveness to the God in whom we live and move and have our being.

In his foreword to Rahner's autobiographical interview with Meinhold Krauss, Harvey Egan, S.J. calls Rahner, "Doctor Orationis," Doctor of Prayer.[45] I find myself wishing to make the same description of John Macquarrie. He too is a Doctor of Prayer. As with Rahner, not just Macquarrie's immediate writing on prayer but the entire *corpus* of his work is mystagogical, drawing us into the heart of the Mystery of Holy Being. Holy Being has poured itself out in creation, has entered human history, so as to make that history "the theater of God's unparalleled intimacy with the human person."[46] For Rahner and Macquarrie the central task of theology, and indeed, the ultimate goal of the entire Christian life is *reductio in mysterium*, being found through being led into the very heart of God.[47]

The Celtic Temperament: Mystical Macquarrie, Mystical Baillie

Writing of himself in 1980 Macquarrie made this comment: "By 'religion' I mean an awareness of the holy, of the depth and mystery of existence. It can be a sense of presence, or, paradoxically, a sense of absence. Perhaps it is part of my Celtic heritage, for it is very close to the sense of presence which John Baillie described, and which he said he had from the beginning of his life and which he took to be the main root of belief in God. Like Baillie too, I thought of this mystery in terms of immanence rather than transcendence."[48] There has, of course, being a renaissance of interest in all things Celtic, including Celtic theology and mysticism. While the interpretation of Celtic theology is challenged in various ways in the world of scholarship, there can be little doubt that one of its key and central features is the immanence of God. "Put in its simplest form this general theology of Celtic Christians thinks of the divine being and act or, better, the divine presence and power, flowing in and through what can only be described as an extended family... An awesomely immanent divine being, presence and power, then, could be experienced and invoked in and through... varied embodiments."[49] This description of Celtic theological thinking from the pen of James P. Mackey, who has become an authority in this area, indicates that the presence of this immanent divine being is mediated and, indeed, experienced through a range of other beings. This engenders a sense of inclusivism within God, a sense of inclusivism that comes close historically to the thought of John Scotus Eriugena. Macquarrie has paid particular attention to this ninth century philosopher-theologian in his Gifford lectures and he has described him as "the greatest Celtic thinker who has ever lived."[50] Not only has God put something of himself into creation, according to Eriugena, but God has manifested himself as a result in theophanies, particular manifestations of God on the finite level. These manifestations are such that the entire world may be considered theophanic.[51] Macquarrie goes so far as to claim that the immanence or indwelling of God in creation is the most important heritage of Celtic Christianity from its pre-Christian ancestors.[52] Mackey's "varied embodiments" seem to be coincident with Eriugena's theophanies, and also with Macquarrie's and Baillie's understanding of the divine immanence. This is the heart of Celtic mysticism.

There are several points of contact between Macquarrie's understanding of prayer and that of John Baillie. It is true that both share what might be called this Celtic sense of God's presence. But there is more to it than that. We have noted above the liturgical shaping of Macquarrie's theology of prayer. The same may be said of John Baillie. Baillie moved away from the traditional Calvinism of his upbringing and towards a liturgical sensibility, although he remained a Presbyterian all his life, unlike John Macquarrie who moved from Presbyterianism to the Anglican Communion. In point of fact, Baillie had a deep appreciation for the liturgical shape of Anglicanism: "Unlike Karl Barth, John Baillie was deeply influenced by liturgical worship, and in particular, through his wife who was a descendent of the Reforming Bishop Jewel of Salisbury, by the Anglican Book of Common Prayer."[53] Without the discipline of daily prayer which, for Baillie was "thinking towards God," theology becomes simply an intellectual engagement, bereft of any sense of communion with the ever present God.[54]

This sense of the presence/absence of God is mysticism. Macquarrie has always been possessed of this mystical sense, something noted from time to time throughout this book. Reminiscing about Macquarrie's time at Union Theological Seminary in New York, Ronald H. Stone, a former student, makes the following comment: "(Macquarrie's) reading of Heidegger on human existence, criticized by Joan Stambaugh, another translator of *Being and* Time... *as almost mystical,* led (Macquarrie) to move through philosophical theology toward a revelation of Being as holy."[55] Inadvertently, Stambaugh --- though her comment is intended to be at least somewhat pejorative --- has hit upon the key insight that John Macquarrie was always something of a mystic, so much so that his reading and exposition of philosophy had this particular flavor to it. Stambaugh is not alone in noting this mystical quality in Macquarrie's writing, even in his translating. The Anglican theologian, Alister E. McGrath, in a brief article on Macquarrie notes that Macquarrie testified to a "constant sense of the divine presence," which he describes as "of a more mystical character," and the New Testament scholar, Leslie Houlden has characterized his work in this way: "Macquarrie's own tendency... seems to be towards mysticism..."[56]

Ten Characteristics of Mysticism

John Macquarrie's final book, *Two Worlds Are Ours: An Introduction to Christian Mysticism,* was published in 2004.[57] Throughout the book he maintains that while he is interested in mysticism he himself is no mystic. We must take him at his word and acknowledge some sense in which this is true. He has not had the experiences of visions or locutions associated with some mystics. Yet if the heart of mysticism is the sheer, grace-filled transforming awareness of God, then John Macquarrie was a mystic, albeit a mystic who refuses to allow mysticism to be separated from reason.[58] In the first chapter of the book, he offers ten characteristics of mysticism.[59]

First is directness. Mystics claim to have a direct relation to God, often mediated by revelations, either visions or locutions, or both visions and locutions. He does not dismiss these phenomena, though one senses that he does not find in them the essence of mysticism. Second is cognition. "The mystical experience has a cognitive aspect and brings an understanding." Throughout his career Macquarrie has consistently affirmed that the emotions have a cognitive dimension. He is utterly opposed to the view that only discursive reason provides access to reality, something recognized earlier in this book. "There are different kinds of knowledge. When I talk of knowing a person, that knowledge is different from knowledge of a fact." He realizes, of course, that these two kinds of knowing cannot be entirely and in every way different. That would make nonsense of knowing, but there is a definitive and self-validating "something more" to knowing a person than purely factual knowledge. The mystic's "knowing" is closer to the former than to the latter. Macquarrie adds here something that most if not all mystics claim to be true and that has emerged forcefully in his research: "Most mystics stress the interrelatedness of knowledge of God and self-knowledge, to such an extent that sometimes it is hard to say where the knowledge of the one leaves off and the other begins." Progress in communion with God not only *may not* but *cannot* be divorced from genuine and authentic progress in knowledge of self. There is no either-or. This is certainly a central truth of Catholic Christianity as a whole, let alone the mystical tradition. There can be no vertical relationship with God that is not in some way mediated and measured by relationship with others. Access to God is never in competition with due regard for our fellows. What we might call mystical theism and prophetic theism may be conceptually distinguished but can never be separated. Catholic Christianity is no Gnostic flight from the messiness of the self or the messiness of the world. In insisting on this point Macquarrie is in good company. Thomas Merton, whom Macquarrie treats as a modern mystic, wrote in a well-known letter: "It is the love of my lover, my brother or my child that sees God in me, makes God credible to myself in me," just as "it is my love for my lover, my child, my brother that enables me to show God to him or her in himself or herself."[60] A similar understanding is to be found, for example, in the philosopher, Walter Kaufman: "Even the difference between theism and atheism is not nearly so profound as that between those who feel and those who do not feel their brothers' torments."[61] This is close to what is meant by the philosophical theologian, Louis K. Dupré, when he insists that there are "spiritual seekers" in our midst to whom the writings of the mystics might speak. These are people who have a sense of the *mysterium tremendum et fascinans*. "To such persons, perhaps for very diverse reasons, the doctrines of the church that are intended to enshrine the mystery may seem instead to entomb it."[62]

Third is ecstasy or rapture. Though the wisest mystics never accentuate ecstasy or the paranormal, ecstasy is a regular aspect of mystical experience, described by Macquarrie as follows: "These are moments of joy and of a sense of union with God or with all reality, though paradoxically there may also be intense pain." Fourth, apophaticism or negative theology. This is the recognition of the sheer limitations of language in speaking of God or in the communication of mystical experiences to others. It is summed up in Gregory of Nyssa's notion of *epektasis*, which Macquarrie particularly likes: "There can be no end to the exploration of God." Sometimes authors so emphasize apophaticism that they maintain nothing can be said of God. This is for Macquarrie something of a performative contradiction. Fifth is self-knowledge or inwardness. To some extent this has been touched on in the first characteristic already noted. The emphasis here is more on the inwardness, on the closeness, the communion of God and the self. It is in this section that Macquarrie cites from the nineteenth century Anglican priest-theologian-poet, John Keble and from whom he got the title for his book:

> "Two worlds are ours: 'tis only sin
> Forbids us to descry
> The mystic heaven and earth within
> Plain as the sea and sky."

Interpreting Keble's words, but fairly, it is sin that keeps us from recognizing our ontological participation in God. This notion of being one-d in God is so strong for mystics that it can give rise to dangers. Macquarrie sees two specific dangers: "There is a danger... of pantheism, and even of confusing God and ourselves. There is also a danger of retreating so far into ourselves that we lose contact with and responsibility for the world." The first danger takes us to the doctrine of God and the second to individualism, characteristics six and seven in his description. In the language of some mystics and in virtue of the communion between God and the self, the difference between God and his creature has almost been eliminated. This is pantheism. Macquarrie will have no part in this lack of differentiation. Drawing upon his decades-long study of the doctrine of God, however, and insisting upon the utter priority of God, he avoids the doctrinal error of pantheism by moving in the direction of panentheism, treated earlier in this book in the chapter on God: "The mystical quest for union with God does not necessarily lead us into pantheism. It may very well, however, demand some form of panentheism or, as I prefer to say, 'dialectical theism,' which can never be free from some element of paradox. It implies an understanding of God which attributes to him both total transcendence and total immanence." Everything that is and especially humankind participates in the reality of God, yet does not add up to God, as it were. God is always prior, and graciously lets creation be and graciously draws creation into the *telos* or finality that he himself is. This way of understanding participation or communion not only recognizes God's utter transcendence but also refuses the total absorption of the creature in God. Ultimately, whatever language is used for the doctrine of God, it must be acknowledged that no language for God works perfectly. There is no precise "fit" between our human language for God and the reality of God. In respect of individualism he acknowledges that there is a certain necessary solitude involved in mystical union with God. Mystical union flows from God's gracious priority but it also is necessarily dependent upon the individual mystic's response. There is no coercion on God's part, only invitation and persuasion. But this is not what is meant by individualism. Individualism occurs when "mysticism becomes a kind of spiritual hedonism." The authentic Christian mystic does not experience the joys of consummate communion with God in order to live as a spiritual solipsist. Rather, "the mystic at least for as long as he or she lives on earth, has, as already noted, a measure of responsibility for the earth and for other human beings."

Macquarrie's eighth characteristic is passivity. He insists that the prayer of the mystic is both passionate and passive. Passionate means that the whole being of the mystic is engaged in something like continuous prayer. Passive means that the mystic's prayer "aims not at mastery but at letting oneself be mastered, immersed in a power and wisdom transcending one's own." God's intimacy to the mystic is not simply the product of prayer but the producer of prayer. Ninth is what he calls the "holistic view." This is "trying to see or understand things in their wholeness or interconnectedness." In a sense, this way of seeing everything as interrelated flows theologically as well as logically from accepting God --- moreover a God whose very being is Communion as Father, Son and Holy Spirit --- as the originating Ground of everything and as the final Goal of everything. If you will, a relational view of reality flows directly from a God who is no divine monad but Persons-in-Communion. Finally there is prayer. Macquarrie's discussion of prayer ranges across the familiar territory of spiritual and mystical authors from purgation through illumination to contemplation. However, the center of prayer for him is to be found in this description: "Prayer is a kind of opening of the self so that the Spirit of God may pray in us and our wills may become attuned to the divine will... Etymologically (adoration) suggests 'praying toward', a kind of reaching out towards God which is also a kind of going out of oneself; yet this reaching out is not brought about simply by our own volition, we are drawn out by the divine Other." Prayer is no therapeutic exercise for self-improvement but the gracious initiative of God luring the human subject into an intimacy through which one becomes attuned to the Other, by the Other, and by means of this grace-filled attunement recognizes the interconnection of everything and everyone in the Communion that is the Other. This prayer of adoration is the highest reach of prayer when the soul "sinks into God and God envelops the soul."

Conclusion

In my judgment both John Macquarrie and Karl Rahner are not only doctors of prayer but mystics. They are mystics because, while coming out of significantly different Christian and ecclesial backgrounds, the reality of God for both of them was overwhelming. It was overwhelming not only in terms of its self-evident conceptual magnitude, but also in terms of its sheer abidingness. They lived, worked and prayed out of this sense of the divine presence, the One in whom they lived, moved and had their being.

[1] John Macquarrie, "The Mystic Way," in Joseph Baunoch, ed., *Foundation Theology 2006: Faculty Essays for Ministry Professionals* (South Bend, IN: Graduate Theological Foundation, 2006), 110.

[2] Allan D. Galloway, "A God I Can Talk To," in Eugene T. Long, ed., *God, Secularization and History* (Columbia, SC: University of South Carolina Press, 1974), 107.

[3] John Macquarrie, *Theology, Church and Ministry* (London: SCM Press, 1986), 48-68.

[4] Philip Endean, SJ, "John Macquarrie and Karl Rahner," in Robert Morgan, ed., *In Search of Humanity and Deity* (London: SCM Press, 2006), 115.

[5] I regret that I have mislaid the source of this quotation from Archbishop Williams.

[6] John Macquarrie, "Prayer as Thinking," in his *Paths in Spirituality*, 2nd ed. (Harrisburg, PA: Morehouse Publishing, 1992), 25.

[7] Simon Tugwell, OP, *Prayer in Practice* (Dublin: Veritas Publications, 1974), 7.

[8] John Macquarrie, "Prayer as Thinking," 26.

[9] Ibid., 27.

[10] Ibid., 30.

[11] Brian E. Daley, SJ, "How Should We Pray? Five Guiding Principles," *Crisis* (March, 1994), 29.

[12] John Macquarrie, "Adoration," in Gordon S. Wakefield, ed., *A Dictionary of Christian Spirituality* (London: SCM Press, 1983), 308.

[13] Esther de Waal, *Lost in Wonder* (Collegeville: The Liturgical Press, 2003), 102.

[14] Herbert McCabe, OP, *God Still Matters* (New York and London: Continuum, 2002), 68.

[15] Chet Raymo, *Climbing Brandon, Science and Faith on Ireland's Holy Mountain* (New York: Walker and Co., 2004), 157, 167.

[16] John Macquarrie, "Prayer as Thinking," 27-28.

[17] Ibid., 33-34.

[18] John Macquarrie, op. cit., 36.

[19] Ibid., 37, slightly adapted.

[20] John Macquarrie, *Principles of Christian Theology*, rev. ed. (London: SCM Press, 1977), 493.

[21] Ibid., 494.

[22] Ibid.

[23] Ibid., 497.

[24] Austin Flannery, O.P., ed., *Vatican Council II: The Conciliar and Postconciliar Documents* (New York: Costello Publishing Company, 1975), 6-7.

[25] John Macquarrie, *Principles of Christian Theology*, 498.

[26] Ibid., 499.

[27] Ibid., 500.

[28] Ibid., 501. For a perspective similar to Macquarrie's, but treating of the eucharistic pattern in the cycle of psychological and faith development, see Owen F. Cummings, "Eucharist, Life-Cycle, Prayer," *Emmanuel* 104 (1998), 203-213.

[29] For a fine evaluation of the relationship between Anglican ecclesiology and Eucharistic ecclesiology, see Paul Avis, *The Identity of Anglicanism: Essentials of Anglican Ecclesiology* (New York: T. & T. Clark, 2007), 81-108.

[30] John Macquarrie, *Principles of Christian Theology*, 501.

[31] For example, see Owen F. Cummings, "Is the Mass Eurocentric? A Response to Gary Riebe-Estrella," *Antiphon, A Journal for Liturgical Renewal* 4 (1999), 5-7.

[32] Karl Rahner, SJ, *On Prayer* (Collegeville: The Liturgical Press, 1993).

[33] Ibid., 9.

[34] Ibid., 8.

[35] Ibid., 10.

[36] Ibid., 12.

[37] Ibid., 13.

[38] Ibid.

[39] Karl Rahner, "Experience of the Holy Spirit," in *Theological Investigations*, vol. 18 (New York: The Crossroad Publishing Company, 1983), 202.

[40] Karl Rahner, *On Prayer*, 18.

[41] Ibid., 19.

[42] Ibid., 21.

[43] Ibid., 39-48.

[44] Karl Rahner, "Experience of the Holy Spirit," 197.

[45] Karl Rahner, *I Remember: Autobiographical Interview with Meinhold Krauss* (New York: The Crossroad Publishing Company, 1984), 11.

[46] Geffrey B. Kelly, ed., *Karl Rahner: Theologian of the Graced Search for Meaning* (Minneapolis: Fortress Press, 1992), 59.

[47] See R. R. Reno, *The Ordinary Transformed: Karl Rahner and the Christian Vision of Transcendence* (Grand Rapids: Eerdmans, 1995), 219-222.

[48] John Macquarrie, "Pilgrimage in Theology," in Alistair Kee and Eugene Thomas Long, ed., *Being and Truth: Essays in Honour of John Macquarrie* (London: SCM Press, 1986), xi. One might contrast Macquarrie's Celtic sense of God's presence with what Archbishop Rowan Williams calls "my Celtic gloom." See Rupert Shortt, *Rowan's Rule: The Biography of the Archbishop of Canterbury* (Grand Rapids: Eerdmans, 2008), 103.

[49] James P. Mackey, "Preface," in *Celtic Christianity*, translated and introduced by Oliver Davies with the collaboration of Thomas O'Loughlin (New York-Mahwah, NJ: Paulist Press, 1999), xvii-xviii.

[50] John Macquarrie, *Two Worlds Are Ours* (London: SCM Press, 2004), 106; John Macquarrie, *On Being a Theologian* (London: SCM Press, 1999), 9.

[51] John Macquarrie, *In Search of Deity* (New York: Crossroad, 1985), 94-95; John Macquarrie, *On Being a Theologian*, 10.

[52] John Macquarrie, *On Being a Theologian*, 8.

[53] Thomas F. Torrance, "John Baillie at Prayer," in David Fergusson, ed., *Christ, Church and Society: Essays on John Baillie and Donald Baillie* (Edinburgh: T. & T. Clark, 1993), 254.

[54] See John Baillie, *Christian Devotion* (London: Oxford University Press, 1962), 23.

[55] Ronald H. Stone, "John Macquarrie at Union Theological Seminary in New York City," in Robert Morgan, ed., *In Search of Humanity and Deity* (London: SCM Press, 2006), 66.

[56] Alister E. McGrath, ed., *The SPCK Handbook of Anglican Theologians* (London: SPCK, 1998), 166. J. Leslie Houlden, Review: John Macquarrie, *Stubborn Theological Questions* (London: SCM Press, 2003), in *Journal of Theological Studies* 54 (2003), 863.

[57] Macquarrie's choice of mystics in the book seems to me to speak more of his own particular interests rather than to provide a comprehensive initial account of Christian mysticism. This becomes evident in the comments he makes on individual mystics.

[58] John Macquarrie, *Two Worlds Are Ours*, 266.

[59] See pages 1-34, and also Owen F. Cummings, "Mystical Macquarrie," *Emmanuel* 111 (2005), 415-425.

[60] Thomas Merton, "A Letter on the Contemplative Life," in his *The Monastic Journey*, ed. P. Hart (Garden City, NY: Doubleday, 1978), 222.

[61] Walter Kaufman, *The Faith of a Heretic* (Garden City, NY: Doubleday, 1963), 168.

[62] Cited in James Wiseman, "Mystical Literature and the Culture of Unbelief," in George Schner and Peter Casarella, ed., *Christian Spirituality and the Culture of Modernity* (Grand Rapids: Eerdmans, 1998), 184.

CONCLUSION

John Macquarrie is not an easy theologian about whom to write.
Maurice Wiles.[1]

(John Macquarrie is) a deeply spiritual theologian and a truly catholic father of the Church in our time.
Paul Fiddes.[2]

Mystical Macquarrie seems the most adequate way to describe this remarkable man. His mysticism, his God-awareness, however, was always within the framework of human reason. His early philosophical training at the University of Glasgow, allied to his natural disposition, never allowed him to neglect reason. But he was never a rationalist.

The range of John Macquarie's theological interests was very comprehensive, and this was matched by his awareness of the so many quite different and contrasting points of view in the theological world. While he maintained his own position, he was also marked, in the Scottish Dominican Fergus Kerr's words, by "his desire to get adversaries to the point where they may be able to tolerate one another's views." Kerr accepts this as an attractive quality in Macquarrie, but adds a qualifier to the effect that "sometimes (it) disqualifies him from fathoming just how deep theological and philosophical arguments often go."[3] In this respect, I believe Kerr is wrong. Macquarrie knew the depth of difference, indeed of conflict and opposition in both philosophical and theological arguments. However, reaching for a non-adversarial perspective, tending towards a tolerance that respected difference without artificially attempting to reduce it to the status of irrelevance seems to me a preeminently satisfactory methodology. It is so not least because of the irreducible pluralism that marks the worlds of philosophy and theology, indeed a fast accelerating pluralism as one engages with other cultures and religious traditions. There is a pluralism at every level of serious philosophical and theological thinking. Perhaps David Tracy is right when he says: "Theology will never again be tameable by any totality system --- any system --- modern or premodern or postmodern." If such tameability is in principle impossible, as well as undesirable, the posture of the Christian theologian will be alertness to "the voice of the Other through all those others who have tasted... the Infinity disclosed in the kenotic reality of Jesus Christ."[4] Macquarrie's habitual desire for tolerance is no easy slide into an enervating though superficially happy despair. Rather, it is the recognition that the accent of truth may be heard in a myriad of ways, and this is not always comfortable. Speaking of the contemporary tensions in Catholic theology Fergus Kerr draws a lesson from the recent past in the history of theology and shows how the future might be faced: "Perhaps one of the lessons we have learnt since the cruel way in which the modernists were treated a century ago is that we have to live with some quite deep divisions and intractable rifts within the Catholic Church..."[5] This is true not just of Catholics but of theology in general, and Macquarrie's way is one of the ways in which this living may be done with a high degree of *sanitas*.

In recent years there have been various attempts to classify theologies and theologians according to a typology. Two of the more successful of these typologies have been constructed by David Tracy of Chicago and the late Hans Frei of Yale.[6] Sometimes people speak of a "Chicago School" and a "Yale School." Tracy stands for a correlational theology, yet a correlational theology that differs from Paul Tillich's. Crudely speaking Tillich's correlational methodology moves through listening to the critical and existential questions raised by the culture, and supplying the responses to these questions from the tradition of Christian faith. Tracy's approach moves beyond this. His method of correlation works out of a dual fidelity, a fidelity to the classics of the Christian tradition, with the Scriptures as the classics *par excellence*, and to contemporary experience. Contemporary experience for Tracy includes the wide range of modern and contemporary philosophies, engaged in a mutually critical correlation with the Christian classics. Frei, on the other hand, maintained that theologies which give philosophy a systematic priority inevitably distort Christian faith. Such theologies appear to permit reality to be defined in terms "external" to the biblical tradition. Where Tracy would be involved in an apologetic for the credibility and livability of Christianity, Frei would have suggested that Christianity's credibility and integrity could only be lived in its self-evident witness, not in reference to some set of extra-Christian criteria. The dialogue/debate between the two so-called "schools" continues. Frei's position concerning the self-evident witness of Christianity over extra-Christian criteria is certainly true. This is "faith" calling forth faith, *ex fide in fidem*. It is the witness of the saint, the one who, embodied in Christ and nurtured on Word and Sacrament, attempts to live out that identity in all its fullness in worship, prayer and the moral life. Countless Christians offer the testimony that they came to Christian commitment and faith through the vibrant and persuasive witness of some Christian whom they knew. At the same time, Tracy's position is also true. Arguably, Tracy's correlational method offers greater scope for Christian theology to interact with life, with experience both personal and communal.[7] People are marked by an innate quest for understanding, "reason" to give it its classical name. It is, at least in part, through this innate reasonable quest that they are able to form an intelligent judgment about the witness provided by a Christian someone, or perhaps by the local Christian community. Both faith and reason are equally central, equally primordial. One may not be had without the other. To attempt to have one without the other is to perform contradiction. Nonetheless, particular ecclesial traditions and particular theologians will tend to emphasize one over the other.

If we had to situate John Macquarrie in this context, he would be closer to David Tracy than to Hans Frei. Macquarrie works from general human experience to the data of Christian revelation and faith. Macquarrie's penchant is for something of Tracy's critical correlation between the classics of Christianity and public discourse, informed primarily for him by philosophy. Thus, his interest in Heidegger's contribution to theology has not abated, as is evidenced by his *Heidegger and Christianity*.[8] Yet, this does not do justice to Macquarrie's contribution. In an interesting essay entitled "Liberal and Radical Theologies Compared," Macquarrie writes, "The wisest theologians avoid getting themselves labeled too precisely."[9] Indeed, he writes: "What is meant by 'liberal theology'? If it means only that the theologian to whom the adjective is applied has an openness to other points of view, then liberal theologians are found in all schools of thought. But if 'liberal' becomes itself a party label, then it usually turns out to be extremely illiberal."[10] While Macquarrie is more of a correlationist than a postliberal theologian in the Yale/Frei tradition, he is not easily labeled as a liberal or a radical. Indeed, in his defense of, for example, the Marian dogmas, some would describe him as a conservative theologian.

Macquarrie is best described in his own terms as a dialectical theologian, that is, a committed Christian theologian possessed of the skill to think dialectically in an habitual fashion, within the Christian ellipse whose two *foci* are "faith" and "reason." He also establishes in his even-handedness and fair treatment of others a real ability to enter into seemingly opposing systems of thought or points of view to see another aspect of the Christian mystery. His theology is not marked by "stifling absorption" in someone else's thought categories, or by "damaging division" in relation to the positions of others. His theological perspective is above all marked by balance. One commentator on his theological method puts it like this: "The balance gives rise to a delicacy and harmony in his theology. Tensions seem not only held together but resolved; divergences and convergences of thought when taken together yield disclosures of God and of us. His balance serves to translate the peace of the Gospel from intellectual interpretations into feeling tones."[11] This leads Macquarrie to avoid what has been called "a regrettable univocity in speech about the divine."[12] Many who have read deeply in Macquarrie would agree.

The Scottish Dominican theologian, Fergus Kerr, O.P. says that there is in Macquarrie a "total lack of *odium theologicum.*"[13] That is quite an accomplishment. This correlational theologian, whose life has been a lesson in real ecumenical conversion, has offered much to the church, to all the Christian churches, not least to Anglicanism and Catholicism. His way of doing theology offers all Christians a successful paradigm for living amicably together, and for drawing closer.

[1] Maurice Wiles, Review of Georgina Morley, *John Macquarrie's Natural Theology* (Bristol, IN: Wyndham Hall Press, 2001), in *Journal of Theological Studies* 53 (2002), 402.

[2] Paul Fiddes, "On God the Incomparable: Thinking about God with John Macquarrie," in Robert Morgan, ed., *In Search of Humanity and Deity* (London: SCM Press, 2006), 179.

[3] Fergus Kerr, OP, Review of John Macquarrie's Festschrift *Being and Truth* and his *Theology, Church and Ministry* in *New Blackfriars* 68 (1987), 420.

[4] David Tracy, "Forms of Divine Disclosure," in James L. Heft, ed., *Believing Scholars* (New York: Fordham University Press, 2005), 57. See also John Macquarrie, "The Figure of Jesus Christ in Contemporary Christianity," in Peter Byrne and Leslie Houlden, ed., *Companion Encyclopedia of Theology* (New York and London: Routledge, 1995), 918.

[5] Fergus Kerr, OP, *Twentieth Century Catholic Theologians* (Oxford: Blackwell Publishing, 2007), 222.

[6] David Tracy, *Blessed Rage for Order: The New Pluralism in Theology* (New York: The Seabury Press, 1975), reprinted with a new preface by the University of Chicago Press, 1996. Other key works by Tracy include: *The Analogical Imagination* (New York: Crossroad, 1981), *Plurality and Ambiguity* (Chicago and London: University of Chicago and London: University of Chicago Press, 1987), and *On Naming the Present: God, Hermeneutics and Church* (Maryknoll, NY: Orbis Books, 1994). For Hans Frei see *Types of Christian Theology* (New Haven and London: Yale University Press, 1992), *The Identity of Jesus Christ: The Hermeneutical Bases of Dogmatic Theology* (Philadelphia: Fortress Press, 1975), and the posthumously published *Theology and Narrative: Selected Essays*, ed., G. Hunsinger and W. C. Placher (New York: Oxford University Press, 1993).

[7] Fergus Kerr seems to make a similar criticism of Frei in his "Frei's Types," *New Blackfriars* 75 (1994), 184-193, especially 193.

[8] (London: SCM Press, 1994).

[9] John Macquarrie, *Thinking About God* (London: SCM Press, 1975), 61.

[10] Ibid.

[11] J. J. Mueller, *What Are They Saying About Theological Method?* (New York-Ramsey: Paulist Press, 1984), 27. See also Marion L. Hendrickson, *Behold the Man! An Anthropological Comparison of the Christologies of John Macquarrie and of Wolfhart Pannenberg* (Lanham-New York-Oxford: University Press of America, 1998), 92-95, and David Jenkins, *The Scope and Limits of John Macquarrie's Existential Theology* (Uppsala: Acta Universitatis Upsaliensis, 1987), 107-125.

[12] Elizabeth A. Johnson, "Response," in Phyllis Zagano and Terrence W. Tilley, ed., *Things New and*

Old: Essays on the Theology of Elizabeth A. Johnson (New York: Crossroad, 1999), 101.

[13] Review of Alistair Kee and Eugene T. Long, ed., *Being and Truth: Essays in Honour of John Macquarrie*, and John Macquarrie, *Theology, Church and Ministry*, in *New Blackfriars* 68 (1987), 420.

BIBLIOGRAPHY

The major books of John Macquarrie cited in the text.

(A complete bibliography may be found in his *On Being a Theologian*.)

An Existentialist Theology, A Comparison of Heidegger and Bultmann, London: SCM Press, 1955.

God Talk, London: SCM Press, 1962.

Twentieth Century Religious Thought, London: SCM Press, 1963, rev. eds. 1971, 1981, 2001.

Principles of Christian Theology, London: SCM Press, 1966, rev. ed., 1977.

God and Secularity, London: Lutterworth, 1967.

Paths in Spirituality, London: SCM Press, 1972, rev. ed., 1992.

The Faith of the People of God, London: SCM Press, 1972.

Thinking About God, London: SCM Press, 1975.

Christian Unity and Christian Diversity, London: SCM Press, 1975.

"Robert Burns: Poet, Prophet, Philosopher," *The Expository Times* 86 (1974-1975), 112-115.

Christian Hope, London: SCM Press, 1978.

The Humility of God, London: SCM Press, 1978.

In Search of Humanity, London: SCM Press, 1982.

Theology, Church and Ministry, London: SCM Press, 1984.

In Search of Deity, London: SCM Press, 1985.

Jesus Christ in Modern Thought, London: SCM Press, 1990.

Mary for All Christians, London: Collins, 1990.

Heidegger and Christianity, London: SCM Press, 1994.

"The Figure of Jesus Christ in Contemporary Christianity," in Peter Byrne and Leslie Houlden, ed., *Companion Encyclopedia of Theology* (New York and London: Routledge, 1995), 917-935.

Mediators Between Human and Divine: From Moses to Muhammad, New York: The Continuum Publishing Company, 1996.

A Guide to the Sacraments, New York: The Continuum Publishing Company, 1997.

"Ebb and Flow of Hope: Christian Theology at the End of the Second Millennium," *The Expository Times* 107 (1995-1996), 205-210.

"Dialogue Among the World Religions," *The Expository Times* 108 (1996-1997), 167-172.

Christology Revisited, London: SCM Press, 1998.

On Being a Theologian, (ed. John H. Morgan), London: SCM Press, 1999.

"Mary and the Saints in Early Scottish Poetry," in William McLoughlin and Jill Pinnock, ed., *Mary for Heaven and Earth, Essays on Mary and Ecumenism* Leominster, UK: Gracewing, 2002), 377-386.

"The Theological Legacy of Maurice Wiles," *Anglican Theological Review* 88 (2006), 597-616.

Other books and articles cited in the text.

Allchin, Arthur M., *The Joy of All Creation, An Anglican Meditation on the Place of Mary* (Cambridge, MA: Cowley Publications, 1984).
_____ *Participation in God: A Forgotten Strand in Anglican Tradition* (Wilton, CT: Morehouse-Barlow, 1988).
Avis, Paul, *The Identity of Anglicanism: Essentials of Anglican Ecclesiology* (New York and London: T. & T. Clark, 2007).
Bacik, James J., *Apologetics and the Eclipse of Mystery* (Notre Dame and London: University of Notre Dame Press, 1980).
_____ *Contemporary Theologians* (New York: Triumph Books, 1989).
Badham, Paul, "Recent Thinking on Christian Beliefs: The Future Life," *The Expository Times* 88 (1976-1977), 197-198.
Baillie, John, *Christian Devotion* (London: Oxford University Press, 1962).
Baker, John Austin, "Wrestling with the Divine Mystery," *Church Times*, May 4, 2007.
Balthasar, Hans Urs von, *The Grain of Wheat* (San Francisco: Ignatius Press, 1995).
Bartlett, Alan, *A Passionate Balance: The Anglican Tradition* (Maryknoll, NY: Orbis Books, 2007).
Bauckham, Richard, Review: John Macquarrie, *Jesus Christ in Modern Thought* (London: SCM Press, 1990), in *Journal of Theological Studies* 42 (1991), 793-797.
Bolen, Donald and Cameron, Gregory, ed., *Mary, Grace and Hope* (The Seattle Statement of the Anglican-Roman Catholic International Commission, The Text with Commentaries and Study Guide), (New York and London: Continuum, 2006).
Booty, John, *Reflections on the Theology of Richard Hooker* (Sewanee, TN: University of the South Press, 1998).
Bowden, John, *Who's Who in Theology?* (New York: Crossroad, 1992).
Bowditch, Gillian, "There's more to me than Rebus, insists novelist Rankin," *Times On Line*, October 19, 2008.
Bouyer, Louis, *Orthodox Spirituality and Protestant and Anglican Spirituality* (New York: Desclée, 1969).
Braaten, Carl E. and Jenson, Robert W., ed., *Mary Mother of God* (Grand Rapids: Eerdmans, 2004).
Bradley, F. H., *The Principles of Logic*, 2nd ed., vol. II (London: Oxford University Press, 1922).
Bradshaw, Timothy, "Macquarrie's Doctrine of God," *Tyndale Bulletin* 44 (1993), 1-32.

_____ "Macquarrie, John," in Alister E. McGrath, ed., *The SPCK Handbook of Anglican Theologians* (London: SPCK, 1998), 167.

Brierley, Michael W., "Naming a Quiet Revolution: The Panentheistic Turn in Modern Theology," in Philip Clayton and Arthur Peacocke, ed., *In Whom We Live and Move and Have Our Being: Panentheistic Reflections on God's Presence in a Scientific World* (Grand Rapids: Eerdmans, 2004), 1-15.

Brown, David, "Philosophical Theology," in Alister E. McGrath, ed., *The Blackwell Encyclopedia of Modern Christian Thought* (Oxford: Blackwell, 1993), 438-440.

Brown, P. Hume, *John Knox, A Biography* (London: A. & C. Black, 1895).

Brown, Raymond E., *The Virginal Conception and Bodily Resurrection of Jesus* (New York-Paramus-Toronto: Paulist Press, 1973).

_____ *The Birth of the Messiah* (New York: Doubleday, 1977).

_____ and others, ed., *Mary in the New Testament* (New York: Paulist Press, 1978).

Browning, W. R. F., "Obituary: The Rev. John Macquarrie," *Church Times*, June 1, 2007.

Buber, Martin, *I and Thou* (New York: Charles Scribner's Sons, 1958).

Burrell, David, *Faith and Freedom, An Interfaith Perspective* (Oxford: Blackwell Publishing, 2004).

Butler, B. C., "Roman Requirements," *The Tablet* (July 5, 1975), 99-100.

Butter, P. H., ed., *Selected Letters of Edwin Muir* (London: The Hogarth Press, 1974).

Caputo, John D., "Meister Eckhart and the later Heidegger: the Mystical Elements in Heidegger's Thought," in Christopher Macann, ed., *Martin Heidegger, Critical Assessments*, vol. II (London and New York: Routledge, 1992),

Carpenter, Humphrey, *Robert Runcie, the Reluctant Archbishop* (London: Hodder and Stoughton, 1996).

Carr, Thomas K., "Only a God Can Save Us: Heidegger and Christianity," *First Things* 55 (1995), 57-62.

Carroll, Denis, *A Pilgrim God for a Pilgrim People* (Dublin: Gill and Macmillan, 1988).

Carroll, Robert P., "Hebrew, Heresy and Hot Air: Biblical Studies in Glasgow Since 1900," in William Ian P. Hazlett, ed., *Traditions of Theology in Glasgow 1450-1990* (Edinburgh: Scottish Academic Press Ltd., 1993), 87-98.

Celtic Spirituality, translated and introduced by Oliver Davies with the collaboration of Thomas O'Loughlin, and a preface by James P. Mackey (New York-Mahwah, NJ: Paulist Press, 1999).

Chadwick, Owen, *Michael Ramsey, A Life* (New York and Oxford: Oxford University Press, 1990).

Chapman, Mark, *Anglicanism* (New York and Oxford: Oxford University Press, 2006).

Clark, Kenneth, *Civilisation, a Personal View* (New York and Evanston: Harper and Row, 1969).

Clarke, SJ, W. Norris, "A New Look at the Immutability of God," in Robert Roth, ed., *God Knowable and Unknowable* (New York: Fordham University Press, 1973), 43-72.

_____ "Fifty Years of Metaphysical Reflection," in Gerald McCool, SJ, ed., *The Universe as Journey: Conversations with W. Norris Clarke, SJ* (New York: Fordham University Press, 1988).

Clayton, Philip, "God and World," in Kevin J. Vanhoozer, ed., *The Cambridge Companion to Postmodern Theology* (Cambridge: Cambridge University Press, 2003).

Cocksworth, Christopher, *Evangelical Eucharistic Thought in the Church of England* (Cambridge: Cambridge University Press, 1993).

Coll, Niall, *Some Anglican Interpretations of Christ's Pre-Existence: A Study of L. S. Thornton, E. L. Mascall, J. A. T. Robinson and J. Macquarrie* (Rome: Gregorian University Press, 1995).

Colledge, Edmund and McGinn, Bernard, trans. and intro., *Meister Eckhart: The Essential Sermons, Commentaries, Treatises, and Defense* (New York-Ramsey-Toronto: Paulist Press, 1981).

Collins, Paul M., *Trinitarian Theology, East and West* (New York and Oxford: Oxford University Press, 2001).

Conway, Eamonn, "The papacy in a Pilgrim Church," in John Macquarrie, *On Being a Theologian* (London: SCM Press, 1999), 173-177.

Cooper, John W., *Panentheism, The Other God of the Philosophers* (Grand Rapids, MI: Baker Academic, 2006).

Coppa, Frank J., *The Papacy, the Jews and the Holocaust* (Washington, DC: Catholic University of America Press, 2006).

Cottingham, John, *The Spiritual Dimension: Religion, Philosophy and Human Value* (Cambridge: Cambridge University Press, 2005).

Cross, F. L. and Livingstone, E. A., ed., *The Oxford Dictionary of the Christian Church*, 2nd ed. (London and New York: Oxford University Press, 1974).

Cross, F. L. and More, P. E., ed., *Anglicanism* (London: SPCK, 1951).

Crowley, Paul G., *Unwanted Wisdom: Suffering, the Cross and Hope* (New York: Continuum, 2005).

Cummings, Owen F., "Toward a Postliberal Religious Education," *The Living Light* 28 (1992), 315-324.

_____ "The Real Mary of Nazareth," *The Priest* 48 (1992), 14-17.

_____ "A Critical Note on Norman Pittenger's Mariology," *New Blackfriars* 78 (1997), 336-340.

_____ "Eucharist, Life Cycle, Prayer," *Emmanuel* 104 (1998), 203-213.

_____ "Is the Mass Eurocentric? A Response to Gary Riebe-Estrella," *Antiphon, A Journal for Liturgical Renewal* 4 (1999), 5-7.

_____ *John Macquarrie, A Master of Theology* (New York-Mahwah, NJ: Paulist Press, 2002).

_____ "The Trinity Today: Some Recent Views of the Social Doctrine of the Trinity," *The Priest* (June, 2003), 13-17.

_____ "Mystical Macquarrie," *Emmanuel* 111 (2005), 415-425.

_____ "The Eucharistic Richard Hooker (1554-1600)," *Emmanuel* 112 (2006), 218-228.

_____ *Prophets, Guardians and Saints: Shapers of Modern Catholic History* (New York-Mahwah, NJ: Paulist Press, 2007).

_____ *Canterbury Cousins: The Eucharist in Contemporary Anglican Theology* (New York-Mahwah, NJ: Paulist Press, 2007).

_____ *The Popes of the Twentieth Century* (Lewiston, NY and Lampeter, UK: The Edwin Mellen Press, 2008).

Curtin, Maurice, "God's Presence in the World: The Metaphysics of Aquinas and Some Recent Thinkers --- Moltmann, Macquarrie, Rahner," in Fran O'Rourke, ed., *At the Heart of the Real* (Dublin: Irish Academic Press, 1992), 123-136.

Daley, Brian E., "How Should We Pray? Five Guiding Principles," *Crisis* (March, 1994).

Daly, Gabriel, "Catholicism and Modernity," *Journal of the American Academy of Religion* 53 (1985), 773-796.

_____ *Creation and Redemption* (Dublin: Gill and Macmillan, 1988).

Davies, Brian, Review of John Macquarrie, *In Search of Deity* in *New Blackfriars* 64 (1984), 439-440.

DiNoia, Joseph A., "Karl Rahner," in David F. Ford, ed., *The Modern Theologians*, 2nd. ed. (Oxford: Blackwell, 1997), 118-133.

Dulles, Avery, *The Resilient Church* (Garden City, NY: Doubleday, 1977).

_____ *The Catholicity of the Church* (New York and Oxford: Oxford University Press, 1985).

_____ "A Roman Catholic Response to *Principles*," in Robert Morgan, ed., *In Search of Humanity and Deity* (London: SCM Press, 2006), 76-82.

Endean, Philip, "Spirituality and Religious Experience: A Perspective from Rahner," in Declan Marmion, ed., *Christian Identity in a Postmodern Age* (Dublin: Veritas Publications, 2005).

_____ "John Macquarrie and Karl Rahner," in Robert Morgan, ed., *In Search of Humanity and Deity* (London: SCM Press, 2006), 107-116.

Fergusson, David, ed., *Christ, Church and Society: Essays on John Baillie and Donald Baillie* (Edinburgh: T. & T. Clark, 1993).

_____ "John Macquarrie as Interpreter of Bultmann," in Robert Morgan, ed., *In Search of Humanity and Deity* (London: SCM Press, 2006), 25-33.

Fiddes, Paul, "On God the Incomparable: Thinking about God with John Macquarrie," in Robert Morgan, ed., *In Search of Humanity and Deity* (London: SCM Press, 2006), 179-199.

Flanagan, Donal, "Mary and the Unremembered Past," *Doctrine and Life* 43 (1993), 259-266.

Flannery, OP, Austin, ed., *Vatican Council II: The Conciliar and Postconciliar Documents* (New York: Costello Publishing Co., 1975).

Ford, David F., ed., *The Modern Theologians*, 2nd ed. (Oxford: Blackwell, 1997).
_____ *The Shape of Living* (London: HarperCollins, 1997).
_____ "Wilderness Wisdom for the Twenty-First Century: Arthur, L'Arche and the Culmination of Christian History, in R. S. Sugitharajah, ed., *Wilderness: Essays in Honor of Frances Young* (New York and London: T. & T. Clark, 2005), 153-165.
Frei, Hans, *Types of Christian Theology* (New Haven and London: Yale University Press, 1992).
Galloway, Allan Douglas, *Faith in a Changing Culture* (London: Allen and Unwin, 1968).
_____ "A God I Can Talk To," in Eugene T. Long, ed., *God, Secularization and History* (Columbia, SC: University of South Carolina Press, 1974), 107-124.
Gathercole, Simon J., *The Pre-Existent Son* (Grand Rapids: Eerdmans, 2006).
Gaventa, Beverly R., *Mary, Glimpses of the Mother of Jesus* (Columbia, SC: University of South Carolina Press, 1995).
Gethmann-Siefert, Annemarie, "Martin Heidegger and Theology: 'Reciprocal Modification'," in Alastair Kee and Eugene Thomas Long, ed., *Being and Truth: Essays in Honor of John Macquarrie* (London: SCM Press, 1986), 18-42.
Gorringe, Timothy, Review: Robert Morgan, ed., *In Search of Humanity and Deity: A Celebration of John Macquarrie's Theology* (London: SCM Press, 2006), in *The Expository Times* 118 (2007), 561-562.
Green, William B., "Profile: John Macquarrie," *Epworth Review* 20 (1997), 13-18.
Grislis, Egil, "Richard Hooker and Mysticism," *Anglican Theological Review* 87 (2005), 253-271.
Groves, Peter, "Body Language: John Macquarrie on the Eucharist," in Robert Morgan, ed., *In Search of Humanity and Deity* (London: SCM Press, 2006), 287-296.
Guignon, Charles, ed., *The Cambridge Companion to Heidegger* (Cambridge: Cambridge University Press, 1993).
Hackett, Jeremiah and Wallulis, Jerald, ed., *Philosophy of Religion for a New Century: Essays in Honor of Eugene Thomas Long* (Dordrecht, The Netherlands: Kluwer Academic Publishers, 2004).
Hager, Hal, "About Muriel Spark," Muriel Spark, *The Prime of Miss Jean Brodie* (New York: HarperPerennial, 1996).
Hanson, Richard P. C., *Christian Priesthood Reexamined* (London: Lutterworth Press, 1979).
_____ *Eucharistic Offering in the Early Church* (Bramcote, Notts.: Grove Books, 1982).
Hardy, Daniel W., "Theology through Philosophy," in David F. Ford, ed., *The Modern Theologians*, vol. II (Oxford: Blackwell, 1989), 48-54.
_____ *Finding the Church: The Dynamic Truth of Anglicanism* (London: SCM Press, 2001).

355

_____ "John Macquarrie's Ecclesiology," in Robert Morgan, ed., *In Search of Humanity and Divinity: A Celebration of John Macquarrie's Theology* (London: SCM Press, 2006), 267-276.

Hazlett, William Ian P., "Ebbs and Flows of Theology in Glasgow 1451-1843," in William Ian P. Hazlett, ed., *Traditions of Theology in Glasgow 1450-1990* (Edinburgh: Scottish Academic Press Ltd., 1993), 1-26.

He, Guanghu, "Professor Macquarrie in China," in Robert Morgan, ed., *In Search of Humanity and Deity* (London: SCM Press, 2006), 141-149.

Hebblethwaite, Brian, *The Christian Hope* (Grand Rapids: Eerdmans, 1984).

Hefling, Charles C., "Reviving Adamic Adoptionism: The Example of John Macquarrie," *Theological Studies* 52 (1991), 476-494.

Henderson, Ian, *Myth in the New Testament* (London: SCM Press, 1952).

Hendrickson, Marion Lars, *Behold the Man! An Anthropological Comparison of the Christologies of John Macquarrie and of Wolfhart Pannenberg* (Lanham-New York-Oxford: University Press of America, 1998).

Heron, Alasdair, *A Century of Protestant Theology* (Philadelphia: The Westminster Press, 1980).

Hill, William J., *The Three Personed God* (Washington, DC: The Catholic University of America Press, 1982).

Hollenweger, Walter J., "Ave Maria: Mary, the Reformers and the Protestants," *One in Christ* 13 (1977), 285-290.

Holloway, Richard, ed., *The Anglican Tradition* (Wilton, CT: Morehouse-Barlow, 1984).

Houlden, J. Leslie, Review: John Macquarrie, *Stubborn Theological Questions* (London: SCM Press, 2003), in *Journal of Theological Studies* 54 (2003), 861-863.

Hughes, Gerard W., *God, Where Are You?* (London: Darton, Longman and Todd, 1997).

Johnson, Elizabeth, *She Who Is* (New York: Crossroad, 1992).

_____ "Mary, Contemporary Issues," in Wolfgang Beinert and Francis S. Fiorenza, ed., *Handbook of Catholic Theology* (New York: Crossroad, 1995), 459-464.

_____ *Quest for the Living God* (New York: Continuum, 2007).

Jones, Alan, *Common Prayer on Common Ground: a Vision of Anglican Orthodoxy* (Harrisburg, PA: Morehouse Publishing, 2006).

Jones, Gareth, *Bultmann* (Cambridge: Polity Press, 1991).

_____ "Existentialism," in Alister E. McGrath, ed., *The Blackwell Encyclopedia of Modern Christian Thought* (Oxford: Blackwell, 1993), 200.

Kaiser, Christopher B., *The Doctrine of God* (London: Marshall, Morgan and Scott, 1982).

Kasper, Walter, *That They May All Be One* (New York: Continuum, 2005).

Kaufman, Walter, *The Faith of a Heretic* (Garden City, NY: Doubleday, 1963).

Kee, Alistair and Long, Eugene T., ed., *Being and Truth: Essays in Honour of John Macquarrie* (London: SCM Press, 1986).

Kee, Alistair, "Deconstructing the Blessed Virgin," in Robert Morgan, ed., *In Search of Humanity and Deity* (London: SCM Press, 2006), 307-313.

Kelly, Geffrey B., ed., *Karl Rahner: Theologian of the Graced Search for Meaning* (Minneapolis: Fortress Press, 1992).

Kenny, Anthony, *What I Believe* (New York: Continuum, 2007).

Kerr, Fergus, Review of *Being and Truth* (Macquarrie Festschrift) and John Macquarrie, *Theology, Church and Ministry*, *New Blackfriars* 68 (1987), 419-420.

_____ "Idealism and Realism," in Kenneth Surin, ed., *Christ, Ethics and Tragedy* (Cambridge: Cambridge University Press, 1989).

_____ "Frei's Types," *New Blackfriars* 75 (1994), 184-192.

_____ Review: John Macquarrie, *Heidegger and Christianity* (London: SCM Press, 1994), in *Journal of Theological Studies* 46 (1995), 791-794.

_____ *After Aquinas: Versions of Thomism* (Oxford: Blackwell Publishing, 2002).

_____ "Editorial," in *New Blackfriars* 83 (2002), 382-383.

_____ Review: *Coming to Be: Towards a Thomistic-Whiteheadian Metaphysics of Becoming* by James W. Felt (Albany, NY: State University of New York Press, 2001), in *Modern Theology* 18 (2002), 413-416.

_____ *After Aquinas: Versions of Thomism* (Oxford: Blackwell Publishing, 2002).

_____ "God in the *Summa Theologiae:* Entity or Event?" in Jeremiah Hackett and Jerald Wallulis, ed., *Philosophy of Religion for a New Century: Essays in Honor of Eugene Thomas Long* (Dordrecht, The Netherlands: Kluwer Academic Publishers, 2004), 63-80.

_____ *Twentieth Century Catholic Theologians* (Oxford: Blackwell Publishing, 2007).

_____ "'A Thomist, but not a Medievalist', An Interview with Fergus Kerr, OP," *The Leuven Philosophy Newsletter* 16 (2007), 15-19.

_____ "Comment: Ratzinger's Thomism," *New Blackfriars* 89 (2008), 367-368.

Kilby, Karen, "Perichoresis and Projection: Problems with Social Doctrines of the Trinity," *New Blackfriars* 81 (2001).

_____ "Balthasar and Karl Rahner," in Edward T. Oakes, SJ and David Moss, ed., *The Cambridge Companion to Hans Urs von Balthasar* (Cambridge: Cambridge University Press, 2004), 256-268.

_____ *Karl Rahner, A Brief Introduction* (New York: Crossroad, 2007).

King, Ursula, *Christian Mystics: The Spiritual Heart of the Christian Tradition* (New York: Simon and Schuster, 1998).

Knox, John, *Never Far From Home* (Waco, TX: Word Books, 1975).

Kress, Robert, "Karl Rahner: A New Father for the Church?" *Emmanuel* 110 (2004), 254-260.

Krieg, Robert, *Romano Guardini, a Precursor of Vatican II* (Notre Dame, IN: University of Notre Dame Press, 1997).

_____ *Catholic Theologians in Nazi Germany* (New York and London: Continuum, 2004).

Küng, Hans, ed., *Post-Ecumenical Christianity* (New York: Herder and Herder, 1970).

Lane, Dermot A., "Karl Rahner's Contribution to Interreligious Dialogue," in Declan Marmion, ed., *Christian Identity in a Postmodern Age* (Dublin: Veritas Publications, 2005).

Lash, Nicholas, *Theology on Dover Beach* (London: Darton, Longman and Todd, 1979).

_____ "Considering the Trinity," *Modern Theology* 2 (1986).

_____ "Are We Born and Do We Die?" *New Blackfriars* 90 (2009), 403-412.

Law, David R., "Existentialism," in Adrian Hastings and others, ed., *The Oxford Companion to Christian Thought* (New York and Oxford: Oxford University Press, 2000), 227-228.

_____ "The Abiding Significance of Existentialist Theology," in Robert Morgan, ed., *In Search of Humanity and Deity* (London: SCM Press, 2006), 34-56.

Lewis, C. S., *English Literature in the Sixteenth Century* (Oxford: Clarendon Press, 1954).

Lindbeck, George, *The Nature of Doctrine* (London: SPCK, 1984).

_____ *The Church in a Postliberal Age* (London: SCM Press, 2002).

Lonergan, SJ, Bernard J. F., *Insight* (London: Longmans Green, 1958).

_____ *Method in Theology* (New York: Herder and Herder, 1972).

Long, Eugene T., *Jaspers and Bultmann: a Dialogue Between Philosophy and Theology in the Existentialist Tradition* (Durham, NC: Duke University Press, 1968).

_____ *Existence, Being and God: An Introduction to the Philosophical Theology of John Macquarrie* (New York: Paragon House Publishers, 1985).

_____ ed., *God, Secularization and History: Essays in Memory of Ronald Gregor Smith* (Columbia, SC: University of South Carolina Press, 1974).

_____ "Self and Other, in Robert Morgan, ed., *In Search of Humanity and Deity* (London: SCM Press, 2006), 159-169.

_____ "Existential Anglican: Remembering John Macquarrie, 1919-2007," *The Weekly Standard*, June 18, 2007.

Louth, Andrew, *Discerning the Mystery* (New York and Oxford: Clarendon Press, 1983).

Ludlow, Morwenna, "'The Task of Theology Is Never Finished': John Macquarrie and Karl Rahner on the Challenges and Limits of Doing Theology," in Robert Morgan, ed., *In Search of Humanity and Deity* (London: SCM Press, 2006), 117-126.

McAdoo, Henry, "Richard Hooker," in Geoffrey Rowell, ed., *The English Religious Tradition and the Genius of Anglicanism* (Nashville: Abingdon Press, 1992), 105-126.

McBrien, Richard P., *Catholicism* (Minneapolis: Winston Press, 1980).

_____ "The Inspiration of John Macquarrie," the-tidings.com, July 13, 2007.

McCabe, OP, Herbert, *God Matters* (London: Geoffrey Chapman, 1987).

_____ *God Still Matters* (New York and London: Continuum, 2002).

McCabe, Michael, "The Mystery of the Human: A Perspective from Rahner," in Declan Marmion, ed., *Christian Identity in a Postmodern Age* (Dublin: Veritas Publications, 2005).

McCready, Douglas, *He Came Down from Heaven: The Preexistence of Christ and the Christian Faith* (Downers Grove, IL: InterVarsity Press, 2005).

MacCulloch, Diarmaid, "Mary and Sixteenth Century Protestants," in R. N. Swanson, ed., *The Church and Mary* (Rochester, NY and Woodbridge, UK: The Boydell Press, 2004), 191-217.

McGrath, Alister E., *Christian Theology, An Introduction* (Oxford, UK and Cambridge, MA: Blackwell Publishers, 1994).

_____ *The SPCK Handbook of Anglican Theologians* (London: SPCK, 1998).

McGrath, S. J., *The Early Heidegger and Medieval Philosophy* (Washington, DC: The Catholic University of America Press, 2006).

Mackey, James P., "Preface," in *Celtic Christianity,* translated and introduced by Oliver Davies with the collaboration of Thomas O'Loughlin (New York-Mahwah, NJ: Paulist Press, 1999).

Mackinnon, Donald M., *Borderlands of Theology and Other Essays* (New York and Philadelphia: J. B. Lippincott Company, 1968).

McIntosh, Mark, *Mystical Theology* (Oxford: Blackwell, 1998).

MacIntyre, Alastair, *After Virtue* (London: Duckworth, 1981).

McIntyre, John, "The Christology of Donald Baillie in Perspective," in David Fergusson, ed., *Christ, Church and Society* (Edinburgh: T. & T. Clark, 1993), 87-114.

McPartlan, Paul, *Sacrament of Salvation* (Edinburgh: T. & T. Clark, 1995).

Macquarrie, Alan, *The Saints of Scotland* (Edinburgh: John Donald, 1997).

Marmion, Declan, "Christian Identity in a Postmodern Age: A Perspective from Rahner," in Declan Marmion, ed., *Christian Identity in a Postmodern Age* (Dublin: Veritas Publications, 2005), 160-175.

Maron, Gottfried, "Mary in Protestant Theology," in Hans Kung and Jurgen Moltmann, ed., *Mary in the Churches* (New York: The Seabury Press, 1983), 40-47.

Mason, Alistair, "Scottish Christian Thought," in Adrian Hastings and others, ed., *The Oxford Companion to Christian Thought* (New York and Oxford: Oxford University Press, 2000), 651-653.

Merton, Thomas, *The Monastic Journey* (Garden City, NY: Doubleday, 1972).

Meyer, Charles R., *A Contemporary Theology of Grace* (Eugene, OR: Wipf and Stock Publishing, 2002).

Miller, J. Michael, *The Divine Right of the Papacy in Recent Ecumenical Theology* (Rome: Gregorian University Press, 1980).

Mitchell, Basil, "I Believe: We Believe," in The Doctrine Commission of the Church of England, *Believing in the Church: The Corporate Nature of Faith* (Wilton, CT: Morehouse-Barlow, 1982), 9-24.

Mitchell, Nathan, *Cult and Controversy: The Worship of the Eucharist Outside the Mass* (New York: Pueblo Publishing Co., 1982).

359

Moehling, Karl A., "Heidegger and the Nazis," in Thomas Sheehan, ed., *Heidegger the Man and the Thinker* (Chicago: Precedent Publishing, Inc., 1981).

Molnar, Paul D., *Incarnation and Resurrection, Toward a Contemporary Understanding* (Grand Rapids: Eerdmans, 2007).

Montefiore, Hugh, *Credible Christianity: The Gospel in Contemporary Society* (Grand Rapids: Eerdmans, 1994).

Moran, Dermot, *Introduction to Phenomenology* (New York and London: Routledge, 2000).

Morgan, Robert, ed., *In Search of Humanity and Deity: A Celebration of John Macquarrie's Theology* (London: SCM Press, 2006).

_____ "John Macquarrie in Oxford," in Robert Morgan ed., *In Search of Humanity and Deity* (London: SCM Press, 2006), 93-106.

_____ "Obituary: The Rev. John Macquarrie," *The Guardian*, June 5, 2007.

Morley, Georgina, *John Macquarrie's Natural Theology: The Grace of Being* (Burlington, VT and Aldershot, UK: Ashgate Publishing, 2003).

_____ "Trailing Clouds of Glory: John Macquarrie on Being Human," in Robert Morgan, ed., *In Search of Humanity and Deity: A Celebration of John Macquarrie's Theology* (London. SCM Press, 2006), 170-177.

Mueller, J. J., *What Are They Saying About Theological Method?* (New York-Ramsey: Paulist Press, 1984).

Muir, Edwin, *Autobiography* (London: The Hogarth Press, 1954).

_____ *Collected Poems*, 2nd ed. (Boston: Faber & Faber, 1984).

Murray, Paul D., *Reason, Truth and Theology in Pragmatist Perspective* (Leuven -Paris-Dudley: Peeters, 2004).

_____ "Roman Catholic Theology After Vatican II," n David F. Ford with Rachel Muers, ed., *The Modern Theologians* (Oxford: Blackwell Publishing, 2005), 265-286.

Need, Stephen W., "Macquarrie, John," in J. Leslie Houlden, ed., *Jesus in History, Thought and Culture* (Santa Barbara, CA and Oxford, UK: ABC-CLIO, 2003), 585-587.

Neuner, Joseph and Dupuis, Jacques, ed., *The Christian Faith in the Doctrinal Documents of the Catholic Church*, rev. ed. (London: Collins, 1983).

Newbigin, Lesslie, "All in One Place or All of One Sort?" in Richard W. A. McKinney, ed., *Creation, Christ and Culture: Studies in Honor of T. F. Torrance* (Edinburgh: T. & T. Clark, 1976), 288-306.

Newlands, George, *John and Donald Baillie: Transatlantic Theology* (Bern: Peter Lang, 2002).

_____ "John Macquarrie in Scotland," in Robert Morgan, ed., *In Search of Humanity and Deity* (London: SCM Press, 2006), 17-24.

Nichols, Aidan, *Epiphany, a Theological Introduction to Catholicism* (Collegeville: The Liturgical Press, 1996).

_____ *Catholic Thought Since the Enlightenment, a Survey* (Pretoria: University of South Africa Press, and Leominster, UK: Gracewing, 1998).

Norris, R. A., ed., *Lux in Lumine: Essays to Honor W. Norman Pittenger* (New York: The Seabury Press, 1966).

O'Connor, David, "On the Viability of Macquarrie's *God-Talk*," *Philosophical Studies* (National University of Ireland) 23 (1974), 107-116.

O'Donovan, Leo J., ""Karl Rahner, SJ (1904-1984): A Theologian for the Twenty-first Century," *Theology Today* 62 (2005), 211-218.

O'Hanlon, Gerard, *The Immutability of God in the Theology of Hans Urs von Balthasar* (Cambridge: Cambridge University Press, 1990).

_____ "The Legacy of Hans Urs von Balthasar," *Doctrine and Life* 41 (1991), 401-407.

O'Malley, John W., *What Happened at Vatican II* (Cambridge, MA: The Belknap Press of Harvard University Press, 2008).

O'Meara, Thomas F., *God in the World: A Guide to Karl Rahner's Theology* (Collegeville: The Liturgical Press, 2007).

One Bread, One Body (London and Dublin: Catholic Truth Society and Veritas Publications, 1998).

Owen, Huw Parri, *Concepts of Deity* (London: Macmillan, 1971).

Pattison, George, *A Short Course in Christian Doctrine* (London: SCM Press, 2005).

_____ "Translating Heidegger," in Robert Morgan, ed., *In Search of Humanity and Deity* (London: SCM Press, 2006), 57-65.

Pierce, J. Kingston, "Interview with Ian Rankin," *January Magazine*, January 2000, on-line.

Pitstick, Alyssa L., *Hans Urs von Balthasar and the Catholic Doctrine of Christ's Descent into Hell* (Grand Rapids: Eerdmans, 2007).

Pittenger, Norman, *The Last Things in a Process Perspective* (London: Epworth Press, 1970).

_____ *After-Death-Life in God* (London: SCM Press, 1980).

_____ *Catholic Faith in a Process Perspective* (Maryknoll, NY: Orbis Books, 1981).

_____ *Our Lady* (London: SCM Press, 1996).

Plantinga, Cornelius, "Social Trinity and Tritheism," in Ronald J. Feenstra and Cornelius Plantinga, ed., *Trinity, Incarnation and Atonement* (Notre Dame: University of Notre Dame Press, 1989).

Pratt, Douglas, *Relational Deity: Hartshorne and Macquarrie on God* (Lanham -New York-Oxford: University Press of America, 2002).

Purdy, Vernon L., *The Christology of John Macquarrie* (New York: Peter Lang Publishing, 2009).

Rahner, SJ, Karl, *Theological Investigations*, vol. 1 (London: Darton, Longman and Todd, 1961).

_____ "The Need for a Short Formula of Christian Faith," *Theological Investigations*, vol. 9 (New York: Crossroad, 1973).

_____ "Theology and the Arts," *Thought* 57 (1982), 24-36.

_____ "Experience of the Holy Spirit," in *Theological Investigations*, vol. 18 (New York: Crossroad, 1983).

_____ *I Remember* (London: SCM Press, 1985).

_____ *On Prayer* (Collegeville: The Liturgical Press, 1993).

Ratzinger, Joseph, *'In the Beginning... ' A Catholic Understanding of the Story of Creation and the Fall* (Grand Rapids: Eerdmans, 1995).

_____ *Salt of the Earth* (San Francisco: Ignatius Press, 1997).

_____ *Milestones* (San Francisco: Ignatius Press, 1998).

Rawlins, Clive, *William Barclay: the Authorized Biography* (Grand Rapids: Eerdmans, 1984).

Raymo, Chet, *Climbing Brandon, Science and Faith on Ireland's Holy Mountain* (New York: Walker and Co., 2004).

Reath, Mary, *Rome and Canterbury, The Elusive Search for Unity* (Lanham -Boulder-New York-Toronto-Plymouth, UK: Rowman and Littlefield Publishers, Inc., 2007).

Reno, R. R., *The Ordinary Transformed* (Grand Rapids: Eerdmans, 1995).

Riches, John K. and Quash, Ben, "Hans Urs von Balthasar," in David F. Ford, ed., *The Modern Theologians*, 2nd. ed. (Oxford: Blackwell, 1997), 134-151.

Rodd, Cyril S., Review: John Macquarrie, *Mary for All Christians* (Edinburgh: T. & T. Clark, 2001), in *The Expository Times* 113 (2001), 73-74.

Rowland, Tracey, *Ratzinger's Faith* (New York and Oxford: Oxford University Press, 2008).

Ryle, Gilbert, "Heidegger's *Sein und Zeit*," in Michael Murray, ed., *Heidegger and Modern Philosophy* (New Haven: Yale University Press, 1978).

Safranski, Rüdiger, *Martin Heidegger, Between Good and Evil* (Cambridge, MA: Harvard University Press, 1998).

Santer, Mark, ed., *Their Lord and Ours* (London: SPCK, 1982).

_____ "Communion, Unity and Primacy: An Anglican Response to *Ut Unum Sint*," *Ecclesiology* 3 (2007), 283-295.

Schaab, Gloria L., *The Creative Suffering of the Triune God* (New York and Oxford: Oxford University Press, 2007).

Schleiermacher, F. D. E., *The Christian Faith* (Edinburgh: T. & T. Clark, 1928).

Schloesser, Stephen, *Jazz Age Catholicism* (Toronto: University of Toronto Press, 2005).

Schumacher, Michele M., "Ecclesial Existence: Person and Community in the Trinitarian Theology of Adrienne von Speyr," *Modern Theology* 24 (2008), 359-385.

Schürmann, Reiner, *Wandering Joy: Meister Eckhart's Mystical Philosophy* (Great Barrington, MA: Lindisfarne Books, 2001).

Sedgwick, Peter, "Anglican Theology," in David F. Ford with Rachel Muers, ed., *The Modern Theologians* (Oxford: Blackwell Publishing, 2005), 178-193.

Sheehan, Thomas, "Heidegger's Early Years: Fragments for a Philosophical Biography," in Thomas Sheehan, ed., *Heidegger the Man and the Thinker* (Chicago: Precedent Publishing Inc., 1981).

Shortt, Rupert, *Rowan's Rule: The Biography of the Archbishop of Canterbury* (Grand Rapids: Eerdmans, 2008).

Sia, Santiago, *God in Process Thought: A Study in Charles Hartshorne's Concept of God* (Dordrecht-Boston-Lancaster: Martinus Nijhoff, 1985).

———, "The Doctrine of God's Immutability: Introducing the Modern Debate," *New Blackfriars* 68 (1987), 220-232.

———, "Charles Hartshorne on Describing God," *Modern Theology* 3 (1987), 193-203.

———, *Religion, Reason and God: Essays in the Philosophies of Charles Hartshorne and A. N. Whitehead* (Frankfurt: Peter Lang, 2004).

Smith, Ronald Gregor, *The Doctrine of God* (Philadelphia: The Westminster Press, 1970).

Soskice, Janet Martin, *The Kindness of God: Metaphor, Gender and Religious Language* (Oxford: Oxford University Press, 2007).

Stevenson, Kenneth, *Covenant of Grace Renewed: A Vision of the Eucharist in the Seventeenth Century* ((London: Darton, Longman and Todd, 1994).

———, *The Mystery of Baptism in the Anglican Tradition* (Harrisburg, PA: Morehouse Publishing, 1998).

Stone, Ronald, "John Macquarrie at Union Theological Seminary in New York City," in Robert Morgan, ed., *In Search of Humanity and Deity* (London: SCM Press, 2006), 66-75.

Sumner, George, "After Dromatine," *Anglican Theological Review* 87 (2005), 559-566.

Surin, Kenneth, *Theology and the Problem of Evil* (Oxford: Blackwell, 1986).

———, "Process Theology," in David F. Ford, ed., *The Modern Theologians*, vol. II (Oxford: Blackwell, 1989), 103-114.

Sykes, Stephen, "The Genius of Anglicanism," in Geoffrey Rowell, ed., *The English Religious Tradition and the Genius of Anglicanism* (Nashville: Abingdon Press, 1992), 227-242.

Tanner, Kathryn, "Towards a New Theology of Confirmation," *Anglican Theological Review* 88 (2006), 85-94.

Tavard, George, *The Thousand Faces of the Blessed Virgin* (Collegeville: The Liturgical Press, 1996).

Taylor, Charles, "Engaged Agency and Background in Heidegger," in Charles Guignon, ed., *The Cambridge Companion to Heidegger* (Cambridge: Cambridge University Press, 1993).

Thiel, John, *God, Evil and Innocent Suffering* (New York: Crossroad, 2000).

Thurian, Max, *Mary, Mother of the Lord, Figure of the Church* (London and Oxford: Mowbray, 1963).

Tillard, Jean M. R., *Church of Churches* (Collegeville: The Liturgical Press, 1992).

Tilley, Terrence W., *Evils of Theodicy* (Washington, DC: Georgetown University Press, 1991).

Torrance, Iain, "A Long Tradition of Engagement: A Tribute to Trinity College, Glasgow, on its 150th Anniversary," in Paul Middleton, ed., *The God of Love and Human Dignity: Essays in Honour of George M. Newlands* (Edinburgh: T. & T. Clark, 2007), 5-18.

363

Torrance, Thomas F., "John Baillie at Prayer," in David Fergusson, ed., *Christ, Church and Society: Essays on John Baillie and Donald Baillie* (Edinburgh: T. & T. Clark, 1993), 153-262,

Tracy, David, *Blessed Rage for Order*, rev. ed. (Chicago: University of Chicago Press, 1996).

_____ *The Analogical Imagination* (New York: Crossroad, 1981).

_____ *Plurality and Ambiguity* (Chicago and London: University of Chicago Press, 1987).

_____ "Kenosis, Sunyata, and Trinity," in John B. Cobb and Christopher Ives, ed., *The Emptying God* (Maryknoll, NY: Orbis Books, 1990), 135- 154.

_____ "Approaching the Christian Understanding of God," in Francis Schussler Fiorenza, ed., *Systematic Theology: Roman Catholic Perspectives*, vol. 1 (Minneapolis: Fortress Press, 1991).

_____ *On Naming the Present* (Maryknoll, NY: Orbis Books, 1994).

_____ "Forms of Divine Disclosure," in James L. Heft, ed , *Believing Scholars* (New York: Fordham University Press, 2005).

Travis, Stephen, *Christian Hope and the Future of Man* (Leicester: Intervarsity Press, 1980).

Trethowan, Illtyd, *Absolute Value: A Study in Christian Theism* (London: Allen and Unwin, 1970).

Tugwell, Simon, *Prayer in Practice* (Dublin: Veritas Publications, 1974).

Vorgrimler, Herbert, *Understanding Karl Rahner* (London: SCM Press, 1986).

Waal, Esther de, *Lost in Wonder* (Collegeville: The Liturgical Press, 2003).

Wainwright, Geoffrey, *Doxology, A Systematic Theology* (New York and Oxford: Oxford University Press, 1984).

_____ *Is the Reformation Over?* (Milwaukee: Marquette University Press, 2000).

_____ *Leslie Newbigin, a Theological Life* (New York and Oxford: Oxford University Press 2000).

_____ "Subjectivity and Objectivity in Theology and Worship," in Robert Morgan, ed., *In Search of Humanity and Deity* (London: SCM Press, 2006), 297-306.

Webster, John, "Principles of Christian Theology," in Robert Morgan, ed., *In Search of Humanity and Deity* (London: SCM Press, 2006), 83-92.

Weigel, George, *God's Choice: Pope Benedict XVI and the Future of the Roman Catholic Church* (New York: HarperCollins, 2005).

Weinandy, Thomas G. Weinandy, "Does God Suffer?" *First Things* 117 (2001), 35-41.

_____ *Does God Suffer?* (Notre Dame, IN: University of Notre Dame Press, 2000).

Welte, Bernhard, "La Métaphysique de Saint Thomas d'Aquin et la pensée de l'histoire de l'être de Heidegger," *Revue des Sciences Philosophiques et Théologiques* 50 (1966), 601-614.

_____ "Seeking and Finding: The Speech at Heidegger's Burial," in Thomas Sheehan, ed., *Heidegger: The Man and the Thinker* (Chicago: Precedent Publishing, Inc., 1981).

_____ "The Question of God in the Thought of Heidegger," *Philosophy Today* 26 (1982), 85-100.

Wiles, Maurice F., Review: Georgina Morley, *John Macquarrie's Natural Theology* (Bristol, IN: Wyndham Hall Press, 2001), in *Journal of Theological Studies* 53 (2002), 403-403.

Williams, Harry A., "Theology and Self-Awareness," in Alec R. Vidler, ed., *Soundings* (Cambridge: Cambridge University Press, 1963).

Williams, Rowan D., *Anglican Identities* (Cambridge, MA: Cowley Publications, 2003).

Wiseman, James, "Mystical Literature and the Culture of Unbelief," in George Schner and Peter Casarella, ed., *Christian Spirituality and the Culture of Modernity* (Grand Rapids: Eerdmans, 1998), 176-188.

Wright, N. T., "God's Way of Acting," *The Christian Century* December 16, 1998.

_____ *The Last Word* (New York: HarperCollins, 2005).

Young, Frances M., *Face to Face: A Narrative Essay in the Theology of Suffering* (Edinburgh: T. & T. Clark, 1990).

Zagano, Phyllis and Tilley, Terrence W., ed., *Things New and Old: Essays on the Theology of Elizabeth A. Johnson* (New York: Crossroad, 1999).

Zaleski, Carol, *The Life of the World to Come* (New York and Oxford: Oxford University Press, 1996).

Zizioulas, John D., *Being as Communion* (London: Darton, Longman and Todd, 1985).

Owen F. Cummings

Dr. Owen F. Cummings is Regents' Professor of Theology at Mount Angel Seminary in St. Benedict, Oregon. Dr. Cummings received his D.D. from the University of Dublin, Trinity College, Ireland.

THE THEOLOGY OF JOHN MACQUARRIE
(1919-2007)
A Comprehensive and Contextual Exploration